THE PROFESSOR'S COMPANION TO TEST PREP

50 SAT® & ACT®
Passages You Will Enjoy

Short Stories, Essays, and Speeches to
Spark Student Interest and Prepare You for the
SAT®, ACT®, and Other Standardized Tests
with 300+ Questions to Train Your Brain

THOMAS CHARLES, PhD

For information regarding bulk order purchases and discounts for classrooms, please contact
tom@professorscompanion.com

ISBN-13: 978-1090293541

www.professorscompanion.com

CONTENTS

WHAT WAS THE LAST BOOK YOU READ FOR FUN?

I ask this question when I start working with new students. They typically laugh, then pause, and finally admit to me (and to themselves) that they can't remember the last time they read something for fun.

Remember when you were young and you enjoyed reading? You read stories of adventure, tales of pirates and wizards and knights, of jungles and deserts and space. New books were devoured like chocolate cake. Library days meant you were entering an unexplored world or going on a new adventure with old friends.

Sooner or later, however, school intervened. Reading became something you had to do. Teachers assigned book reports, reflection papers, essays. Midterms sap the fun out of reading faster than anything. Anything except standardized tests, that is. The reading sections of the SAT and ACT not only take the fun out of reading, they also inject a healthy dose of anxiety into your already chaotic and busy world.

But the best way to improve your reading score is to read. It's hard to study for the reading section of standardized tests. The passages are not the types of books and essays you would typically choose to read. Sometimes, the content can trip you up. Other times, the archaic words and phrases of nineteenth-century literature slow you to a crawl. There are lots of strategies you can deploy to help yourself with the passages but nothing will improve your score faster than reading regularly.

This book will help you prepare for the test in three ways. First, you will (re)-learn to **read for fun**. You'll get more out of reading when you read something you want to read. Second, you'll **know what to expect** on the test. The passages here, more or less, conform to the types of passages you'll see on test day. Third, you'll learn to **focus, relax, and pace yourself**. These tests are stressful enough as it is. Preparing will remove some anxiety and give you the confidence to succeed.

TIP #1: READ FOR FUN (AGAIN)

The passages in this book are, more or less, the kinds of passages you would find on standardized tests. However, I have chosen these particular passages because I think that they may be more interesting than those you'll find on test day.

On the left-hand column, you'll find a list of things that students have told me they like over the years, from binge-watching TV shows to their favorite history subjects. In the right-hand columns are readings that are associated with each of these things. So, if you like *Stranger Things*, you could start with H. P. Lovecraft's short-story *Ex Oblivione*. If you're a fan of the Cold War, you might like to read Kennedy and Reagan on the Berlin Wall. If you like comic book movies, try Thomas Malthus's essay on overpopulation (which is the basis of Thanos's philosophy in the *Avengers* movies). There are enough options here that you're bound to find passages that are fun.

Like this?	Short Reads	Medium Reads	Long Reads
The Handmaid's Tale	❑ "The Story of an Hour" ❑ "On Nomination to the Supreme Court"	❑ "Silly Novels by Lady Novelists" ❑ "Women's Rights are Human Rights"	❑ The Yellow Wallpaper ❑ Emma (Abridged)
Stranger Things	❑ "Ex Oblivione"	❑ "An Occurrence at Owl Creek Bridge" ❑ "2-B-R-0-2-B"	❑ The Pit and the Pendulum
The Outdoors	❑ "Yosemite Fall"	❑ "Where I Lived, And What I Lived For"	❑ To Build a Fire
Satire	❑ "Advice to Youth"	❑ "A Modest Proposal"	❑ Three Satirical Short Stories from Saki
Math and Science	❑ Flatland ❑ The Dangers of Spaceflight (paired)	❑ On Marie Curie's Discovery of Radium (paired)	❑ Earthquakes
House of Cards	❑ "The King of Vultures" ❑ Selection from The Prince	❑ Macbeth: A Prose Adaptation	❑ "The Fad of the Fisherman"
Comic Book Movies	❑ The Young Edda	❑ A History of the Amazons	❑ An Essay on the Principle of Population

Like this?	Short Reads	Medium Reads	Long Reads
Parks and Recreation	❑ "Yosemite Fall"	❑ "Government is the Problem" ❑ "Women's Rights are Human Rights"	❑ The Inaugural Addresses of Abraham Lincoln
Hamilton	❑ "On My Impending Duel with Aaron Burr" (paired)	❑ On the Separation of Power (paired)	❑ The Farmer and the Farmer Refuted (paired)
Science Fiction and Dystopian Literature	❑ The War of the Worlds ❑ The Dangers of Spaceflight (paired)	❑ "2-B-R-0-2-B" ❑ "The Pendulum"	❑ The Hanging Stranger
Game of Thrones and Lord of the Rings	❑ The Young Edda ❑ Selection from The Prince	❑ "Macbeth: A Prose Adaptation"	❑ The Death of King Arthur (Le Morte d'Arthur)
Literature	❑ "The Story of an Hour"	❑ Macbeth: A Prose Adaptation	❑ Emma (Abridged)
African American History	❑ "What to the Slave Is the Fourth of July?"	❑ Editorials from The Crisis (paired)	❑ "Letter from Birmingham Jail"
The American Revolution	❑ "On My Impending Interview with Burr" (paired)	❑ "On the Separation of Powers" (paired)	❑ The Farmer and the Farmer Refuted (paired)
The American Civil War	❑ "What to the Slave Is the Fourth of July?"	❑ "An Occurrence at Owl Creek Bridge"	❑ The Inaugural Addresses of Abraham Lincoln (paired)
The Cold War	❑ "Don't Wait for the Translation!"	❑ "Ich bin ein Berliner" and "Tear Down this Wall" (paired)	❑ National Security Council Report 68
Economics	❑ "The Division of Labor"	❑ "Government is the Problem"	❑ On the Principle of Population
Philosophy	❑ "The King of Vultures"	❑ "Where I Lived, And What I Lived For"	❑ On the Principle of Population

You can find a quick reference to this table on the last page of the book.

TIP #2: KNOW WHAT TO EXPECT

The length, content, and complexity of the SAT and ACT are quite similar. Here's how both test makers describe their test in their official study guides and test specifications with regards to the length, content, and complexity of the passages.

	SAT[1]	ACT[2]
Length	500 to 750 words per passage 5 passages with 10-11 questions each 65 minutes (about 13 minutes per passage)	About 800 words per passage 4 passages with 10 question each 35 minutes (about 9 minutes per passage)
Content	All passages are taken from high-quality, previously published sources; all graphics are either also taken from such sources or created for the test based on authentic, accurate data. **Literature (1)** selections come from classic and contemporary works by authors working in the United States and around the world. **History & social studies (2)** selections include portions of U.S.-based founding documents and texts in the Great Global Conversation—engaging, often historically and culturally important works grappling with issues at the heart of civic and political life—and explorations of topics in the social sciences, including anthropology, communication studies, economics, education, human geography, law, linguistics, political science, psychology, and sociology (and their subfields). **Science (2)** selections examine both foundational concepts and recent developments in the natural sciences, including Earth science, biology, chemistry, and physics (and their subfields).	The passages on the reading test come from published materials, such as books and magazines. The ACT reading test may contain passages from each of the following categories: **Prose fiction (1):** Passages from short stories or novels **Social studies (1):** Passages that cover topics such as anthropology, archaeology, biography, business, economics, education, geography, history, political science, psychology, and sociology **Humanities (1):** Articles about topics including architecture, art, dance, ethics, film, language, literary criticism, memoir, music, personal essays, philosophy, radio, television, and theater **Natural science (1):** Passages related to subjects such as anatomy, astronomy, biology, botany, chemistry, ecology, geology, medicine, meteorology, microbiology, natural history, physiology, physics, technology, and zoology
Complexity	The SAT Reading Test includes passages that span a specified range of text complexity levels from **grades 9-10 to postsecondary entry**.	The passages are representative of the level and kinds of text commonly encountered in **first-year college curricula**.

---

[1] The College Board, <u>The Official SAT Study Guide, 2018 Edition.</u>(New York: College Board, 2018), 44-45
[2] The ACT Inc., <u>The Official ACT Prep Guide.</u> (San Francisco: John Wiley & Sons, 2019), 194.

🎓 www.professorscompanion.com

You'll notice substantial overlap between the tests. The passages on the ACT are longer, though only by a few sentences. Both have prose fiction, social studies, and science, with the SAT having a second social studies and science passage and the ACT having a humanities passage.

The biggest differences come not on the content of the passages, but in the formatting. For example, the SAT has passages with limited questions on data, while the ACT reserves those for the Science section of the test. The biggest difference in formatting is probably with the amount of time per passage. The SAT gives you about 13 minutes to read each passage and answer the questions associated with it, while the ACT gives you about 9 minutes for the passage and its questions. The questions on the SAT are a little more complex, so the time disparity is not as radical as it may first appear.

The passages in this book are designed to improve your reading abilities for either the SAT or ACT. You'll find a diversity of passage complexity as well as a good variety of topics that represent the full range of topics that appear on the test. Some of the passages are also a little more fun than what you'd see on test day. Sadly, you're unlikely to open the test booklet and find a passage about Odin, Loki, Thor, and the Norse tradition of Ragnarok. Then again, it doesn't do you any good to have a book of practice passages if you can't motivate yourself to sit down and read!

TIP #3: FOCUS, RELAX, AND PACE YOURSELF

Standardized tests require you to stay focused. This doesn't have to mean a constant vigilance, as if you are on guard for a marauding army or a spy returning from the front, even if the army is your parents and the spy is your little brother. But you have to maintain focus for three and a half hours. You can do any of these things in less time to do than it takes to sit through either the SAT or ACT:

- Watch the longest Best Picture winner from the last sixty years (*The Return of the King*, 3:13)
- Binge the first season of *The Jersey Shore* (3:26)
- Fly from New York to the Bahamas (3:05)
- Drive from Los Angeles to Mexico (3:21)
- Hike along the rapids above Niagara Falls (about 3:00)
- Cook a 13-pound turkey, stuffing (dressing in the South), mashed potatoes, cranberry sauce, corn-on-the-cob, and pumpkin pie for Thanksgiving dinner (3:15)

If the first goal of this book is to get you to like reading again and the second goal is to teach you what to expect, the third goal is to help you focus, relax, and pace yourself. Preparing now will keep you relaxed on test day so you do your best.

	Full Test	Passages	Time per Passage
SAT	65 minutes with 5 passages	5 passages with 10-11 questions	About 13 minutes
ACT	35 minutes with 4 passages	4 passages with 10 questions	About 9 minutes

If you don't have your pacing down on the SAT, you'll come out of the first section exhausted, just in time for a bunch of grammar and math. On the ACT, you'll have just finished the grammar and math, so if you lose your focus on the reading section you can suddenly be behind.

If you want to work on...	then you should read...
Passages and Questions	Short Reads
Passage Pacing	Medium Reads
Full Section Pacing	Long Reads

The passages in this book are broken up into test-length passages with questions, passages that take about 9 to 13 minutes to read, and passages that take 35 to 65 minutes to read. It can be difficult to force yourself to read the longer passages. Try to read at least one long passage a week as you prepare for the test. You can start with the passages that interest you most, but make sure you work through passages that will push you as well.

Studying for standardized tests can feel a little daunting at times, but I hope this will make things a little less scary. Feel free to drop me a note by email at tom@professorscompanion.com if you have questions or comments on the book, especially if you spot an error. I've also left couple of **Easter Eggs** in the book for you to find. If you want more materials in a digital space, shoot me an email and I'll send you some exclusive online-only materials.

Remember: **There is nothing you can do to improve your reading score more than reading**. The more you read, the better you will do.

Good luck and remember to enjoy yourself!

– Tom

SHORT READS WITH QUESTIONS

Let's start with the short passages. These short passages replicate the passages on the test in terms of their length, content. and difficulty. After each passage you'll be asked questions based on what you read.

Short Reads

There are three steps to reading short passages.

1. **Underline** anything that you think *might* be relevant.

2. **Annotate** the passage.

3. **Identify** the author's purpose.

Students sometimes stress about the amount of time it takes to read a passage. I understand their feelings. It's a timed test, and you don't want to waste any time. But the time you spend on the passage isn't wasted time. In fact, every second you spend on the passage will save you two seconds when you are reading and answering the questions, so you'll know where to go.

This doesn't mean you should dawdle. You want to read efficiently and keep pace, so don't get bogged down on any section of the passage. **Keep yourself moving**. You can come back to anything you miss.

Step 1: Underline

Underline as you read. One of the things I look for when I first meet with a student is whether or not they underlined the passages on their diagnostic test. I've looked at hundreds of diagnostic tests and the students who underline score higher than students who don't. Here's the weird part: *It doesn't matter what you underline, just that you underline.*

I have found that the more underlining a student does, the better they remember not just the information that they underlined, but the information around the underlining as well. So, while you should try to underline things you think will be useful, if you think something might be important, underline it.

One other thing: I **circle the names** that appear in the passage so I can keep track of the various literary characters, scientific researchers, and historical figures when I get to the questions. I'll also **box or star dates** in case I need to track what happened when.

Step 2: Annotate

As you go, **annotate the passage so you know the main idea of each paragraph**. Keep your annotations brief. Strive for two or three words, four if you must.

The goal isn't to cram all the information into the margins that you can or convince your English teacher that you read the passage. That isn't the point. Rather, you are setting yourself up to quickly answer the questions that follow, sketching out the passage for yourself so you can bounce back and forth between the questions and the passage.

Your annotations can also help you answer questions that deal with smaller segments of the passage. If they ask "what is he main idea of the fourth paragraph," and you've already written down some keywords in the margins, it makes sorting between the correct and incorrect answers that much faster. If you need to identify where the author talks about virtue ethics, you've already got notations telling you where to go.

Step 3: Identify

The last and most important step is to identify the author's purpose in writing the passage. **Why did the author write this?**

There are three main reasons that the authors of test passages write the things that they write.

1. **To explain something**: the ethics of economics; DNA; flight and bird physiology. Science and Social Studies passages are well suited to explanatory passages.

2. **To argue something**: women should be educated like men; public transportation can be better; civil disobedience is good. The paired passages are often argument passages—two authors debating each other—though you will also find them on Social Studies and History passages.

3. **To describe literary characters**: a man asks a woman for her daughter's hand in marriage; a man hates his boss; a woman pretends to be somebody she is not. The literature passages, which typically focus on the interactions of two or three characters, are descriptive passages.

If you're looking for help identifying the author's purpose, read line 0. *Where is line zero?* That's the blurb in the paragraph before the passage itself begins.

Reading for purpose helps with a lot of questions on the test. Many passages will have questions that straight up ask you "what's the purpose of the passage?" Other questions ask you to identify the function of a word or image as it relates to the author's argument. It's a lot easier to identify why an author used some phrase or metaphor if you look for what they are trying to do overall.

Questions

Each of these passages is accompanied by a set of questions that mimic the questions from the test with two important distinctions:

1. The questions here are all **free response**, meaning they don't have multiple choice answers. You should do your best to give coherent answers, but don't focus too much on "correct" answers. On the real test, one useful strategy is to try to answer the question before you look at the answer choices so you can then answer them more quickly and with greater accuracy.

2. Each passage focuses on one kind of question, meaning you will be asked a bunch of the same type of question for each passage. It can be helpful to work on one type of question and see the different ways you might be asked about a paragraph's function or the rhetoric an author uses.

Type	Core Question	Passages
Function	How does this part of the passage fit the overall purpose?	☑ The Dangers of Spaceflight ❑ The Division of Labor ❑ *Flatland: A Romance of Many Dimensions*
Main Idea	What is this passage or paragraph about?	☑ "Advice to Youth" ❑ "Yosemite Fall" ❑ Selection from *War of the Worlds* ❑ "On My Impending Interview with Aaron Burr" by Alexander Hamilton
Attitude	How does the author feel?	❑ *Common Sense* ❑ "The Story of an Hour"
Rhetoric	How does the author support their thesis?	❑ "What to the Slave is the Fourth of July?" ❑ "The King of the Vultures" ❑ "On Nomination to the Supreme Court"
Vocabulary	What does this word mean?	❑ "*Ex Oblivione*" ❑ Don't Wait for the Translation!
Detail	What does the author say? How do you know?	❑ Selection from *The Prince* ❑ Selection from *The Young Edda*

You'll also be asked three general questions on every passage:

1. **What is the author's main purpose**? Are they trying to *describe* literary characters or an encounter, *explain* something, or *argue* for a position?

2. **What is the author's thesis** or **how would you summarize the passage**?

3. **What is the tone of the passage overall**?

On the test, you'll sometimes be asked questions this directly. Even if you are not, however, you will be able to answer questions more quickly and accurately if you try to figure out the answers to these questions as you read.

As a reminder, on the real tests there will be 10 or 11 questions for each passage.

	Full Test	Passages	Time per Passage
SAT	65 minutes with 5 passages	**5 passages with 10-11 questions**	About 13 minutes
ACT	35 minutes with 4 passages	**4 passages with 10 questions**	About 9 minutes

"ADVICE TO YOUTH" – MARK TWAIN (MAIN IDEA)

Mark Twain, born Samuel Clemens, is the premier American humorist. Best-known for *The Adventures of Huckleberry Finn* and *Tom Sawyer*, Twain wrote dozens of short stores, including the satirical "Advice to Youth," published in 1882. Be careful with satire: if you miss the joke and take things seriously, you'll miss everything!

Being told I would be expected to talk here, I inquired what sort of talk I ought to make. They said it should be something suitable to youth-something didactic, instructive, or something in the nature of

5 good advice. Very well. I have a few things in my mind which I have often longed to say for the instruction of the young; for it is in one's tender early years that such things will best take root and be most enduring and most valuable. First, then. I will say to you my young

10 friends -- and I say it beseechingly, urgently --
Always obey your parents, when they are present. This is the best policy in the long run, because if you don't, they will make you. Most parents think they know better than you do, and you can generally make

15 more by humoring that superstition than you can by acting on your own better judgment.
Be respectful to your superiors, if you have any, also to strangers, and sometimes to others. If a person offend you, and you are in doubt as to whether it was

20 intentional or not, do not resort to extreme measures; simply watch your chance and hit him with a brick. That will be sufficient. If you shall find that he had not intended any offense, come out frankly and confess yourself in the wrong when you struck him;

25 acknowledge it like a man and say you didn't mean to. Yes, always avoid violence; in this age of charity and kindliness, the time has gone by for such things. Leave dynamite to the low and unrefined.
Go to bed early, get up early -- this is wise. Some

30 authorities say get up with the sun; some say get up with one thing, others with another. But a lark is really the best thing to get up with. It gives you a splendid reputation with everybody to know that you get up with the lark; and if you get the right kind of lark, and

35 work at him right, you can easily train him to get up at half past nine, every time -- it's no trick at all.
Now as to the matter of lying. You want to be very careful about lying; otherwise you are nearly sure to get caught. Once caught, you can never again be in the

40 eyes to the good and the pure, what you were before. Many a young person has injured himself permanently through a single clumsy and ill finished lie, the result of carelessness born of incomplete training. Some authorities hold that the young out not to lie at all.

45 That of course, is putting it rather stronger than necessary; still while I cannot go quite so far as that, I

do maintain, and I believe I am right, that the young ought to be temperate in the use of this great art until practice and experience shall give them that

50 confidence, elegance, and precision which alone can make the accomplishment graceful and profitable. Patience, diligence, painstaking attention to detail -- these are requirements; these in time, will make the student perfect; upon these only, may he rely as the

55 sure foundation for future eminence. Think what tedious years of study, thought, practice, experience, went to the equipment of that peerless old master who was able to impose upon the whole world the lofty and sounding maxim that "Truth is mighty and will

60 prevail" -- the most majestic compound fracture of fact which any of woman born has yet achieved. For the history of our race, and each individual's experience, are sewn thick with evidences that a truth is not hard to kill, and that a lie well told is immortal. There is in

65 Boston a monument of the man who discovered anesthesia; many people are aware, in these latter days, that that man didn't discover it at all, but stole the discovery from another man. Is this truth mighty, and will it prevail? Ah no, my hearers, the monument is

70 made of hardy material, but the lie it tells will outlast it a million years. An awkward, feeble, leaky lie is a thing which you ought to make it your unceasing study to avoid; such a lie as that has no more real permanence than an average truth. Why, you might as well tell the

75 truth at once and be done with it. A feeble, stupid, preposterous lie will not live two years -- except it be a slander upon somebody. It is indestructible, then of course, but that is no merit of yours. A final word: begin your practice of this gracious and beautiful art

80 early -- begin now. If I had begun earlier, I could have learned how.
There are many sorts of books; but good ones are the sort for the young to read. Remember that. They are a great, an inestimable, and unspeakable means of

85 improvement. Therefore be careful in your selection, my young friends; be very careful; confine yourselves exclusively to Robertson's *Sermons*, Baxter's *Saints' Rest*, Twain's *The Innocents Abroad*, and works of that kind.

90 But I have said enough. I hope you will treasure up the instructions which I have given you, and make them a guide to your feet and a light to your understanding. Build your character thoughtfully and painstakingly upon these precepts, and by and by,

95 when you have got it built, you will be surprised and gratified to see how nicely and sharply it resembles everybody else's.

[Handwritten margin annotations: "purpose of passage"; "less hassle to obey"; "violence ≠ sol'n"; "humor/satire/irony"; "reputation isn't everything"; "caught in lie damages rep"; "exaggeration for future advice"; "unexpected satire"; "think before you act; why apologize after?"; "early is relative"; "balance b/w submissiveness + individual/freedom"; "is this true?"; "books are good"; "lying/rumors can do lasting damage"; "is it good to be like everybody else?"]

1

What is the main purpose of this passage?

To satirically criticize society while giving advice to youth, but not in the way you'd expect

2

What is the main idea of the first paragraph (lines 1-10)?

States purpose of passage: to teach youth a lesson

3

What is the main idea of the second paragraph (lines 11-16)?

obey your parents even when they're not present

4

What is the central claim of the third paragraph (lines 17-28)?

people often resort to violence/aggression to solve problems

5

What is the main idea of the fourth paragraph (lines 29-36)?

People care too much about what others think, getting up early ≠ success

6

What is the central topic of the fifth paragraph (lines 37-82)?

the repercussions/efforts of lying

7

What is the thesis of the sixth paragraph (lines 83-89)?

Books help us improve/grow, but we shouldn't limit our reading to what others tell us to read.

8

What is the central idea in the seventh paragraph (lines 90-97)

Following his advice will help youth develop a char. like everyone else's

9

What is the overall tone of the passage?

humorous, light-hearted, satirical

10

What is the author's central claim? We too often follow advice given by elders/others, but fail to be our own person/find your own identity. copy

2) advice best when young

5) society thinks we are "splendid" if we wake up early / says something about our char. but why should it matter when we get up / what others think?

6) associates good qualities w/ lying... using reverse psychology to get ppl to change their behavior? good liars practice... is it worth the effort?

Lying = bad bc always caught esp. if not good

7) what makes a book good? good, so don't do it → bad rep. uses irony to state that good books are for everyone, not just youth, and come in many diff. titles/genres

8) do we want to succumb to all of society's expectations?

10) irony = develop char. by playing by rules/fitting in w/ society, but that's not really building char.

Adam Smith (1723-1790) was a Scottish philosopher and economist. The principle of the division of Labor is the opening chapter in his essay *The Wealth of Nations*, one of the most influential books on economics

The greatest improvements in the productive powers of labour, and the greater part of the skill, dexterity, and judgment, with which it is anywhere directed, or applied, seem to have been the effects of
5 the division of labour. The effects of the division of labour, in the general business of society, will be more easily understood, by considering in what manner it operates in some particular manufactures. It is commonly supposed to be carried furthest in some
10 very trifling ones; not perhaps that it really is carried further in them than in others of more importance: but in those trifling manufactures which are destined to supply the small wants of but a small number of people, the whole number of workmen must
15 necessarily be small; and those employed in every different branch of the work can often be collected into the same workhouse, and placed at once under the view of the spectator.

In those great manufactures, on the contrary,
20 which are destined to supply the great wants of the great body of the people, every different branch of the work employs so great a number of workmen, that it is impossible to collect them all into the same workhouse. We can seldom see more, at one time,
25 than those employed in one single branch. Though in such manufactures, therefore, the work may really be divided into a much greater number of parts, than in those of a more trifling nature, the division is not near so obvious, and has accordingly been much less
30 observed.

To take an example, therefore, from a very trifling manufacture, but one in which the division of labour has been very often taken notice of, the trade of a pin-maker: a workman not educated to this business
35 (which the division of labour has rendered a distinct trade), nor acquainted with the use of the machinery employed in it (to the invention of which the same division of labour has probably given occasion), could scarce, perhaps, with his utmost industry, make one
40 pin in a day, and certainly could not make twenty.

But in the way in which this business is now carried on, not only the whole work is a peculiar trade, but it is divided into a number of branches, of which the greater part are likewise peculiar trades. One man
45 draws out the wire; another straights it; a third cuts it; a fourth points it; a fifth grinds it at the top for receiving the head; to make the head requires two or

three distinct operations; to put it on is a peculiar business; to whiten the pins is another; it is even a
50 trade by itself to put them into the paper; and the important business of making a pin is, in this manner, divided into about eighteen distinct operations, which, in some manufactories, are all performed by distinct hands, though in others the same man will sometimes
55 perform two or three of them.

I have seen a small manufactory of this kind, where ten men only were employed, and where some of them consequently performed two or three distinct operations. But though they were very poor, and
60 therefore but indifferently accommodated with the necessary machinery, they could, when they exerted themselves, make among them about twelve pounds of pins in a day. There are in a pound upwards of four thousand pins of a middling size. Those ten persons,
65 therefore, could make among them upwards of forty-eight thousand pins in a day.

Each person, therefore, making a tenth part of forty-eight thousand pins, might be considered as making four thousand eight hundred pins in a day.
70 But if they had all wrought separately and independently, and without any of them having been educated to this peculiar business, they certainly could not each of them have made twenty, perhaps not one pin in a day; that is, certainly, not the two hundred
75 and fortieth, perhaps not the four thousand eight hundredth, part of what they are at present capable of performing, in consequence of a proper division and combination of their different operations.

1

What is the main purpose of the passage?

To argue for to div. of labor

2

What is the purpose of the first paragraph (lines 1-18)?

To state the necessity of division of labor

3

What is the function of the second paragraph (lines 19-30)?

To inform audience of large industries

4

What is the function of describing pin-making as "trifling" (line 31)?

To acknowledge that it seems like a trivial job, but actually involves a highly complex process

5

What is the function of the example of the solitary pin-makers in lines 34-40 ("a workman... twenty")?

To show the disadvantage of solitary work

6

The main purpose of the fourth paragraph (lines 41-55) is to?

To show this complex process involved in pinmaking as beneficial

7

What is the function of the description of the pin-makers as poor in line 59 and uneducated in lines 71-72?

Alone = poor/uneducated, so better to work together

8

What is the primary function of the final paragraph (lines 67-78)?

To drive home the point that collaborating/using all skills together > working independently

9

What is the author's thesis?

Labor has been most improved in its division of labor as seen in large industries

10

What is the author's tone?

Argumentative

alone = unproductive; together = efficient

THE DANGERS OF SPACEFLIGHT – NASA (FUNCTION)

The triumphs of the Apollo 11 moon landing often obscure the dangers of space flight. In the following passages from the historical archives at NASA.gov, we get a glimpse of what could go wrong.

Passage 1

One of the worst tragedies in the history of spaceflight occurred on January 27, 1967 when the crew of Gus Grissom, Ed White, and Roger Chaffee were killed in a fire in the Apollo Command Module during a preflight test at Cape Canaveral. They were training for the first crewed Apollo flight, an Earth orbiting mission scheduled to be launched on February 21st. They were taking part in a "plugs-out" test, in which the Command Module was mounted on the Saturn 1B on the launch pad just as it would be for the actual launch, but the Saturn 1B was not fueled. The plan was to go through an entire countdown sequence.

At 1 p.m. on Friday, 27 January 1967 the astronauts entered the capsule on Pad 34 to begin the test. A number of minor problems cropped up which delayed the test considerably and finally a failure in communications forced a hold in the count at 5:40 p.m. At 6:31 p.m. one of the astronauts (probably Chaffee) reported, "Fire, I smell fire." Two seconds later White was heard to say, "Fire in the cockpit." The fire spread throughout the cabin in a matter of seconds. The last crew communication ended 17 seconds after the start of the fire, followed by loss of all telemetry. The Apollo hatch could only open inward and was held closed by a number of latches which had to be operated by ratchets. It was also held closed by the interior pressure, which was higher than outside atmospheric pressure and required venting of the command module before the hatch could be opened. It took at least 90 seconds to get the hatch open under ideal conditions. Because the cabin had been filled with a pure oxygen atmosphere at normal pressure for the test and there had been many hours for the oxygen to permeate all the material in the cabin, the fire spread rapidly and the astronauts had no chance to get the hatch open. Nearby technicians tried to get to the hatch but were repeatedly driven back by the heat and smoke. By the time they succeeded in getting the hatch open roughly 5 minutes after the fire started the astronauts had already perished, probably within the first 30 seconds, due to smoke inhalation and burns.

The mission, originally designated Apollo 204 but commonly referred to as Apollo 1, was officially assigned the name "Apollo 1" in honor of Grissom, White, and Chaffee. The Apollo 1 Command Module capsule 012 was impounded and studied after the accident and was then locked away in a storage facility at NASA Langley Research Center. The changes made to the Apollo Command Module as a result of the tragedy resulted in a highly reliable craft which, with the exception of Apollo 13, helped make the complex and dangerous trip to the Moon almost commonplace.

Passage 2

On May 6, 1968, astronaut Neil A. Armstrong, then assigned as backup commander for the Apollo 9 mission, took off on a simulated lunar landing mission in Lunar Landing Research Vehicle #1 (LLRV-1) at Ellington Air Force Base near the Manned Spacecraft Center (MSC) in Houston, his 22nd flight of the test vehicle. Armstrong had been airborne about five minutes when he suddenly lost control of the vehicle. About 200 feet above the ground, he chose to eject. While the LLRV crashed and burned on impact Armstrong parachuted safely to Earth and was not injured. A crash investigation showed that a loss of helium pressure caused depletion of the hydrogen peroxide used for the reserve attitude thrusters. The vehicle's instrumentation did not provide adequate warning about the adverse situation. Engineers corrected the problems before flights resumed in October.

One of the most difficult tasks to accomplish President John F. Kennedy's goal of landing a man on the Moon and returning him safely to the Earth was the actual lunar landing. Astronauts used several tools to train for the landing, and possibly the most critical was the LLRV and its successor the Lunar Landing Training Vehicle (LLTV). Using these vehicles, astronauts mastered the intricacies of landing on the Moon by simulating the Lunar Module's (LM) performance. Dubbed the "flying bedstead," the ungainly contraption is "a much unsung hero of the Apollo Program," according to Apollo 8 astronaut Bill Anders. The open-framed LLRV and LLTV used a downward pointing turbofan engine to counteract five-sixths of the vehicle's weight to simulate lunar gravity and LM-like thrusters for attitude control. The astronauts were thus able to simulate maneuvering and landing on the lunar surface while still on Earth.

Bell Aerosystems of Buffalo, NY, built the LLRV, the first pure fly-by-wire aircraft to fly in Earth's atmosphere, meaning it relied exclusively on an interface with three analog computers to convert the pilot's movements to digital signals transmitted by wire and then execute his commands. These early research and test vehicles aided in the development

digital fly-by-wire technology for future aircraft. The
100 LLTVs were overall similar to the LLRVs, but used
newer electronic technologies that made them lighter
and allowed for improvements in their structural
integrity. Armstrong made the first LLRV flight by an
astronaut on March 27, 1967. Later, as commander of
105 Apollo 11, Armstrong completed his lunar landing
training in LLTV-2, making his final flight just three
weeks before the historic Moon landing mission.

 Armstrong said of the LLTV: "(The LM) Eagle
flew very much like the Lunar Landing Training
110 Vehicle which I had flown more than 30 times…. I
had made from 50 to 60 landings in the trainer, and
the final trajectory I flew to the landing was very
much like those flown in practice. That of course gave
me a good deal of confidence – a comfortable
115 familiarity." Summarizing its usefulness to the Apollo
training program, Armstrong said: "It was a contrary
machine, and a risky machine, but a very useful one."
All prime and backup Moon landing commanders
completed training in the LLTV, and those who
120 landed a LM on the Moon attributed their success to
this training.

1

What is the main purpose of the first passage?

To show how dangerous flying can be

2

What is main purpose of the first paragraph
(lines 1-13)?

To introduce failed mission/tragedy

3

What is the function of the second paragraph
(lines 14-43)?

To explain the mishaps of
this failed space mission

4

What is the function of the third paragraph
(lines 44-55)?

To show effects of this mission →
resulted in a safer aircraft

5

What is the function of lines 44-47 ("The
mission… Chaffee")?

To show respect for the crew

6

What is the tone of the first passage?

Cautious, informative, respectful

7

What is the main purpose of the second
passage?

To explain how training helps improve
safety of flight in space

8

What is the purpose of describing Armstrong's
crash in lines 62-67?

To provide example of dangerous flight

9

What is the function of the quotation marks
around the phrase "flying bedstead" in line 83?

Nickname/title for the machine

10

What is the primary purpose of the final
paragraph (lines 108-121)?

To praise the usefulness of training

11

What is the tone of the second passage?

informational

12

What is the relationship between passage 1 and
passage 2?

Both note the dangers of flying
and offer solutions. Passage
2 goes into more specifics
about how to improve safety

In October 1962, President John F. Kennedy sent United Nations Ambassador Adlai Steven to New York to confront the Soviet Ambassador Valerian Zorin on their installation of nuclear missiles in Cuba.

I want to say to you, Mr. Zorin, that I do not have your talent for obfuscation, for distortion, for confusing language, and for doubletalk. And I must confess to you that I am glad that I do not!

5   But if I understood what you said, you said that my position had changed, that today I was defensive because we did not have the evidence to prove our assertions, that your Government had installed long-range missiles in Cuba.

10   Well, let me say something to you, Mr. Ambassador—we do have the evidence. We have it, and it is clear and it is incontrovertible. And let me say something else—those weapons must be taken out of Cuba.

15   Next, let me say to you that, if I understood you, with a trespass on credibility that excels your best, you said that our position had changed since I spoke here the other day because of the pressures of world opinion and the majority of the United Nations. Well,

20   let me say to you, sir, you are wrong again. We have had no pressure from anyone whatsoever. We came in here today to indicate our willingness to discuss Mr. U Thant's proposals, and that is the only change that has taken place.

25   But let me also say to you, sir, that there has been a change. You—the Soviet Union has sent these weapons to Cuba. You—the Soviet Union has upset the balance of power in the world. You—the Soviet Union has created this new danger, not the United States.

30   And you ask with a fine show of indignation why the President did not tell Mr. Gromyko on last Thursday about our evidence, at the very time that Mr. Gromyko was blandly denying to the President that the U.S.S.R. was placing such weapons on sites in the

35   new world.

Well, I will tell you why—because we were assembling the evidence, and perhaps it would be instructive to the world to see how a Soviet official— how far he would go in perfidy. Perhaps we wanted to

40   know if this country faced another example of nuclear deceit like that one a year ago, when in stealth, the Soviet Union broke the nuclear test moratorium.

And while we are asking questions, let me ask you why your Government—your Foreign Minister—

45   deliberately, cynically deceived us about the nuclear build-up in Cuba.

And, finally, the other day, Mr. Zorin, I remind you that you did not deny the existence of these weapons. Instead, we heard that they had suddenly

50   become defensive weapons. But today again if I heard you correctly, you now say that they do not exist, or that we haven't proved they exist, with another fine flood of rhetorical scorn.

All right, sir, let me ask you one simple question:

55   Do you, Ambassador Zorin, deny that the U.S.S.R. has placed and is placing medium- and intermediate-range missiles and sites in Cuba? Yes or no—don't wait for the translation—yes or no? (*The Soviet representative waited for translation, then responded.*)

60   "This is not a court of law, I do not need to provide a yes or no answer..." (*Mr. Stevenson cuts him off*)

You can answer yes or no. You have denied they exist. I want to know if I understood you correctly. I am prepared to wait for my answer until hell freezes

65   over, if that's your decision. And I am also prepared to present the evidence in this room. (*The President called on the representative of Chile to speak, who instead let Ambassador Stevenson continue as follows.*)

70   I have not finished my statement. I asked you a question. I have had no reply to the question, and I will now proceed, if I may, to finish my statement.

I doubt if anyone in this room, except possibly the representative of the Soviet Union, has any doubt

75   about the facts. But in view of his statements and the statements of the Soviet Government up until last Thursday, when Mr. Gromyko denied the existence or any intention of installing such weapons in Cuba, I am going to make a portion of the evidence available right

80   now. If you will indulge me for a moment, we will set up an easel here in the back of the room where I hope it will be visible to everyone. (*Stephenson shows a number of photos clearly showing the build-up of munitions and military personnel...*)

85   These weapons, gentlemen, these launching pads, these planes—of which we have illustrated only a fragment—are a part of a much larger weapons complex, what is called a weapons system.

To support this build-up, to operate these

90   advanced weapons systems, the Soviet Union has sent a large number of military personnel to Cuba—a force now amounting to several thousand men.

These photographs, as I say, are available to members for detailed examination in the Trusteeship

95   Council room following this meeting. There I will have one of my aides who will gladly explain them to you in such detail as you may require.

I have nothing further to say at this time. (*After another statement by the Soviet representative,*

100 *Ambassador Stevenson replied as follows:*)

Mr. President and gentlemen, I won't detain you ~keep from; hold back~ but one minute. I have not had a direct answer to my question. The representative of the Soviet Union says that the official answer of the U.S.S.R. was the Tass
105 statement that they don't need to locate missiles in Cuba. Well, I agree—they don't need to. But the question is, have they missiles in Cuba—and that question remains unanswered. I knew it would be.

~realness~ As to the authenticity of the photographs, which
110 Mr. Zorin has spoken about with such scorn, I wonder ~contempt; negativity~ if the Soviet Union would ask its Cuban colleague to permit a U.N. team to go to these sites. If so, I can assure you that we can direct them to the proper places very quickly.

115 And now I hope that we can get down to business, that we can stop this sparring. We know the facts, and ~quarrel; fight; argument~ so do you, sir, and we are ready to talk about them. Our job here is not to score debating points. Our job, Mr. Zorin, is to save the peace. And if you are ready to
120 try, we are.

1

What is the main purpose of the passage?

To confront the Soviet Ambassador about his installation of nuclear weapons in Cuba

2

As used in line 2, the word "distortion" most nearly means

misinterpretation; twisting; falsification

3

The word "excels" in line 16 most nearly means

goes beyond/further; surpass

4

As it is used in line 27, the word "upset" most nearly means

disturb; overturn; tip; disrupt

5

As used in line 31, the word "fine" most nearly means

intense; explicit; visible

6

As used in line 54, the word "flood" most nearly means

constant string/series; outpouring; excess barrage

7

As used in line 54, the word "flood" most nearly means

[crossed out]

8

In line 82, the word "indulge" most nearly means

humor; yield to; satisfy

9

As it is used in line 117, the word "business" most nearly means

serious work; "busy-ness"

10

What is the author's thesis?

Due to constant deceit and info distortion, a direct confrontation is necessary to reveal the truth.

11

What is the author's tone?

critical; accusatory; warning

Thomas Paine (1736-1809) emigrated to the United States in 1774. *Common Sense* was a pamphlet written in 1775 and 1776 to support American independence from Britain.

The blood of the slain, the weeping voice of nature cries, "'tis time to part." Even the distance at which the Almighty hath placed England and America, is a strong and natural proof that the authority of the one

5 over the other was never the design of heaven. The time, likewise, at which the continent was discovered, adds weight to the argument, and the manner in which it was peopled, increases the force of it. The Reformation was preceded by the discovery

10 of America, as if the Almighty graciously meant to open a sanctuary to the persecuted in future years, when home should afford neither friendship nor safety.

The authority of Great Britain over this continent

15 is a form of government which sooner or later must have an end: and a serious mind can draw no true pleasure by looking forward, under the painful and positive conviction that what he calls "the present constitution" is merely temporary. As parents, we can

20 have no joy knowing that this government is not sufficiently lasting to insure anything which we may bequeath to posterity; and by a plain method of argument, as we are running the next generation into debt, we ought to do the work of it, otherwise we use

25 them meanly and pitifully. In order to discover the line of our duty rightly, we should take our children in our hand, and fix our station a few years farther into life; that eminence will present a prospect which a few present fears and prejudices conceal from our sight.

30 Tho I would carefully avoid giving unnecessary offense, yet I am inclined to believe that all those who espouse the doctrine of reconciliation may be included within the following descriptions:

Interested men, who are not to be trusted; weak

35 men, who can not see; prejudiced men, who will not see; and a certain set of moderate men, who think better of the European world than it deserves: and this last class, by an ill-judged deliberation, will be the cause of more calamities to this continent than all the

40 other three.

It is the good fortune of many to live distant from the scene of sorrow; the evil is not sufficiently brought to their doors to make them feel the precariousness with which all American property is possest. But let

45 our imaginations transport us a few moments to Boston; that seat of wretchedness will teach us wisdom, and instruct us forever to renounce a power in whom we can have no trust. The inhabitants of that unfortunate city, who but a few months ago were in

50 ease and affluence, have now no other alternative than to stay and starve, or turn out to beg. Endangered by the fire of their friends if they continue within the city, and plundered by the soldiery if they leave it. In their present situation they are prisoners without the hope

55 of redemption, and in a general attack for their relief they would be exposed to the fury of both armies.

Men of passive tempers look somewhat lightly over the offenses of Britain, and, still hoping for the best, are apt to call out, "Come, come, we shall be friends again

60 for all this." But examine the passions and feelings of mankind, bring the doctrine of reconciliation to the touchstone of nature, and then tell me whether you can hereafter love, honor, and faithfully serve the power that hath carried fire and sword into your land?

65 If you can not do all these, then are you only deceiving yourselves, and by your delay bringing ruin upon your posterity. Your future connection with Britain, whom you can neither love nor honor, will be forced and unnatural, and being formed only on the plan of

70 present convenience, will in a little time fall into a relapse more wretched than the first. But if you say you can still pass the violations over, then I ask, hath your house been burnt? Hath your property been destroyed before your face? Are your wife and children destitute

75 of a bed to lie on, or bread to live on? Have you lost a parent or a child by their hands, and yourself the ruined and wretched survivor? If you have not, then are you not a judge of those who have. But if you have, and can still shake hands with the murderers, then are

80 you unworthy the name of husband, father, friend, or lover, and, whatever may be your rank or title in life, you have the heart of a coward and the spirit of a sycophant.

1

What is the main purpose of this passage?

2

In lines 6-11 ("the time… safety"), what is the author's attitude toward the events of history?

3

What is the author's attitude toward British rule in the future?

4

How does the author characterize those who would reconcile with Britain?

5

What is the author's attitude toward the citizens of Boston?

6

What is the author's attitude toward "Men of passive tempers"?

7

What lines support your answer to the previous question?

8

What is the author's attitude toward those who have not suffered at the hands of the British?

9

What is the author's attitude toward England?

10

What is the author's attitude toward America?

11

What is the tone of the passage on the whole?

12

What is the author's central claim?

H. P. Lovecraft (1890-1937) was an American author of surrealist and horror fiction. *Ex Oblivione* was published in 1921.

When the last days were upon me, and the ugly trifles of existence began to drive me to madness like the small drops of water that torturers let fall ceaselessly upon one spot of their victim's body, I
5   loved the irradiate refuge of sleep. In my dreams I found a little of the beauty I had vainly sought in life, and wandered through old gardens and enchanted woods.

Once when the wind was soft and scented I heard
10   the south calling, and sailed endlessly and languorously under strange stars.

Once when the gentle rain fell I glided in a barge down a sunless stream under the earth till I reached another world of purple twilight, iridescent arbours,
15   and undying roses.

And once I walked through a golden valley that led to shadowy groves and ruins, and ended in a mighty wall green with antique vines, and pierced by a little gate of bronze.
20   Many times I walked through that valley, and longer and longer would I pause in the spectral half-light where the giant trees squirmed and twisted grotesquely, and the grey ground stretched damply from trunk to trunk, sometimes disclosing the mould-
25   stained stones of buried temples. And always the goal of my fancies was the mighty vine-grown wall with the little gate of bronze therein.

After a while, as the days of waking became less and less bearable from their greyness and sameness, I
30   would often drift in opiate peace through the valley and the shadowy groves, and wonder how I might seize them for my eternal dwelling-place, so that I need no more crawl back to a dull world stript of interest and new colours. And as I looked upon the little gate in the
35   mighty wall, I felt that beyond it lay a dream-country from which, once it was entered, there would be no return.

So each night in sleep I strove to find the hidden latch of the gate in the ivied antique wall, though it was
40   exceedingly well hidden. And I would tell myself that the realm beyond the wall was not more lasting merely, but more lovely and radiant as well.

Then one night in the dream-city of Zakarion, I found a yellowed papyrus filled with the thoughts of
45   dream-sages who dwelt of old in that city, and who were too wise ever to be born in the waking world. Therein were written many things concerning the world of dream, and among them was lore of a golden valley and a sacred grove with temples, and a high wall

50   pierced by a little bronze gate. When I saw this lore, I knew that it touched on the scenes I had haunted, and I therefore read long in the yellowed papyrus.

Some of the dream-sages wrote gorgeously of the wonders beyond the irrepassable gate, but others told
55   of horror and disappointment. I knew not which to believe, yet longed more and more to cross forever into the unknown land; for doubt and secrecy are the lure of lures, and no new horror can be more terrible than the daily torture of the commonplace. So when I
60   learned of the drug which would unlock the gate and drive me through, I resolved to take it when next I awaked.

Last night I swallowed the drug and floated dreamily into the golden valley and the shadowy
65   groves; and when I came this time to the antique wall, I saw that the small gate of bronze was ajar. From beyond came a glow that weirdly lit the giant twisted trees and the tops of the buried temples, and I drifted on songfully, expectant of the glories of the land from
70   whence I should never return.

But as the gate swung wider and the sorcery of drug and dream pushed me through, I knew that all sights and glories were at an end; for in that new realm was neither land nor sea, but only the white void of
75   unpeopled and illimitable space. So, happier than I had ever dared hoped to be, I dissolved again into that native infinity of crystal oblivion from which the daemon Life had called me for one brief and desolate hour.

1

What is the author's primary purpose?

to show that nothingness > life ; oblivion

2

In line 2, the word "trifles" most nearly means

unimportant/trivial matters

3

As it is used in line 24, the word "disclosing" most nearly means

↳ other def: make known, reveal, tell (disclose info)

expose ; uncover physically

4

In line 26, the word "fancies" most nearly means

desires ; whim

5

As used in line 32, the word "seize" most nearly means

take ; get a hold of

6

As it is used in line 51, the word "touched" most nearly means _on_

mention ; come close to/resemble

7

In line 51, the word "haunted" most nearly means

appeared in ; frequented

8

As used in line 79, the word "called" most nearly means

summoned

9

How would you summarize this passage?

10

What is the overall tone of this passage?

haunting, mysterious, spiritual

Edward A. Abbott (1838-1926) was an English schoolmaster. *Flatland* is an abstract novella of the hypothetical world "Flatland," a two-dimensional country. In it, Abbott presents an allegorical satire about the English class structure.

I call our world Flatland, not because we call it so, but to make its nature clearer to you, my happy readers, who are privileged to live in Space.

Imagine a vast sheet of paper on which straight
5 Lines, Triangles, Squares, Pentagons, Hexagons, and other figures, instead of remaining fixed in their places, move freely about, on or in the surface, but without the power of rising above or sinking below it, very much like shadows—only hard and with luminous edges—
10 and you will then have a pretty correct notion of my country and countrymen. Alas, a few years ago, I should have said "my universe": but now my mind has been opened to higher views of things.

In such a country, you will perceive at once that it
15 is impossible that there should be anything of what you call a "solid" kind; but I dare say you will suppose that we could at least distinguish by sight the Triangles, Squares, and other figures, moving about as I have described them. On the contrary, we could see nothing
20 of the kind, not at least so as to distinguish one figure from another. Nothing was visible, nor could be visible, to us, except Straight Lines; and the necessity of this I will speedily demonstrate.

Place a penny on the middle of one of your tables
25 in Space; and leaning over it, look down upon it. It will appear a circle.

But now, drawing back to the edge of the table, gradually lower your eye (thus bringing yourself more and more into the condition of the inhabitants of
30 Flatland), and you will find the penny becoming more and more oval to your view, and at last when you have placed your eye exactly on the edge of the table (so that you are, as it were, actually a Flatlander) the penny will then have ceased to appear oval at all, and will have
35 become, so far as you can see, a straight line.

The same thing would happen if you were to treat in the same way a Triangle, or Square, or any other figure cut out of pasteboard. As soon as you look at it with your eye on the edge on the table, you will find
40 that it ceases to appear to you a figure, and that it becomes in appearance a straight line. Take for example an equilateral Triangle—who represents with us a Tradesman of the respectable class. Fig. 1 represents the Tradesman as you would see him while
45 you were bending over him from above; figs. 2 and 3 represent the Tradesman, as you would see him if your eye were close to the level, or all but on the level of the table; and if your eye were quite on the level of the table (and that is how we see him in Flatland) you
50 would see nothing but a straight line.

When I was in Spaceland I heard that your sailors have very similar experiences while they traverse your seas and discern some distant island or coast lying on the horizon. The far-off land may have bays, forelands,
55 angles in and out to any number and extent; yet at a distance you see none of these (unless indeed your sun shines bright upon them revealing the projections and retirements by means of light and shade), nothing but a grey unbroken line upon the water.

60 Well, that is just what we see when one of our triangular or other acquaintances comes toward us in Flatland. As there is neither sun with us, nor any light of such a kind as to make shadows, we have none of the helps to the sight that you have in Spaceland. If our
65 friend comes closer to us we see his line becomes larger; if he leaves us it becomes smaller: but still he looks like a straight line; be he a Triangle, Square, Pentagon, Hexagon, Circle, what you will—a straight Line he looks and nothing else.

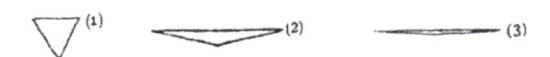

Figures 1, 2, and 3

· What or who do the shapes represent?

· Pay attention to bigger picture

1

What is the main purpose of the passage?

to surmise about what society would be like in a 2D world

2

What is main purpose of the first paragraph (lines 1-3)?

to introduce/describe this world

3

What is the function of the penny in lines 27-35?

to compare the view to perspective of Spaceland

4

What is the function of lines 39-54?

to compare the penny example to tradesman

5

What is the function of figures 1, 2, and 3?

to help readers visualize the view of the Tradesman

6

How does the example of sailors in lines 51-60 contribute to the passage's overall meaning?

the sailors experience similar things to the author/inhabitants of Flatland

7

What is the purpose of the final paragraph (lines 60-69)?

to describe how outsiders are viewed in Flatland

8

What is the main idea of this passage?

society views gender in a superficial way

9

What is the tone of this passage?

critical

- *Satire of Victorian England — not really Flatland*
- *Flatland = 2D world where men are many-sided figures and woman (represented as lines) are 2nd class citizens*
- *Author uses these geometric shapes to explore diffs. b/w 2 genders*
- *describes social stratification in Flatland, which resembles our world in its attitude toward gender*
- *everyone in Flatland sees each other in the same way*
  ↳ *view each other as lines since they have no perception of depth*

"THE KING OF VULTURES" – JOHN STUART MILL (RHETORIC)

John Stuart Mill (1806-1873) was one of the most influential political philosophers of the nineteenth century. This passage, from Mill's *On Liberty* (1859), explores the necessity of protecting the weak of society without overpowering the mighty.

The struggle between Liberty and Authority is the most conspicuous feature in the portions of history with which we are earliest familiar, particularly in that of Greece, Rome, and England. But in old times this

5 contest was between subjects, or some classes of subjects, and the Government. By liberty, was meant protection against the tyranny of the political rulers. The rulers were conceived (except in some of the popular governments of Greece) as in a necessarily

10 antagonistic position to the people whom they ruled. They consisted of a governing One, or a governing tribe or caste, who derived their authority from inheritance or conquest, who, at all events, did not hold it at the pleasure of the governed, and whose

15 supremacy men did not venture, perhaps did not desire, to contest, whatever precautions might be taken against its oppressive exercise. Their power was regarded as necessary, but also as highly dangerous; as a weapon which they would attempt to use against

20 their subjects, no less than against external enemies. To prevent the weaker members of the community from being preyed on by innumerable vultures, it was needful that there should be an animal of prey stronger than the rest, commissioned to keep them down. But

25 as the king of the vultures would be no less bent upon preying upon the flock than any of the minor harpies, it was indispensable to be in a perpetual attitude of defence against his beak and claws.

The aim, therefore, of patriots was to set limits to

30 the power which the ruler should be suffered to exercise over the community; and this limitation was what they meant by liberty. It was attempted in two ways. First, by obtaining a recognition of certain immunities, called political liberties or rights, which it

35 was to be regarded as a breach of duty in the ruler to infringe, and which, if he did infringe, specific resistance, or general rebellion, was held to be justifiable. A second, and generally a later expedient, was the establishment of constitutional checks, by

40 which the consent of the community, or of a body of some sort, supposed to represent its interests, was made a necessary condition to some of the more important acts of the governing power.

To the first of these modes of limitation, the ruling

45 power, in most European countries, was compelled, more or less, to submit. It was not so with the second; and, to attain this, or when already in some degree

possessed, to attain it more completely, became everywhere the principal object of the lovers of liberty.

50 And so long as mankind were content to combat one enemy by another, and to be ruled by a master, on condition of being guaranteed more or less efficaciously against his tyranny, they did not carry their aspirations beyond this point.

55 A time, however, came, in the progress of human affairs, when men ceased to think it a necessity of nature that their governors should be an independent power, opposed in interest to themselves. It appeared to them much better that the various magistrates of the

60 State should be their tenants or delegates, revocable at their pleasure. In that way alone, it seemed, could they have complete security that the powers of government would never be abused to their disadvantage. By degrees this new demand for elective and temporary

65 rulers became the prominent object of the exertions of the popular party, wherever any such party existed; and superseded, to a considerable extent, the previous efforts to limit the power of rulers.

As the struggle proceeded for making the ruling

70 power emanate from the periodical choice of the ruled, some persons began to think that too much importance had been attached to the limitation of the power itself. That (it might seem) was a resource against rulers whose interests were habitually opposed

75 to those of the people. What was now wanted was, that the rulers should be identified with the people; that their interest and will should be the interest and will of the nation. The nation did not need to be protected against its own will. There was no fear of its

80 tyrannizing over itself. Let the rulers be effectually responsible to it, promptly removable by it, and it could afford to trust them with power of which it could itself dictate the use to be made. Their power was but the nation's own power, concentrated, and in a form

85 convenient for exercise.

1

What is the main purpose of the passage?

_____

2

What does Mill assume about the monarchs of history ?

_____

3

What lines provide evidence for the previous question?

_____

4

How does Mill's argument shift in lines 29-33?

_____

5

What assumptions lie behind lines 44-54?

_____

6

How does Mill shift his argument in line 55?

_____

7

What are the central claims of the people discussed in the fourth paragraph (lines 55-68)?

_____

8

What assumptions lie behind the claims made in lines 80-85?

_____

9

What is the overall tone of this passage?

_____

10

What is the main thesis of this passage?

_____

"ON NOMINATION TO THE SUPREME COURT" – SONIA SOTOMAYOR (RHETORIC)

Born in the Bronx to Puerto Rican parents, Justice Sonia Sotomayor is the first person of Hispanic descent and first Latina to serve on the US Supreme Court. The following passage is adapted from her opening statements to the US Senate during her confirmation hearings.

The progression of my life has been uniquely American. My parents left Puerto Rico during World War II. I grew up in modest circumstances in a Bronx housing project. My father, a factory worker with a
5 third-grade education, passed away when I was 9 years old.

On her own, my mother raised my brother and me. She taught us that the key to success in America is a good education. And she set the example, studying
10 alongside my brother and me at our kitchen table so that she could become a registered nurse.

We worked hard. I poured myself into my studies at Cardinal Spellman High School, earning scholarships to Princeton University and then Yale
15 Law School, while my brother went on to medical school. Our achievements are due to the values that we learned as children, and they have continued to guide my life's endeavors. I try to pass on this legacy by serving as a mentor and friend to my many
20 godchildren and to students of all backgrounds.

Over the past three decades, I have seen our judicial system from a number of different perspectives—as a big-city prosecutor, as a corporate litigator, as a trial judge, and as an appellate judge. My
25 first job after law school was as an assistant district attorney in New York. There I saw children exploited and abused. I felt the pain and suffering of families torn apart by the needless death of loved ones. I saw and learned the tough job law enforcement has in
30 protecting the public. In my next legal job, I focused on commercial instead of criminal matters. I litigated issues on behalf of national and international businesses and advised them on matters ranging from contracts to trademarks.

35 My career as an advocate ended, and my career as a judge began, when I was appointed by President George H.W. Bush to the United States District Court for the Southern District of New York. As a trial judge, I did decide over 450 cases and presided over dozens of
40 trials, with perhaps my most famous case being the Major League Baseball strike in 1995.

After six extraordinary years on the district court, I was appointed by President Clinton to the United States Court of Appeals for the Second Circuit. On that
45 court, I have enjoyed the benefit of sharing ideas and perspectives with wonderful colleagues as we have

worked together to resolve the issues before us. I have now served as an appellate judge for over a decade, deciding a wide range of constitutional, statutory and
50 other legal questions. Throughout my 17 years on the bench, I have witnessed the human consequences of my decisions. Those decisions have not been made to serve the interests of any one litigant, but always to serve the larger interests of impartial justice.

55 In the past month, many senators have asked me about my judicial philosophy. Simple: fidelity to the law. The task of a judge is not to make law. It is to apply the law. And it is clear, I believe, that my record in two courts reflects my rigorous commitment to
60 interpreting the constitution according to its terms, interpreting statutes according to their terms and Congress's intent, and hewing faithfully to precedents established by the Supreme Court and by my circuit court.

65 In each case I have heard, I have applied the law to the facts at hand. The process of judging is enhanced when the arguments and concerns of the parties to the litigation are understood and acknowledged.

That is why I generally structure my opinions by
70 setting out what the law requires and then explaining why a contrary position, sympathetic or not, is accepted or rejected. That is how I seek to strengthen both the rule of law and faith in the impartiality of our judicial system. My personal and professional
75 experiences helped me to listen and understand, with the law always commanding the result in every case.

Since President Obama announced my nomination in May, I have received letters from people all over this country. Many tell a unique story of hope in spite of
80 struggle. Each letter has deeply touched me. Each reflects a dream—a belief in the dream that led my parents to come to New York all those years ago. It is our Constitution that makes that dream possible, and I now seek the honor of upholding the Constitution as a
85 justice on the Supreme Court.

Senators, I look forward in the next few days to answering your questions, to having the American people learn more about me, and to being part of a process that reflects the greatness of our Constitution
90 and of our nation.

1

What is the main purpose of the passage?

_____

2

What is unstated assumption about family in the first two paragraphs (lines 1-11)?

_____

3

What objections to Sotomayor's appointment does the third paragraph (lines 13-20) anticipate and counter?

_____

4

How did Sotomayor's experience as an advocate influence her view of the judicial system?

_____

5

How do lines 35-54 suggest that Sotomayor has bipartisan support?

_____

6

What does the sixth paragraph (lines 55-64) suggest about Sotomayor's judicial approach?

_____

7

In the seventh paragraph (lines 65-68), what does Sotomayor assume about the arguments and concerns of litigants?

_____

8

What objections to her appointment does the eighth paragraph (lines 69-76) anticipate and counter?

_____

9

How does the ninth paragraph (lines 77-85) reflect the ideas of the first two paragraphs (lines 1-11)?

_____

10

What is the overall rhetorical structure of the passage?

_____

11

What is the overall tone of the passage?

_____

12

What is the main topic of the passage?

_____

"ON MY IMPENDING INTERVIEW WITH BURR" – ALEXANDER HAMILTON (DETAIL)

Passage 1 is adapted from a statement former Treasury Secretary Alexander Hamilton written the day before he dueled Vice President Aaron Burr. The duel took place in Weehawken, NJ, on July 11, 1804. Passage 2 is from a letter Hamilton wrote to his wife Eliza in the event of his death.

Passage 1

On my expected interview with Col. Burr, I think it proper to make some remarks explanatory of my conduct, motives, and views. I was certainly desirous
5 of avoiding this interview for the most urgent reasons:

1. My religious and moral principles are strongly opposed to the practise of duelling, and it would ever give me pain to be obliged to shed the blood of a fellow creature in a private combat forbidden by the law.

10 2. My wife and children are extremely dear to me, and my life is of the utmost importance to them in various views.

3. I feel a sense of obligation toward my creditors, who, in case of accident to me, by the forced sale of my
15 property, may be in some degree sufferers. I did not think myself at liberty, as a man of probity, lightly to expose them to this hazard.

4. I am conscious of no ill-will toward Col. Burr, distinct from political opposition, which, as I trust, has
20 proceeded from pure and upright motives.

Lastly, I shall hazard much and can probably gain nothing by the issue of this interview.

But it was, as I conceive, impossible to avoid it. There were intrinsic difficulties in the thing, an
25 artificial embarrassment from the manner of proceeding on the part of Col. Burr.

Intrinsic, because it is not to be denied that my animadversion on the political principles, character and views of Col. Burr have been extremely severe; and
30 on different occasions I, in common with many others, have made very unfavorable criticisms on particular instances of the private conduct of this gentleman. In proportion as these impressions were entertained with sincerity and uttered with motives and for purposes
35 which might appear to me commendable would be the difficulty (until they could be removed by evidence of their being erroneous) of explanation or apology. The disavowal required of me by Col. Burr in a general and indefinite form was out of my power, if it had really
40 been proper for me to submit to be questioned, but I was sincerely of the opinion that this could not be, and in this opinion I was confirmed by a very moderate and judicious friend whom I consulted. Besides that, Col. Burr appeared to me to assume, in the first
45 instance, a tone unnecessarily peremptory and menacing, and, in the second, positively offensive. Yet

I wished as far as might be practicable to leave a door open to accommodation....

It is also my ardent wish that I may have been more
50 mistaken than I think I have been, and that he, by his future conduct, may show himself worthy of all confidence and esteem and prove an ornament and a blessing to the country as well, because it is possible I may have injured Col. Burr, however convinced myself
55 that my opinions and declarations may have been well founded.

As for my general principles and temper in relation to similar affairs, I have resolved, if our interview is conducted in the usual manner, and it pleases God to
60 give me the opportunity, to reserve and throw away my first shot, and I have thoughts even of reserving my second shot, and thus giving a double opportunity to Col. Burr to pause and reflect. It is not, however, my intention to enter into any explanation on the ground.
65 Apology, from principle, I hope, rather than pride, is out of the question. To those who, with me abhorring the practise of duelling, may think that I ought on no account to have added to the number of examples, I answer that my relative situation as well in public as in
70 private, enforcing all the considerations which constitute what men of the world denominate honor, inspired in me (as I thought) a peculiar necessity not to decline the call. The ability to be useful in future, whether in resisting mischief or in effecting good, in
75 those crises of our public affairs which seem lately to happen would probably be inseparable from a conformity with public prejudice in this particular.

Passage 2

"This letter, my dear Eliza, will not be delivered to
80 you unless I shall first have terminated my earthly career, to begin, as I humbly hope from redeeming grace and divine mercy, a happy immortality. If it had been possible for me to have avoided the interview, my love for you and my precious children would have
85 been alone a decisive motive. But it was not possible without sacrifice which would have rendered me unworthy of your esteem. I need not tell you of the pangs I feel from the idea of quitting you and exposing you to the anguish I know you would feel. Nor could I
90 dwell on the topic lest it should unman me. The consolations of religion, my beloved, can alone support you; and these you have a right to enjoy. Fly to the bosom of your God and be comforted. With my last idea I shall cherish the sweet hope of meeting you in a
95 better world. Adieu, best of wives, best of women. Embrace all my darling children for me."

1

What is the main purpose of the first passage?

_____

2

What does Hamilton indicate that he has to gain from his duel with Col. Burr?

_____

3

According to passage 1, why was the debate unavoidable?

_____

4

What lines provide evidence for your previous answer?

_____

5

What do lines 27-48 indicate about Hamilton's opinion of Col. Burr?

_____

6

What reasons does Hamilton give for refusing to explain or apologize for his comments?

_____

7

What does Hamilton say he will do with his shot?

_____

8

According to passage 1, why must Hamilton duel Col. Burr?

_____

9

What is the main purpose of passage 2?

_____

10

According to passage 2, why must Hamilton duel Col. Burr?

_____

12

What is the relationship between the passages?

_____

Niccolò Machiavelli's classic, *The Prince*, was first published in 1532. *The Prince* is one of the first books of modern political theory and philosophy.

Coming now to the other qualities mentioned above, I say that every prince ought to desire to be considered clement and not cruel. Nevertheless he ought to take care not to misuse this clemency. Cesare

5   Borgia was considered cruel; notwithstanding, his cruelty reconciled the Romagna, unified it, and restored it to peace and loyalty. And if this be rightly considered, he will be seen to have been much more merciful than the Florentine people, who, to avoid a

10 reputation for cruelty, permitted Pistoia[11] to be destroyed. Therefore a prince, so long as he keeps his subjects united and loyal, ought not to mind the reproach of cruelty; because with a few examples he will be more merciful than those who, through too

15 much mercy, allow disorders to arise, from which follow murders or robberies; for these are wont to injure the whole people, whilst those executions which originate with a prince offend the individual only.

And of all princes, it is impossible for the new

20 prince to avoid the imputation of cruelty, owing to new states being full of dangers. Hence Virgil, through the mouth of Dido, excuses the inhumanity of her reign owing to its being new, saying: Hard fortune in a strange realm forces me to this task, to keep watch and

25 ward on my wide frontiers

Nevertheless he ought to be slow to believe and to act, nor should he himself show fear, but proceed in a temperate manner with prudence and humanity, so that too much confidence may not make him

30 incautious and too much distrust render him intolerable.

Upon this a question arises: whether it be better to be loved than feared or feared than loved? It may be answered that one should wish to be both, but, because

35 it is difficult to unite them in one person, it is much safer to be feared than loved, when, of the two, either must be dispensed with. Because this is to be asserted in general of men, that they are ungrateful, fickle, false, cowardly, covetous, and as long as you succeed they

40 are yours entirely; they will offer you their blood, property, life, and children, as is said above, when the need is far distant; but when it approaches they turn against you. And that prince who, relying entirely on their promises, has neglected other precautions, is

45 ruined; because friendships that are obtained by payments, and not by greatness or nobility of mind,

may indeed be earned, but they are not secured, and in time of need cannot be relied upon; and men have less scruple in offending one who is beloved than one who

50 is feared, for love is preserved by the link of obligation which, owing to the baseness of men, is broken at every opportunity for their advantage; but fear preserves you by a dread of punishment which never fails.

55 Nevertheless a prince ought to inspire fear in such a way that, if he does not win love, he avoids hatred; because he can endure very well being feared whilst he is not hated, which will always be as long as he abstains from the property of his citizens and subjects and from

60 their women. But when it is necessary for him to proceed against the life of someone, he must do it on proper justification and for manifest cause, but above all things he must keep his hands off the property of others, because men more quickly forget the death of

65 their father than the loss of their patrimony. Besides, pretexts for taking away the property are never wanting; for he who has once begun to live by robbery will always find pretexts for seizing what belongs to others; but reasons for taking life, on the contrary, are

70 more difficult to find and sooner lapse. But when a prince is with his army, and has under control a multitude of soldiers, then it is quite necessary for him to disregard the reputation of cruelty, for without it he would never hold his army united or disposed to its

75 duties.

As to the question of being feared or loved, I come to the conclusion that, men loving according to their own will and fearing according to that of the prince, a wise prince should establish himself on that which is in

80 his own control and not in that of others; he must endeavour only to avoid hatred, as is noted.

---

[1] Pistoia was a nearby town beholden to the city-state of Florence. When Pistoria rebelled, the Florentines did not punish the rebels, who subsequently broke into factions.

1

What is the main purpose of the passage?

_____

2

According to lines 11-18, what is the problem with mercy?

_____

3

What does the passages say about the benefits of a temperate manner?

_____

4

What does Machiavelli indicate about being loved?

_____

5

What lines provide evidence for your previous answer?

_____

6

How does the passage describe the difference between fear and hatred?

_____

7

According to the passage, how do people respond differently to the death of a parent and the loss of wealth?

_____

8

According to Machiavelli, when is it appropriate for a prince to be cruel?

_____

9

What is the central thesis of the passage?

_____

10

What is the tone of the passage overall?

_____

Kate Chopin (1850-1904) was an author from the American South. This 1894 short story was originally published in *Vogue* magazine.

Knowing that Mrs. Mallard was afflicted with a heart trouble, great care was taken to break to her as gently as possible the news of her husband's death.

5 It was her sister Josephine who told her, in broken sentences; veiled hints that revealed in half concealing. Her husband's friend Richards was there, too, near her. It was he who had been in the newspaper office when intelligence of the railroad disaster was received, with Brently Mallard's name leading the list of "killed." He
10 had only taken the time to assure himself of its truth by a second telegram, and had hastened to forestall any less careful, less tender friend in bearing the sad message.

She did not hear the story as many women have
15 heard the same, with a paralyzed inability to accept its significance. She wept at once, with sudden, wild abandonment, in her sister's arms. When the storm of grief had spent itself she went away to her room alone. She would have no one follow her.
20 There stood, facing the open window, a comfortable, roomy armchair. Into this she sank, pressed down by a physical exhaustion that haunted her body and seemed to reach into her soul.

She could see in the open square before her house
25 the tops of trees that were all aquiver with the new spring life. The delicious breath of rain was in the air. In the street below a peddler was crying his wares. The notes of a distant song which someone was singing reached her faintly, and countless sparrows were
30 twittering in the eaves.

There were patches of blue sky showing here and there through the clouds that had met and piled one above the other in the west facing her window.

She sat with her head thrown back upon the
35 cushion of the chair, quite motionless, except when a sob came up into her throat and shook her, as a child who has cried itself to sleep continues to sob in its dreams.

She was young, with a fair, calm face, whose lines
40 bespoke repression and even a certain strength. But now there was a dull stare in her eyes, whose gaze was fixed away off yonder on one of those patches of blue sky. It was not a glance of reflection, but rather indicated a suspension of intelligent thought.
45 There was something coming to her and she was waiting for it, fearfully. What was it? She did not know; it was too subtle and elusive to name. But she felt it, creeping out of the sky, reaching toward her through the sounds, the scents, the color that filled the air.

50 Now her bosom rose and fell tumultuously. She was beginning to recognize this thing that was approaching to possess her, and she was striving to beat it back with her will—as powerless as her two white slender hands would have been. When she
55 abandoned herself a little whispered word escaped her slightly parted lips. She said it over and over under the breath: "free, free, free!" The vacant stare and the look of terror that had followed it went from her eyes. They stayed keen and bright. Her pulses beat fast, and the
60 coursing blood warmed and relaxed every inch of her body.

She did not stop to ask if it were or were not a monstrous joy that held her. A clear and exalted perception enabled her to dismiss the suggestion as
65 trivial. She knew that she would weep again when she saw the kind, tender hands folded in death; the face that had never looked save with love upon her, fixed and gray and dead. But she saw beyond that bitter moment a long procession of years to come that would
70 belong to her absolutely. And she opened and spread her arms out to them in welcome.

There would be no one to live for during those coming years; she would live for herself. There would be no powerful will bending hers in that blind
75 persistence with which men and women believe they have a right to impose a private will upon a fellow-creature. A kind intention or a cruel intention made the act seem no less a crime as she looked upon it in that brief moment of illumination.
80 And yet she had loved him—sometimes. Often she had not. What did it matter! What could love, the unsolved mystery, count for in the face of this possession of self-assertion which she suddenly recognized as the strongest impulse of her being!
85 "Free! Body and soul free!" she kept whispering.

Josephine was kneeling before the closed door with her lips to the keyhole, imploring for admission. "Louise, open the door! I beg; open the door—you will make yourself ill. What are you doing, Louise? For
90 heaven's sake open the door."

"Go away. I am not making myself ill." No; she was drinking in a very elixir of life through that open window.

Her fancy was running riot along those days ahead
95 of her. Spring days, and summer days, and all sorts of days that would be her own. She breathed a quick prayer that life might be long. It was only yesterday she had thought with a shudder that life might be long.

She arose at length and opened the door to her
100 sister's importunities. There was a feverish triumph in her eyes, and she carried herself unwittingly like a goddess of Victory. She clasped her sister's waist, and

together they descended the stairs. Richards stood waiting for them at the bottom.

105   Someone was opening the front door with a latchkey. It was Brently Mallard who entered, a little travel-stained, composedly carrying his grip-sack and umbrella. He had been far from the scene of the accident, and did not even know there had been one.

110 He stood amazed at Josephine's piercing cry; at Richards' quick motion to screen him from the view of his wife.

    When the doctors came they said she had died of heart disease—of the joy that kills.

1

What is the main purpose of this passage?

_____

2

What is Josephine's and Richards's attitude toward Mrs. Mallard?

_____

3

What is Mrs. Mallard's initial response to the death of her husband?

_____

4

What lines support your answer to the previous question?

_____

5

How does Mrs. Mallard's attitude shift in line 54-57?

_____

6

What is Mrs. Mallard's attitude in lines 80-84?

_____

7

What do lines 99-104 indicate about Mrs. Mallard's attitude toward widowhood?

_____

8

What is Mrs. Mallard's response to her husband's sudden reappearance?

_____

9

How would you summarize the passage?

_____

10

What is the tone of the passage on the whole?

_____

12/9

This passage is adapted from a speech by Frederick Douglass given on July 5, 1852 to the Ladies' Anti-Slavery Society in Rochester, NY. Douglass was an abolitionist and former slave who taught himself to read and write.

But I fancy I hear some one of my audience say, it is just in this circumstance that you and your brother abolitionists fail to make a favorable impression on the public mind. Would you argue more, and denounce
5   less, would you persuade more, and rebuke less, your cause would be much more likely to succeed. But, I submit, where all is plain there is nothing to be argued. What point in the anti-slavery creed would you have me argue? On what branch of the subject do the people
10   of this country need light? Must I undertake to prove that the slave is a man? That point is conceded already. Nobody doubts it. The slaveholders themselves acknowledge it in the enactment of laws for their government. They acknowledge it when they punish
15   disobedience on the part of the slave. There are seventy-two crimes in the State of Virginia, which, if committed by a black man, (no matter how ignorant he be), subject him to the punishment of death; while only two of the same crimes will subject a white man to
20   the like punishment. What is this but the acknowledgement that the slave is a moral, intellectual and responsible being? The manhood of the slave is conceded. It is admitted in the fact that Southern statute books are covered with enactments forbidding,
25   under severe fines and penalties, the teaching of the slave to read or to write. When you can point to any such laws, in reference to the beasts of the field, then I may consent to argue the manhood of the slave. When the dogs in your streets, when the fowls of the air,
30   when the cattle on your hills, when the fish of the sea, and the reptiles that crawl, shall be unable to distinguish the slave from a brute, then will I argue with you that the slave is a man!

For the present, it is enough to affirm the equal
35   manhood of the Negro race. Is it not astonishing that, while we are ploughing, planting and reaping, using all kinds of mechanical tools, erecting houses, constructing bridges, building ships, working in metals of brass, iron, copper, silver and gold; that, while we
40   are reading, writing and cyphering, acting as clerks, merchants and secretaries, having among us lawyers, doctors, ministers, poets, authors, editors, orators and teachers; that, while we are engaged in all manner of enterprises common to other men, digging gold in
45   California, capturing the whale in the Pacific, feeding sheep and cattle on the hill-side, living, moving, acting, thinking, planning, living in families as husbands, wives and children, and, above all, confessing and worshipping the Christian's God, and looking
50   hopefully for life and immortality beyond the grave, we are called upon to prove that we are men!

Would you have me argue that man is entitled to liberty? That he is the rightful owner of his own body? You have already declared it. Must I argue the
55   wrongfulness of slavery? Is that a question for Republicans? Is it to be settled by the rules of logic and argumentation, as a matter beset with great difficulty, involving a doubtful application of the principle of justice, hard to be understood? How should I look
60   today, in the presence of Americans, dividing, and subdividing a discourse, to show that men have a natural right to freedom? Speaking of it relatively, and positively, negatively, and affirmatively. To do so, would be to make myself ridiculous, and to offer an
65   insult to your understanding.—There is not a man beneath the canopy of heaven that does not know that slavery is wrong for him.

What, am I to argue that it is wrong to make men brutes, to rob them of their liberty, to work them
70   without wages, to keep them ignorant of their relations to their fellow men, to beat them with sticks, to flay their flesh with the lash, to load their limbs with irons, to hunt them with dogs, to sell them at auction, to sunder their families, to knock out their teeth, to burn
75   their flesh, to starve them into obedience and submission to their masters? Must I argue that a system thus marked with blood, and stained with pollution, is wrong? No! I will not. I have better employments for my time and strength than such
80   arguments would imply.

What, then, remains to be argued? Is it that slavery is not divine; that God did not establish it; that our doctors of divinity are mistaken? There is blasphemy in the thought. That which is inhuman, cannot be
85   divine! Who can reason on such a proposition? They that can, may; I cannot. The time for such argument is passed.

1

What is the main purpose of the passage?

_____

2

Why does Douglass say that even the slave owners acknowledge that slaves are human?

_____

3

What lines provide evidence for the previous question?

_____

4

How does Douglass support his claim for the equal humanity of slaves?

_____

5

What is the effect of Douglass's rhetorical questions in the third paragraph (lines 52-67)?

_____

6

What is the tone of the fourth paragraph (lines 68-80)?

_____

7

How does the final paragraph support Douglass's claims?

_____

8

What assumptions does Douglass make about his audience?

_____

9

What lines provide evidence for the previous question?

_____

10

What is the main thesis of this passage?

_____

11

What is the tone of the passage?

_____

This passage is the opening chapter of H. G. Wells, *The War of the Worlds*. Wells (1866-1946) was one of the founders of science fiction and fantasy literature.

No one would have believed in the last years of the nineteenth century that this world was being watched keenly and closely by intelligences greater than man's and yet as mortal as his own; that as men busied
5 themselves about their various concerns they were scrutinised and studied, perhaps almost as narrowly as a man with a microscope might scrutinise the transient creatures that swarm and multiply in a drop of water. With infinite complacency men went to and fro over
10 this globe about their little affairs, serene in their assurance of their empire over matter. It is possible that the infusoria[1] under the microscope do the same. No one gave a thought to the older worlds of space as sources of human danger, or thought of them only to
15 dismiss the idea of life upon them as impossible or improbable.

It is curious to recall some of the mental habits of those departed days. At most terrestrial men fancied there might be other men upon Mars, perhaps inferior
20 to themselves and ready to welcome a missionary enterprise. Yet across the gulf of space, minds that are to our minds as ours are to those of the beasts that perish, intellects vast and cool and unsympathetic, regarded this earth with envious eyes, and slowly and
25 surely drew their plans against us. And early in the twentieth century came the great disillusionment.

The planet Mars, I scarcely need remind the reader, revolves about the sun at a mean distance of 140,000,000 miles, and the light and heat it receives
30 from the sun is barely half of that received by this world. It must be, if the nebular hypothesis has any truth, older than our world; and long before this earth ceased to be molten, life upon its surface must have begun its course. The fact that it is scarcely one seventh
35 of the volume of the earth must have accelerated its cooling to the temperature at which life could begin. It has air and water and all that is necessary for the support of animated existence.

Yet so vain is man, and so blinded by his vanity,
40 that no writer, up to the very end of the nineteenth century, expressed any idea that intelligent life might have developed there far, or indeed at all, beyond its earthly level. Nor was it generally understood that since Mars is older than our earth, with scarcely a
45 quarter of the superficial area and remoter from the sun, it necessarily follows that it is not only more distant from time's beginning but nearer its end.

The secular cooling that must someday overtake our planet has already gone far indeed with our
50 neighbour. Its physical condition is still largely a mystery, but we know now that even in its equatorial region the midday temperature barely approaches that of our coldest winter. Its air is much more attenuated than ours, its oceans have shrunk until they cover but a
55 third of its surface, and as its slow seasons change huge snowcaps gather and melt about either pole and periodically inundate its temperate zones. That last stage of exhaustion, which to us is still incredibly remote, has become a present-day problem for the
60 inhabitants of Mars.

The immediate pressure of necessity has brightened their intellects, enlarged their powers, and hardened their hearts. And looking across space with instruments, and intelligences such as we have scarcely
65 dreamed of, they see, at its nearest distance only 35,000,000 of miles sunward of them, a morning star of hope, our own warmer planet, green with vegetation and grey with water, with a cloudy atmosphere eloquent of fertility, with glimpses through its drifting
70 cloud wisps of broad stretches of populous country and narrow, navy-crowded seas.

And we men, the creatures who inhabit this earth, must be to them at least as alien and lowly as are the monkeys and lemurs to us. The intellectual side of man
75 already admits that life is an incessant struggle for existence, and it would seem that this too is the belief of the minds upon Mars. Their world is far gone in its cooling and this world is still crowded with life, but crowded only with what they regard as inferior
80 animals. To carry warfare sunward is, indeed, their only escape from the destruction that, generation after generation, creeps upon them.

And before we judge of them too harshly we must remember what ruthless and utter destruction our own
85 species has wrought, not only upon animals, such as the vanished bison and the dodo, but upon its inferior races. The Tasmanians, in spite of their human likeness, were entirely swept out of existence in a war of extermination waged by European immigrants, in
90 the space of fifty years. Are we such apostles of mercy as to complain if the Martians warred in the same spirit?

---

[1] A single-celled organism

1

What is the main purpose of this passage?

_____

2

What is the main idea of the first paragraph (lines 1-16)?

_____

3

What claim does the author make in the second paragraph (lines 17-26)?

_____

4

What is the main idea of the third paragraph (lines 27-38)?

_____

5

What is the author's central claim in the fourth paragraph (lines 39-47)?

_____

6

What does the author indicate about the planet Mars In the fifth paragraph (lines 48-60)?

_____

7

What does the sixth paragraph (lines 61-71) indicate about the planet Earth?

_____

8

What is the primary idea of the seventh paragraph (lines 72-82)?

_____

9

What is the central claim in the ninth paragraph (lines 83-92)?

_____

10

What is the main thesis of this passage?

_____

11

What is the overall tone of the passage?

_____

"YOSEMITE FALL" – JOHN MUIR (MAIN IDEA)

This passage is adapted from John Muir, *Our National Parks*, 1901. Muir (1838-1914) was a Scottish-American naturalist, co-founder of the Sierra Club, and the father of the American National Park system.

5 Yosemite Fall is a prominent waterfall in Yosemite National Park in California.

The views developed in a walk up the zigzags of the trail leading to the foot of the Upper Fall are about as varied and impressive as those displayed along the
10 favorite Glacier Point Trail. One rises as if on wings. The groves, meadows, fern-flats and reaches of the river gain new interest, as if never seen before; all the views changing in a most striking manner as we go higher from point to point. The foreground also
15 changes every few rods in the most surprising manner, although the earthquake talus and the level bench on the face of the wall over which the trail passes seem monotonous and commonplace as seen from the bottom of the Valley.

20 Up we climb with glad exhilaration, through shaggy fringes of laurel, ceanothus, glossy-leaved manzanita and live-oak, from shadow to shadow across bars and patches of sunshine, the leafy openings making charming frames for the Valley pictures beheld
25 through gem, and for the glimpses of the high peaks that appear in the distance. The higher we go the farther we seem to be from the summit of the vast granite wall. Here we pass a projecting buttress hose grooved and rounded surface tells a plain story of the
30 time when the Valley, now filled with sunshine, was filled with ice, when the grand old Yosemite Glacier, flowing river-like from its distant fountains, swept through it, crushing, grinding, wearing its way ever deeper, developing and fashioning these sublime rocks.

35 Again we cross a white, battered gully, the pathway of rock avalanches or snow avalanches. Farther on we come to a gentle stream slipping down the face of the Cliff in lace-like strips, and dropping from ledge to ledge—too small to be called a fall—trickling, dripping,
40 oozing, a pathless wanderer from one of the upland meadow lying a little way back of the Valley rim, seeking a way century after century to the depths of the Valley without any appreciable channel. Every morning after a cool night, evaporation being checked,
45 it gathers strength and sings like a bird, but as the day advances and the sun strikes its thin currents outspread on the heated precipices, most of its waters vanish ere the bottom of the Valley is reached.

Many a fine, hanging-garden aloft on breezy
50 inaccessible heights awes to it its freshness and fullness of beauty; ferneries in shady nooks, filled with Adiantum, Woodwardia, Woodsia, Aspidium, Pellaea, and Cheilanthes, rosetted and tufted and ranged in

lines, daintily overlapping, thatching the stupendous
55 cliffs with softest beauty, some of the delicate fronds seeming to float on the warm moist air, without any connection with rock or stream. Nor is there any lack of colored plants wherever they can find a place to cling to; lilies and mints, the showy cardinal mimulus,
60 and glowing cushions of the golden bahia, enlivened with butterflies and bees and all the other small, happy humming creatures that belong to them.

After the highest point on the lower division of the trail is gained it leads up into the deep recess occupied
65 by the great fall, the noblest display of falling water to be found in the Valley, or perhaps in the world. When it first comes in sight it seems almost within reach of one's hand, so great in the spring is its volume and velocity, yet it is still nearly a third of a mile away and
70 appears to recede as we advance. The sculpture of the walls about it is on a scale of grandeur, according nobly with the fall plain and massive, though elaborately finished, like all the other cliffs about the Valley.

In the afternoon an immense shadow is cast
75 athwart the plateau in front of the fall, and over the chaparral bushes that clothe the slopes and benches of the walls to the eastward, creeping upward until the fall is wholly overcast, the contrast between the shaded and illumined sections being very striking in these near
80 views.

Under this shadow, during the cool centuries immediately following the breaking-up of the Glacial Period, dwelt a small residual glacier, one of the few that lingered on this sun-beaten side of the Valley after
85 the main trunk glacier had vanished. It sent down a long winding current through the narrow cañon on the west side of the fall, and must have formed a striking feature of the ancient scenery of the Valley; the lofty fall of ice and fall of water side by side, yet separate and
90 distinct.

The coolness of the afternoon shadow and the abundant dewy spray make a fine climate for the plateau ferns and grasses, and for the beautiful azalea bushes that grow here in profusion and bloom in
95 September, long after the warmer thickets down on the floor of the Valley have withered and gone to seed. Even close to the fall, and behind it at the base of the cliff, a few venturesome plants may be found undisturbed by the rock-shaking torrent.

1

What is the main purpose of the passage?

_____

2

How does Muir's narrative shift at line 14?

_____

3

How does the description shift between the second and third paragraphs and the fourth paragraph?

_____

4

What features of the ascent does Muir discuss throughout?

_____

5

How does Muir's description shift in line 61?

_____

6

What is the overall narrative structure of the passage?

_____

7

How would you summarize the passage?

_____

8

What is the tone of this passage?

_____

9

What is the main topic of this passage?

_____

THE YOUNG EDDA – SNORRI STURLUSON (DETAIL)

This passage is adapted from Rasmus B. Anderson's preface to *The Young (or Prose) Edda*. *The Young Edda* is a medieval collection of Islandic and Norse mythology written around 1220 CE. In this preface, Anderson outlines the Norse myths of the beginning and the end of the world (cosmogony and eschatology).

In the beginning, before the heaven and the earth and the sea were created, the great abyss Ginungagap was without form and void, and the spirit of Fimbultyr moved upon the face of the deep, until the ice-cold
5 rivers, the Elivogs, flowing from Niflheim, came in contact with the dazzling flames from Muspelheim. This was before Chaos.

And Fimbultyr said: Let the melted drops of vapor quicken into life, and the giant Ymer was born in the
10 midst of Ginungagap. He was not a god, but the father of all the race of evil giants. This was Chaos.

And Fimbultyr said: Let Ymer be slain and let order be established. And straightway Odin and his brothers—the bright sons of Bure—gave Ymer a
15 mortal wound, and from his body made they the universe; from his flesh, the earth; from his blood, the sea; from his bones, the rocks; from his hair, the trees; from his skull, the vaulted heavens; from his eyebrows, the bulwark called Midgard. And the gods
20 formed man and woman in their own image of two trees, and breathed into them the breath of life. Ask and Embla became living souls, and they received a garden in Midgard as a dwelling-place for themselves and their children until the end of time. This was
25 Cosmos.

The world's last day approaches. All bonds and fetters that bound the forces of heaven and earth together are severed, and the powers of good and of evil are brought together in an internecine feud. Loki
30 advances with the Fenris-wolf and the Midgard-serpent, his own children, with all the hosts of the giants, and with Surt, who flings fire and flame over the world. Odin advances with all the asas and all the blessed einherjes.1 They meet, contend, and fall. The
35 wolf swallows Odin, but Vidar, the Silent, sets his foot upon the monster's lower jaw, he seizes the other with his hand, and thus rends him till he dies. Frey encounters Surt, and terrible blows are given ere Frey falls. Heimdal and Loki fight and kill each other, and
40 so do Tyr and the dog Garm from the Gnipa Cave. Thor fells the Midgard-serpent with his Mjolner, but he retreats only nine paces when he himself falls dead, suffocated by the serpent's venom. Then smoke

wreathes up around the ash Ygdrasil, the high flames
45 play against the heavens, the graves of the gods, of the giants and of men are swallowed up by the sea, and the end has come. This is Ragnarok, the twilight of the gods.

But the radiant dawn follows the night. The earth,
50 completely green, rises again from the sea, and where the mews have but just been rocking on restless waves, rich fields unplowed and unsown, now wave their golden harvests before the gentle breezes. The asas awake to a new life, Balder is with them again. Then
55 comes the mighty Fimbultyr, the god who is from everlasting to everlasting; the god whom the Edda skald dared not name. The god of gods comes to the asas. He comes to the great judgment and gathers all the good into Gimle to dwell there forever, and
60 evermore delights enjoy; but the perjurers and murderers and adulterers he sends to Nastrand, that terrible hall, to be torn by Nidhug until they are purged from their wickedness. This is Regeneration.

These are the outlines of the Norse religion. Such
65 were the doctrines established by Odin among our ancestors. Thus do we find it recorded in the Eddas of Iceland.

---

[1] The *asa* and *einherjes* were the Norse gods and divine fighters.

1

What is the main purpose of the passage?

_____

2

According to the passage, what are Elivogs?

_____

3

Which lines provide evidence for your previous answer?

_____

4

In lines 12-25, the author indicates that the cosmos was created from

_____

5

From what did the gods make humans?

_____

6

What does the passage state will precede Ragnarok?

_____

7

Why can it be inferred from the passage that the _Prose Edda_ did not mention Fimbultyr?

_____

8

According to the passage, who provided the doctrines of Norse religion?

_____

9

How would you describe the passage overall?

_____

10

What is the tone of the passage?

_____

MEDIUM READS

The following short stories and essays are between 8 and 15 minutes long, the approximate time you have for the passages on the SAT and ACT.

	Full Test	Passages	Time per Passage
SAT	65 minutes with 5 passages	5 passages with 10-11 questions	**About 13 minutes**
ACT	35 minutes with 4 passages	4 passages with 10 questions	**About 9 minutes**

These passages are not exactly 9 or 13 minutes, in part because your reading times may vary, but they should take around that long to read, give or take a few minutes.

You can practice your annotations here, but your primary goal is to stay focused as you read the passage. At the end, be able to answer the basic questions the test asks:

- What is the author's purpose?

- What is the author's tone?

- How would you summarize the passage?

- For literature passages, how would you describe the main characters?

- For non-fiction passages, what is the central thesis or main idea of the passage?

- For paired passages, how are the two passages related?

Notice that we don't have the extensive questions that we did on the short reads. Rather, we're working on your reading pace and your big-picture comprehension.

Keep yourself moving by reading the passages that are most interesting to you. Refer back to the table on page 6 at the beginning of the book if you are looking for suggestions.

Kurt Vonnegut (1922-2007) was an American author of satire, dark humor, and science fiction. The title (pronounced "two bee are naught two bee") hints at the dystopia of a world without death.

Everything was perfectly swell.

There were no prisons, no slums, no insane asylums, no cripples, no poverty, no wars.

All diseases were conquered. So was old age.

Death, barring accidents, was an adventure for volunteers.

The population of the United States was stabilized at forty-million souls.

One bright morning in the Chicago Lying-in Hospital, a man named Edward K. Wehling, Jr., waited for his wife to give birth. He was the only man waiting. Not many people were born a day any more.

Wehling was fifty-six, a mere stripling in a population whose average age was one hundred and twenty-nine.

X-rays had revealed that his wife was going to have triplets. The children would be his first.

Young Wehling was hunched in his chair, his head in his hand. He was so rumpled, so still and colorless as to be virtually invisible. His camouflage was perfect, since the waiting room had a disorderly and demoralized air, too. Chairs and ashtrays had been moved away from the walls. The floor was paved with spattered dropcloths.

The room was being redecorated. It was being redecorated as a memorial to a man who had volunteered to die.

A sardonic old man, about two hundred years old, sat on a stepladder, painting a mural he did not like. Back in the days when people aged visibly, his age would have been guessed at thirty-five or so. Aging had touched him that much before the cure for aging was found.

The mural he was working on depicted a very neat garden. Men and women in white, doctors and nurses, turned the soil, planted seedlings, sprayed bugs, spread fertilizer.

Men and women in purple uniforms pulled up weeds, cut down plants that were old and sickly, raked leaves, carried refuse to trash-burners.

Never, never, never—not even in medieval Holland nor old Japan—had a garden been more formal, been better tended. Every plant had all the loam, light, water, air and nourishment it could use.

A hospital orderly came down the corridor, singing under his breath a popular song:

If you don't like my kisses, honey,
Here's what I will do:

I'll go see a girl in purple,
Kiss this sad world toodle-oo.
If you don't want my lovin',
Why should I take up all this space?
I'll get off this old planet,
Let some sweet baby have my place.

The orderly looked in at the mural and the muralist. "Looks so real," he said, "I can practically imagine I'm standing in the middle of it."

"What makes you think you're not in it?" said the painter. He gave a satiric smile. "It's called 'The Happy Garden of Life,' you know."

"That's good of Dr. Hitz," said the orderly.

He was referring to one of the male figures in white, whose head was a portrait of Dr. Benjamin Hitz, the hospital's Chief Obstetrician. Hitz was a blindingly handsome man.

"Lot of faces still to fill in," said the orderly. He meant that the faces of many of the figures in the mural were still blank. All blanks were to be filled with portraits of important people on either the hospital staff or from the Chicago Office of the Federal Bureau of Termination.

"Must be nice to be able to make pictures that look like something," said the orderly.

The painter's face curdled with scorn. "You think I'm proud of this daub?" he said. "You think this is my idea of what life really looks like?"

"What's your idea of what life looks like?" said the orderly.

The painter gestured at a foul dropcloth. "There's a good picture of it," he said. "Frame that, and you'll have a picture a damn sight more honest than this one."

"You're a gloomy old duck, aren't you?" said the orderly.

"Is that a crime?" said the painter.

The orderly shrugged. "If you don't like it here, Grandpa—" he said, and he finished the thought with the trick telephone number that people who didn't want to live any more were supposed to call. The zero in the telephone number he pronounced "naught."

The number was: "2-B-R-0-2-B."

It was the telephone number of an institution whose fanciful sobriquets included: "Automat," "Birdland," "Cannery," "Catbox," "De-louser," "Easy-go," "Good-by, Mother," "Happy Hooligan," "Kiss-me-quick," "Lucky Pierre," "Sheepdip," "Waring Blendor," "Weep-no-more" and "Why Worry?"

"To be or not to be" was the telephone number of the municipal gas chambers of the Federal Bureau of Termination.

The painter thumbed his nose at the orderly. "When I decide it's time to go," he said, "it won't be at the Sheepdip."

"A do-it-yourselfer, eh?" said the orderly. "Messy business, Grandpa. Why don't you have a little consideration for the people who have to clean up after you?"

The painter expressed with an obscenity his lack of concern for the tribulations of his survivors. "The world could do with a good deal more mess, if you ask me," he said.

The orderly laughed and moved on.

Wehling, the waiting father, mumbled something without raising his head. And then he fell silent again.

A coarse, formidable woman strode into the waiting room on spike heels. Her shoes, stockings, trench coat, bag and overseas cap were all purple, the purple the painter called "the color of grapes on Judgment Day."

The medallion on her purple musette bag was the seal of the Service Division of the Federal Bureau of Termination, an eagle perched on a turnstile.

The woman had a lot of facial hair—an unmistakable mustache, in fact. A curious thing about gas-chamber hostesses was that, no matter how lovely and feminine they were when recruited, they all sprouted mustaches within five years or so.

"Is this where I'm supposed to come?" she said to the painter.

"A lot would depend on what your business was," he said. "You aren't about to have a baby, are you?"

"They told me I was supposed to pose for some picture," she said. "My name's Leora Duncan." She waited.

"And you dunk people," he said.

"What?" she said.

"Skip it," he said.

"That sure is a beautiful picture," she said. "Looks just like heaven or something."

"Or something," said the painter. He took a list of names from his smock pocket. "Duncan, Duncan, Duncan," he said, scanning the list. "Yes—here you are. You're entitled to be immortalized. See any faceless body here you'd like me to stick your head on? We've got a few choice ones left."

She studied the mural bleakly. "Gee," she said, "they're all the same to me. I don't know anything about art."

"A body's a body, eh?" he said, "All righty. As a master of fine art, I recommend this body here." He indicated a faceless figure of a woman who was carrying dried stalks to a trash-burner.

"Well," said Leora Duncan, "that's more the disposal people, isn't it? I mean, I'm in service. I don't do any disposing."

The painter clapped his hands in mock delight. "You say you don't know anything about art, and then you prove in the next breath that you know more about it than I do! Of course the sheave-carrier is wrong for a hostess! A snipper, a pruner—that's more your line." He pointed to a figure in purple who was sawing a dead branch from an apple tree. "How about her?" he said. "You like her at all?"

"Gosh—" she said, and she blushed and became humble." That—that puts me right next to Dr. Hitz."

"That upsets you?" he said.

"Good gravy, no!" she said. "It's—it's just such an honor."

"Ah, You admire him, eh?" he said.

"Who doesn't admire him?" she said, worshiping the portrait of Hitz. It was the portrait of a tanned, white-haired, omnipotent Zeus, two hundred and forty years old. "Who doesn't admire him?" she said again. "He was responsible for setting up the very first gas chamber in Chicago."

"Nothing would please me more," said the painter, "than to put you next to him for all time. Sawing off a limb—that strikes you as appropriate?"

"That is kind of like what I do," she said. She was demure about what she did. What she did was make people comfortable while she killed them.

And, while Leora Duncan was posing for her portrait, into the waitingroom bounded Dr. Hitz himself. He was seven feet tall, and he boomed with importance, accomplishments, and the joy of living.

"Well, Miss Duncan! Miss Duncan!" he said, and he made a joke. "What are you doing here?" he said. "This isn't where the people leave. This is where they come in!"

"We're going to be in the same picture together," she said shyly.

"Good!" said Dr. Hitz heartily. "And, say, isn't that some picture?"

"I sure am honored to be in it with you," she said.

"Let me tell you," he said, "I'm honored to be in it with you. Without women like you, this wonderful world we've got wouldn't be possible."

He saluted her and moved toward the door that led to the delivery rooms. "Guess what was just born," he said.

"I can't," she said.

"Triplets!" he said.

"Triplets!" she said. She was exclaiming over the legal implications of triplets.

The law said that no newborn child could survive unless the parents of the child could find someone who would volunteer to die. Triplets, if they were all to live, called for three volunteers.

"Do the parents have three volunteers?" said Leora Duncan.

"Last I heard," said Dr. Hitz, "they had one, and were trying to scrape another two up."

"I don't think they made it," she said. "Nobody made three appointments with us. Nothing but singles going through today, unless somebody called in after I left. What's the name?"

"Wehling," said the waiting father, sitting up, red-eyed and frowzy. "Edward K. Wehling, Jr., is the name of the happy father-to-be."

He raised his right hand, looked at a spot on the wall, gave a hoarsely wretched chuckle. "Present," he said.

"Oh, Mr. Wehling," said Dr. Hitz, "I didn't see you."

"The invisible man," said Wehling.

"They just phoned me that your triplets have been born," said Dr. Hitz. "They're all fine, and so is the mother. I'm on my way in to see them now."

"Hooray," said Wehling emptily.

"You don't sound very happy," said Dr. Hitz.

"What man in my shoes wouldn't be happy?" said Wehling. He gestured with his hands to symbolize care-free simplicity. "All I have to do is pick out which one of the triplets is going to live, then deliver my maternal grandfather to the Happy Hooligan, and come back here with a receipt."

Dr. Hitz became rather severe with Wehling, towered over him. "You don't believe in population control, Mr. Wehling?" he said.

"I think it's perfectly keen," said Wehling tautly.

"Would you like to go back to the good old days, when the population of the Earth was twenty billion—about to become forty billion, then eighty billion, then one hundred and sixty billion? Do you know what a drupelet is, Mr. Wehling?" said Hitz.

"Nope," said Wehling sulkily.

"A drupelet, Mr. Wehling, is one of the little knobs, one of the little pulpy grains of a blackberry," said Dr. Hitz. "Without population control, human beings would now be packed on this surface of this old planet like drupelets on a blackberry! Think of it!"

Wehling continued to stare at the same spot on the wall.

"In the year 2000," said Dr. Hitz, "before scientists stepped in and laid down the law, there wasn't even enough drinking water to go around, and nothing to eat but sea-weed—and still people insisted on their right to reproduce like jackrabbits. And their right, if possible, to live forever."

"I want those kids," said Wehling quietly. "I want all three of them."

"Of course you do," said Dr. Hitz. "That's only human."

"I don't want my grandfather to die, either," said Wehling.

"Nobody's really happy about taking a close relative to the Catbox," said Dr. Hitz gently, sympathetically.

"I wish people wouldn't call it that," said Leora Duncan.

"What?" said Dr. Hitz.

"I wish people wouldn't call it 'the Catbox,' and things like that," she said. "It gives people the wrong impression."

"You're absolutely right," said Dr. Hitz. "Forgive me." He corrected himself, gave the municipal gas chambers their official title, a title no one ever used in conversation. "I should have said, 'Ethical Suicide Studios,'" he said.

"That sounds so much better," said Leora Duncan.

"This child of yours—whichever one you decide to keep, Mr. Wehling," said Dr. Hitz. "He or she is going to live on a happy, roomy, clean, rich planet, thanks to population control. In a garden like that mural there." He shook his head. "Two centuries ago, when I was a young man, it was a hell that nobody thought could last another twenty years. Now centuries of peace and plenty stretch before us as far as the imagination cares to travel."

He smiled luminously.

The smile faded as he saw that Wehling had just drawn a revolver.

Wehling shot Dr. Hitz dead. "There's room for one—a great big one," he said.

And then he shot Leora Duncan. "It's only death," he said to her as she fell. "There! Room for two."

And then he shot himself, making room for all three of his children.

Nobody came running. Nobody, seemingly, heard the shots.

The painter sat on the top of his stepladder, looking down reflectively on the sorry scene.

The painter pondered the mournful puzzle of life demanding to be born and, once born, demanding to be fruitful ... to multiply and to live as long as possible—to do all that on a very small planet that would have to last forever.

All the answers that the painter could think of were grim. Even grimmer, surely, than a Catbox, a Happy Hooligan, an Easy Go. He thought of war. He thought of plague. He thought of starvation.

He knew that he would never paint again. He let his paintbrush fall to the drop-cloths below. And then he decided he had had about enough of life in the Happy Garden of Life, too, and he came slowly down from the ladder.

He took Wehling's pistol, really intending to shoot himself.

But he didn't have the nerve.

And then he saw the telephone booth in the corner of the room. He went to it, dialed the well-remembered number: "2 B R 0 2 B."

"Federal Bureau of Termination," said the very warm voice of a hostess.

"How soon could I get an appointment?" he asked, speaking very carefully.

"We could probably fit you in late this afternoon, sir," she said. "It might even be earlier, if we get a cancellation."

"All right," said the painter, "fit me in, if you please." And he gave her his name, spelling it out.

"Thank you, sir," said the hostess. "Your city thanks you; your country thanks you; your planet thanks you. But the deepest thanks of all is from future generations."

1

What is the main purpose of this passage?

_____

2

What is the passage's tone?

_____

3

How would you summarize the passage?

_____

4

How would you describe Mr. Wehling?

_____

5

How would you describe Dr. Hitz?

_____

THE DISCOVERY OF RADIUM – TOWER, SMITH & CHARLES AND MARIE CURIE

Passage 1 is adapted from Willis Tower, Charles Smith, and Charles Turton, *Physics*, 1920. Passage 2 is adapted from a speech given by Marie Curie to the students of Vassar College in May of 1921.

Passage 1

In 1896 Henri Becquerel of Paris discovered that uranium and its compounds emit a form of radiation that produces an effect upon a photographic plate that is similar to that resulting from the action of "X" rays. These rays are often called Becquerel rays in honor of their discoverer. The property of emitting such rays is called radio-activity, and the substances producing them are called radio-active.

In 1898, Professor [Pierre] and Madame [Marie] Curie after an investigation of all the elements found that thorium, one of the chief constituents of incandescent gas mantles, together with its compounds, was also radio-active. This may be shown by the following experiment:

Place a flattened gas mantle upon a photographic plate and leave in a light tight-box for several days. Upon developing the plate in the usual way a distinct image of the mantle will be found upon the plate.

Madame Curie discovered also that pitch-blende possessed much greater radio-active power than either thorium or uranium. After prolonged chemical experiments she obtained from several tons of the ore a few milligrams of a substance more than a million times as active as thorium or uranium. She called this new substance radium. Radium is continually being decomposed, this decomposition being accompanied by the production of a great deal of heat. It has been calculated that it will take about 300 years for a particle of radium to be entirely decomposed and separated into other substances. It is also believed that radium itself is the product of the decomposition of uranium, atomic weight 238, and that the final product of successive decompositions may be some inert metal, like lead, atomic weight 207.

The radiation given off by radio-active substances consists of three kinds: (A) Positively charged particles of helium called alpha rays: (B) negatively charged particles called beta rays: (C) gamma rays.

The alpha rays have little penetrating power, a sheet of paper or a sheet of aluminum 0.05 mm. stopping them. Upon losing their charges they become atoms of helium. Their velocity is about 1/10 of that of light or 18,000 miles a second. The spinthariscope is a little instrument devised by Sir Williams Crookes in 1903 to show direct evidence that particles are continually being shot off from radium. In this instrument, a speck of radium is placed on the under side of a wire placed a few millimeters above a screen covered with crystals of zinc sulphide. Looking in the dark at this screen through the lens, a continuous succession of sparks is seen like a swarm of fireflies on a warm summer night. Each flash is due to an alpha particle striking the screen. The beta rays are supposed to be cathode rays or electrons with velocities of from 40,000 to 170,000 miles a second. The gamma rays are supposed to be "X" rays produced by the beta rays striking solid objects.

The discovery of radio-activity has revolutionized the ideas of the constitution of matter. Further, the results of experiments upon radio-active materials reveals the presence of immense quantities of sub-atomic energy. If man ever discovers a means of utilizing this, he will enter a storehouse of energy of far greater extent and value than any of which he has as yet made use. A consideration of this unexplored region gives zest to the work of those who day by day are striving to understand and control forces of nature.

Passage 2

I could tell you many things about radium and radioactivity and it would take a long time. But as we can not do that, I shall only give you a short account of my early work about radium. Radium is no more a baby, it is more than twenty years old, but the conditions of the disc

overy were somewhat peculiar, and so it is always of interest to remember them and to explain them.

We must go back to the year 1897. Professor [Pierre] Curie and I worked at that time in the laboratory of the school of Physics and Chemistry where Professor Curie held his lectures. I was engaged in some work on uranium rays which had been discovered two years before by Professor [Henri] Becquerel. I shall tell you how these uranium rays may be detected. If you take a photographic plate and wrap it in black paper and then on this plate, protected from ordinary light, put some uranium salt and leave it a day, and the next day the plate is developed, you notice on the plate a black spot at the place where the uranium salt was. This spot has been made by special rays which are given out by the uranium and are able to make an impression on the plate in the same way as ordinary light. You can also test those rays in another way, by placing them on an electroscope. You know what an electroscope is. If you charge it, you can keep it charged several hours and more, unless uranium salts are placed near to it. But if this is the case the electroscope loses its charge and the gold or aluminum leaf falls gradually in a progressive way. The speed with which the leaf moves may be used as a measure of the intensity of the rays; the greater the speed, the greater the intensity.

I spent some time in studying the way of making good measurements of the uranium rays, and then I wanted to know if there were other elements, giving out rays of the same kind. So I took up a work about all known elements, and their compounds and found that uranium compounds are active and also all thorium compounds, but other elements were not found active, nor were their compounds. As for the uranium and thorium compounds, I found that they were active in proportion to their uranium or thorium content. The more uranium or thorium, the greater the activity, the activity being an atomic property of the elements, uranium and thorium.

Then I took up measurements of minerals and I found that several of those which contain uranium or thorium or both were active. But then the activity was not what I could expect, it was greater than for uranium or thorium compounds like the oxides which are almost entirely composed of these elements. Then I thought that there should be in the minerals some unknown element having a much greater radioactivity than uranium or thorium. And I wanted to find and to separate that element, and I settled to that work with Professor Curie. We thought it would be done in several weeks or months, but it was not so. It took many years of hard work to finish that task. There was not one new element, there were several of them. But the most important is radium which could be separated in a pure state.

All the tests for the separation were done by the method of electrical measurements with some kind of electroscope. We just had to make chemical separations and to examine all products obtained with respect to their activity. The product which retained the radioactivity was considered as that one which had kept the new element; and, as the radioactivity was more strong in some products, we knew that we had succeeded in concentrating the new element. The radioactivity was used in the same way as a spectroscopical test.

The difficulty was that there is not much radium in a mineral; this we did not know at the beginning. But we now know that there is not even one part of radium in a million parts of good ore. And too, to get a small quantity of pure radium salt, one is obliged to work up a huge quantity of ore. And that was very hard in a laboratory.

We had not even a good laboratory at that time. We worked in a hangar where there were no improvements, no good chemical arrangements. We had no help, no money. And because of that the work could not go on as it would have done under better conditions. I did myself the numerous crystalizations

which were wanted to get the radium salt separated from the barium salt with which it is obtained out of the ore. And in 1902 I finally succeeded in getting pure radium chloride and determining the atomic weight of the new element radium, which is 226 while that of barium is only 137.

Later I could also separate the metal radium, but that was a very difficult work; and, as it is not necessary for the use of radium to have it in this state, it is not generally prepared that way.

Now, the special interest of radium is in the intensity of its rays which is several million times greater than the uranium rays. And the effects of the rays make the radium so important. If we take a practical point of view, then the most important property of the rays is the production of physiological effects on the cells of the human organism. These effects may be used for the cure of several diseases. Good results have been obtained in many cases. What is considered particularly important is the treatment of cancer. The medical utilization of radium makes it necessary to get that element in sufficient quantities. And so a factory of radium was started to begin with in France, and later in America where a big quantity of ore named carnotite is available. America does produce many grams of radium every year but the price is still very high because the quantity of radium contained in the ore is so small. The radium is more than a hundred thousand times dearer than gold.

But we must not forget that when radium was discovered no one knew that it would prove useful in hospitals. The work was one of pure science. And this is a proof that scientific work must not be considered from the point of view of the direct usefulness of it. It must be done for itself, for the beauty of science, and then there is always the chance that a scientific discovery may become like the radium a benefit for humanity.

But science is not rich, it does not dispose of important means, it does not generally meet recognition before the material usefulness of it has been proved. The factories produce many grams of radium every year, but the laboratories have very small quantities. It is the same for my laboratory and I am very grateful to the American women who wish me to have more of radium and give me the opportunity of doing more work with it.

The scientific history of radium is beautiful. The properties of the rays have been studied very closely. We know that particles are expelled from radium with a very great velocity near to that of the light. We know that the atoms of radium are destroyed by expulsion of these particles, some of which are atoms of helium. And in that way it has been proved that the radioactive elements are constantly disintegrating and that they produce at the end ordinary elements, principally helium and lead. That is, as you see, a theory of transformation of atoms which are not stable, as was believed before, but may undergo spontaneous changes.

Radium is not alone in having these properties. Many having other radioelements are known already, the polonium, the mesothorium, the radiothorium, the actinium. We know also radioactive gases, named emanations. There is a great variety of substances and effects in radioactivity. There is always a vast field left to experimentation and I hope that we may have some beautiful progress in the following years. It is my earnest desire that some of you should carry on this scientific work and keep for your ambition the determination to make a permanent contribution to science.

1

What is the main purpose of the first passage?

_____

2

What is the first passage's tone?

_____

3

What is the main purpose of the second passage?

_____

4

What is the tone of the second passage?

_____

5

What is the relationship between the passages?

_____

The Crisis is the official magazine of the National Association for the Advancement of Colored People (NAACP). It was founded by W. E. B. Du Bois, the African American sociologist, historian, activist, and author. The first passage is an open letter Du Bois wrote to President Woodrow Wilson in March, 1913. The second passage is an open letter Du Bois wrote in August 1913.

Passage 1

Sir: Your inauguration to the Presidency of the United States is to the colored people, to the white South and to the nation a momentous people, to the white South and to the nation a momentous occasion. For the first time since the emancipation of slaves the government of this nation—the Presidency, the Senate, the House of Representatives—passes on the 4th of March into the hands of the party which a half century ago fought desperately to keep black men as real estate in the eyes of the law.

Your elevation to the chief magistracy of the nation at this time shows not simply a splendid national faith in the perpetuity of free government in this land, but even more, a personal faith in you.

We black men by our votes helped to put you in your high position. It is true that in your overwhelming triumph at the polls that you might have succeeded without our aid, but the fact remains that our votes helped elect you this time, and that the time may easily come in the near future when without our 500,000 ballots neither you nor your party can control the government.

True as this is, we would not be misunderstood. We do not ask or expect special consideration or treatment in return for our franchises. We did not vote for you and your party because you represented our best judgment. It was not because we loved Democrats more, but Republicans less and Roosevelt least, that led to our action.

Calmly reviewing our action we are glad of it. It was a step toward political independence, and it was helping to put into power a man who has today the power to become the greatest benefactor of his country since Abraham Lincoln.

We say this to you, sir, advisedly. We believe that the Negro problem is in many respects the greatest problem facing the nation, and we believe that you have the opportunity of beginning a just and righteous solution of this burning human wrong. This opportunity is yours because, while a Southerner in birth and tradition, you have escaped the provincial training of the South and you have not had burned into your soul desperate hatred and despising of your darker fellow men.

You start when where no Northerner could start, and perhaps your only real handicap is peculiar lack of personal acquaintance with individual black men, a lack which is the pitiable cause of much social misery and hurt. A president of Harvard or Columbia would have known a few black men as men. It is sad that this privilege is denied a president of Princeton, sad for him and his students.

But waiving this, you face no insoluble problem. The only time when the Negro problem is insoluble is when men insist on settling it wrong by asking absolutely contradictory things. You cannot make 10,000,000 people at one and the same time servile and dignified, docile and self-reliant, servants and independent leaders, segregated and yet part of the industrial organism, disfranchised and citizens of a democracy, ignorant and intelligent. This is impossible and the impossibility is not factitious; it is in the very nature of things.

On the other hand, a determination on the part of intelligent and decent Americans to see that no man is denied a reasonable chance for life, liberty, and happiness simply because of the color of his skin is simple, sane and practical solution of the race problem in this land. The education of colored children, the opening of the gates of industrial opportunity to colored workers, absolute equality of all citizens before law, the civil rights of all decently behaving citizens in places of public accommodation and entertainment, absolute impartiality in the granting of the right of suffrage—these things are the bedrock of a just solution of the rights of man in the American Republic.

Nor does this solution of color, race and class discrimination abate one jot or tittle the just fight of humanity against crime, ignorance, inefficiency and the right to choose one's own wife and dinner companions.

Against this plan straight truth the forces of hell in this country are fighting a terrific and momentarily successful battle. You may not realize this, Mr. Wilson. To the quiet walls of Princeton where no Negro student is admitted the noise of the fight and the reek of its blood may have penetrated but vaguely and dimly.

But the fight is on, and you, sir, are this month stepping into its arena. Its virulence will doubtless surprise you and it may scare you as it scared one William Howard Taft. But we trust not; we think not.

First you will be urged to surrender your conscience and intelligence in these matters to the keeping of your Southern friends. They "know the Negro," as they will continually tell you. And this is true. They do know "the Negro," but the question for you to settle is whether or not the Negro whom they know is the real Negro or the Negro of their vivid imaginations and violent prejudices.

Whatever Negro it is that your Southern friends know, it is your duty to know the real Negro and know him personally. This will be no easy task. The embattle Bourbons, from the distinguished Blease to the gifted Hoke Smith, will evince grim determination to keep you from contact with any colored person. It will take more than general good will on your part to foil the wide conspiracy to make Negroes known to their fellow Americans not as flesh and blood but as beasts of fiction.

You must remember that the ability, sincerity and worth of one-tenth of the population of your country will be absolutely veiled from you unless you make effort to lift the veil. When you make that effort, then more trouble will follow. If you tell your Southern friends that you have discovered that the internal revenue of New York is well collected and administered, they are going to regard you in pained surprise. Can a Negro administrator! they will exclaim, ignoring the fact that he does.

But it is not the offices at your disposal, President Woodrow Wilson, that is the burden of our great cry to you. We want to be treated as men. We want to vote. We want our children educated. We want lynching stopped. We want no longer to be herded as cattle on street cars and railroads. We want the right to earn a living, to own our own property and to spend our income unhindered and uncursed. Your power is limited? We know that, but the power of the American people is unlimited. Today you embody that power, you typify its ideals. In the name then of that common country for which your fathers and ours have bled and toiled, be not untrue, President Wilson, to the highest ideals of American Democracy.

Respectfully yours,
The Crisis

Passage 2

Sir: On the occasion of your inauguration as President of the United States, The Crisis took the liberty of addressing to you an open letter. The Crisis spoke for no inconsiderable part of ten millions of human beings, American born, American citizens. The Crisis said in that letter, among other things:

"The only time when the Negro problem is insoluble is when men insist on settling it wrong by asking absolutely contradictory things. You cannot make 10,000,000 people at one and the same time servile and dignified, docile and self-reliant, servants and independent leaders, segregated and yet part of the industrial organism, disfranchised and citizens of a democracy, ignorant and intelligent. This is impossible and the impossibility is not factitious; it is in the very nature of things."

"On the other hand, a determination on the part of intelligent and decent Americans to see that no man is denied a reasonable chance for life, liberty, and happiness simply because of the color of his skin is a simple, sane, and practical solution of the race problem in this land."

Sir, you have now been President of the United States for six months and what is the result? It is no exaggeration to say that every enemy of the Negro race is greatly encouraged; that every man who dreams of making the Negro race a group of menials and pariahs is alert and hopeful. Vardaman, Tillman, Hoke Smith, Cole Blease, and Burleson are evidently assuming that their theory of the place and destiny of the Negro race is the theory of your administration, They and others are assuming this because not a single act and not a single word of yours since election has given anyone reason to infer that that you have the slightest interest in the colored people or desire to alleviate their intolerable position, A dozen worthy Negro officials have been removed from office, and you have nominated but on black man for office, and he such a contemptible cur, that his very nomination was an insult to every Negro in the land.

To this negative appearance of indifference has been added positive action on the part of your advisers, with or without your knowledge, which constitutes the gravest attack on the liberties of our people since emancipation, Public segregation of civil servants in government employ, necessarily involving personal insult and humiliation, has for the first time in history been made the policy of the United States government.

In the Treasury and Post Office Departments colored clerks have been herded to themselves as though they were not human beings. We are told that one colored clerk who could not actually be segregated on account of the nature of his work has consequently had a cage built around him to separate him from his white companions of many years. Mr. Wilson, do you know these things? Are you responsible for them? Did you advise them? Do you not know that no other group of American citizens has ever been treated in this way and that no President of the United States ever dared to propose such treatment? Here is a plain, flat, disgraceful spitting in the face of people whose darkened countenances are already dark with the slime of insult. Do you consent to this, President Wilson? Do you believe in it? Have you been able to persuade yourself that national insult is best for a people struggling into self-respect?

President Wilson, we do not, we cannot believe this. The Crisis still clings to the conviction that a vote for Woodrow Wilson was NOT a vote for Cole Blease or Hoke Smith. But whether it was or not segregation is going to be resented as it ought to be resented by the colored people. We would not be men if we did not resent it. The policy adopted, whether with your consent of knowledge or not, is an indefensible attack on a people who have in the past been shamefully humiliated. There are foolish people who think that such policy has no limit and that lynching "Jim Crowism," segregation and insult are to be permanent institutions in America.

We have appealed in the past, Mr. Wilson, to you as a man and statesmen; to your sense of fairness and broad cosmopolitan outlook on the world. We renew this appeal and to it we venture to add some plain considerations of political expediency.

We black men still vote. In spite of the fact that the triumph of your party last fall was possible only because Southern white men have, through our disfranchisement, from twice to seven times the political power of Northern white men notwithstanding this, we black men of the North have a growing nest egg of 500,000 ballots, and ballots that are counted, which no sane party can ignore. Does your Mr. Burleson expect the Democratic Party to carry New York, New Jersey, Pennsylvania, Ohio, Indiana, Illinois, by 200,000 votes? If he does will it not be well for him to remember that there are 237,942 black voters in these states. We have been trying to tell these voters that the Democratic Party wants their votes. Have we been wrong, Mr. Wilson? Have we assumed too great and quick a growth of intelligence in the party that once made slavery its cornerstone?

In view of all this, we beg to ask the President of the United States and the leader of the Democratic Party a few plain questions: (1) Do you want Negro votes? (2) Do you think that "Jim Crow" civil service will get these votes?
(3) Is your Negro policy to be dictated by Tillman and Vardaman? (4) Are you going to appoint black men to office on the same terms that you choose white men?

This is information, Mr. Wilson, which we are very anxious to have.

The Crisis advocated sincerely and strongly your election to the Presidency. The Crisis has no desire to be compelled to apologize to its constituency for this course. But at the present rate it looks as though some apology or explanation was going to be in order very soon.

We are still hoping that present indications are deceptive. We are still trying to believe that the President of the United States is the President of 10,000,000 as well as of 90,000,000 and that though the 10,000,000 are black and poor, he is too honest and cultured a gentleman to yield to the clamors of

ignorance and prejudice and hatred. We are still hoping all this, Mr. Wilson, but hope deferred maketh the heart sick.

Very respectfully yours,
The Crisis

1

What is the main purpose of the first passage?

_____

2

What is the first passage's tone?

_____

3

What is the central claim of the first passage?

_____

4

What is the main purpose of the second passage?

_____

5

What is the second passage's tone?

_____

6

What is the central claim of the second passage?

_____

7

What is the relationship between the passages?

_____

The Amazons, a legendary tribe of warrior women, were a staple of ancient histories and human geographies. In this passage from *Female Warriors: Memorials of Female Valour and Heroism, from the Mythologiocal Ages to the Present Era,* Ellen C. Clayton summarizes the various Greek and Roman traditions about the Amazon.

It is the fashion nowadays to sneer at the traditions venerated by our grandfathers. Those chapters in the world's history which have not been proved by facts, have passed, in the opinion of many well educated people, into the category of fable and nursery-rhyme. The early histories of Greece and Rome, and of our own country too, are now taken, if taken at all, *cum grano salis.* King Arthur, Hengist and Horsa, and many another hero of whom we were once so proud, have been cast, by most matter-of-fact writers, on the same dusty shelf with Achilles and Hector, Romulus and Remus, side by side with Jupiter and Mercury, Jack the Giant-Killer and Blue Beard. Scarcely anybody in our days is so credulous as to believe that the Amazons ever existed. "Amongst barbarous nations," observes Gibbon, "women have often combated by the side of their husbands; but it is almost impossible that a society of Amazons could have existed in the old or new world." His opinion has been endorsed by most subsequent writers, some of whom are even more positive in their expressions of incredulity.

Ancient writers are divided on the question. Strabo denies that there ever was or could have been such a community, and adds, to believe in their existence we must suppose "in those days the women were men and the men women." Plutarch, more moderate, half believes they did exist, but doubts most of their marvellous achievements, which, he thinks, "clearly resemble fable and fiction." Amongst those who speak for the defence, Herodotus, Diodorus Siculus, Justin, and Quintus Curtius stand prominently forward.

Their origin, as related by Justin, though curious, is far from being impossible or even improbable in the remote days when they lived. Some years previous to the reign of Ninus, king of Assyria, two young princes of the Scythian blood-royal, Hylinos and Scolopitos, being driven from their native country by a faction of the nobility, induced several hundred young men and women to emigrate with them. After a toilsome march through barren wilds they settled at last in Cappadocia, on the rugged banks of the Thermodon. This little river, which now bears the name of Termeh or Karmili, falls into the Black Sea, between Trebisond and Sinope.

For a number of years, the new-comers carried on a species of border warfare with the natives of the Themiscyrean plains—stealing their cattle, tearing up their corn, destroying their homes by fire and sword. At last the aborigines surprised and massacred the male settlers, by means of an ambush. The wives of the latter, having now no one to whom they could look for protection, armed themselves and expelled the foe from their territory.

From this time they laid aside all thoughts of marriage, "calling it slavery and not matrimony." And, to enforce this law, it is said, they murdered a few men who had escaped the fury of the natives in the general massacre. The Amazons were thenceforth forbidden even to speak to men, save during certain days in the year. At the appointed time, throwing aside their military character, they visited the surrounding nations, and were permitted, by special treaties, to depart again unmolested. Justin says they strangled all their male children directly they were born; Diodorus, that they distorted their limbs; while Philastratus and others affirm that they sent them back, uninjured, to the fathers.

The girls were bred, like their mothers, "not in idleness, nor spinning, but in exercises of war, such as hunting and riding." In early childhood the right breast was burnt off, that they might, when grown up, be more easily able to bend the bow and hurl the dart. From whence, some say, they derived the name of Amazon, which is formed of two Greek words, signifying "wanting a breast." Bryant, the antiquarian, rejects this theory, and suggests, though with less probability, that the name comes from Zon, the Sun, which was the national object of worship.

The bow was their favourite weapon, and from constant practice they acquired such proficiency as to equal, if not surpass the Scythians and Parthians, who were the most skilful archers of ancient times. With the Greeks and Romans it was not uncommon to speak of a very superior bow or quiver as "Amazonian."

The nation soon became formidable, and in due time grew famous throughout the world. At one time the dominion of the Amazons extended over the entire of Asia Minor and Ionia, besides a great part of Italy. So renowned did they at last become, that Jobates, king of Lycia, commanded Bellerophon to effect their subjugation, feeling certain that the hero would never return; great indeed was his astonishment to see the redoubtable conqueror of the Chimera return victorious, and he no longer hesitated to confess the divine origin of the hero. It is said that Cadmus, the founder of Thebes, was married to an Amazon named

Sphynx when he carried letters from Egypt to Greece, about 1550 B.C.

Lampedo and Marpesia were the first Amazon queens whose names became known beyond their own dominions. To give greater éclat to their numerous victories, they claimed to be daughters of the God Mars—a common expedient in the olden times. Taking it in turn to defend the frontier and invade foreign countries, they speedily conquered Iberia (Georgia), Colchis (Mingrelia), Albania, the Tauric Chersonese (the Crimea), and a great part of Asia.

To commemorate the achievements of Queen Marpesia during her passage over the craggy and snow-capped Caucasus, when every peak, every ridge was bravely defended by hordes of desperate mountaineers, the name of Mount Marpesia was bestowed upon one of the loftiest rocks.

It was Marpesia who founded Themiscyra, the capital of the Amazons, on the banks of the Thermodon. She adorned this city with many stately buildings, conspicuous amongst which was the royal palace. Many cities in Asia Minor owed their origin to the same queen—amongst others, Ephesus, Thyatira, Smyrna, and Magnesia.

On the death of Marpesia, who was surrounded by the barbarians during an expedition into Asia, and, together with her entire army, put to the sword, Orithya, Orseria, or Sinope, and her sister Antiope, or Hippolyte, ascended the throne. Orithya, the most famous of all the Amazon queens, inherited the beauty, together with the military skill of her mother, Marpesia. Under her rule the nation became so renowned, that Eurystheus, fancying he had at last found a task beyond the powers of Hercules, commanded the hero, as his ninth labour, to bring him the girdle of the Amazon queen. The hero succeeded, however.

Hercules, accompanied by Theseus, Castor and Pollux, and most of the young princes of Greece, sailed to the Euxine with a fleet of nine ships, landed at the mouth of the Thermodon, during the temporary absence of Orithya with the best part of the army, and gained an easy victory over Antiope, whose sister Menalippe he made prisoner; restoring her to liberty in exchange for a suit of the royal armour, including, of course, the girdle.

Historians differ as to the expedition of Theseus. Some say he took away Hippolyte or Antiope, at the same time that Hercules captured her sister; others, however, relate that he undertook a separate voyage many years after that of Hercules, and carried Antiope to Greece, where he made her his queen. Plutarch, in his life of Theseus, gives many details of this latter expedition.

When Orithya heard of the invasion, and of the part which the Athenian prince had acted in it, she vowed not to rest till she was revenged. Calling her subjects together, she soon found herself at the head of many thousand warriors. At her entreaty, Sagillus, king of Scythia, furnished a squadron of horse, commanded by his nephew, Panasagorus. Passing through Colchis, over Mount Caucasus, and crossing an arm of the Cimmerian Bosphorus, which, tradition says, was frozen, the Amazons marched victoriously through Taurica, Thrace, Thessaly, Macedonia, Attica, and entered the city of Athens. A hard-fought battle in the streets—described in detail by old Plutarch—ended by the total rout of the Amazons, who were compelled to take refuge in the camp of the Scythians—the latter, in consequence of a quarrel, having taken no part in the engagement.

The fate of Orithya is unknown, and historians differ as to that of Antiope. Some say she fell in the battle by the hand of an Amazon, while fighting in the Athenian ranks, side by side with Theseus; but according to others, it was her mediation which brought about a treaty of peace some four months later.

Theseus and the Amazon queen had a son named Hippolytus, or Demophoon, who afterwards ascended the throne of Athens.

That the Amazons survived this defeat is evident, since, years after this, we find the Phrygians imploring aid of Priam, king of Troy, against Myrene, queen of the Amazons. Little is known about this war, save that the queen lost her life, and was succeeded by the beautiful Penthesilea, who not only made peace with Priam, but led a chosen band of Amazons to the assistance of Troy when it was besieged by the Greeks. She arrived shortly after the death of Hector, and, some declare, seemed, in the eyes of the old king, destined to take the place of the deceased hero. New life was infused into the dejected Trojans. But, alas! their joy was short-lived. The morning after her arrival Penthesilea fell by the hand of the invincible Achilles, who, struck by her exquisite beauty, repented too late of what he had done. The sarcastic Thersites jeered and derided, as usual, till the hero, in a fury, turned on the sneering old wretch and slew him. Diomedes, enraged at the death of his mocking old comrade, dragged the corpse of the Amazon queen from the camp, and flung it into the Scamander.

Pliny ascribes the invention of the battle-axe to this queen.

After the death of Penthesilea we learn nothing of the Amazons until the days of Alexander the Great. When that conqueror arrived at Zadracarta, the capital of Hyrcania, about the year B.C. 330, he is said to have been visited by an Amazon queen named Minithya, or

Thalestris, who—like another Queen of Sheba—having heard of his mighty achievements, travelled through many lands to see him, followed by an army of female warriors. After staying thirteen days she returned home, greatly disappointed with the personal appearance of the Macedonian king, who, contrary to her expectations, proved, 'tis said, to be a little man.

This is the last we ever hear of the great female nation. Some Roman authors affirm that the Amazons, in alliance with the Albanians, fought most valiantly in a battle against Pompey the Great, B.C. 66. But the only ground for this assertion consisted in the fact that some painted shields and buskins were found on the battle-field.

1

What is the main purpose of this passage?

2

What is the passage's tone?

3

How would you summarize the passage?

4

What is the author's central thesis?

5

How would you describe the Amazons?

GOVERNMENT IS THE PROBLEM – RONALD REAGAN

This passage is adapted from Ronald Reagan's first inaugural address. Reagan (1911-2004) was the fortieth president of the United States.

Senator Hatfield, Mr. Chief Justice, Mr. President, Vice President Bush, Vice President Mondale, Senator Baker, Speaker O'Neill, Reverend Moomaw, and my fellow citizens: To a few of us here today, this is a solemn and most momentous occasion; and yet, in the history of our Nation, it is a commonplace occurrence. The orderly transfer of authority as called for in the Constitution routinely takes place as it has for almost two centuries and few of us stop to think how unique we really are. In the eyes of many in the world, this every-4-year ceremony we accept as normal is nothing less than a miracle.

Mr. President, I want our fellow citizens to know how much you did to carry on this tradition. By your gracious cooperation in the transition process, you have shown a watching world that we are a united people pledged to maintaining a political system which guarantees individual liberty to a greater degree than any other, and I thank you and your people for all your help in maintaining the continuity which is the bulwark of our Republic.

The business of our nation goes forward. These United States are confronted with an economic affliction of great proportions. We suffer from the longest and one of the worst sustained inflations in our national history. It distorts our economic decisions, penalizes thrift, and crushes the struggling young and the fixed- income elderly alike. It threatens to shatter the lives of millions of our people.

Idle industries have cast workers into unemployment, causing human misery and personal indignity. Those who do work are denied a fair return for their labor by a tax system which penalizes successful achievement and keeps us from maintaining full productivity.

But great as our tax burden is, it has not kept pace with public spending. For decades, we have piled deficit upon deficit, mortgaging our future and our children's future for the temporary convenience of the present. To continue this long trend is to guarantee tremendous social, cultural, political, and economic upheavals.

You and I, as individuals, can, by borrowing, live beyond our means, but for only a limited period of time. Why, then, should we think that collectively, as a nation, we are not bound by that same limitation?

We must act today in order to preserve tomorrow. And let there be no misunderstanding—we are going to begin to act, beginning today.

The economic ills we suffer have come upon us over several decades. They will not go away in days, weeks, or months, but they will go away. They will go away because we, as Americans, have the capacity now, as we have had in the past, to do whatever needs to be done to preserve this last and greatest bastion of freedom.

In this present crisis, government is not the solution to our problem, government is the problem.

From time to time, we have been tempted to believe that society has become too complex to be managed by self-rule, that government by an elite group is superior to government for, by, and of the people. But if no one among us is capable of governing himself, then who among us has the capacity to govern someone else? All of us together, in and out of government, must bear the burden. The solutions we seek must be equitable, with no one group singled out to pay a higher price.

We hear much of special interest groups. Our concern must be for a special interest group that has been too long neglected. It knows no sectional boundaries or ethnic and racial divisions, and it crosses political party lines. It is made up of men and women who raise our food, patrol our streets, man our mines and our factories, teach our children, keep our homes, and heal us when we are sick—professionals, industrialists, shopkeepers, clerks, cabbies, and truckdrivers. They are, in short, "We the people," this breed called Americans.

Well, this administration's objective will be a healthy, vigorous, growing economy that provides equal opportunity for all Americans, with no barriers born of bigotry or discrimination. Putting America back to work means putting all Americans back to work. Ending inflation means freeing all Americans from the terror of runaway living costs. All must share in the productive work of this "new beginning" and all must share in the bounty of a revived economy. With the idealism and fair play which are the core of our system and our strength, we can have a strong and prosperous America at peace with itself and the world.

So, as we begin, let us take inventory. We are a nation that has a government—not the other way around. And this makes us special among the nations of the Earth. Our Government has no power except that granted it by the people. It is time to check and reverse the growth of government which shows signs of having grown beyond the consent of the governed.

It is my intention to curb the size and influence of the Federal establishment and to demand recognition of the distinction between the powers granted to the Federal Government and those reserved to the States or to the people. All of us need to be reminded that the Federal Government did not create the States; the States created the Federal Government.

Now, so there will be no misunderstanding, it is not my intention to do away with government. It is, rather, to make it work-work with us, not over us; to stand by our side, not ride on our back. Government can and must provide opportunity, not smother it; foster productivity, not stifle it.

If we look to the answer as to why, for so many years, we achieved so much, prospered as no other people on Earth, it was because here, in this land, we unleashed the energy and individual genius of man to a greater extent than has ever been done before. Freedom and the dignity of the individual have been more available and assured here than in any other place on Earth. The price for this freedom at times has been high, but we have never been unwilling to pay that price.

It is no coincidence that our present troubles parallel and are proportionate to the intervention and intrusion in our lives that result from unnecessary and excessive growth of government. It is time for us to realize that we are too great a nation to limit ourselves to small dreams. We are not, as some would have us believe, doomed to an inevitable decline. I do not believe in a fate that will fall on us no matter what we do. I do believe in a fate that will fall on us if we do nothing. So, with all the creative energy at our command, let us begin an era of national renewal. Let us renew our determination, our courage, and our strength. And let us renew; our faith and our hope.

We have every right to dream heroic dreams. Those who say that we are in a time when there are no heroes just don't know where to look. You can see heroes every day going in and out of factory gates. Others, a handful in number, produce enough food to feed all of us and then the world beyond. You meet heroes across a counter—and they are on both sides of that counter. There are entrepreneurs with faith in themselves and faith in an idea who create new jobs, new wealth and opportunity. They are individuals and families whose taxes support the Government and whose voluntary gifts support church, charity, culture, art, and education. Their patriotism is quiet but deep. Their values sustain our national life.

I have used the words "they" and "their" in speaking of these heroes. I could say "you" and "your" because I am addressing the heroes of whom I speak—you, the citizens of this blessed land. Your dreams, your hopes, your goals are going to be the dreams, the hopes, and the goals of this administration, so help me God.

We shall reflect the compassion that is so much a part of your makeup. How can we love our country and not love our countrymen, and loving them, reach out a hand when they fall, heal them when they are sick, and provide opportunities to make them self-sufficient so they will be equal in fact and not just in theory?

Can we solve the problems confronting us? Well, the answer is an unequivocal and emphatic "yes." To paraphrase Winston Churchill, I did not take the oath I have just taken with the intention of presiding over the dissolution of the world's strongest economy.

In the days ahead I will propose removing the roadblocks that have slowed our economy and reduced productivity. Steps will be taken aimed at restoring the balance between the various levels of government. Progress may be slow—measured in inches and feet, not miles—but we will progress. It is time to reawaken this industrial giant, to get government back within its means, and to lighten our punitive tax burden. And these will be our first priorities, and on these principles, there will be no compromise.

On the eve of our struggle for independence a man who might have been one of the greatest among the Founding Fathers, Dr. Joseph Warren, President of the Massachusetts Congress, said to his fellow Americans, "Our country is in danger, but not to be despaired of.... On you depend the fortunes of America. You are to decide the important questions upon which rests the happiness and the liberty of millions yet unborn. Act worthy of yourselves."

Well, I believe we, the Americans of today, are ready to act worthy of ourselves, ready to do what must be done to ensure happiness and liberty for ourselves, our children and our children's children.

And as we renew ourselves here in our own land, we will be seen as having greater strength throughout the world. We will again be the exemplar of freedom and a beacon of hope for those who do not now have freedom.

To those neighbors and allies who share our freedom, we will strengthen our historic ties and assure them of our support and firm commitment. We will match loyalty with loyalty. We will strive for mutually beneficial relations. We will not use our friendship to impose on their sovereignty, for our own sovereignty is not for sale.

As for the enemies of freedom, those who are potential adversaries, they will be reminded that peace is the highest aspiration of the American people. We will negotiate for it, sacrifice for it; we will not surrender for it—now or ever.

Our forbearance should never be misunderstood. Our reluctance for conflict should not be misjudged as a failure of will. When action is required to preserve our national security, we will act. We will maintain sufficient strength to prevail if need be, knowing that if we do so we have the best chance of never having to use that strength.

Above all, we must realize that no arsenal, or no weapon in the arsenals of the world, is so formidable as the will and moral courage of free men and women. It is a weapon our adversaries in today's world do not have. It is a weapon that we as Americans do have. Let that be understood by those who practice terrorism and prey upon their neighbors.

I am told that tens of thousands of prayer meetings are being held on this day, and for that I am deeply grateful. We are a nation under God, and I believe God intended for us to be free. It would be fitting and good, I think, if on each Inauguration Day in future years it should be declared a day of prayer.

This is the first time in history that this ceremony has been held, as you have been told, on this West Front of the Capitol. Standing here, one faces a magnificent vista, opening up on this city's special beauty and history. At the end of this open mall are those shrines to the giants on whose shoulders we stand.

Directly in front of me, the monument to a monumental man: George Washington, Father of our country. A man of humility who came to greatness reluctantly. He led America out of revolutionary victory into infant nationhood. Off to one side, the stately memorial to Thomas Jefferson. The Declaration of Independence flames with his eloquence.

And then beyond the Reflecting Pool the dignified columns of the Lincoln Memorial. Whoever would understand in his heart the meaning of America will find it in the life of Abraham Lincoln.

Beyond those monuments to heroism is the Potomac River, and on the far shore the sloping hills of Arlington National Cemetery with its row on row of simple white markers bearing crosses or Stars of David. They add up to only a tiny fraction of the price that has been paid for our freedom.

Each one of those markers is a monument to the kinds of hero I spoke of earlier. Their lives ended in places called Belleau Wood, The Argonne, Omaha Beach, Salerno and halfway around the world on Guadalcanal, Tarawa, Pork Chop Hill, the Chosin Reservoir, and in a hundred rice paddies and jungles of a place called Vietnam.

Under one such marker lies a young man—Martin Treptow—who left his job in a small town barber shop in 1917 to go to France with the famed Rainbow Division. There, on the western front, he was killed trying to carry a message between battalions under heavy artillery fire.

We are told that on his body was found a diary. On the flyleaf under the heading, "My Pledge," he had written these words: "America must win this war.

Therefore, I will work, I will save, I will sacrifice, I will endure, I will fight cheerfully and do my utmost, as if the issue of the whole struggle depended on me alone."

The crisis we are facing today does not require of us the kind of sacrifice that Martin Treptow and so many thousands of others were called upon to make. It does require, however, our best effort, and our willingness to believe in ourselves and to believe in our capacity to perform great deeds; to believe that together, with God's help, we can and will resolve the problems which now confront us.

And, after all, why shouldn't we believe that? We are Americans. God bless you, and thank you.

1

What is the main purpose of this passage?

_____

2

What is the passage's tone?

_____

3

How would you summarize the passage?

_____

4

What is the author's central thesis?

_____

"ICH BIN EIN BERLINER" AND "TEAR DOWN THIS WALL" – JOHN F. KENNEDY AND RONALD REAGAN

The first passage is adapted from John F. Kennedy's speech in Berlin on June 26, 1963. The second passage is adapted from Ronald Reagan's speech in Berlin on June 12, 1987. The wall would come down in 1989.

Passage 1

I am proud to come to this city as the guest of your distinguished mayor, who has symbolized throughout the world the fighting spirit of West Berlin. And I am proud to visit the Federal Republic with your distinguished chancellor, who for so many years has committed Germany to democracy and freedom and progress, and to come here in the company of my fellow American, General Clay, who has been in this city during its great moments of crisis and will come again if ever needed.

Two thousand years ago, the proudest boast was "*civis romanus sum*."[1] Today, in the world of freedom, the proudest boast is "*Ich bin ein Berliner*."[2]

I appreciate my interpreter translating my German!

There are many people in the world who really don't understand, or say they don't, what is the great issue between the free world and the communist world. Let them come to Berlin. There are some who say that communism is the wave of the future. Let them come to Berlin. And there are some who say in Europe and elsewhere we can work with the communists. Let them come to Berlin. And there are even a few who say that it is true that communism is an evil system, but it permits us to make economic progress. *Lasst sie nach Berlin kommen*. Let them come to Berlin.

Freedom has many difficulties and democracy is not perfect, but we have never had to put a wall up to keep our people in, to prevent them from leaving us. I want to say, on behalf of my countrymen, who live many miles away on the other side of the Atlantic, who are far distant from you, that they take the greatest pride that they have been able to share with you, even from a distance, the story of the last 18 years. I know of no town, no city, that has been besieged for 18 years that still lives with the vitality and the force and the hope and the determination of the city of West Berlin. While the wall is the most obvious and vivid demonstration of the failures of the communist system, for all the world to see, we take no satisfaction in it, for it is, as your mayor has said, an offense not only against history but an offense against humanity, separating families, dividing husbands and wives and brothers and sisters, and dividing a people who wish to be joined together.

What is true of this city is true of Germany--real, lasting peace in Europe can never be assured as long as one German out of four is denied the elementary right of free men, and that is to make a free choice. In 18 years of peace and good faith, this generation of Germans has earned the right to be free, including the right to unite their families and their nation in lasting peace, with good will to all people. You live in a defended island of freedom, but your life is part of the main. So let me ask you as I close, to lift your eyes beyond the dangers of today, to the hopes of tomorrow, beyond the freedom merely of this city of Berlin, or your country of Germany, to the advance of freedom everywhere, beyond the wall to the day of peace with justice, beyond yourselves and ourselves to all mankind.

Freedom is indivisible, and when one man is enslaved, all are not free. When all are free, then we can look forward to that day when this city will be joined as one and this country and this great Continent of Europe in a peaceful and hopeful globe. When that day finally comes, as it will, the people of West Berlin can take sober satisfaction in the fact that they were in the front lines for almost two decades.

All free men, wherever they may live, are citizens of Berlin, and therefore, as a free man, I take pride in the words "*Ich bin ein Berliner*."

Passage 2

Thank you. Thank you very much. Chancellor Kohl, Governing Mayor Diepgen, ladies and gentlemen: Twenty-four years ago, President John F. Kennedy visited Berlin, speaking to the people of this city and the world at the City Hall. Well, since then two other presidents have come, each in his turn, to Berlin. And today I, myself, make my second visit to your city.

We come to Berlin, we American presidents, because it's our duty to speak, in this place, of freedom. But I must confess, we're drawn here by other things as well: by the feeling of history in this city, more than 500 years older than our own nation; by the beauty of the Grunewald and the Tiergarten; most of all, by your courage and determination. Perhaps the composer Paul Lincke understood something about American presidents. You see, like so many presidents before me,

---

[1] I am a Roman citizen.

[2] I am a citizen of Berlin

I come here today because wherever I go, whatever I do: *Ich hab noch einen Koffer* in Berlin. [I still have a suitcase in Berlin.] Our gathering today is being broadcast throughout Western Europe and North America. I understand that it is being seen and heard as well in the East. To those listening throughout Eastern Europe, I extend my warmest greeting and the goodwill of the American people. To those listening in Eastern Berlin, a special word: Although I cannot be with you, I address my remarks to you just as surely as to those standing here before me. For I join you, as I join your fellow countrymen in the West, in this firm, this unalterable belief: *Es gibt nur ein Berlin.*[3]

Behind me stands a wall that encircles the free sectors of this city, part of a vast system of barriers that divides the entire continent of Europe. From the Baltic, south, those barriers cut across Germany in a gash of barbed wire, concrete, dog runs, and guard towers. Farther south, there may be no visible, no obvious wall. But there remain armed guards and checkpoints all the same—still a restriction on the right to travel, still an instrument to impose upon ordinary men and women the will of a totalitarian state. Yet it is here in Berlin where the wall emerges most clearly; here, cutting across your city, where the news photo and the television screen have imprinted this brutal division of a continent upon the mind of the world. Standing before the Brandenburg Gate, every man is a German, separated from his fellow men. Every man is a Berliner, forced to look upon a scar. President Von Weizsacker has said, "The German question is open as long as the Brandenburg Gate is closed." Today I say: As long as the gate is closed, as long as this scar of a wall is permitted to stand, it is not the German question alone that remains open, but the question of freedom for all mankind. Yet I do not come here to lament. For I find in Berlin a message of hope, even in the shadow of this wall, a message of triumph.

In this season of spring in 1945, the people of Berlin emerged from their air-raid shelters to find devastation. Thousands of miles away, the people of the United States reached out to help. And in 1947 Secretary of State—as you've been told—George Marshall announced the creation of what would become known as the Marshall Plan. Speaking precisely 40 years ago this month, he said: "Our policy is directed not against any country or doctrine, but against hunger, poverty, desperation, and chaos." In the Reichstag a few moments ago, I saw a display

commemorating this 40th anniversary of the Marshall Plan. I was struck by the sign on a burnt-out, gutted structure that was being rebuilt. I understand that Berliners of my own generation can remember seeing signs like it dotted throughout the western sectors of the city. The sign read simply: "The Marshall Plan is helping here to strengthen the free world." A strong, free world in the West, that dream became real. Japan rose from ruin to become an economic giant. Italy, France, Belgium— virtually every nation in Western Europe saw political and economic rebirth; the European Community was founded.

In West Germany and here in Berlin, there took place an economic miracle, the *Wirtschaftswunder.*[4] Adenauer, Erhard, Reuter,[5] and other leaders understood the practical importance of liberty—that just as truth can flourish only when the journalist is given freedom of speech, so prosperity can come about only when the farmer and businessman enjoy economic freedom. The German leaders reduced tariffs, expanded free trade, lowered taxes. From 1950 to 1960 alone, the standard of living in West Germany and Berlin doubled.

Where four decades ago there was rubble, today in West Berlin there is the greatest industrial output of any city in Germany—busy office blocks, fine homes and apartments, proud avenues, and the spreading lawns of parkland. Where a city's culture seemed to have been destroyed, today there are two great universities, orchestras and an opera, countless theaters, and museums. Where there was want, today there's abundance—food, clothing, automobiles—the wonderful goods of the Ku'damm. From devastation, from utter ruin, you Berliners have, in freedom, rebuilt a city that once again ranks as one of the greatest on earth. The Soviets may have had other plans. But my friends, there were a few things the Soviets didn't count on—*Berliner Herz, Berliner Humor, ja, und Berliner Schnauze.*[6] In the 1950s, Khrushchev predicted: "We will bury you." But in the West today, we see a free world that has achieved a level of prosperity and well-being unprecedented in all human history. In the Communist world, we see failure, technological backwardness, declining standards of health, even want of the most basic kind—too little food. Even today, the Soviet Union still cannot feed itself. After these four decades, then, there stands before the entire world one great and inescapable conclusion: Freedom leads to prosperity. Freedom

---

[3] "There is only one Berlin."

[4] "The Miracle on the Rhine." After WWII, West Germany and Austria were revitalized quickly.

[5] Konrad Adenauer and Ludwig Erhard were the Chancellors of West Germany from 1949-1963 and 1963-1966 respectively; Ernst Reuter was mayor of West Berlin from 1947-1953.

[6] Berliner heart, Berliner humor, yes, and a Berliner Schnauze" [an expression for Berliner's attitude]

Medium Reads 🎓

replaces the ancient hatreds among the nations with comity and peace. Freedom is the victor.

And now the Soviets themselves may, in a limited way, be coming to understand the importance of freedom. We hear much from Moscow about a new policy of reform and openness. Some political prisoners have been released. Certain foreign news broadcasts are no longer being jammed. Some

economic enterprises have been permitted to operate with greater freedom from state control. Are these the beginnings of profound changes in the Soviet state? Or are they token gestures, intended to raise false hopes in the West, or to strengthen the Soviet system without changing it? We welcome change and openness; for we believe that freedom and security go together, that the advance of human liberty can only strengthen the cause of world peace. There is one sign the Soviets can make that would be unmistakable, that would advance dramatically the cause of freedom and peace.

General Secretary Gorbachev, if you seek peace, if you seek prosperity for the Soviet Union and Eastern Europe, if you seek liberalization: Come here to this gate! Mr. Gorbachev, open this gate! Mr. Gorbachev, tear down this wall!

I understand the fear of war and the pain of division that afflict this continent— and I pledge to you my country's efforts to help overcome these burdens. To be sure, we in the West must resist Soviet expansion. So we must maintain defenses of unassailable strength. Yet we seek peace; so we must strive to reduce arms on both sides. Beginning 10 years ago, the Soviets challenged the Western alliance with a grave new threat, hundreds of new and more deadly SS-20 nuclear missiles, capable of striking every capital in Europe. The Western alliance responded by committing itself to a counter-deployment unless the Soviets agreed to negotiate a better solution; namely, the elimination of such weapons on both sides. For many months, the Soviets refused to bargain in earnestness. As the alliance, in turn, prepared to go forward with its counter-deployment, there were difficult days—days of protests like those during my 1982 visit to this city—and the Soviets later walked away from the table.

But through it all, the alliance held firm. And I invite those who protested then— I invite those who protest today—to mark this fact: Because we remained strong, the Soviets came back to the table. And because we remain strong today, we have within reach the possibility, not merely of limiting the growth of arms, but of eliminating, for the first time, an entire class of nuclear weapons from the face of the earth.

As I speak, NATO ministers are meeting in Iceland to review the progress of our proposals for eliminating

these weapons. At the talks in Geneva, we have also proposed deep cuts in strategic offensive weapons. And the Western allies have likewise made far-reaching proposals to reduce the danger of conventional war and to place a total ban on chemical weapons.

While we pursue these arms reductions, I pledge to you that we will maintain the capacity to deter Soviet aggression at any level at which it might occur. And in cooperation with many of our allies, the United States is pursuing the Strategic Defense Initiative—research to base deterrence not on the threat of offensive retaliation, but on defenses that truly defend; on systems, in short, that will not target populations, but shield them. By these means we seek to increase the safety of Europe and all the world. But we must remember a crucial fact: East and West do not mistrust each other because we are armed; we are armed because we mistrust each other. And our differences are not about weapons but about liberty. When President Kennedy spoke at the City Hall those 24 years ago, freedom was encircled, Berlin was under siege. And today, despite all the pressures upon this city, Berlin stands secure in its liberty. And freedom itself is transforming the globe.

In the Philippines, in South and Central America, democracy has been given a rebirth. Throughout the Pacific, free markets are working miracle after miracle of economic growth. In the industrialized nations, a technological revolution is taking place—a revolution marked by rapid, dramatic advances in computers and telecommunications.

In Europe, only one nation and those it controls refuse to join the community of freedom. Yet in this age of redoubled economic growth, of information and innovation, the Soviet Union faces a choice: It must make fundamental changes, or it will become obsolete. Today thus represents a moment of hope. We in the West stand ready to cooperate with the East to promote true openness, to break down barriers that separate people, to create a safe, freer world. And surely there is no better place than Berlin, the meeting place of East and West, to make a start. Free people of Berlin: Today, as in the past, the United States stands for the strict observance and full implementation of all parts of the Four Power Agreement of 1971. Let us use this occasion, the 750th anniversary of this city, to usher in a new era, to seek a still fuller, richer life for the Berlin of the future. Together, let us maintain and develop the ties between the Federal Republic and the Western sectors of Berlin, which is permitted by the 1971 agreement.

And I invite Mr. Gorbachev: Let us work to bring the Eastern and Western parts of the city closer together, so that all the inhabitants of all Berlin can enjoy the benefits that come with life in one of the great cities of the world. To open Berlin still further to all Europe, East and West, let us expand the vital air access to this city, finding ways of making commercial air service to Berlin more convenient, more comfortable, and more economical. We look to the day when West Berlin can become one of the chief aviation hubs in all central Europe.

With our French and British partners, the United States is prepared to help bring international meetings to Berlin. It would be only fitting for Berlin to serve as the site of United Nations meetings, or world conferences on human rights and arms control or other issues that call for international cooperation.

There is no better way to establish hope for the future than to enlighten young minds, and we would be honored to sponsor summer youth exchanges, cultural events, and other programs for young Berliners from the East. Our French and British friends, I'm certain, will do the same. And it's my hope that an authority can be found in East Berlin to sponsor visits from young people of the Western sectors.

One final proposal, one close to my heart: Sport represents a source of enjoyment and ennoblement, and you may have noted that the Republic of Korea—South Korea—has offered to permit certain events of the 1988 Olympics to take place in the North. International sports competitions of all kinds could take place in both parts of this city. And what better way to demonstrate to the world the openness of this city than to offer in some future year to hold the Olympic games here in Berlin, East and West? In these four decades, as I have said, you Berliners have built a great city. You've done so in spite of threats—the Soviet attempts to impose the Ostmark, the blockade. Today the city thrives in spite of the challenges implicit in the very presence of this wall. What keeps you here? Certainly there's a great deal to be said for your fortitude, for your defiant courage. But I believe there's something deeper, something that involves Berlin's whole look and feel and way of life—not mere sentiment. No one could live long in Berlin without being completely disabused of illusions. Something instead, that has seen the difficulties of life in Berlin but chose to accept them, that continues to build this good and proud city in contrast to a surrounding totalitarian presence that refuses to release human energies or aspirations. Something that speaks with a powerful voice of affirmation, that says yes to this city, yes to the future, yes to freedom. In a word, I would submit that what keeps you in Berlin is love—love both profound and abiding.

Perhaps this gets to the root of the matter, to the most fundamental distinction of all between East and West. The totalitarian world produces backwardness because it does such violence to the spirit, thwarting the human impulse to create, to enjoy, to worship. The totalitarian world finds even symbols of love and of worship an affront. Years ago, before the East Germans began rebuilding their churches, they erected a secular structure: the television tower at Alexander Platz. Virtually ever since, the authorities have been working to correct what they view as the tower's one major flaw, treating the glass sphere at the top with paints and chemicals of every kind. Yet even today when the sun strikes that sphere—that sphere that towers over all Berlin— the light makes the sign of the cross. There in Berlin, like the city itself, symbols of love, symbols of worship, cannot be suppressed.

As I looked out a moment ago from the Reichstag, that embodiment of German unity, I noticed words crudely spray-painted upon the wall, perhaps by a young Berliner: "This wall will fall. Beliefs become reality." Yes, across Europe, this wall will fall. For it cannot withstand faith; it cannot withstand truth. The wall cannot withstand freedom.

And I would like, before I close, to say one word. I have read, and I have been questioned since I've been here about certain demonstrations against my coming. And I would like to say just one thing, and to those who demonstrate so. I wonder if they have ever asked themselves that if they should have the kind of government they apparently seek, no one would ever be able to do what they're doing again.

Thank you and God bless you all.

1

What is the main purpose of the first passage?

_____

2

What is the first passage's tone?

_____

3

What is the central claim of the first passage?

_____

4

What is the main purpose of the second passage?

_____

5

What is the second passage's tone?

_____

6

What is the central claim of the second passage?

_____

7

What is the relationship between the passages?

_____

The following passage is adapted from E. Nesbit's *Beautiful Stories from Shakespeare* (1907). Nesbit (1858-1924) was at the forefront of writing novels for children that have adult themes, a tradition carried on by, among others, C. S. Lewis and J. K. Rowling.

When a person is asked to tell the story of Macbeth, he can tell two stories. One is of a man called Macbeth who came to the throne of Scotland by a crime in the year of our Lord 1039, and reigned justly and well, on the whole, for fifteen years or more. This story is part of Scottish history. The other story issues from a place called Imagination; it is gloomy and wonderful, and you shall hear it.

A year or two before Edward the Confessor began to rule England, a battle was won in Scotland against a Norwegian King by two generals named Macbeth and Banquo. After the battle, the generals walked together towards Forres, in Elginshire, where Duncan, King of Scotland, was awaiting them.

While they were crossing a lonely heath, they saw three bearded women, sisters, hand in hand, withered in appearance and wild in their attire.

"Speak, who are you?" demanded Macbeth.

"Hail, Macbeth, chieftain of Glamis," said the first woman.

"Hail, Macbeth, chieftain of Cawdor," said the second woman.

"Hail, Macbeth, King that is to be," said the third woman.

Then Banquo asked, "What of me?" and the third woman replied, "You shalt be the father of kings."

"Tell me more," said Macbeth. "By my father's death I am chieftain of Glamis, but the chieftain of Cawdor lives, and the King lives, and his children live. Speak, I charge you!"

The women replied only by vanishing, as though suddenly mixed with the air.

Banquo and Macbeth knew then that they had been addressed by witches, and were discussing their prophecies when two nobles approached. One of them thanked Macbeth, in the King's name, for his military services, and the other said, "He bade me call you chieftain of Cawdor."

Macbeth then learned that the man who had yesterday borne that title was to die for treason, and he could not help thinking, "The third witch called me, 'King that is to be.'"

"Banquo," he said, "you see that the witches spoke truth concerning me. Do you not believe, therefore, that your child and grandchild will be kings?"

Banquo frowned. Duncan had two sons, Malcolm and Donalbain, and he deemed it disloyal to hope that his son Fleance should rule Scotland. He told Macbeth

that the witches might have intended to tempt them both into villainy by their prophecies concerning the throne. Macbeth, however, thought the prophecy that he should be King too pleasant to keep to himself, and he mentioned it to his wife in a letter.

Lady Macbeth was the grand-daughter of a King of Scotland who had died in defending his crown against the King who preceded Duncan, and by whose order her only brother was slain. To her, Duncan was a reminder of bitter wrongs. Her husband had royal blood in his veins, and when she read his letter, she was determined that he should be King.

When a messenger arrived to inform her that Duncan would pass a night in Macbeth's castle, she nerved herself for a very base action.

She told Macbeth almost as soon as she saw him that Duncan must spend a sunless morrow. She meant that Duncan must die, and that the dead are blind. "We will speak further," said Macbeth uneasily, and at night, with his memory full of Duncan's kind words, he would gladly have spared his guest.

"Would you live a coward?" demanded Lady Macbeth, who seems to have thought that morality and cowardice were the same.

"I dare do all that may become a man," replied Macbeth; "who dare do more is none."

"Why did you write that letter to me?" she inquired fiercely, and with bitter words she egged him on to murder, and with cunning words she showed him how to do it.

After supper Duncan went to bed, and two grooms were placed on guard at his bedroom door. Lady Macbeth caused them to drink wine till they were stupefied. She then took their daggers and would have killed the King herself if his sleeping face had not looked like her father's.

Macbeth came later, and found the daggers lying by the grooms; and soon with red hands he appeared before his wife, saying, "Methought I heard a voice cry, 'Sleep no more! Macbeth destroys the sleeping.'"

"Wash your hands," said she. "Why did you not leave the daggers by the grooms? Take them back, and smear the grooms with blood."

"I dare not," said Macbeth.

His wife dared, and she returned to him with hands red as his own, but a heart less white, she proudly told him, for she scorned his fear.

The murderers heard a knocking, and Macbeth wished it was a knocking which could wake the dead. It was the knocking of Macduff, the chieftain of Fife, who had been told by Duncan to visit him early. Macbeth went to him, and showed him the door of the King's room.

Macduff entered, and came out again crying, "O horror! horror! horror!"

Macbeth appeared as horror-stricken as Macduff, and pretending that he could not bear to see life in Duncan's murderers, he slew the two grooms with their own daggers before they could proclaim their innocence.

These murders did not shriek out, and Macbeth was crowned at Scone. One of Duncan's sons went to Ireland, the other to England. Macbeth was King. But he was discontented. The prophecy concerning Banquo oppressed his mind. If Fleance were to rule, a son of Macbeth would not rule. Macbeth determined, therefore, to murder both Banquo and his son. He hired two ruffians, who slew Banquo one night when he was on his way with Fleance to a banquet which Macbeth was giving to his nobles. Fleance escaped.

Meanwhile Macbeth and his Queen received their guests very graciously, and he expressed a wish for them which has been uttered thousands of times since his day—"Now good digestion wait on appetite, and health on both."

"We pray your Majesty to sit with us," said Lennox, a Scotch noble; but ere Macbeth could reply, the ghost of Banquo entered the banqueting hall and sat in Macbeth's place.

Not noticing the ghost, Macbeth observed that, if Banquo were present, he could say that he had collected under his roof the choicest chivalry of Scotland. Macduff, however, had curtly declined his invitation.

The King was again pressed to take a seat, and Lennox, to whom Banquo's ghost was invisible, showed him the chair where it sat.

But Macbeth, with his eyes of genius, saw the ghost. He saw it like a form of mist and blood, and he demanded passionately, "Which of you have done this?"

Still none saw the ghost but he, and to the ghost Macbeth said, "You canst not say I did it."

The ghost glided out, and Macbeth was impudent enough to raise a glass of wine "to the general joy of the whole table, and to our dear friend Banquo, whom we miss."

The toast was drunk as the ghost of Banquo entered for the second time.

"Begone!" cried Macbeth. "You are senseless, mindless! Hide in the earth, you horrible shadow."

Again none saw the ghost but he.

"What is it your Majesty sees?" asked one of the nobles.

The Queen dared not permit an answer to be given to this question. She hurriedly begged her guests to quit a sick man who was likely to grow worse if he was obliged to talk.

Macbeth, however, was well enough next day to converse with the witches whose prophecies had so depraved him.

He found them in a cavern on a thunderous day. They were revolving round a cauldron in which were boiling particles of many strange and horrible creatures, and they knew he was coming before he arrived.

"Answer me what I ask you," said the King.

"Would you rather hear it from us or our masters?" asked the first witch.

"Call them," replied Macbeth.

Thereupon the witches poured blood into the cauldron and grease into the flame that licked it, and a helmeted head appeared with the visor on, so that Macbeth could only see its eyes.

He was speaking to the head, when the first witch said gravely, "He knows your thought," and a voice in the head said, "Macbeth, beware Macduff, the chieftain of Fife." The head then descended Into the cauldron till it disappeared.

"One word more," pleaded Macbeth.

"He will not be commanded," said the first witch, and then a crowned child ascended from the cauldron bearing a tree in his hand The child said—

"Macbeth shall be unconquerable till
The Wood of Birnam climbs Dunsinane Hill."

"That will never be," said Macbeth; and he asked to be told if Banquo's descendants would ever rule Scotland.

The cauldron sank into the earth; music was heard, and a procession of phantom kings filed past Macbeth; behind them was Banquo's ghost. In each king, Macbeth saw a likeness to Banquo, and he counted eight kings.

Then he was suddenly left alone.

His next proceeding was to send murderers to Macduff's castle. They did not find Macduff, and asked Lady Macduff where he was. She gave a stinging answer, and her questioner called Macduff a traitor. "You liest!" shouted Macduff's little son, who was immediately stabbed, and with his last breath entreated his mother to fly. The murderers did not leave the castle while one of its inmates remained alive.

Macduff was in England listening, with Malcolm, to a doctor's tale of cures wrought by Edward the Confessor when his friend Ross came to tell him that his wife and children were no more. At first Ross dared not speak the truth, and turn Macduff's bright sympayour with sufferers relieved by royal virtue into sorrow and hatred. But when Malcolm said that England was sending an army into Scotland against Macbeth, Ross blurted out his news, and Macduff cried, "All dead, did you say? All my pretty ones and their mother? Did you say all?"

His sorry hope was in revenge, but if he could have looked into Macbeth's castle on Dunsinane Hill, he would have seen at work a force more solemn than revenge. Retribution was working, for Lady Macbeth was mad. She walked in her sleep amid ghastly dreams. She was wont to wash her hands for a quarter of an hour at a time; but after all her washing, would still see a red spot of blood upon her skin. It was pitiful to hear her cry that all the perfumes of Arabia could not sweeten her little hand.

"Canst you not minister to a mind diseased?" inquired Macbeth of the doctor, but the doctor replied that his patient must minister to her own mind. This reply gave Macbeth a scorn of medicine. "Throw physic to the dogs," he said; "I'll none of it."

One day he heard a sound of women crying. An officer approached him and said, "The Queen, your Majesty, is dead." "Out, brief candle," muttered Macbeth, meaning that life was like a candle, at the mercy of a puff of air. He did not weep; he was too familiar with death.

Presently a messenger told him that he saw Birnam Wood on the march. Macbeth called him a liar and a slave, and threatened to hang him if he had made a mistake. "If you are right you can hang me," he said.

From the turret windows of Dunsinane Castle, Birnam Wood did indeed appear to be marching. Every soldier of the English army held aloft a bough which he had cut from a tree in that wood, and like human trees they climbed Dunsinane Hill.

Macbeth had still his courage. He went to battle to conquer or die, and the first thing he did was to kill the English general's son in single combat. Macbeth then felt that no man could fight him and live, and when Macduff came to him blazing for revenge, Macbeth said to him, "Go back; I have spilt too much of your blood already."

"My voice is in my sword," replied Macduff, and hacked at him and bade him yield.

"I will not yield!" said Macbeth, but his last hour had struck. He fell.

Macbeth's men were in retreat when Macduff came before Malcolm holding a King's head by the hair.

"Hail, King!" he said; and the new King looked at the old.

So Malcolm reigned after Macbeth; but in years that came afterwards the descendants of Banquo were kings.

1

What is the main purpose of this passage?

_____

2

What is the passage's tone?

_____

3

How would you summarize the passage?

_____

4

How does Nesbit describe Macbeth?

_____

5

How does Nesbit portray Lady Macbeth?

_____

6

What is the conflict between Macbeth and Lady Macbeth?

_____

Ambrose Bierce's short story "An Occurrence at Owl Creek Bridge" (1890) is a classic of the American short stories. Kurt Vonnegut described it as "a flawless example of American genius, like 'Sophisticated Lady' by Duke Ellington or the Franklin stove."

I

A man stood upon a railroad bridge in northern Alabama, looking down into the swift water twenty feet below. The man's hands were behind his back, the wrists bound with a cord. A rope closely encircled his neck. It was attached to a stout cross-timber above his head and the slack fell to the level of his knees. Some loose boards laid upon the sleepers supporting the metals of the railway supplied a footing for him and his executioners—two private soldiers of the Federal army, directed by a sergeant who in civil life may have been a deputy sheriff. At a short remove upon the same temporary platform was an officer in the uniform of his rank, armed. He was a captain. A sentinel at each end of the bridge stood with his rifle in the position known as "support," that is to say, vertical in front of the left shoulder, the hammer resting on the forearm thrown straight across the chest—a formal and unnatural position, enforcing an erect carriage of the body. It did not appear to be the duty of these two men to know what was occurring at the center of the bridge; they merely blockaded the two ends of the foot planking that traversed it. Beyond one of the sentinels nobody was in sight; the railroad ran straight away into a forest for a hundred yards, then, curving, was lost to view. Doubtless there was an outpost farther along. The other bank of the stream was open ground—a gentle acclivity topped with a stockade of vertical tree trunks, loopholed for rifles, with a single embrasure through which protruded the muzzle of a brass cannon commanding the bridge. Midway of the slope between the bridge and fort were the spectators—a single company of infantry in line, at "parade rest," the butts of the rifles on the ground, the barrels inclining slightly backward against the right shoulder, the hands crossed upon the stock. A lieutenant stood at the right of the line, the point of his sword upon the ground, his left hand resting upon his right. Excepting the group of four at the center of the bridge, not a man moved. The company faced the bridge, staring stonily, motionless. The sentinels, facing the banks of the stream, might have been statues to adorn the bridge. The captain stood with folded arms, silent, observing the work of his subordinates, but making no sign. Death is a dignitary who when he comes announced is to be received with formal manifestations of respect, even by those most familiar with him. In the code of military etiquette silence and fixity are forms of deference.

The man who was engaged in being hanged was apparently about thirty-five years of age. He was a civilian, if one might judge from his habit, which was that of a planter. His features were good—a straight nose, firm mouth, broad forehead, from which his long, dark hair was combed straight back, falling behind his ears to the collar of his well-fitting frock coat. He wore a mustache and pointed beard, but no whiskers; his eyes were large and dark gray, and had a kindly expression which one would hardly have expected in one whose neck was in the hemp. Evidently this was no vulgar assassin. The liberal military code makes provision for hanging many kinds of persons, and gentlemen are not excluded.

The preparations being complete, the two private soldiers stepped aside and each drew away the plank upon which he had been standing. The sergeant turned to the captain, saluted and placed himself immediately behind that officer, who in turn moved apart one pace. These movements left the condemned man and the sergeant standing on the two ends of the same plank, which spanned three of the cross-ties of the bridge. The end upon which the civilian stood almost, but not quite, reached a fourth. This plank had been held in place by the weight of the captain; it was now held by that of the sergeant. At a signal from the former the latter would step aside, the plank would tilt and the condemned man go down between two ties. The arrangement commended itself to his judgment as simple and effective. His face had not been covered nor his eyes bandaged. He looked a moment at his "unsteadfast footing," then let his gaze wander to the swirling water of the stream racing madly beneath his feet. A piece of dancing driftwood caught his attention and his eyes followed it down the current. How slowly it appeared to move, What a sluggish stream!

He closed his eyes in order to fix his last thoughts upon his wife and children. The water, touched to gold by the early sun, the brooding mists under the banks at some distance down the stream, the fort, the soldiers, the piece of drift—all had distracted him. And now he became conscious of a new disturbance. Striking through the thought of his dear ones was a sound which he could neither ignore nor understand, a sharp, distinct, metallic percussion like the stroke of a blacksmith's hammer upon the anvil; it had the same ringing quality. He wondered what it was, and whether immeasurably distant or near by—it seemed both. Its recurrence was regular, but as slow as the tolling of a death knell. He awaited each stroke with impatience and—he knew not why—apprehension. The intervals of silence grew progressively longer, the delays became maddening. With their greater infrequency the sounds increased in strength and sharpness. They hurt his ear like the thrust of a knife; he feared he would shriek. What he heard was the ticking of his watch.

He unclosed his eyes and saw again the water below him. "If I could free my hands," he thought, "I might throw off the noose and spring into the stream. By diving I could evade the bullets and, swimming vigorously, reach the bank, take to the woods and get away home. My home, thank God, is as yet outside their lines; my wife and little ones are still beyond the invader's farthest advance."

As these thoughts, which have here to be set down in words, were flashed into the doomed man's brain rather than evolved from it the captain nodded to the sergeant. The sergeant stepped aside.

II

Peyton Farquhar was a well-to-do planter, of an old and highly respected Alabama family. Being a slave owner and like other slave owners a politician he was naturally an original secessionist and ardently devoted to the Southern cause. Circumstances of an imperious nature, which it is unnecessary to relate here, had prevented him from taking service with the gallant army that had fought the disastrous campaigns ending with the fall of Corinth, and he chafed under the inglorious restraint, longing for the release of his energies, the larger life of the soldier, the opportunity for distinction. That opportunity, he felt, would come, as it comes to all in war time. Meanwhile he did what he could. No service was too humble for him to perform in aid of the South, no adventure too perilous for him to undertake if consistent with the character of a civilian who was at heart a soldier, and who in good faith and without too much qualification assented to at least a part of the frankly villainous dictum that all is fair in love and war.

One evening while Farquhar and his wife were sitting on a rustic bench near the entrance to his grounds, a gray-clad soldier rode up to the gate and asked for a drink of water. Mrs. Farquhar was only too happy to serve him with her own white hands. While she was fetching the water her husband approached the dusty horseman and inquired eagerly for news from the front.

"The Yanks are repairing the railroads," said the man, "and are getting ready for another advance. They have reached the Owl Creek bridge, put it in order and built a stockade on the north bank. The commandant has issued an order, which is posted everywhere, declaring that any civilian caught interfering with the railroad, its bridges, tunnels or trains will be summarily hanged. I saw the order."

"How far is it to the Owl Creek bridge?" Farquhar asked.

"About thirty miles."

"Is there no force on this side the creek?"

"Only a picket post half a mile out, on the railroad, and a single sentinel at this end of the bridge."

"Suppose a man—a civilian and student of hanging—should elude the picket post and perhaps get the better of the sentinel," said Farquhar, smiling, "what could he accomplish?"

The soldier reflected. "I was there a month ago," he replied. "I observed that the flood of last winter had lodged a great quantity of driftwood against the wooden pier at this end of the bridge. It is now dry and would burn like tow."

The lady had now brought the water, which the soldier drank. He thanked her ceremoniously, bowed to her husband and rode away. An hour later, after nightfall, he repassed the plantation, going northward in the direction from which he had come. He was a Federal scout.

III

As Peyton Farquhar fell straight downward through the bridge he lost consciousness and was as one already dead. From this state he was awakened—ages later, it seemed to him—by the pain of a sharp pressure upon his throat, followed by a sense of suffocation. Keen, poignant agonies seemed to shoot from his neck downward through every fiber of his body and limbs. These pains appeared to flash along well-defined lines of ramification and to beat with an inconceivably rapid periodicity. They seemed like streams of pulsating fire heating him to an intolerable temperature. As to his head, he was conscious of nothing but a feeling of fulness—of congestion. These sensations were unaccompanied by thought. The intellectual part of his nature was already effaced; he had power only to feel, and feeling was torment. He was conscious of motion. Encompassed in a luminous cloud, of which he was now merely the fiery heart, without material substance, he swung through unthinkable arcs of oscillation, like a vast pendulum. Then all at once, with terrible suddenness, the light about him shot upward with the noise of a loud splash; a frightful roaring was in his ears, and all was cold and dark. The power of thought was restored; he knew that the rope had broken and he had fallen into the stream. There was no additional strangulation; the noose about his neck was already suffocating him and kept the water from his lungs. To die of hanging at the bottom of a river!—the idea seemed to him ludicrous. He opened his eyes in the darkness and saw above him a gleam of light, but how distant, how inaccessible! He was still sinking, for the light became fainter and fainter until it was a mere glimmer. Then it began to grow and brighten, and he knew that he was rising toward the surface—knew it with reluctance, for he was now very comfortable. "To be hanged and drowned," he thought? "that is not so bad; but I do not wish to be shot. No; I will not be shot; that is not fair."

He was not conscious of an effort, but a sharp pain in his wrist apprised him that he was trying to free his hands. He gave the struggle his attention, as an idler might observe the feat of a juggler, without interest in the outcome. What splendid effort!—what magnificent, what superhuman strength! Ah, that was a fine endeavor! Bravo! The cord fell away; his arms parted and floated upward, the hands dimly seen on each side in the growing light. He watched them with a new interest as first one and then the other pounced upon the noose at his neck. They tore it away and thrust it fiercely aside, its undulations resembling those of a water snake. "Put it back, put it back!" He thought he shouted these words to his hands, for the undoing of the noose had been succeeded by the direst pang that he had yet experienced. His neck ached horribly; his brain was on fire; his heart, which had been fluttering faintly, gave a great leap, trying to force itself out at his mouth. His whole body was racked and wrenched with an insupportable anguish! But his disobedient hands gave no heed to the command. They beat the water vigorously with quick, downward strokes, forcing him to the surface. He felt his head emerge; his eyes were blinded by the sunlight; his chest expanded convulsively, and with a supreme and crowning agony his lungs engulfed a great draught of air, which instantly he expelled in a shriek!

He was now in full possession of his physical senses. They were, indeed, preternaturally keen and alert. Something in the awful disturbance of his organic system had so exalted and refined them that they made record of things never before perceived. He felt the ripples upon his face and heard their separate sounds as they struck. He looked at the forest on the bank of the stream, saw the individual trees, the leaves and the veining of each leaf—saw the very insects upon them: the locusts, the brilliant-bodied flies, the grey spiders stretching their webs from twig to twig. He noted the prismatic colors in all the dewdrops upon a million blades of grass. The humming of the gnats that danced above the eddies of the stream, the beating of the dragon flies' wings, the strokes of the water-spiders' legs, like oars which had lifted their boat—all these made audible music. A fish slid along beneath his eyes and he heard the rush of its body parting the water.

He had come to the surface facing down the stream; in a moment the visible world seemed to wheel slowly round, himself the pivotal point, and he saw the bridge, the fort, the soldiers upon the bridge, the captain, the sergeant, the two privates, his executioners. They were in silhouette against the blue sky. They shouted and gesticulated, pointing at him. The captain had drawn his pistol, but did not fire; the others were unarmed. Their movements were grotesque and horrible, their forms gigantic.

Suddenly he heard a sharp report and something struck the water smartly within a few inches of his head, spattering his face with spray. He heard a second report, and saw one of the sentinels with his rifle at his shoulder, a light cloud of blue smoke rising from the muzzle. The man in the water saw the eye of the man on the bridge gazing into his own through the sights of the rifle. He observed that it was a grey eye and remembered having read that grey eyes were keenest, and that all famous marksmen had them. Nevertheless, this one had missed.

A counter-swirl had caught Farquhar and turned him half round; he was again looking into the forest on the bank opposite the fort. The sound of a clear, high voice in a monotonous singsong now rang out behind him and came across the water with a distinctness that pierced and subdued all other sounds, even the beating of the ripples in his ears. Although no soldier, he had frequented camps enough to know the dread significance of that deliberate, drawling, aspirated chant; the lieutenant on shore was taking a part in the morning's work. How coldly and pitilessly—with what an even, calm intonation, presaging, and enforcing tranquillity in the men—with what accurately measured intervals fell those cruel words:

"Attention, company!... Shoulder arms!... Ready!... Aim!... Fire!"

Farquhar dived—dived as deeply as he could. The water roared in his ears like the voice of Niagara, yet he heard the dulled thunder of the volley and, rising again toward the surface, met shining bits of metal, singularly flattened, oscillating slowly downward. Some of them touched him on the face and hands, then fell away, continuing their descent. One lodged between his collar and neck; it was uncomfortably warm and he snatched it out.

As he rose to the surface, gasping for breath, he saw that he had been a long time under water; he was perceptibly farther down stream nearer to safety. The soldiers had almost finished reloading; the metal ramrods flashed all at once in the sunshine as they were drawn from the barrels, turned in the air, and thrust into their sockets. The two sentinels fired again, independently and ineffectually.

The hunted man saw all this over his shoulder; he was now swimming vigorously with the current. His brain was as energetic as his arms and legs; he thought with the rapidity of lightning.

The officer," he reasoned, "will not make that martinet's error a second time. It is as easy to dodge a volley as a single shot. He has probably already given the command to fire at will. God help me, I cannot dodge them all!"

An appalling splash within two yards of him was followed by a loud, rushing sound, diminuendo, which seemed to travel back through the air to the fort and died in an explosion which stirred the very river to its deeps!

A rising sheet of water curved over him, fell down upon him, blinded him, strangled him! The cannon had taken a hand in the game. As he shook his head free from the commotion of the smitten water he heard the deflected shot humming through the air ahead, and in an instant it was cracking and smashing the branches in the forest beyond.

"They will not do that again," he thought; "the next time they will use a charge of grape. I must keep my eye upon the gun; the smoke will apprise me—the report arrives too late; it lags behind the missile. That is a good gun."

Suddenly he felt himself whirled round and round—spinning like a top. The water, the banks, the forests, the now distant bridge, fort and men—all were commingled and blurred. Objects were represented by their colors only; circular horizontal streaks of color— that was all he saw. He had been caught in a vortex and was being whirled on with a velocity of advance and gyration that made him giddy and sick. In a few moments he was flung upon the gravel at the foot of the left bank of the stream—the southern bank—and behind a projecting point which concealed him from his enemies. The sudden arrest of his motion, the abrasion of one of his hands on the gravel, restored him, and he wept with delight. He dug his fingers into the sand, threw it over himself in handfuls and audibly blessed it. It looked like diamonds, rubies, emeralds; he could think of nothing beautiful which it did not resemble. The trees upon the bank were giant garden plants; he noted a definite order in their arrangement, inhaled the fragrance of their blooms. A strange, roseate light shone through the spaces among their trunks and the wind made in their branches the music of olian harps. He had no wish to perfect his escape— was content to remain in that enchanting spot until retaken.

A whiz and rattle of grapeshot among the branches high above his head roused him from his dream. The baffled cannoneer had fired him a random farewell. He sprang to his feet, rushed up the sloping bank, and plunged into the forest.

All that day he traveled, laying his course by the rounding sun. The forest seemed interminable; nowhere did he discover a break in it, not even a woodman's road. He had not known that he lived in so wild a region. There was something uncanny in the revelation.

By nightfall he was fatigued, footsore, famishing. The thought of his wife and children urged him on. At last he found a road which led him in what he knew to be the right direction. It was as wide and straight as a city street, yet it seemed untraveled. No fields bordered it, no dwelling anywhere. Not so much as the barking of a dog suggested human habitation. The black bodies of the trees formed a straight wall on both sides, terminating on the horizon in a point, like a diagram in a lesson in perspective. Overhead, as he looked up through this rift in the wood, shone great garden stars looking unfamiliar and grouped in strange constellations. He was sure they were arranged in some order which had a secret and malign significance. The wood on either side was full of singular noises, among which—once, twice, and again—he distinctly heard whispers in an unknown tongue.

His neck was in pain and lifting his hand to it found it horribly swollen. He knew that it had a circle of black where the rope had bruised it. His eyes felt congested; he could no longer close them. His tongue was swollen with thirst; he relieved its fever by thrusting it forward from between his teeth into the cold air. How softly the turf had carpeted the untraveled avenue—he could no longer feel the roadway beneath his feet!

Doubtless, despite his suffering, he had fallen asleep while walking, for now he sees another scene— perhaps he has merely recovered from a delirium. He stands at the gate of his own home. All is as he left it, and all bright and beautiful in the morning sunshine. He must have traveled the entire night. As he pushes open the gate and passes up the wide white walk, he sees a flutter of female garments; his wife, looking fresh and cool and sweet, steps down from the veranda to meet him. At the bottom of the steps she stands waiting, with a smile of ineffable joy, an attitude of matchless grace and dignity. Ah, how beautiful she is! He springs forward with extended arms. As he is about to clasp her he feels a stunning blow upon the back of the neck; a blinding white light blazes all about him with a sound like the shock of a cannon—then all is darkness and silence!

Peyton Farquhar was dead; his body, with a broken neck, swung gently from side to side beneath the timbers of the Owl Creek bridge.

1

What is the main purpose of this passage?

_____

2

What is the passage's tone?

_____

3

How would you summarize the passage?

_____

4

How would you describe Peyton?

_____

ON THE SEPARATION OF POWERS – JAMES MADISON AND DAVID HUME

Passage 1 is from David Hume, "Of the Independency of Parliament," 1742. Passage 2 is adapted from James Madison, *Federalist 51*, 1788.

Passage 1

Political writers have established it as a maxim, that, in contriving any system of government, and fixing the several checks and controls of the constitution, every man ought to be supposed a knave, and to have no other end, in all his actions, than private interest. By this interest we must govern him, and, by means of it, make him, notwithstanding his insatiable avarice and ambition, cooperate to public good. Without this, say they, we shall in vain boast of the advantages of any constitution, and shall find, in the end, that we have no security for our liberties or possessions, except the good-will of our rulers; that is, we shall have no security at all.

It is, therefore, a just political maxim, that every man must be supposed a knave; though, at the same time, it appears somewhat strange, that a maxim should be true in politics which is false in fact. But to satisfy us on this head, we may consider, that men are generally more honest in their private than in their public capacity, and will go greater lengths to serve a party, than when their own private interest is alone concerned. Honour is a great check upon mankind: but where a considerable body of men act together, this check is in a great measure removed, since a man is sure to be approved of by his own party, for what promotes the common interest; and he soon learns to despise the clamours of adversaries. To which we may add, that every court or senate is determined by the greater number of voices; so that, if self-interest influences only the majority (as it will always do), the whole senate follows the allurements of this separate interest and acts as if it contained not one member who had any regard to public interest and liberty.

When there offers, therefore, to our censure and examination, any plan of government, real or imaginary, where the power is distributed among several courts, and several orders of men, we should always consider the separate interest of each court, and each order; and if we find that, by the skilful division of power, this interest must necessarily, in its operation, concur with the public, we may pronounce that government to be wise and happy. If, on the contrary, separate interest be not checked, and be not directed to the public, we ought to look for nothing but faction, disorder, and tyranny from such a government. In this opinion I am justified by experience, as well as by the authority of all philosophers and politicians, both ancient and modern.

How much, therefore, would it have surprised such a genius as Cicero or Tacitus, to have been told, that in a future age there should arise a very regular system of mixed government, where the authority was so distributed, that one rank, whenever it pleased, might swallow up all the rest, and engross the whole power of the constitution! Such a government, they would say, will not be a mixed government. For so great is the natural ambition of men, that they are never satisfied with power; and if one order of men, by pursuing its own interest, can usurp upon every other order, it will certainly do so, and render itself, as far as possible, absolute and uncontrollable.

But, in this opinion, experience shows they would have been mistaken. For this is actually the case with the British constitution. The share of power allotted by our constitution to the House of Commons, is so great, that it absolutely commands all the other parts of the government. The king's legislative power is plainly no proper check to it. For though the king has a negative in framing laws, yet this, in fact, is esteemed of so little moment, that whatever is voted by the two Houses, is always sure to pass into a law, and the royal assent is little better than a form. The principal weight of the crown lies in the executive; power. But, besides that the executive power in every government is altogether subordinate to the legislative; besides this, I say, the exercise of this power requires an immense expense, and the Commons have assumed to themselves the sole right of granting money. How easy, therefore, would it be for that house to wrest from the crown all these powers, one after another, by making every grant conditional, and choosing their time so well, that their refusal of supply should only distress the government, without giving foreign powers any advantage over us! Did the House of Commons depend in the same manner upon the king, and had none of the members any property but from his gift, would not he command all their resolutions, and be from that moment absolute? As to the House of Lords, they are a very powerful support to the crown, so long as they are, in their turn, supported by it; but both experience and reason show, that they have no force or authority sufficient to maintain themselves alone, without such support.

How, therefore, shall we solve this paradox? And by what means is this member of our constitution confined within the proper limits, since, from our very constitution, it must necessarily have as much power as it demands, and can only be confined by itself? How is this consistent with our experience of human nature? I answer, that the interest of the body is here restrained by that of the individuals, and that the

House of Commons stretches not its power, because such an usurpation would be contrary to the interest of the majority of its members. The crown has so many offices at its disposal, that, when assisted by the honest and disinterested part of the House, it will always command the resolutions of the whole, so far, at least, as to preserve the ancient constitution from danger. We may, therefore, give to this influence what name we please; we may call it by the invidious appellations of corruption and dependence; but some degree and some kind of it are inseparable from the very nature of the constitution, and necessary to the preservation of our mixed government.

Instead, then, of asserting absolutely, that the dependence of parliament, in every degree, is an infringement of British liberty, the country party should have made some concessions to their adversaries, and have only examined what was the proper degree of this dependence, beyond which it became dangerous to liberty. But such a moderation is not to be expected in party men of any kind. After a concession of this nature, all declamation must be abandoned; and a calm inquiry into the proper degree of court influence and parliamentary dependence would have been expected by the readers. And though the advantage, in such a controversy, might possibly remain to the country party, yet the victory would not be so complete as they wish for, nor would a true patriot have given an entire loose to his zeal, for fear of running matters into a contrary extreme, by diminishing too far the influence of the crown. It was, therefore, thought best to deny that this extreme could ever be dangerous to the constitution, or that the crown could ever have too little influence over members of parliament.

All questions concerning the proper medium between extremes are difficult to be decided; both because it is not easy to find words proper to fix this medium, and because the good and ill, in such cases, run so gradually into each other, as even to render our sentiments doubtful and uncertain. But there is a peculiar difficulty in the present case, which would embarrass the most knowing and most impartial examiner. The power of the crown is always lodged in a single person, either king or minister; and as this person may have either a greater or less degree of ambition, capacity, courage, popularity, or fortune, the power, which is too great in one hand, may become too little in another. In pure republics, where the authority is distributed among several assemblies or senates, the checks and controls are more regular in their operation; because the members of such numerous assemblies may be presumed to be always nearly equal in capacity and virtue; and it is only their number, riches, or authority, which enter into

consideration. But a limited monarchy admits not of any such stability; nor is it possible to assign to the crown such a determinate degree of power, as will, in every hand, form a proper counterbalance to the other parts of the constitution. This is an unavoidable disadvantage, among the many advantages attending that species of government.

Passage 2

In order to lay a due foundation for that separate and distinct exercise of the different powers of Government, which to a certain extent is admitted on all hands to be essential to the preservation of liberty, it is evident that each department should have a will of its own; and consequently should be so constituted, that the members of each should have as little agency as possible in the appointment of the members of the others. Were this principle rigorously adhered to, it would require that all the appointments for the supreme Executive, Legislative, and Judiciary magistracies should be drawn from the same fountain of authority, the People, through channels having no communication whatever with one another. Perhaps such a plan of constructing the several departments would be less difficult in practice, than it may in contemplation appear. Some difficulties, however, and some additional expense would attend the execution of it. Some deviations, therefore, from the principle must be admitted. In the constitution of the Judiciary department in particular, it might be inexpedient to insist rigorously on the principle: first, because peculiar qualifications being essential in the members, the primary consideration ought to be to select that mode of choice which best secures these qualifications; secondly, because the permanent tenure by which the appointments are held in that department, must soon destroy all sense of dependence on the authority conferring them.

It is equally evident, that the members of each department should be as little dependent as possible on those of the others, for the emoluments annexed to their offices. Were the Executive magistrate, or the Judges, not independent of the Legislature in this particular, their independence in every other would be merely nominal.

But the great security against a gradual concentration of the several powers in the same department, consists in giving to those who administer each department the necessary constitutional means, and personal motives, to resist encroachments of the others. The provision for defence must in this, as in all other cases, be made commensurate to the danger of attack. Ambition must be made to counteract ambition. The interest of the man must be connected with the constitutional rights of the place. It may be a reflection on human nature, that such devices should be necessary to control the abuses of Government. But what is Government itself, but the greatest of all reflections on human nature? If men were angels, no Government would be necessary. If angels were to govern men, neither external nor internal controls on Government would be necessary. In framing a Government which is to be administered by men over men, the great difficulty lies in this: you must first enable the Government to control the governed; and in the next place oblige it to control itself. A dependence on the People is, no doubt, the primary control on the Government; but experience has taught mankind the necessity of auxiliary precautions.

This policy of supplying, by opposite and rival interests, the defect of better motives, might be traced through the whole system of human affairs, private as well as public. We see it particularly displayed in all the subordinate distributions of power; where the constant aim is, to divide and arrange the several offices in such a manner as that each may be a check on the other; that the private interest of every individual may be a sentinel over the public rights. These inventions of prudence cannot be less requisite in the distribution of the supreme powers of the State.

But it is not possible to give to each department an equal power of self-defence. In republican Government, the Legislative authority necessarily predominates. The remedy for this inconveniency is, to divide the Legislature into different branches; and to render them, by different modes of election, and different principles of action, as little connected with each other, as the nature of their common functions, and their common dependence on the society, will admit. It may even be necessary to guard against dangerous encroachments by still further precautions. As the weight of the Legislative authority requires that it should be thus divided, the weakness of the Executive may require, on the other hand, that it should be fortified. An absolute negative on the Legislature appears, at first view, to be the natural defence with which the Executive magistrate should be armed. But perhaps it would be neither altogether safe, nor alone sufficient. On ordinary occasions, it might not be exerted with the requisite firmness; and on extraordinary occasions, it might be perfidiously abused. May not this defect of an absolute negative be supplied by some qualified connection between this weaker department and the weaker branch of the stronger department, by which the latter may be led to support the constitutional rights of the former, without being too much detached from the rights of its own department?

If the principles on which these observations are founded be just, as I persuade myself they are, and they be applied as a criterion to the several State Constitutions, and to the Federal Constitution, it will be found, that if the latter does not perfectly correspond with them, the former are infinitely less able to bear such a test.

There are moreover two considerations particularly applicable to the Federal system of America, which place that system in a very interesting point of view.

First. In a single republic, all the power surrendered by the People is submitted to the administration of a single Government; and the usurpations are guarded against, by a division of the Government into distinct and separate departments. In the compound republic of America, the power surrendered by the People is first divided between two distinct Governments, and then the portion allotted to each, subdivided among distinct and separate departments. Hence a double security arises to the rights of the People. The different Governments will control each other, at the same time that each will be controlled by itself.

Second. It is of great importance in a republic, not only to guard the society against the oppression of its rulers, but to guard one part of the society against the injustice of the other part. Different interests necessarily exist in different classes of citizens. If a majority be united by a common interest, the rights of the minority will be insecure. There are but two methods of providing against this evil: the one by creating a will in the community independent of the majority, that is, of the society itself; the other, by comprehending in the society so many separate descriptions of citizens as will render an unjust combination of a majority of the whole very improbable, if not impracticable. The first method prevails in all Governments possessing an hereditary or self-appointed authority. This, at best, is but a precarious security; because a power independent of the society may as well espouse the unjust views of the major, as the rightful interests of the minor party, and may possibly be turned against both parties. The second method will be exemplified in the Federal republic of the United States. Whilst all authority in it will be derived from and dependent on the society, the society itself will be broken into so many parts, interests, and classes of citizens, that the rights of individuals, or of the minority, will be in little danger from interested combinations of the majority. In a free Government, the security for civil rights must be the same as that for religious rights. It consists in the one case in the multiplicity of interests, and in the other in the multiplicity of sects. The degree of security in both cases, will depend on the number of interests and sects; and this may be presumed to depend on the extent of country and number of People comprehended under the same Government. This view of the subject must particularly recommend a proper Federal system to all the sincere and considerate friends of republican government; since it shows, that in exact proportion as the territory of the Union may be formed into more circumscribed Confederacies, or States, oppressive combinations of a majority will be facilitated; the best security, under the republican forms, for the rights of every class of citizens, will be diminished; and consequently, the stability and independence of some member of the Government, the only other security, must be proportionately increased. Justice is the end of Government. It is the end of civil society. It ever has been, and ever will be pursued, until it be obtained, or until liberty be lost in the pursuit. In a society, under the forms of which the stronger faction can readily unite and oppress the weaker, anarchy may as truly be said to reign, as in a state of nature, where the weaker individual is not secured against the violence of the stronger; and as in the latter state, even the stronger individuals are prompted, by the uncertainty of their condition, to submit to a Government which may protect the weak, as well as themselves: so, in the former state, will the more powerful factions or parties be gradually induced, by a like motive, to wish for a Government which will protect all parties, the weaker as well as the more powerful. It can be little doubted, that if the State of Rhode Island was separated from the Confederacy, and left to itself, the insecurity of rights under the popular form of Government within such narrow limits would be displayed by such reiterated oppressions of factious majorities, that some power altogether independent of the People would soon be called for by the voice of the very factions whose misrule had proved the necessity of it. In the extended republic of the United States, and among the great variety of interests, parties, and sects which it embraces, a coalition of a majority of the whole society could seldom take place on any other principles than those of justice and the general good; whilst there being thus less danger to a minor from the will of a major party, there must be less pretext, also, to provide for the security of the former, by introducing into the Government a will not dependent on the latter: or, in other words, a will independent of the society itself. It is no less certain than it is important, notwithstanding the contrary opinions which have been entertained, that the larger the society, provided it lie within a practical sphere, the more duly capable it will be of self-government. And happily for the republican cause, the practicable sphere may be carried to a very great extent, by a judicious modification and mixture of the Federal principle.

1

What is the main purpose of the first passage?

_____

2

What is the first passage's tone?

_____

3

What is the central claim of the first passage?

_____

4

What is the main purpose of the second passage?

_____

5

What is the second passage's tone?

_____

6

What is the central claim of the second passage?

_____

7

What is the relationship between the passages?

_____

"THE PENDULUM" – RAY BRADBURY

Ray Bradbury (1920-2012) was an American author. His novel *Fahrenheit 451* is a classic of dystopian literature. The ACT included a section of his novel *Dandelion Wine* and an autobiographical essay on writing in their sample test.

Up and down, back and forth, up and down. First the quick flite skyward, gradually slowing, reaching the pinnacle of the curve, poising a moment, then flashing earthward again, faster and faster at a nauseating speed, reaching the bottom and hurtling aloft on the opposite side. Up and down. Back and forth. Up and down.

How long it had continued this way Layeville didn't know. It might have been millions of years he'd spent sitting here in the massive glass pendulum watching the world tip one way and another, up and down, dizzily before his eyes until they ached. Since first they had locked him in the pendulum's round glass head and set if swinging it had never stopped or changed. Continuous, monotonous movements over and above the ground. So huge was this pendulum that it shadowed one hundred feet or more with every majestic sweep of its gleaming shape, dangling from the metal intestines of the shining machine overhead. It took three or four seconds for it to traverse the one hundred feet one way, three or four seconds to come back.

THE PRISONER OF TIME! That's what they called him now! Now, fettered to the very machine he had planned and constructed. A pri—son—er—of—time! A—pris—on—er—of—Time! With every swing of the pendulum it echoed in his thoughts. For ever like this until he went insane. He tried to focus his eyes on the arching hotness of the earth as it swept past beneath him.

They had laughed at him a few days before. Or was it a week? A month? A year? He didn't know. This ceaseless pitching had filled him with an aching confusion. They had laughed at him when he said, some time before all this, he could bridge time gaps and travel into futurity. He had designed a huge machine to warp space, invited thirty of the worlds most gifted scientists to help him finish his colossal attempt to scratch the future wall of time.

The hour of the accident spun back to him now thru misted memory. The display of the time machine to the public. The exact moment when he stood on the platform with the thirty scientists and pulled the main switch! The scientists, all of them, blasted into ashes from wild electrical flames! Before the eyes of two million witnesses who had come to the laboratory or were tuned in by television at home! He had slain the world's greatest scientists!

He recalled the moment of shocked horror that followed. Something radically wrong had happened to the machine. He, Layeville, the inventor of the machine, had staggered backward, his clothes flaming and eating up about him. No time for explanations. Then he had collapsed in the blackness of pain and numbing defeat.

Swept to a hasty trial, Layeville faced jeering throngs calling out for his death. "Destroy the Time Machine!" they cried. "And destroy this MURDERER with it!"

Murderer! And he had tried to help humanity. This was his reward.

One man had leaped onto the tribunal platform at the trial, crying, "No! Don't destroy the machine! I have a better plan! A revenge for this—this man!" His finger pointed at Layeville where the inventor sat unshaven and haggard, his eyes failure glazed. "We shall rebuild his machine, take his precious metals, and put up a monument to his slaughtering! We'll put him on exhibition for life within his executioning device!" The crowd roared approval like thunder shaking the tribunal hall.

Then, pushing hands, days in prison, months. Finally, led forth into the hot sunshine, he was carried in a small rocket car to the center of the city. The shock of what he saw brought him back to reality. THEY had rebuilt his machine into a towering timepiece with a pendulum. He stumbled forward, urged on by thrusting hands, listening to the roar of thousands of voices damning him. Into the transparent pendulum head they pushed him and clamped it tight with weldings.

Then they set the pendulum swinging and stood back. Slowly, very slowly, it rocked back and forth, increasing in speed. Layeville had pounded futilely at the glass, screaming. The faces became blurred, were only tearing pink blobs before him.

On and on like this—for how long?

He hadn't minded it so much at first, that first nite. He couldn't sleep, but it was not uncomfortable. The lites of the city were comets with tails that pelted from rite to left like foaming fireworks. But as the nite wore on he felt a gnawing in his stomach, that grew worse. He got very sick and vomited. The next day he couldn't eat anything.

They never stopped the pendulum, not once. Instead of letting him eat quietly, they slid the food down the stem of the pendulum in a special tube, in little round parcels that plunked at his feet. The first time he attempted eating he was unsuccessful, it wouldn't stay down. In desperation he hammered against the cold glass with his fists until they bled, crying hoarsely, but he heard nothing but his own weak, fear-wracked words muffled in his ears.

After some time had elapsed he got so that he could eat, even sleep while travelling back and forth this way. They allowed him small glass loops on the floor and leather thongs with which he tied himself down at nite and slept a soundless slumber without sliding.

People came to look at him. He accustomed his eyes to the swift flite and followed their curiosity-etched faces, first close by in the middle, then far away to the right, middle again, and to the left.

He saw the faces gaping, speaking soundless words, laughing and pointing at the prisoner of time traveling forever nowhere. But after awhile the town people vanished and it was only tourists who came and read the sign that said: THIS IS THE PRISONER OF TIME—JOHN LAYEVILLE—WHO KILLED THIRTY OF THE WORLDS FINEST SCIENTISTS! The school children, on the electrical moving sidewalk stopped to stare in childish awe. THE PRISONER OF TIME!

Often he thot of that title. God, but it was ironic, that he should invent a time machine and have it converted into a clock, and that he, in its pendulum, should mete out the years—traveling with Time.

He couldn't remember how long it had been. The days and nites ran together in his memory. His unshaven checks had developed a short beard and then ceased growing. How long a time? How long?

Once a day they sent down a tube after he ate and vacuumed up the cell, disposing of any wastes. Once in a great while they sent him a book, but that was all.

The robots took care of him now. Evidently the humans thot it a waste of time to bother over their prisoner. The robots brot the food, cleaned the pendulum cell, oiled the machinery, worked tirelessly from dawn until the sun crimsoned westward. At this rate it could keep on for centuries.

But one day as Layeville stared at the city and its people in the blur of ascent and descent, he perceived a swarming darkness that extended in the heavens. The city rocket ships that crossed the sky on pillars of scarlet flame darted helplessly, frightenedly for shelter. The people ran like water splashed on tiles, screaming soundlessly. Alien creatures fluttered down, great gelatinous masses of black that sucked out the life of all. They clustered thickly over everything, glistened momentarily upon the pendulum and its body above, over the whirling wheels and roaring bowels of the metal creature once a Time Machine. An hour later they dwindled away over the horizon and never came back. The city was dead.

Up and down, Layeville went on his journey to nowhere, in his prison, a strange smile etched on his lips. In a week or more, he knew, he would be the only man alive on earth.

Elation flamed within him. This was his victory! Where the other men had planned the pendulum as a prison it had been an asylum against annihilation now!

Day after day the robots still came, worked, unabated by the visitation of the black horde. They came every week, brot food, tinkered, checked, oiled, cleaned. Up and down, back and forth—THE PENDULUM!

…a thousand years must have passed before the sky again showed life over the dead Earth. A silvery bullet of space dropped from the clouds, steaming, and hovered over the dead city where now only a few solitary robots performed their tasks. In the gathering dusk the lites of the metropolis glimmered on. Other automatons appeared on the rampways like spiders on twisting webs, scurrying about, checking, oiling, working in their crisp mechanical manner.

And the creatures in the alien projectile found the time mechanism, the pendulum swinging up and down, back and forth, up and down. The robots still cared for it, oiled it, tinkering.

A thousand years this pendulum had swung. Made of glass the round disk at the bottom was, but now when food was lowered by the robots through the tube it lay untouched. Later, when the vacuum tube came down and cleaned out the cell it took that very food with it.

Back and \forth—up and down.

The visitors saw something inside the pendulum. Pressed closely to the glass side of the cell was the face of a whitened skull—a skeleton visage that stared out over the city with empty sockets and an enigmatical smile wreathing its lipless teeth.

Back and forth—up and down.

The strangers from the void stopped the pendulum in its course, ceased its swinging and cracked open the glass cell, exposing the skeleton to view. And in the gleaming light of the stars the skull face continued its weird grinning as if it knew that it had conquered something. Had conquered time.

The Prisoner Of Time, Layeville, had indeed travelled along the centuries.

And the journey was at an end.

1

What is the main purpose of this passage?

_____

2

What is the passage's tone?

_____

3

How would you summarize the passage?

_____

4

How would you describe the prisoner?

_____

George Eliot was the *nom de plume* of Mary Anne Evans. Her novel *Middlemarch* (1872) is regarded as masterpiece of Victorian literature. Another of her novels, *Silas Marner*, appeared on SAT Practice Test #6. Eliot adopted a male pen name (much like the Bronte sisters and J. K. Rowling) to escape prejudicial reviews.

Silly Novels by Lady Novelists are a genus with many species, determined by the particular quality of silliness that predominates in them—the frothy, the prosy, the pious, or the pedantic. But it is a mixture of all these—a composite order of feminine fatuity—that produces the largest class of such novels, which we shall distinguish as the *mind-and-millinery* species. The heroine is usually an heiress, probably a peeress in her own right, with perhaps a vicious baronet, an amiable duke, and an irresistible younger son of a marquis as lovers in the foreground, a clergyman and a poet sighing for her in the middle distance, and a crowd of undefined adorers dimly indicated beyond. Her eyes and her wit are both dazzling; her nose and her morals are alike free from any tendency to irregularity; she has a superb *contralto* and a superb intellect; she is perfectly well dressed and perfectly religious; she dances like a sylph, and reads the Bible in the original tongues. Or it may be that the heroine is not an heiress—that rank and wealth are the only things in which she is deficient; but she infallibly gets into high society, she has the triumph of refusing many matches and securing the best, and she wears some family jewels or other as a sort of crown of righteousness at the end. Rakish men either bite their lips in impotent confusion at her repartees, or are touched to penitence by her reproofs, which, on appropriate occasions, rise to a lofty strain of rhetoric; indeed, there is a general propensity in her to make speeches, and to rhapsodize at some length when she retires to her bedroom. In her recorded conversations she is amazingly eloquent, and in her unrecorded conversations amazingly witty. She is understood to have a depth of insight that looks through and through the shallow theories of philosophers, and her superior instincts are a sort of dial by which men have only to set their clocks and watches, and all will go well. The men play a very subordinate part by her side. You are consoled now and then by a hint that they have affairs, which keeps you in mind that the working-day business of the world is somehow being carried on, but ostensibly the final cause of their existence is that they may accompany the heroine on her "starring" expedition through life. They see her at a ball, and they are dazzled; at a flower-show, and they are fascinated;

on a riding excursion, and they are witched by her noble horsemanship; at church, and they are awed by the sweet solemnity of her demeanor. She is the ideal woman in feelings, faculties, and flounces. For all this she as often as not marries the wrong person to begin with, and she suffers terribly from the plots and intrigues of the vicious baronet; but even death has a soft place in his heart for such a paragon, and remedies all mistakes for her just at the right moment. The vicious baronet is sure to be killed in a duel, and the tedious husband dies in his bed requesting his wife, as a particular favor to him, to marry the man she loves best, and having already dispatched a note to the lover informing him of the comfortable arrangement. Before matters arrive at this desirable issue our feelings are tried by seeing the noble, lovely, and gifted heroine pass through many *mauvais moments*, but we have the satisfaction of knowing that her sorrows are wept into embroidered pocket-handkerchiefs, that her fainting form reclines on the very best upholstery, and that whatever vicissitudes she may undergo, from being dashed out of her carriage to having her head shaved in a fever, she comes out of them all with a complexion more blooming and locks more redundant than ever.

We may remark, by the way, that we have been relieved from a serious scruple by discovering that silly novels by lady novelists rarely introduce us into any other than very lofty and fashionable society. We had imagined that destitute women turned novelists, as they turned governesses, because they had no other "ladylike" means of getting their bread. On this supposition, vacillating syntax, and improbable incident had a certain pathos for us, like the extremely supererogatory pincushions and ill-devised nightcaps that are offered for sale by a blind man. We felt the commodity to be a nuisance, but we were glad to think that the money went to relieve the necessitous, and we pictured to ourselves lonely women struggling for a maintenance, or wives and daughters devoting themselves to the production of "copy" out of pure heroism—perhaps to pay their husband's debts or to purchase luxuries for a sick father. Under these impressions we shrank from criticising a lady's novel: her English might be faulty, but we said to ourselves her motives are irreproachable; her imagination may be uninventive, but her patience is untiring. Empty writing was excused by an empty stomach, and twaddle was consecrated by tears. But no! This theory of ours, like many other pretty theories, has had to give way before observation. Women's silly novels, we are now convinced, are written under totally different circumstances. The fair writers have evidently never talked to a tradesman except from a carriage window;

www.professorscompanion.com

they have no notion of the working-classes except as "dependents;" they think five hundred a year a miserable pittance; Belgravia and "baronial halls" are their primary truths; and they have no idea of feeling interest in any man who is not at least a great landed proprietor, if not a prime minister. It is clear that they write in elegant boudoirs, with violet-colored ink and a ruby pen; that they must be entirely indifferent to publishers' accounts, and inexperienced in every form of poverty except poverty of brains. It is true that we are constantly struck with the want of verisimilitude in their representations of the high society in which they seem to live; but then they betray no closer acquaintance with any other form of life. If their peers and peeresses are improbable, their literary men, tradespeople, and cottagers are impossible; and their intellect seems to have the peculiar impartiality of reproducing both what they *have* seen and heard, and what they have *not* seen and heard, with equal unfaithfulness.

***

"Be not a baker if your head be made of butter," says a homely proverb, which, being interpreted, may mean, let no woman rush into print who is not prepared for the consequences. We are aware that our remarks are in a very different tone from that of the reviewers who, with perennial recurrence of precisely similar emotions, only paralleled, we imagine, in the experience of monthly nurses, tell one lady novelist after another that they "hail" her productions "with delight." We are aware that the ladies at whom our criticism is pointed are accustomed to be told, in the choicest phraseology of puffery, that their pictures of life are brilliant, their characters well drawn, their style fascinating, and their sentiments lofty. But if they are inclined to resent our plainness of speech, we ask them to reflect for a moment on the chary praise, and often captious blame, which their panegyrists give to writers whose works are on the way to become classics. No sooner does a woman show that she has genius or effective talent, than she receives the tribute of being moderately praised and severely criticised. By a peculiar thermometric adjustment, when a woman's talent is at zero, journalistic approbation is at the boiling pitch; when she attains mediocrity, it is already at no more than summer heat; and if ever she reaches excellence, critical enthusiasm drops to the freezing point. Harriet Martineau, Currer Bell, and Mrs. Gaskell have been treated as cavalierly as if they had been men. And every critic who forms a high estimate of the share women may ultimately take in literature, will on principle abstain from any exceptional indulgence toward the productions of literary women. For it must be plain to every one who looks impartially and extensively into feminine literature that its greatest deficiencies are due hardly more to the want of intellectual power than to the want of those moral qualities that contribute to literary excellence—patient diligence, a sense of the responsibility involved in publication, and an appreciation of the sacredness of the writer's art. In the majority of woman's books you see that kind of facility which springs from the absence of any high standard; that fertility in imbecile combination or feeble imitation which a little self-criticism would check and reduce to barrenness; just as with a total want of musical ear people will sing out of tune, while a degree more melodic sensibility would suffice to render them silent. The foolish vanity of wishing to appear in print, instead of being counterbalanced by any consciousness of the intellectual or moral derogation implied in futile authorship, seems to be encouraged by the extremely false impression that to write *at all* is a proof of superiority in a woman. On this ground we believe that the average intellect of women is unfairly represented by the mass of feminine literature, and that while the few women who write well are very far above the ordinary intellectual level of their sex, the many women who write ill are very far below it. So that, after all, the severer critics are fulfilling a chivalrous duty in depriving the mere fact of feminine authorship of any false prestige which may give it a delusive attraction, and in recommending women of mediocre faculties— as at least a negative service they can render their sex— to abstain from writin…

The standing apology for women who become writers without any special qualification is that society shuts them out from other spheres of occupation. Society is a very culpable entity, and has to answer for the manufacture of many unwholesome commodities, from bad pickles to bad poetry. But society, like "matter," and Her Majesty's Government, and other lofty abstractions, has its share of excessive blame as well as excessive praise. Where there is one woman who writes from necessity, we believe there are three women who write from vanity; and besides, there is something so antiseptic in the mere healthy fact of working for one's bread, that the most trashy and rotten kind of feminine literature is not likely to have been produced under such circumstances. "In all labor there is profit;" but ladies' silly novels, we imagine, are less the result of labor than of busy idleness.

Happily, we are not dependent on argument to prove that Fiction is a department of literature in which women can, after their kind, fully equal men. A cluster of great names, both living and dead, rush to our memories in evidence that women can produce novels not only fine, but among the very finest— novels, too, that have a precious speciality, lying quite apart from masculine aptitudes and experience. No educational restrictions can shut women out from the materials of fiction, and there is no species of art which is so free from rigid requirements. Like crystalline masses, it may take any form, and yet be beautiful; we have only to pour in the right elements—genuine observation, humor, and passion. But it is precisely this absence of rigid requirement which constitutes the fatal seduction of novel-writing to incompetent women. Ladies are not wont to be very grossly deceived as to their power of playing on the piano; here certain positive difficulties of execution have to be conquered, and incompetence inevitably breaks down. Every art which had its absolute *technique* is, to a certain extent, guarded from the intrusions of mere left-handed imbecility. But in novel-writing there are no barriers for incapacity to stumble against, no external criteria to prevent a writer from mistaking foolish facility for mastery. And so we have again and again the old story of La Fontaine's ass, who pats his nose to the flute, and, finding that he elicits some sound, exclaims, "Moi, aussie, je joue de la flute"—a fable which we commend, at parting, to the consideration of any feminine reader who is in danger of adding to the number of "silly novels by lady novelists."

1 What is the main purpose of this passage?

_____

2 What is the passage's tone?

_____

3 How would you summarize the passage?

_____

4 What is the author's central thesis?

_____

"WHERE I LIVED, AND WHAT I LIVED FOR" FROM *WALDEN* – HENRY DAVID THOREAU

In the 1840s, Henry David Thoreau left the hustle and bustle of Boston for the sylvan Walden pond in nearby Concord, Massachusetts. There, he tried to live a simple and self-reliant life. Thoreau chronicled his experience in *Walden: Or A Life in the Woods*, 1854. This is one Thoreau's most well-known chapters.

Every morning was a cheerful invitation to make my life of equal simplicity, and I may say innocence, with Nature herself. I have been as sincere a worshipper of Aurora as the Greeks. I got up early and bathed in the pond; that was a religious exercise, and one of the best things which I did. They say that characters were engraven on the bathing tub of King Tchingthang to this effect: "Renew yourself completely each day; do it again, and again, and forever again." I can understand that. Morning brings back the heroic ages. I was as much affected by the faint hum of a mosquito making its invisible and unimaginable tour through my apartment at earliest dawn, when I was sitting with door and windows open, as I could be by any trumpet that ever sang of fame. It was Homer's requiem; itself an Iliad and Odyssey in the air, singing its own wrath and wanderings. There was something cosmical about it; a standing advertisement, till forbidden, of the everlasting vigor and fertility of the world. The morning, which is the most memorable season of the day, is the awakening hour. Then there is least somnolence in us; and for an hour, at least, some part of us awakes which slumbers all the rest of the day and night. Little is to be expected of that day, if it can be called a day, to which we are not awakened by our Genius, but by the mechanical nudgings of some servitor, are not awakened by our own newly acquired force and aspirations from within, accompanied by the undulations of celestial music, instead of factory bells, and a fragrance filling the air—to a higher life than we fell asleep from; and thus the darkness bear its fruit, and prove itself to be good, no less than the light. That man who does not believe that each day contains an earlier, more sacred, and auroral hour than he has yet profaned, has despaired of life, and is pursuing a descending and darkening way. After a partial cessation of his sensuous life, the soul of man, or its organs rather, are reinvigorated each day, and his Genius tries again what noble life it can make. All memorable events, I should say, transpire in morning time and in a morning atmosphere. The Vedas say, "All intelligences awake with the morning." Poetry and art, and the fairest and most memorable of the actions of men, date from such an hour. All poets and heroes, like Memnon, are the children of Aurora, and emit their music at sunrise. To him whose elastic and vigorous thought keeps pace with the sun, the day is a perpetual morning. It matters not what the clocks say or the attitudes and labors of men. Morning is when I am awake and there is a dawn in me. Moral reform is the effort to throw off sleep. Why is it that men give so poor an account of their day if they have not been slumbering? They are not such poor calculators. If they had not been overcome with drowsiness, they would have performed something. The millions are awake enough for physical labor; but only one in a million is awake enough for effective intellectual exertion, only one in a hundred millions to a poetic or divine life. To be awake is to be alive. I have never yet met a man who was quite awake. How could I have looked him in the face?

We must learn to reawaken and keep ourselves awake, not by mechanical aids, but by an infinite expectation of the dawn, which does not forsake us in our soundest sleep. I know of no more encouraging fact than the unquestionable ability of man to elevate his life by a conscious endeavor. It is something to be able to paint a particular picture, or to carve a statue, and so to make a few objects beautiful; but it is far more glorious to carve and paint the very atmosphere and medium through which we look, which morally we can do. To affect the quality of the day, that is the highest of arts. Every man is tasked to make his life, even in its details, woryour of the contemplation of his most elevated and critical hour. If we refused, or rather used up, such paltry information as we get, the oracles would distinctly inform us how this might be done.

I went to the woods because I wished to live deliberately, to front only the essential facts of life, and see if I could not learn what it had to teach, and not, when I came to die, discover that I had not lived. I did not wish to live what was not life, living is so dear; nor did I wish to practise resignation, unless it was quite necessary. I wanted to live deep and suck out all the marrow of life, to live so sturdily and Spartan-like as to put to rout all that was not life, to cut a broad swath and shave close, to drive life into a corner, and reduce it to its lowest terms, and, if it proved to be mean, why then to get the whole and genuine meanness of it, and publish its meanness to the world; or if it were sublime, to know it by experience, and be able to give a true account of it in my next excursion. For most men, it appears to me, are in a strange uncertainty about it, whether it is of the devil or of God, and have somewhat hastily concluded that it is the chief end of man here to "glorify God and enjoy him forever."

Still we live meanly, like ants; though the fable tells us that we were long ago changed into men; like pygmies we fight with cranes; it is error upon error, and clout upon clout, and our best virtue has for its occasion a superfluous and evitable wretchedness. Our life is frittered away by detail. An honest man has hardly need to count more than his ten fingers, or in extreme cases he may add his ten toes, and lump the rest. Simplicity, simplicity, simplicity! I say, let your affairs be as two or three, and not a hundred or a thousand; instead of a million count half a dozen, and keep your accounts on your thumb-nail. In the midst of this chopping sea of civilized life, such are the clouds and storms and quicksands and thousand-and-one items to be allowed for, that a man has to live, if he would not founder and go to the bottom and not make his port at all, by dead reckoning, and he must be a great calculator indeed who succeeds. Simplify, simplify. Instead of three meals a day, if it be necessary eat but one; instead of a hundred dishes, five; and reduce other things in proportion. Our life is like a German Confederacy, made up of petty states, with its boundary forever fluctuating, so that even a German cannot tell you how it is bounded at any moment. The nation itself, with all its so-called internal improvements, which, by the way are all external and superficial, is just such an unwieldy and overgrown establishment, cluttered with furniture and tripped up by its own traps, ruined by luxury and heedless expense, by want of calculation and a woryour aim, as the million households in the land; and the only cure for it, as for them, is in a rigid economy, a stern and more than Spartan simplicity of life and elevation of purpose. It lives too fast. Men think that it is essential that the Nation have commerce, and export ice, and talk through a telegraph, and ride thirty miles an hour, without a doubt, whether they do or not; but whether we should live like baboons or like men, is a little uncertain. If we do not get out sleepers, and forge rails, and devote days and nights to the work, but go to tinkering upon our lives to improve them, who will build railroads? And if railroads are not built, how shall we get to heaven in season? But if we stay at home and mind our business, who will want railroads? We do not ride on the railroad; it rides upon us. Did you ever think what those sleepers are that underlie the railroad? Each one is a man, an Irishman, or a Yankee man. The rails are laid on them, and they are covered with sand, and the cars run smoothly over them. They are sound sleepers, I assure you. And every few years a new lot is laid down and run over; so that, if some have the pleasure of riding on a rail, others have the misfortune to be ridden upon. And when they run over a man that is walking in his sleep, a supernumerary sleeper in the wrong position, and wake him up, they suddenly stop the cars, and make a hue and cry about it, as if this were an exception. I am glad to know that it takes a gang of men for every five miles to keep the sleepers down and level in their beds as it is, for this is a sign that they may sometime get up again.

Why should we live with such hurry and waste of life? We are determined to be starved before we are hungry. Men say that a stitch in time saves nine, and so they take a thousand stitches today to save nine tomorrow. As for work, we haven't any of any consequence. We have the Saint Vitus' dance, and cannot possibly keep our heads still. If I should only give a few pulls at the parish bell-rope, as for a fire, that is, without setting the bell, there is hardly a man on his farm in the outskirts of Concord, notwithstanding that press of engagements which was his excuse so many times this morning, nor a boy, nor a woman, I might almost say, but would forsake all and follow that sound, not mainly to save property from the flames, but, if we will confess the truth, much more to see it burn, since burn it must, and we, be it known, did not set it on fire—or to see it put out, and have a hand in it, if that is done as handsomely; yes, even if it were the parish church itself. Hardly a man takes a half-hour's nap after dinner, but when he wakes he holds up his head and asks, "What's the news?" as if the rest of mankind had stood his sentinels. Some give directions to be waked every half-hour, doubtless for no other purpose; and then, to pay for it, they tell what they have dreamed. After a night's sleep the news is as indispensable as the breakfast. "Pray tell me anything new that has happened to a man anywhere on this globe"—and he reads it over his coffee and rolls, that a man has had his eyes gouged out this morning on the Wachito River; never dreaming the while that he lives in the dark unfathomed mammoth cave of this world, and has but the rudiment of an eye himself.

For my part, I could easily do without the post-office. I think that there are very few important communications made through it. To speak critically, I never received more than one or two letters in my life—I wrote this some years ago—that were worth the postage. The penny-post is, commonly, an institution through which you seriously offer a man that penny for his thoughts which is so often safely offered in jest. And I am sure that I never read any memorable news in a newspaper. If we read of one man robbed, or murdered, or killed by accident, or one house burned, or one vessel wrecked, or one steamboat blown up, or one cow run over on the Western Railroad, or one mad dog killed, or one lot of grasshoppers in the winter—we never need read of another. One is enough. If you are acquainted with the principle, what do you care for a myriad instances and applications? To a philosopher all news, as it is called, is gossip, and they who edit and read it are old women over their tea. Yet not a few are greedy after this gossip. There was such a rush, as I hear, the other day at one of the offices to learn the foreign news by the last arrival, that several large squares of plate glass belonging to the establishment were broken by the pressure—news which I seriously think a ready wit might write a twelve-month, or twelve years, beforehand with sufficient accuracy. As for Spain, for instance, if you know how to throw in Don Carlos and the Infanta, and Don Pedro and Seville and Granada, from time to time in the right proportions—they may have changed the names a little since I saw the papers—and serve up a bull-fight when other entertainments fail, it will be true to the letter, and give us as good an idea of the exact state or ruin of things in Spain as the most succinct and lucid reports under this head in the newspapers: and as for England, almost the last significant scrap of news from that quarter was the revolution of 1649; and if you have learned the history of her crops for an average year, you never need attend to that thing again, unless your speculations are of a merely pecuniary character. If one may judge who rarely looks into the newspapers, nothing new does ever happen in foreign parts, a French revolution not excepted.

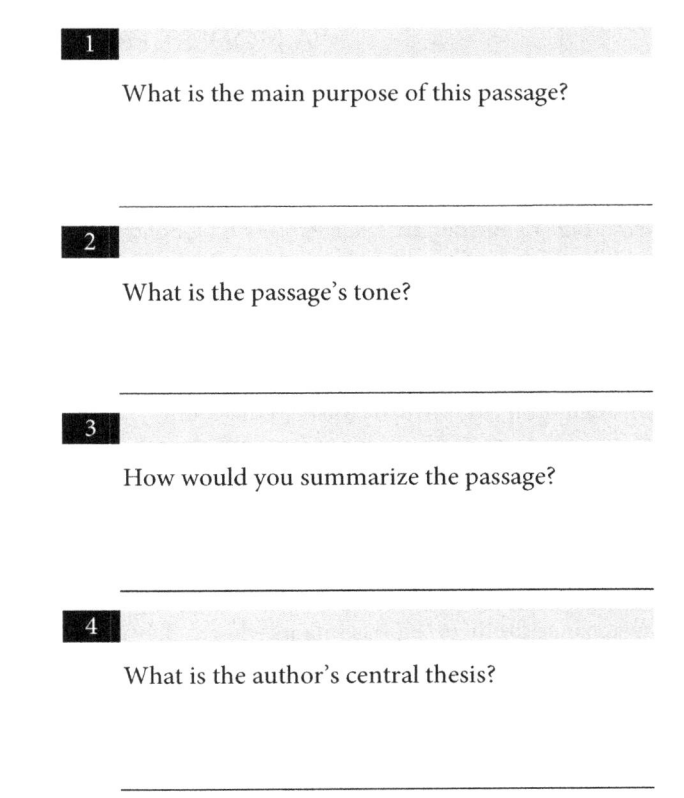

1

What is the main purpose of this passage?

_____

2

What is the passage's tone?

_____

3

How would you summarize the passage?

_____

4

What is the author's central thesis?

_____

"A MODEST PROPOSAL" – JONATHAN SWIFT

The works of Jonathan Swift, the Anglo-Irish author best-known for *Gulliver's Travels* (1726) and "A Modest Proposal," exemplify prose satire. In "A Modest Proposal for Preventing the Children of Poor People from Being a Burden to Their Parents or Country, and For Making Them Beneficial to the Public," commonly known as "A Modest Proposal," Swift aims his wit at the English aristocracy.

It is a melancholy object to those, who walk through this great town, or travel in the country, when they see the streets, the roads and cabbin-doors crowded with beggars of the female sex, followed by three, four, or six children, all in rags, and importuning every passenger for an alms. These mothers instead of being able to work for their honest livelihood, are forced to employ all their time in strolling to beg sustenance for their helpless infants who, as they grow up, either turn thieves for want of work, or leave their dear native country, to fight for the Pretender in Spain, or sell themselves to the Barbadoes.

I think it is agreed by all parties, that this prodigious number of children in the arms, or on the backs, or at the heels of their mothers, and frequently of their fathers, is in the present deplorable state of the kingdom, a very great additional grievance; and therefore whoever could find out a fair, cheap and easy method of making these children sound and useful members of the common-wealth, would deserve so well of the public, as to have his statue set up for a preserver of the nation.

But my intention is very far from being confined to provide only for the children of professed beggars: it is of a much greater extent, and shall take in the whole number of infants at a certain age, who are born of parents in effect as little able to support them, as those who demand our charity in the streets.

As to my own part, having turned my thoughts for many years, upon this important subject, and maturely weighed the several schemes of our projectors, I have always found them grossly mistaken in their computation. It is true, a child just dropt from its dam, may be supported by her milk, for a solar year, with little other nourishment: at most not above the value of two shillings, which the mother may certainly get, or the value in scraps, by her lawful occupation of begging; and it is exactly at one year old that I propose to provide for them in such a manner, as, instead of being a charge upon their parents, or the parish, or wanting food and raiment for the rest of their lives, they shall, on the contrary, contribute to the feeding, and partly to the clothing of many thousands.

There is likewise another great advantage in my scheme, that it will prevent those voluntary abortions, and that horrid practice of women murdering their bastard children, alas! too frequent among us, sacrificing the poor innocent babes, I doubt, more to avoid the expense than the shame, which would move tears and pity in the most savage and inhuman breast.

The number of souls in this kingdom being usually reckoned one million and a half, of these I calculate there may be about two hundred thousand couple whose wives are breeders; from which number I subtract thirty thousand couple, who are able to maintain their own children, (although I apprehend there cannot be so many, under the present distresses of the kingdom) but this being granted, there will remain an hundred and seventy thousand breeders. I again subtract fifty thousand, for those women who miscarry, or whose children die by accident or disease within the year. There only remain an hundred and twenty thousand children of poor parents annually born. The question therefore is, How this number shall be reared, and provided for? which, as I have already said, under the present situation of affairs, is utterly impossible by all the methods hitherto proposed. For we can neither employ them in handicraft or agriculture; they neither build houses, (I mean in the country) nor cultivate land: they can very seldom pick up a livelihood by stealing till they arrive at six years old; except where they are of towardly parts, although I confess they learn the rudiments much earlier; during which time they can however be properly looked upon only as probationers: As I have been informed by a principal gentleman in the county of Cavan, who protested to me, that he never knew above one or two instances under the age of six, even in a part of the kingdom so renowned for the quickest proficiency in that art.

I am assured by our merchants, that a boy or a girl before twelve years old, is no saleable commodity, and even when they come to this age, they will not yield above three pounds, or three pounds and half a crown at most, on the exchange; which cannot turn to account either to the parents or kingdom, the charge of nutriments and rags having been at least four times that value.

I shall now therefore humbly propose my own thoughts, which I hope will not be liable to the least objection.

I have been assured by a very knowing American of my acquaintance in London, that a young healyour child well nursed, is, at a year old, a most delicious nourishing and wholesome food, whether stewed, roasted, baked, or boiled; and I make no doubt that it will equally serve in a fricassee, or a ragout.

I do therefore humbly offer it to public consideration, that of the hundred and twenty thousand children, already computed, twenty thousand may be reserved for breed, whereof only one fourth part to be males; which is more than we allow to sheep, black cattle, or swine, and my reason is, that these children are seldom the fruits of marriage, a circumstance not much regarded by our savages, therefore, one male will be sufficient to serve four females. That the remaining hundred thousand may, at a year old, be offered in sale to the persons of quality and fortune, through the kingdom, always advising the mother to let them suck plentifully in the last month, so as to render them plump, and fat for a good table. A child will make two dishes at an entertainment for friends, and when the family dines alone, the fore or hind quarter will make a reasonable dish, and seasoned with a little pepper or salt, will be very good boiled on the fourth day, especially in winter.

I have reckoned upon a medium, that a child just born will weigh 12 pounds, and in a solar year, if tolerably nursed, increases to 28 pounds.

I grant this food will be somewhat dear, and therefore very proper for landlords, who, as they have already devoured most of the parents, seem to have the best title to the children.

Infant's flesh will be in season throughout the year, but more plentiful in March, and a little before and after; for we are told by a grave author, an eminent French physician, that fish being a prolific diet, there are more children born in Roman Catholic countries about nine months after Lent, the markets will be more glutted than usual, because the number of Popish infants, is at least three to one in this kingdom, and therefore it will have one other collateral advantage, by lessening the number of Papists among us.

I have already computed the charge of nursing a beggar's child (in which list I reckon all cottagers, laborers, and four-fifths of the farmers) to be about two shillings per annum, rags included; and I believe no gentleman would repine to give ten shillings for the carcass of a good fat child, which, as I have said, will make four dishes of excellent nutritive meat, when he hath only some particular friend, or his own family to dine with him. Thus the squire will learn to be a good landlord, and grow popular among his tenants, the mother will have eight shillings neat profit, and be fit for work till she produces another child.

Those who are more thrifty (as I must confess the times require) may flea the carcass; the skin of which, artificially dressed, will make admirable gloves for ladies, and summer boots for fine gentlemen.

As to our City of Dublin, shambles may be appointed for this purpose, in the most convenient parts of it, and butchers we may be assured will not be wanting; although I rather recommend buying the children alive, and dressing them hot from the knife, as we do roasting pigs.

A very woryour person, a true lover of his country, and whose virtues I highly esteem, was lately pleased, in discoursing on this matter, to offer a refinement upon my scheme. He said, that many gentlemen of this kingdom, having of late destroyed their deer, he conceived that the want of venison might be well supply'd by the bodies of young lads and maidens, not exceeding fourteen years of age, nor under twelve; so great a number of both sexes in every country being now ready to starve for want of work and service: And these to be disposed of by their parents if alive, or otherwise by their nearest relations. But with due deference to so excellent a friend, and so deserving a patriot, I cannot be altogether in his sentiments; for as to the males, my American acquaintance assured me from frequent experience, that their flesh was generally tough and lean, like that of our school-boys, by continual exercise, and their taste disagreeable, and to fatten them would not answer the charge. Then as to the females, it would, I think, with humble submission, be a loss to the public, because they soon would become breeders themselves: And besides, it is not improbable that some scrupulous people might be apt to censure such a practice, (although indeed very unjustly) as a little bordering upon cruelty, which, I confess, hath always been with me the strongest objection against any project, however intended.

But in order to justify my friend, he confessed, that this expedient was put into his head by the famous Salmanaazor, a native of the island Formosa, who came from thence to London, above twenty years ago, and in conversation told my friend, that in his country, when any young person happened to be put to death, the executioner sold the carcass to persons of quality, as a prime dainty; and that, in his time, the body of a plump girl of fifteen, who was crucified for an attempt to poison the Emperor, was sold to his imperial majesty's prime minister of state, and other great mandarins of the court in joints from the gibbet, at four hundred crowns. Neither indeed can I deny, that if the same use were made of several plump young girls in this town, who without one single groat to their fortunes, cannot stir abroad without a chair, and appear at a play-house and assemblies in foreign fineries which they never will pay for; the kingdom would not be the worse.

Some persons of a desponding spirit are in great concern about that vast number of poor people, who are aged, diseased, or maimed; and I have been desired to employ my thoughts what course may be taken, to ease the nation of so grievous an incumbrance. But I am not in the least pain upon that matter, because it is very well known, that they are every day dying, and rotting, by cold and famine, and filth, and vermin, as fast as can be reasonably expected. And as to the young laborers, they are now in almost as hopeful a condition. They cannot get work, and consequently pine away from want of nourishment, to a degree, that if at any time they are accidentally hired to common labor, they have not strength to perform it, and thus the country and themselves are happily delivered from the evils to come.

I have too long digressed, and therefore shall return to my subject. I think the advantages by the proposal which I have made are obvious and many, as well as of the highest importance.

For first, as I have already observed, it would greatly lessen the number of Papists, with whom we are yearly over-run, being the principal breeders of the nation, as well as our most dangerous enemies, and who stay at home on purpose with a design to deliver the kingdom to the Pretender, hoping to take their advantage by the absence of so many good Protestants, who have chosen rather to leave their country, than stay at home and pay tithes against their conscience to an episcopal curate.

Secondly, The poorer tenants will have something valuable of their own, which by law may be made liable to a distress, and help to pay their landlord's rent, their corn and cattle being already seized, and money a thing unknown.

Thirdly, Whereas the maintenance of an hundred thousand children, from two years old, and upwards, cannot be computed at less than ten shillings a piece per annum, the nation's stock will be thereby increased fifty thousand pounds per annum, besides the profit of a new dish, introduced to the tables of all gentlemen of fortune in the kingdom, who have any refinement in taste. And the money will circulate among ourselves, the goods being entirely of our own growth and manufacture.

Fourthly, The constant breeders, besides the gain of eight shillings sterling per annum by the sale of their children, will be rid of the charge of maintaining them after the first year.

Fifthly, This food would likewise bring great custom to taverns, where the vintners will certainly be so prudent as to procure the best receipts for dressing it to perfection; and consequently have their houses frequented by all the fine gentlemen, who justly value themselves upon their knowledge in good eating; and a skillful cook, who understands how to oblige his guests, will contrive to make it as expensive as they please.

Sixthly, This would be a great inducement to marriage, which all wise nations have either encouraged by rewards, or enforced by laws and penalties. It would increase the care and tenderness of mothers towards their children, when they were sure of a settlement for life to the poor babes, provided in some sort by the public, to their annual profit instead of expense. We should soon see an honest emulation among the married women, which of them could bring the fattest child to the market. Men would become as fond of their wives, during the time of their pregnancy, as they are now of their mares in foal, their cows in calf, or sow when they are ready to farrow; nor offer to beat or kick them (as is too frequent a practice) for fear of a miscarriage.

Many other advantages might be enumerated. For instance, the addition of some thousand carcasses in our exportation of barreled beef: the propagation of swine's flesh, and improvement in the art of making good bacon, so much wanted among us by the great destruction of pigs, too frequent at our tables; which are no way comparable in taste or magnificence to a well grown, fat yearly child, which roasted whole will make a considerable figure at a Lord Mayor's feast, or any other public entertainment. But this, and many others, I omit, being studious of brevity.

Supposing that one thousand families in this city, would be constant customers for infants flesh, besides others who might have it at merry meetings, particularly at weddings and christenings, I compute that Dublin would take off annually about twenty thousand carcasses; and the rest of the kingdom (where probably they will be sold somewhat cheaper) the remaining eighty thousand.

I can think of no one objection, that will possibly be raised against this proposal, unless it should be urged, that the number of people will be thereby much lessened in the kingdom. This I freely own, and 'twas indeed one principal design in offering it to the world. I desire the reader will observe, that I calculate my remedy for this one individual Kingdom of Ireland, and for no other that ever was, is, or, I think, ever can be upon Earth. Therefore let no man talk to me of other expedients: Of taxing our absentees at five shillings a pound: Of using neither clothes, nor household furniture, except what is of our own growth and manufacture: Of utterly rejecting the materials and instruments that promote foreign luxury: Of curing the expensiveness of pride, vanity, idleness, and gaming in our women: Of introducing a vein of parsimony, prudence and temperance: Of learning to love our country, wherein we differ even from Laplanders, and the inhabitants of Topinamboo: Of quitting our animosities and factions, nor acting any longer like the Jews, who were murdering one another at the very moment their city was taken: Of being a little cautious not to sell our country and consciences for nothing: Of teaching landlords to have at least one degree of mercy towards their tenants. Lastly, of putting a spirit of honesty, industry, and skill into our shop-keepers, who, if a resolution could now be taken to buy only our native goods, would immediately unite to cheat and exact upon us in the price, the measure, and the goodness, nor could ever yet be brought to make one fair proposal of just dealing, though often and earnestly invited to it.

Therefore I repeat, let no man talk to me of these and the like expedients, 'till he hath at least some glimpse of hope, that there will ever be some hearty and sincere attempt to put them into practice.

But, as to my self, having been wearied out for many years with offering vain, idle, visionary thoughts, and at length utterly despairing of success, I fortunately fell upon this proposal, which, as it is wholly new, so it hath something solid and real, of no expense and little trouble, full in our own power, and whereby we can incur no danger in disobliging England. For this kind of commodity will not bear exportation, and flesh being of too tender a consistence, to admit a long continuance in salt, although perhaps I could name a country, which would be glad to eat up our whole nation without it.

After all, I am not so violently bent upon my own opinion, as to reject any offer, proposed by wise men, which shall be found equally innocent, cheap, easy, and effectual. But before something of that kind shall be advanced in contradiction to my scheme, and offering a better, I desire the author or authors will be pleased maturely to consider two points. First, As things now stand, how they will be able to find food and raiment for a hundred thousand useless mouths and backs. And secondly, There being a round million of creatures in humane figure throughout this kingdom, whose whole subsistence put into a common stock, would leave them in debt two million of pounds sterling, adding those who are beggars by profession, to the bulk of farmers, cottagers and laborers, with their wives and children, who are beggars in effect; I desire those politicians who dislike my overture, and may perhaps be so bold to attempt an answer, that they will first ask the parents of these mortals, whether they would not at this day think it a great happiness to have been sold for food at a year old, in the manner I prescribe, and thereby have avoided such a perpetual scene of misfortunes, as they have since gone through, by the oppression of landlords, the impossibility of paying rent without money or trade, the want of common sustenance, with neither house nor clothes to cover them from the inclemencies of the weather, and

the most inevitable prospect of entailing the like, or greater miseries, upon their breed for ever.

I profess, in the sincerity of my heart, that I have not the least personal interest in endeavoring to promote this necessary work, having no other motive than the publics good of my country, by advancing our trade, providing for infants, relieving the poor, and giving some pleasure to the rich. I have no children, by which I can propose to get a single penny; the youngest being nine years old, and my wife past child-bearing.

1

What is the main purpose of this passage?

_____

2

What is the passage's tone?

_____

3

How would you summarize the passage?

_____

4

What is the author's central thesis?

_____

5

How does the author's tone affect the meaning of the passage?

_____

"WOMEN'S RIGHTS ARE HUMAN RIGHTS" – HILLARY RODHAM CLINTON

This passage is adapted from a speech by then-First Lady Hillary Rodham Clinton. She delivered these remarks to the United Nations Fourth World Conference on Women in Beijing, China, September 5, 1995.

Mrs. Mongella, Distinguished delegates and guests,

I would like to thank the Secretary General of the United Nations for inviting me to be part of the United Nations Fourth World Conference on Women. This is truly a celebration -- a celebration of the contributions women make in every aspect of life: in the home, on the job, in their communities, as mothers, wives, sisters, daughters, learners, workers, citizens and leaders.

It is also a coming together, much the way women come together every day in every country.

We come together in fields and in factories. In village markets and supermarkets. In living rooms and board rooms.

Whether it is while playing with our children in the park or washing clothes in a river, or taking a break at the office water cooler, we come together and talk about our aspirations and concerns. And time and again, our talk turns to our children and our families.

However different we may be, there is far more that unites us than divides us. We share a common future. And we are here to find common ground so that we may help bring new dignity and respect to women and girls all over the world -- and in so doing, bring new strength and stability to families as well.

By gathering in Beijing, we are focusing world attention on issues that matter most in the lives of women and their families: access to education, health care, jSobs, and credit, the chance to enjoy basic legal and human rights and participate fully in the political life of their countries.

There are some who question the reason for this conference. Let them listen to the voices of women in their homes, neighborhoods, and workplaces.

There are some who wonder whether the lives of women and girls matter to economic and political progress around the globe. . .Let them look at the women gathered here and at Huairou. . .the homemakers, nurses, teachers, lawyers, policymakers, and women who run their own businesses.

It is conferences like this that compel governments and peoples everywhere to listen, look and face the world's most pressing problems.

Wasn't it after the women's conference in Nairobi ten years ago that the world focused for the first time on the crisis of domestic violence?

Earlier today, I participated in a World Health Organization forum, where government officials, NGOs, and individual citizens are working on ways to address the health problems of women and girls.

Tomorrow, I will attend a gathering of the United Nations Development Fund for Women. There, the discussion will focus on local -- and highly successful -- programs that give hard-working women access to credit so they can improve their own lives and the lives of their families.

What we are learning around the world is that, if women are healthy and educated, their families will flourish. If women are free from violence, their families will flourish. If women have a chance to work and earn as full and equal partners in society, their families will flourish.

And when families flourish, communities and nations will flourish.

That is why every woman, every man, every child, every family, and every nation on our planet has a stake in the discussion that takes place here.

Over the past 25 years, I have worked persistently on issues relating to women, children and families. Over the past two-and-a-half years, I have had the opportunity to learn more about the challenges facing women in my own country and around the world.

I have met new mothers in Jojakarta, Indonesia, who come together regularly in their village to discuss nutrition, family planning, and baby care.

I have met working parents in Denmark who talk about the comfort they feel in knowing that their children can be cared for in creative, safe, and nurturing after-school centers.

I have met women in South Africa who helped lead the struggle to end apartheid and are now helping build a new democracy.

I have met with the leading women of the Western Hemisphere who are working every day to promote literacy and better health care for the children of their countries.

I have met women in India and Bangladesh who are taking out small loans to buy milk cows, rickshaws, thread and other materials to create a livelihood for themselves and their families. '

I have met doctors and nurses in Belarus and Ukraine who are trying to keep children alive in the aftermath of Chernobyl.

The great challenge of this conference is to give voice to women everywhere whose experiences go unnoticed, whose words go unheard.

Women comprise more than half the world's population. Women are 70t percent of the world's poor, and two-thirds of those who are not taught to read and write.

Women are the primary caretakers for most of the world's children and elderly. Yet much of the work we do is not valued -not by economists, not by historians, not by popular culture, not by government leaders.

At this very moment, as we sit here, women around the world are giving birth, raising children, cooking meals, washing clothes, cleaning houses, planting crops, working on assembly lines, running companies, and running countries.

Women also are dying from diseases that should have been prevented or treated; they are watching their children succumb to malnutrition caused by poverty and economic deprivation; they are being denied the right to go to school by their own fathers and brothers; they are being forced into prostitution, and they are being barred from the ballot box and the bank lending office.

Those of us who have the opportunity to be here have the responsibility to speak for those who could not.

As an American, I want to speak up for women in my own country -- women who are raising children on the minimum wage, women who can't afford health care or child care, women whose lives are threatened by violence, including violence in their own homes.

I want to speak up for mothers who are fighting for good schools, safe neighborhoods, clean air and clean airwaves. . . for older women, some of them widows, who have raised their families and now find that their skills and life experiences are not valued in the workplace. . . for women who are working all night as nurses, hotel clerks, and fast food chefs so that they can be at home during the day with their kids. . . and for women everywhere who simply don't have time to do everything they are called upon to do each day.

Speaking to you today, I speak for them, just as each of us speaks for women around the world who are denied the chance to go to school, or see a doctor, or own property, or have a say about the direction of their lives, simply because they are women.

The truth is that most women around the world work both inside and outside the home, usually by necessity.

We need to understand that there is ho formula for how women should lead their lives. That is why we must respect the choices that each woman makes for herself and her family. Every woman deserves the chance to realize her God-given potential.

We also must recognize that women will never gain full dignity until their human rights are respected and protected.

Our goals for this conference, to strengthen families and societies by empowering women to take greater control over their own destinies, cannot be fully achieved unless all governments -here and around the world -- accept their responsibility to protect and promote internationally recognized human rights.

The international community has long acknowledged -- and recently affirmed at Vienna -- that both women and men are entitled to a range of protections and personal freedoms, from the right of personal security to the right to determine freely the number and spacing of the children they bear.

No one should be forced to remain silent for fear of religious or political persecution, arrest, abuse or torture.

Tragically, women are most often the ones whose human rights are violated. Even in the late 20th century, the rape of women continues to be used as an instrument of armed conflict. Women and children make up a large majority of the world's refugees. And when women are excluded from the political process, they become even more vulnerable to abuse.

I believe that, on the eve of a new millennium, it is time to break our silence. It is time for us to say here in Beijing, and the world to hear, that it is no longer acceptable to discuss women's rights as separate from human rights.

These abuses have continued because, for too long, the history of women has been a history of silence. Even today, there are those who are trying to silence our words.

The voices of this conference and of the women at Huairou must be heard loud and clear:

It is a violation of human rights when babies are denied food, or drowned, or suffocated, or their spines broken, simply because they are born girls. '

It is a violation of human rights when women and girls are sold into the slavery of prostitution.

It is a violation of human rights when women are doused with gasoline, set on fire and burned to death because their marriage dowries are deemed too small.

It is a violation of human rights when individual women are raped in their own communities and when thousands of women are subjected to rape as a tactic or prize of war.

It is a violation of human rights when a leading cause of death worldwide among women ages 14 to 44 is the violence they are subjected to in their own homes.

It is a violation of human rights when young girls are brutalized by the painful and degrading practice of genital mutilation.

It is a violation of human rights when women are denied the right to plan their own families, and that includes being forced to have abortions or being sterilized against their will.

If there is one message that echoes forth from this conference, it is that human rights are women's rights.... And women's rights are human rights.

Let us not forget that among those rights are the right to speak freely. And the right to be heard.

Women must enjoy the right to participate fully in the social and political lives of their countries if we want freedom and democracy to thrive and endure.

It is indefensible that many women in non-governmental organizations who wished to participate in this conference have not been able to attend -- or have been prohibited from fully taking part.

Let me be clear. Freedom means the right of people to assemble, organize, and debate openly. It means respecting the views of those who may disagree with the views of their governments. It means not taking citizens away from their loved ones and jailing them, mistreating them, or denying them their freedom or dignity because of the peaceful expression of their ideas and opinions.

In my country, we recently celebrated the 75th anniversary of women's suffrage. It took 150 years after the signing of our Declaration of Independence for women to win the right to vote. It took 72 years of organized struggle on the part of many courageous women and men.

It was one of America's most divisive philosophical wars. But it was also a bloodless war. Suffrage was achieved without a shot fired.

We have also been reminded, in V-J Day observances last weekend, of the good that comes when men and women join together to combat the forces of tyranny and build a better world.

We have seen peace prevail in most places for a half century. We have avoided another world war.

But we have not solved older, deeply-rooted problems that continue to diminish the potential of half the world's population.

Now it is time to act on behalf of women everywhere.

If we take bold steps to better the lives of women, we will be taking bold steps to better the lives of children and families too. Families rely on mothers and wives for emotional support and care; families rely on women for labor in the home; and increasingly, families rely on women for income needed to raise healthy children and care for other relatives.

As long as discrimination and inequities remain so commonplace around the world -- as long as girls and women are valued less, fed less, fed last, overworked, underpaid, not schooled and subjected to violence in and out of their homes -the potential of the human family to create a peaceful, prosperous world will not be realized.

Let this conference be our -- and the world's -- call to action.

And let us heed the call so that we can create a world in which every woman is treated with respect and dignity, every boy and girl is loved and cared for equally, and every family has the hope of a strong and stable future.

Thank you very much.

God's blessings on you, your work and all who will benefit from it.

1

What is the main purpose of this passage?

_____

2

What is the passage's tone?

_____

3

How would you summarize the passage?

_____

4

What is the author's central thesis?

_____

LONG READS

Here they come: the long reads.

The following passages are between 35 and 65 minutes long, the length of the ACT and SAT reading sections, respectively.

	Full Test	Passages	Time per Passage
SAT	65 minutes with 5 passages	5 passages with 10-11 questions	About 13 minutes
ACT	35 minutes with 4 passages	4 passages with 10 questions	About 9 minutes

Once again, you should be able to answer the general questions the test asks at the end of the passages:

- What is the author's purpose?

- What is the author's tone?

- How would you summarize the passage?

- For **literature** passages, how would you describe the main characters?

- For **non-fiction** passages, what is the central claim (or main idea) of the passage?

- For **paired** passages, how are the two passages related?

As you are practicing, make sure you are keeping up with the long reads in addition to the short and medium reads. Sure, they take more time, but practicing the long reads can make test day a little less painful. You can, of course, start with the passages that most interest you (pg. 6), but you should also stretch yourself. After all, you aren't going to like all the passages on test day.

It's the golden age of procrastination. Stay focused!

TO BUILD A FIRE – JACK LONDON

Jack London's *To Build a Fire* was published 1902. London went to the Yukon during the Klondike Gold Rush in 1897.

He travels fastest who travels alone ... but not after the frost has dropped below zero fifty degrees or more.
—Yukon Code

Day had broken cold and gray, exceedingly cold and gray, when the man turned aside from the main Yukon trail and climbed the high earth-bank, where a dim and little-traveled trail led eastward through the fat spruce timberland. It was a steep bank, and he paused for breath at the top, excusing the act to himself by looking at his watch. It was nine o'clock. There was no sun nor hint of sun, though there was not a cloud in the sky. It was a clear day, and yet there seemed an intangible pall over the face of things, a subtle gloom that made the day dark, and that was due to the absence of sun. This fact did not worry the man. He was used to the lack of sun. It had been days since he had seen the sun, and he knew that a few more days must pass before that cheerful orb, due south, would just peep above the sky-line and dip immediately from view.

The man flung a look back along the way he had come. The Yukon lay a mile wide and hidden under three feet of ice. On top of this ice were as many feet of snow. It was all pure white, rolling in gentle, snow-covered undulations where the ice-jams of the freeze-up had formed. North and south, as far as his eye could see, it was unbroken white, save for a dark hair-line that curved and twisted from around the spruce-covered island to the south, and that curved and twisted away into the north, where it disappeared behind another spruce-covered island. This dark hair-line was the trail—the main trail—that led south five hundred miles to the Chilcoot Pass, Dyea, and salt water; and that led north seventy miles to Dawson, and still on to the north a thousand miles to Nulato, and finally to St. Michael on Bering Sea, a thousand miles and half a thousand more.

But all this—the mysterious, far-reaching hair-line trail, the absence of sun from the sky, the tremendous cold, and the strangeness and weirdness of it all—made no impression on the man. It was not because he was long used to it. He was a new-comer in the land, a chechaquo, and this was his first winter. The trouble with him was that he was without imagination. He was quick and alert in the things of life, but only in the things, and not in the significances. Fifty degrees below zero meant eighty-odd degrees of frost. Such fact impressed him as being cold and uncomfortable, and that was all. It did not lead him to meditate upon his frailty as a creature of temperature, and upon man's frailty in general, able only to live within certain narrow limits of temperature; and from there on it did not lead him to the conjectural field of immortality and man's place in the universe. Fifty degrees below zero stood for a bite of frost that hurt and that must be guarded against by the use of mittens, ear-flaps, warm moccasins, and thick socks. Fifty degrees below zero was to him just precisely fifty degrees below zero. That there should be anything more to it than that was a thought that never entered his head.

As he turned to go on, he spat speculatively. There was a sharp, explosive crackle that startled him. He spat again. And again, in the air, before it could fall to the snow, the spittle crackled. He knew that at fifty below spittle crackled on the snow, but this spittle had crackled in the air. Undoubtedly it was colder than fifty below—how much colder he did not know. But the temperature did not matter. He was bound for the old claim on the left fork of Henderson Creek, where the boys were already. They had come over across the divide from the Indian Creek country, while he had come the roundabout way to take a look at the possibilities of getting out logs in the spring from the islands in the Yukon. He would be in to camp by six o'clock; a bit after dark, it was true, but the boys would be there, a fire would be going, and a hot supper would be ready. As for lunch, he pressed his hand against the protruding bundle under his jacket. It was also under his shirt, wrapped up in a handkerchief and lying against the naked skin. It was the only way to keep the biscuits from freezing. He smiled agreeably to himself as he thought of those biscuits, each cut open and sopped in bacon grease, and each enclosing a generous slice of fried bacon.

He plunged in among the big spruce trees. The trail was faint. A foot of snow had fallen since the last sled had passed over, and he was glad he was without a sled, traveling light. In fact, he carried nothing but the lunch wrapped in the handkerchief. He was surprised, however, at the cold. It certainly was cold, he concluded as he rubbed his numb nose and cheek-bones with his mittened hand. He was a warm-whiskered man, but the hair on his face did not protect the high cheek-bones and the eager nose that thrust itself aggressively into the frosty air.

At the man's heels trotted a dog, a big native husky, the proper wolfdog, gray-coated and without any visible or temperamental difference from its brother, the wild wolf. The animal was depressed by the tremendous cold. It knew that it was no time for traveling. Its instinct told it a truer tale than was told to the man by the man's judgment. In reality, it was not merely colder than fifty below zero; it was colder than sixty below, than seventy below. It was seventy-five below zero. Since the freezing point is thirty-two above zero, it meant that one hundred and seven degrees of frost obtained. The dog did not know anything about thermometers. Possibly in its brain there was no sharp consciousness of a condition of very cold such as was in the man's brain. But the brute had its instinct. It experienced a vague but menacing apprehension that subdued it and made it slink along at the man's heels, and that made it question eagerly every unwonted movement of the man as if expec\ting him to go into camp or to seek shelter somewhere and build a fire. The dog had learned fire, and it wanted fire, or else to burrow under the snow and cuddle its warmth away from the air.

The frozen moisture of its breathing had settled on its fur in a fine powder of frost, and especially were its jowls, muzzle, and eyelashes whitened by its crystalled breath. The man's red beard and mustache were likewise frosted, but more solidly, the deposit taking the form of ice and increasing with every warm, moist breath he exhaled. Also, the man was chewing tobacco, and the muzzle of ice held his lips so rigidly that he was unable to clear his chin when he expelled the juice. The result was that a crystal beard of the color and solidity of amber was increasing its length on his chin. If he fell down it would shatter itself, like glass, into brittle fragments. But he did not mind the appendage. It was the penalty all tobacco-chewers paid in that country, and he had been out before in two cold snaps. They had not been so cold as this, he knew, but by the spirit thermometer at Sixty Mile he knew they had been registered at fifty below and at fifty-five.

He held on through the level stretch of woods for several miles, crossed a wide flat of rigger-heads, and dropped down a bank to the frozen bed of a small stream. This was Henderson Creek, and he knew he was ten miles from the forks. He looked at his watch. It was ten o'clock. He was making four miles an hour, and he calculated that he would arrive at the forks at half-past twelve. He decided to celebrate that event by eating his lunch there.

The dog dropped in again at his heels, with a tail drooping discouragement, as the man swung along the creek-bed. The furrow of the old sled-trail was plainly visible, but a dozen inches of snow covered the marks of the last runners. In a month no man had come up or down that silent creek. The man held steadily on. He was not much given to thinking, and just then particularly he had nothing to think about save that he would eat lunch at the forks and that at six o'clock he

would be in camp with the boys. There was nobody to talk to; and, had there been, speech would have been impossible because of the ice-muzzle on his mouth. So he continued monotonously to chew tobacco and to increase the length of his amber beard.

Once in a while the thought reiterated itself that it was very cold and that he had never experienced such cold. As he walked along he rubbed his cheek-bones and nose with the back of his mittened hand. He did this automatically, now and again changing hands. But rub as he would, the instant he stopped his cheek-bones went numb, and the following instant the end of his nose went numb. He was sure to frost his cheeks; he knew that, and experienced a pang of regret that he had not devised a nose-strap of the sort Bud wore in cold snaps. Such a strap passed across the cheeks, as well, and saved them. But it didn't matter much, after all. What were frosted cheeks? A bit painful, that was all; they were never serious.

Empty as the man's mind was of thoughts, he was keenly observant, and he noticed the changes in the creek, the curves and bends and timber jams, and always he sharply noted where he placed his feet. Once coming around a bend, he shied abruptly, like a startled horse, curved away from the place where he had been walking, and retreated several paces back along the trail. The creek he knew was frozen clear to the bottom—no creek could contain water in that arctic winter—but he knew also that there were springs that bubbled out from the hillsides and ran along under the snow and on top the ice of the creek. He knew that the coldest snaps never froze these springs, and he knew likewise their danger. They were traps. They hid pools of water under the snow that might be three inches deep, or three feet. Sometimes a skin of ice half an inch thick covered them, and in turn was covered by the snow. Sometimes there were alternate layers of water and ice-skin, so that when one broke through he kept on breaking through for a while, sometimes wetting himself to the waist.

That was why he had shied in such panic. He had felt the give under his feet and heard the crackle of a snow-hidden ice-skin. And to get his feet wet in such a temperature meant trouble and danger. At the very least it meant delay, for he would be forced to stop and build a fire, and under its protection to bare his feet while he dried his socks and moccasins. He stood and studied the creek-bed and its banks, and decided that the flow of water came from the right. He reflected a while, rubbing his nose and cheeks, then skirted to the left, stepping gingerly and testing the footing for each step. Once clear of the danger, he took a fresh chew of tobacco and swung along at his four-mile gait.

In the course of the next two hours he came upon several similar traps. Usually the snow above the hidden pools had a sunken, candied appearance that advertised the danger. Once again, however, he had a close call; and once, suspecting danger, he compelled the dog to go on in front. The dog did not want to go. It hung back until the man shoved it forward, and then it went quickly across the white, unbroken surface. Suddenly it broke through, floundered to one side, and got away to firmer footing. It had wet its forefeet and legs, and almost immediately the water that clung to it turned to ice. It made quick efforts to lick the ice off its legs, then dropped down in the snow and began to bite out the ice that had formed between the toes. This was a matter of instinct. To permit the ice to remain would mean sore feet. It did not know this. It merely obeyed the mysterious prompting that arose from the deep crypts of its being. But the man knew, having achieved a judgment on the subject, and he removed the mitten from his right hand and helped tear out the ice-particles. He did not expose his fingers more than a minute, and was astonished at the swift numbness that smote them. It certainly was cold. He pulled on the mitten hastily, and beat the hand savagely across his chest.

At twelve o'clock the day was at its brightest. Yet the sun was too far south in its winter journey to clear the horizon. The bulge of the earth intervened between it and Henderson Creek, where the man walked under a clear sky at noon and cast no shadow. At half-past twelve, to the minute, he arrived at the forks of the creek. He was pleased at the speed he had made. If he kept it up, he would certainly be with the boys by six. He unbuttoned his jacket and shirt and drew forth his lunch. The action consumed no more than a quarter of a minute, yet in that brief moment the numbness laid hold of the exposed fingers. He did not put the mitten on, but instead struck the fingers a dozen sharp smashes against his leg. Then he sat down on a snow-covered log to eat. The sting that followed upon the striking of his fingers against his leg ceased so quickly that he was startled. He had had no chance to take a bite of biscuit. He struck the fingers repeatedly and returned them to the mitten, baring the other hand for the purpose of eating, He tried to take a mouthful, but the ice-muzzle prevented. He had forgotten to build a fire and thaw out. He chuckled at his foolishness, and as he chuckled he noted the numbness creeping into the exposed fingers. Also, he noted that the stinging which had first come to his toes when he sat down was already passing away. He wandered whether the toes were warm or numb. He moved them inside the moccasins and decided that they were numb.

He pulled the mitten on hurriedly and stood up. He was a bit frightened. He stamped up and down until the stinging returned into the feet. It certainly was

cold, was his thought. That man from Sulphur Creek had spoken the truth when telling how cold it sometimes got in the country. And he had laughed at him at the time! That showed one must not be too sure of things. There was no mistake about it, it was cold. He strode up and down, stamping his feet and threshing his arms, until reassured by the returning warmth. Then he got out matches and proceeded to make a fire. From the undergrowth, where high water of the previous spring had lodged a supply of seasoned twigs, he got his firewood. Working carefully from a small beginning, he soon had a roaring fire, over which he thawed the ice from his face and in the protection of which he ate his biscuits. For the moment the cold of space was outwitted. The dog took satisfaction in the fire, stretching out close enough for warmth and far enough away to escape being singed.

When the man had finished, he filled his pipe and took his comfortable time over a smoke. Then he pulled on his mittens, settled the ear-flaps of his cap firmly about his ears, and took the creek trail up the left fork. The dog was disappointed and yearned back toward the fire. This man did not know cold. Possibly all the generations of his ancestry had been ignorant of cold, of real cold, of cold one hundred and seven degrees below freezing point. But the dog knew; all its ancestry knew, and it had inherited the knowledge. And it knew that it was not good to walk abroad in such fearful cold. It was the time to lie snug in a hole in the snow and wait for a curtain of cloud to be drawn across the face of outer space whence this cold came. On the other hand, there was no keen intimacy between the dog and the man. The one was the toil-slave of the other, and the only caresses it had ever received were the caresses of the whiplash and of harsh and menacing throat-sounds that threatened the whiplash. So, the dog made no effort to communicate its apprehension to the man. It was not concerned in the welfare of the man, it was for its own sake that it yearned back toward the fire. But the man whistled, and spoke to it with the sound of whiplashes and the dog swung in at the man's heel and followed after.

The man took a chew of tobacco and proceeded to start a new amber beard. Also, his moist breath quickly powdered with white his mustache, eyebrows, and lashes. There did not seem to be so many springs on the left fork of the Henderson, and for half an hour the man saw no signs of any. And then it happened. At a place where there were no signs, where the soft, unbroken snow seemed to advertise solidity beneath, the man broke through. It was not deep. He wet himself halfway to the knees before he floundered out to the firm crust.

He was angry, and cursed his luck aloud. He had hoped to get into camp with the boys at six o'clock, and this would delay him an hour, for he would have to build a fire and dry out his foot-gear. This was imperative at that low temperature--he knew that much; and he turned aside to the bank, which he climbed. On top, tangled in the underbrush about the trunks of several small spruce trees, was a high-water deposit of dry firewood--sticks and twigs, principally, but also larger portions of seasoned branches and fine, dry, last-year's grasses. He threw down several large pieces on top of the snow. This served for a foundation and prevented the young flame from drowning itself in the snow it otherwise would melt. The flame he got by touching a match to a small shred of birch bark that he took from his pocket. This burned even more readily than paper. Placing it on the foundation, he fed the young flame with wisps of dry grass and with the tiniest dry twigs.

He worked slowly and carefully, keenly aware of his danger. Gradually, as the flame grew stronger, he increased the size of the twigs with which he fed it. He squatted in the snow, pulling the twigs out from their entanglement in the brush and feeding directly to the flame. He knew there must be no failure. When it is seventy-five below zero, a man must not fail in his first attempt to build a fire--that is, if his feet are wet. If his feet are dry, and he fails, he can run along the trail for half a mile and restore his circulation. But the circulation of wet and freezing feet cannot be restored by running when it is seventy-five below. No matter how fast he runs, the wet feet will freeze the harder.

All this the man knew. The old-timer on Sulphur Creek had told him about it the previous fall, and now he was appreciating the advice. Already all sensation had gone out of his feet. To build the fire he had been forced to remove his mittens, and the fingers had quickly gone numb. His pace of four miles an hour had kept his heart pumping blood to the surface of his body and to all the extremities. But the instant he stopped, the action of the pump eased down. The cold of space smote the unprotected tip of the planet, and he, being on that unprotected tip, received the full force of the blow. The blood of his body recoiled before it. The blood was alive, like the dog, and like the dog it wanted to hide away and cover itself up from the fearful cold. So long as he walked four miles an hour, he pumped that blood, willy-nilly, to the surface; but now it ebbed away and sank down into the recesses of his body. The extremities were the first to feel its absence. His wet feet froze the faster, and his exposed fingers numbed the faster, though they had not yet begun to freeze. Nose and cheeks were already freezing, while the skin of all his body chilled as it lost its blood.

But he was safe. Toes and nose and cheeks would be only touched by the frost, for the fire was beginning to burn with strength. He was feeding it with twigs the size of his finger. In another minute he would be able to feed it with branches the size of his wrist, and then he could remove his wet foot-gear, and, while it dried, he could keep his naked feet warm by the fire, rubbing them at first, of course, with snow. The fire was a success. He was safe. He remembered the advice of the old timer on Sulphur Creek, and smiled. The old-timer had been very serious in laying down the law that no man must travel alone in the Klondike after fifty below. Well, here he was; he had had the accident; he was alone; and he had saved himself. Those old-timers were rather womanish, some of them, he thought. All a man had to do was to keep his head, and he was all right. Any man who was a man could travel alone. But it was surprising, the rapidity with which his cheeks and nose were freezing. And he had not thought his fingers could go lifeless in so short a time. Lifeless they were, for he could scarcely make them move together to grip a twig, and they seemed remote from his body and from him. When he touched a twig, he had to look and see whether or not he had hold of it. The wires were pretty well down between him and his finger-ends.

All of which counted for little. There was the fire, snapping and crackling and promising life with every dancing flame. He started to untie his moccasins. They were coated with ice; the thick German socks were like sheaths of iron halfway to the knees; and the moccasin strings were like rods of steel all twisted and knotted as by some conflagration. For a moment he tugged with his numb fingers, then, realizing the folly of it, he drew his sheath-knife.

But before he could cut the strings, it happened. It was his own fault or, rather, his mistake. He should not have built the fire under the spruce tree. He should have built it in the open. But it had been easier to pull the twigs from the brush and drop them directly on the fire. Now the tree under which he had done this carried a weight of snow on its boughs. No wind had blown for weeks, and each bough was fully freighted. Each time he had pulled a twig he had communicated a slight agitation to the tree--an imperceptible agitation, so far as he was concerned, but an agitation sufficient to bring about the disaster. High up in the tree one bough capsized its load of snow. This fell on the boughs beneath, capsizing them. This process continued, spreading out and involving the whole tree. It grew like an avalanche, and it descended without warning upon the man and the fire, and the fire was blotted out! Where it had burned was a mantle of fresh and disordered snow.

The man was shocked. It was as though he had just heard his own sentence of death. For a moment he sat and stared at the spot where the fire had been. Then he grew very calm. Perhaps the old-timer on Sulphur Creek was right. If he had only had a trail-mate he would have been in no danger now. The trail-mate could have built the fire. Well, it was up to him to build the fire over again, and this second time there must be no failure. Even if he succeeded, he would most likely lose some toes. His feet must be badly frozen by now, and there would be some time before the second fire was ready.

Such were his thoughts, but he did not sit and think them. He was busy all the time they were passing through his mind. He made a new foundation for a fire, this time in the open, where no treacherous tree could blot it out. Next, he gathered dry grasses and tiny twigs from the high-water flotsam. He could not bring his fingers together to pull them out, but he was able to gather them by the handful. In this way he got many rotten twigs and bits of green moss that were undesirable, but it was the best he could do. He worked methodically, even collecting an armful of the larger branches to be used later when the fire gathered strength. And all the while the dog sat and watched him, a certain yearning wistfulness in its eyes, for it looked upon him as the fire-provider, and the fire was slow in coming.

When all was ready, the man reached in his pocket for a second piece of birch bark. He knew the bark was there, and, though he could not feel it with his fingers, he could hear its crisp rustling as he fumbled for it. Try as he would, he could not clutch hold of it. And all the time in his consciousness, was the knowledge that each instant his feet were freezing. This thought tended to put him in a panic, but he fought against it and kept calm. He pulled on his mittens with his teeth, and threshed his arms back and forth, beating his hands with all his might against his sides. He did this sitting down, and he stood up to do it; and all the while the dog sat in the snow, its wolf-brush of a tail curled around warmly over its forefeet, its sharp wolf-ears pricked forward intently as it watched the man. And the man, as he beat and threshed with his arms and hands, felt a great surge of envy as he regarded the creature that was warm and secure in its natural covering.

After a time he was aware of the first far-away signals of sensation in his beaten fingers. The faint tingling grew stronger till it evolved into a stinging ache that was excruciating, but which the man hailed with satisfaction. He stripped the mitten from his right hand and fetched forth the birch bark. The exposed fingers were quickly going numb again. Next he

brought out his bunch of sulphur matches. But the tremendous cold had already driven the life out of his fingers. In his effort to separate one match from the others, the whole bunch fell in the snow. He tried to pick it out of the snow, but failed. The dead fingers could neither touch nor clutch. He was very careful. He drove the thought of his freezing feet, and nose, and cheeks, out of his mind, devoting his whole soul to the matches. He watched, using the sense of vision in place of that of touch, and when he saw his fingers on each side the bunch, he closed them--that is, he willed to close them, for the wires were down, and the fingers did not obey. He pulled the mitten on the right hand and beat it fiercely against his knee. Then, with both mittened hands, he scooped the bunch of matches, along with much snow, into his lap. Yet he was no better off.

After some manipulation he managed to get the bunch between the heels of his mittened hands. In this fashion he carried it to his mouth. The ice crackled and snapped when by a violent effort he opened his mouth. He drew the lower jaw in, curled the upper lip out of the way, and scraped the bunch with his upper teeth in order to separate a match. He succeeded in getting one, which he dropped on his lap. He was no better off. He could not pick it up. Then he devised a way. He picked it up in his teeth and scratched it on his leg. Twenty times he scratched before he succeeded in lighting it. As it flamed he held it with his teeth to the birch bark. But the burning brimstone went up his nostrils and into his lungs, causing him to cough spasmodically. The match fell into the snow and went out.

The old-timer on Sulphur Creek was right, he thought in the moment of controlled despair that ensued after fifty below, a man should travel with a partner. He beat his hands, but failed in exciting any sensation. Suddenly he bared both hands, removing the mittens with his teeth. He caught the whole bunch between the heels of his hands. His arm muscles not being frozen enabled him to press the hand-heels tightly against the matches. Then he scratched the bunch along his leg. It flared into flame, seventy sulphur matches at once! There was no wind to blow them out. He kept his head to one side to escape the strangling fumes, and held the blazing bunch to the birth bark. As he so held it, he became aware of sensation in his hand. His flesh was burning. He could smell it. Deep down below the surface he could feel it. The sensation developed into pain that grew acute. And still he endured it, holding the flame of the matches clumsily to the bark that would not light readily because his own burning hands were in the way, absorbing most of the flame.

At last, when he could endure no more, he jerked his hands apart. The blazing matches fell sizzling into the snow, but the birch bark was alight. He began laying dry grasses and the tiniest twigs on the flame. He could not pick and choose, for he had to lift the fuel between the heels of his hands. Small pieces of rotten wood and green moss clung to the twigs, and he bit them off as well as he could with his teeth. He cherished the flame carefully and awkwardly. It meant life, and it must not perish. The withdrawal of blood from the surface of his body now made him begin to shiver, and he grew more awkward. A large piece of green moss fell squarely on the little fire. He tried to poke it out with his fingers, but his shivering frame made him poke too far and he disrupted the nucleus of the little fire, the burning grasses and tiny twigs separating and scattering. He tried to poke them together again, but in spite of the tenseness of the effort, his shivering got away with him, and the twigs were hopelessly scattered. Each twig gushed a puff of smoke and went out. The fire-provider had failed. As he looked apathetically about him, his eyes chanced on the dog, sitting across the ruins of the fire from him, in the snow, making restless, hunching movements, slightly lifting one forefoot and then the other, shifting its weight back and forth on them with wistful eagerness.

The sight of the dog put a wild idea into his head. He remembered the tale of the man, caught in a blizzard, who killed a steer and crawled inside the carcass, and so was saved. He would kill the dog and bury his hands in the warm body until the numbness went out of them. Then he could build another fire. He spoke to the dog, calling it to him; but in his voice was a strange note of fear that frightened the animal, who had never known the man to speak in such way before. Something was the matter, and its suspicious nature sensed danger--it knew not what danger, but somewhere, somehow, in its brain arose an apprehension of the man. It flattened its ears down at the sound of the man's voice, and its restless, hunching movements and the liftings and shiftings of its forefeet became more pronounced; but it would not come to the man. He got on his hands and knees and crawled toward the dog. This unusual posture again excited suspicion, and the animal sidled mincingly away.

The man sat up in the snow for a moment and struggled for calmness. Then he pulled on his mittens, by means of his teeth, and got upon his feet. He glanced down at first in order to assure himself that he was really standing up, for the absence of sensation in his feet left him unrelated to the earth. His erect position in itself started to drive the webs of suspicion from the dog's mind; and when he spoke peremptorily, with the sound of whiplashes in his voice, the dog

rendered its customary allegiance and came to him. As it came within reaching distance, the man lost his control. His arms flashed out to the dog, and he experienced genuine surprise when he discovered that his hands could not clutch, that there was neither bend nor feeling in the fingers. He had forgotten for the moment that they were frozen and that they were freezing more and more. All this happened quickly, and before the animal could get away, he encircled its body with his arms. He sat down in the snow, and in this fashion held the dog, while it snarled and whined and struggled.

But it was all he could do, hold its body encircled in his arms and sit there. He realized that he could not kill the dog. There was no way to do it. With his helpless hands he could neither draw nor hold his sheath knife nor throttle the animal. He released it, and it plunged wildly away, with tail between its legs, and still snarling. It halted forty feet away and surveyed him curiously, with ears sharply pricked forward. The man looked down at his hands in order to locate them, and found them hanging on the ends of his arms. It struck him as curious that one should have to use his eyes in order to find out where his hands were. He began threshing his arms back and forth, beating the mittened hands against his sides. He did this for five minutes, violently, and his heart pumped enough blood up to the surface to put a stop to his shivering. But no sensation was aroused in the hands. He had an impression that they hung like weights on the ends of his arms, but when he tried to run the impression down, he could not find it.

A certain fear of death, dull and oppressive, came to him. This fear quickly became poignant as he realized that it was no longer a mere matter of freezing his fingers and toes, or of losing his hands and feet, but that it was a matter of life and death with the chances against him. This threw him into a panic, and he turned and ran up the creek-bed along the old, dim trail. The dog joined in behind and kept up with him. He ran blindly, without intention, in fear such as he had never known in his life. Slowly, as he plowed and floundered through the snow, he began to see things again, the banks of the creek, the old timber-jams, the leafless aspens, and the sky. The running made him feel better. He did not shiver. Maybe, if he ran on, his feet would thaw out; and, anyway, if he ran far enough, he would reach camp and the boys. Without doubt he would lose some fingers and toes and some of his face; but the boys would take care of him, and save the rest of him when he got there. And at the same time there was another thought in his mind that said he would never get to the camp and the boys; that it was too many miles away, that the freezing had too great a start on him, and that he would soon be stiff and dead. This thought he kept in the background and refused to consider. Sometimes it pushed itself forward and demanded to be heard, but he thrust it back and strove to think of other things.

It struck him as curious that he could run at all on feet so frozen that he could not feel them when they struck the earth and took the weight of his body. He seemed to himself to skim along above the surface, and to have no connection with the earth. Somewhere he had once seen a winged Mercury, and he wondered if Mercury felt as he felt when skimming over the earth.

His theory of running until he reached camp and the boys had one flaw in it: he lacked the endurance. Several times he stumbled, and finally he tottered, crumpled up, and fell. When he tried to rise, he failed. He must sit and rest, he decided, and next time he would merely walk and keep on going. As he sat and regained his breath, he noted that he was feeling quite warm and comfortable. He was not shivering, and it even seemed that a warm glow had come to his chest and trunk. And yet, when he touched his nose or cheeks, there was no sensation. Running would not thaw them out. Nor would it thaw out his hands and feet. Then the thought came to him that the frozen portions of his body must be extending. He tried to keep this thought down, to forget it, to think of something else; he was aware of the panicky feeling that it caused, and he was afraid of the panic. But the thought asserted itself, and persisted, until it produced a vision of his body totally frozen. This was too much, and he made another wild run along the trail. Once he slowed down to a walk, but the thought of the freezing extending itself made him run again.

And all the time the dog ran with him, at his heels. When he fell down a second time, it curled its tail over its forefeet and sat in front of him, facing him, curiously eager and intent. The warmth and security of the animal angered him, and he cursed it till it flattened down its ears appealingly. This time the shivering came more quickly upon the man. He was losing in his battle with the frost. It was creeping into his body from all sides. The thought of it drove him on, but he ran no more than a hundred feet, when he staggered and pitched headlong. It was his last panic. When he had recovered his breath and control, he sat up and entertained in his mind the conception of meeting death with dignity. However, the conception did not come to him in such terms. His idea of it was that he had been making a fool of himself, running around like a chicken with its head cut off--such was the simile that occurred to him. Well, he was bound to freeze anyway, and he might as well take it decently. With this new-found peace of mind came the first glimmerings of drowsiness. A good idea, he thought,

to sleep off to death. It was like taking an anaesthetic. Freezing was not so bad as people thought. There were lots worse ways to die.

He pictured the boys finding his body next day. Suddenly he found himself with them, coming along the trail and looking for himself. And, still with them, he came around a turn in the trail and found himself lying in the snow. He did not belong with himself any more, for even then he was out of himself, standing with the boys and looking at himself in the snow. It certainly was cold, was his thought. When he got back to the States he could tell the folks what real cold was. He drifted on from this to a vision of the old-timer on Sulphur Creek. He could see him quite clearly, warm and comfortable, and smoking a pipe.

"You were right, old hoss; you were right," the man mumbled to the old-timer of Sulphur Creek.

Then the man drowsed off into what seemed to him the most comfortable and satisfying sleep he had ever known. The dog sat facing him and waiting. The brief day drew to a close in a long, slow twilight. There were no signs of a fire to be made, and, besides, never in the dog's experience had it known a man to sit like that in the snow and make no fire. As the twilight drew on, its eager yearning for the fire mastered it, and with a great lifting and shifting of forefeet, it whined softly, then flattened its ears down in anticipation of being chidden by the man. But the man remained silent. Later, the dog whined loudly. And still later it crept close to the man and caught the scent of death. This made the animal bristle and back away. A little longer it delayed, howling under the stars that leaped and danced and shone brightly in the cold sky. Then it turned and trotted up the trail in the direction of the camp it knew, where were the other food-providers and fire-providers.

1

What is the main purpose of this passage?

_____

2

What is the passage's tone?

_____

3

How would you summarize the passage?

_____

4

How would you describe the main character?

_____

RTHQUAKES – KAYE M. SHEDLOCK AND LOUIS C. PAKISER

This passage is adapted from Kaye M. Shedlock and Louis C. Pakiser, *Earthquakes*, published by the United States Geological Service. An earthquake is a sudden movement of the Earth, caused by the abrupt release of strain that has accumulated over a long time.

One of the most frightening and destructive phenomena of nature is a severe earthquake and its terrible after-effects. For hundreds of millions of years, the forces of plate tectonics have shaped the Earth as the huge plates that form the Earth's surface slowly move over, under, and past each other. Sometimes the movement is gradual. At other times, the plates are locked together, unable to release the accumulating energy. When the accumulated energy grows strong enough, the plates break free. If the earthquake occurs in a populated area, it may cause many deaths and injuries and extensive property damage.

Today we are challenging the assumption that earthquakes must present an uncontrollable and unpredictable hazard to life and property. Scientists have begun to estimate the locations and likelihoods of future damaging earthquakes. Sites of greatest hazard are being identified, and definite progress is being made in designing structures that will withstand the effects of earthquakes.

The scientific study of earthquakes is comparatively new. Until the 18th century, few factual descriptions of earthquakes were recorded, and the natural cause of earthquakes was little understood. Those who did look for natural causes often reached conclusions that seem fanciful today; one popular theory was that earthquakes were caused by air rushing out of caverns deep in the Earth's interior.

The earliest earthquake for which we have descriptive information occurred in China in 1177 B.C. The Chinese earthquake catalog describes several dozen large earthquakes in China during the next few thousand years. Earthquakes in Europe are mentioned as early as 580 B.C., but the earliest for which we have some descriptive information occurred in the mid-16th century. The earliest known earthquakes in the Americas were in Mexico in the late 14th century and in Peru in 1471, but descriptions of the effects were not well documented. By the 17th century, descriptions of the effects of earthquakes were being published around the world—although these accounts were often exaggerated or distorted.

The most widely felt earthquakes in the recorded history of North America were a series that occurred in 1811-12 near New Madrid, Mo. A great earthquake, whose magnitude is estimated to be about 8, occurred on the morning of December 16, 1811. Another great earthquake occurred on January 23, 1812, and a third, the strongest yet, on February 7, 1812. Aftershocks were nearly continuous between these great earthquakes and continued for months afterwards. These earthquakes were felt by people as far away as Boston and Denver. Because the most intense effects were in a sparsely populated region, the destruction of human life and property was slight. If just one of these enormous earthquakes occurred in the same area today, millions of people and buildings and other structures worth billions of dollars would be affected.

The San Francisco earthquake north of 1906 was one of the most destructive in the recorded history of North America—the earthquake and the fire that followed killed nearly 700 people and left the city in ruins. The Alaska earthquake of March 27, 1964, was of greater magnitude than the San Francisco earthquake; it released perhaps twice as much energy and was felt over an area of almost 500,000 square miles. The ground motion near the epicenter was so violent that the tops of some trees were snapped off. One hundred and fourteen people (some as far away as California) died as a result of this earthquake, but loss of life and property would have been far greater had Alaska been more densely populated.

The Earth is formed of several layers that have very different physical and chemical properties. The outer layer, which averages about 75 kilometers in thickness, consists of about a dozen large, irregularly shaped plates that slide over, under, and past each other on top of the partly molten inner layer. Most earthquakes occur at the boundaries where the plates meet. In fact, the locations of earthquakes and the kinds of ruptures they produce help scientists define the plate boundaries.

There are three types of plate boundaries: spreading zones, transform faults, and subduction zones. At spreading zones, molten rock rises, pushing two plates apart and adding new material at their edges. Most spreading zones are found in oceans; for example, the North American and Eurasian plates are spreading apart along the mid-Atlantic ridge. Spreading zones usually have earthquakes at shallow depths (within 30 kilometers of the surface).

Transform faults are found where plates slide past one another. An example of a transform-fault plate boundary is the San Andreas fault, along the coast of California and northwestern Mexico. Earthquakes at transform faults tend to occur at shallow depths and form fairly straight linear patterns.

Subduction zones are found where one plate overrides, or subducts, another, pushing it downward into the mantle where it melts. An example of a subduction-zone plate boundary is found along the northwest coast of the United States, western Canada, and southern Alaska and the Aleutian Islands. Subduction zones are characterized by deep-ocean trenches, shallow to deep earthquakes, and mountain ranges containing active volcanoes.

Earthquakes can also occur within plates, although plate-boundary earthquakes are much more common. Less than 10 percent of all earthquakes occur within plate interiors. As plates continue to move and plate boundaries change over geologic time, weakened boundary regions become part of the interiors of the plates. These zones of weakness within the continents can cause earthquakes in response to stresses that originate at the edges of the plate or in the deeper crust. The New Madrid earthquakes of 1811-12 and the 1886 Charleston earthquake occurred within the North American plate.

An earthquake is the vibration, sometimes violent, of the Earth's surface that follows a release of energy in the Earth's crust. This energy can be generated by a sudden dislocation of segments of the crust, by a volcanic eruption, or even by manmade explosions. Most destructive quakes, however, are caused by dislocations of the crust. The crust may first bend and then, when the stress exceeds the strength of the rocks, break and "snap" to a new position. In the process of breaking, vibrations called "seismic waves" are generated. These waves travel outward from the source of the earthquake along the surface and through the Earth at varying speeds depending on the material through which they move. Some of the vibrations are of high enough frequency to be audible, while others are of very low frequency. These vibrations cause the entire planet to quiver or ring like a bell or a tuning fork.

A fault is a fracture in the Earth's crust along which two blocks of the crust have slipped with respect to each other. Faults are divided into three main groups, depending on how they move. Normal faults occur in response to pulling or tension; the overlying block moves down the dip of the fault plane. Thrust (reverse) faults occur in response to squeezing or compression; the overlying block moves up the dip of the fault plane. Strike-slip (lateral) faults occur in response to either type of stress; the blocks move horizontally past one another. Most faulting along spreading zones is normal, along subduction zones is thrust, and along transform faults is strike-slip.

Geologists have found that earthquakes tend to reoccur along faults, which reflect zones of weakness in the Earth's crust. Even if a fault zone has recently experienced an earthquake, however, there is no guarantee that all the stress has been relieved. Another earthquake could still occur. In New Madrid, a great earthquake was followed by a large aftershock within 6 hours on December 16, 1811. Furthermore, relieving stress along one part of the fault may increase stress in another part; the New Madrid earthquakes in January and February 1812 may have resulted from this phenomenon.

The focal depth of an earthquake is the depth from the Earth's surface to the region where an earthquake's energy originates (the focus). Earthquakes with focal depths from the surface to about 75 kilometers (43.5 miles) are classified as shallow. Earthquakes with focal depths from 70 to 300 kilometers (43.5 to 186 miles) are classified as intermediate. The focus of deep earthquakes may reach depths of more than 700 kilometers (435 miles). The focuses of most earthquakes are concentrated in the crust and upper mantle. The depth to the center of the Earth's core is about 6,370 kilometers (3,960 miles), so even the deepest earthquakes originate in relatively shallow parts of the Earth's interior.

The epicenter of an earthquake is the point on the Earth's surface directly above the focus. The location of an earthquake is commonly described by the geographic position of its epicenter and by its focal depth.

Earthquakes beneath the ocean floor sometimes generate immense sea waves or tsunamis (Japan's dread "huge wave"). These waves travel across the ocean at speeds as great as 960 kilometers per hour (597 miles per hour) and may be 15 meters (49 feet) high or higher by the time they reach the shore. During the 1964 Alaska earthquake, tsunamis engulfing coastal areas caused most of the destruction at Kodiak, Cordova, and Seward and caused severe damage along the west coast of North America, particularly at Crescent City, Calif. Some waves raced across the ocean to the coasts of Japan.

Liquefaction, which happens when loosely packed, water-logged sediments lose their strength in response to strong shaking, causes major damage during earthquakes. During the 1989 Loma Prieta earthquake, liquefaction of sthe soils and debris used to fill in a lagoon caused major subsidence, fracturing, and horizontal sliding of the ground surface in the Marina district in San Francisco.

Landslides triggered by earthquakes often cause more destruction than the earthquakes themselves. During the 1964 Alaska quake, shock-induced landslides devastated the Turnagain Heights residential development and many downtown areas in Anchorage. An observer gave a vivid report of the breakup of the unstable earth materials in the

Turnagain Heights region: I got out of my car, ran northward toward my driveway, and then saw that the bluff had broken back approximately 300 feet southward from its original edge. Additional slumping of the bluff caused me to return to my car and back southward approximately 180 feet to the corner of McCollie and Turnagain Parkway. The bluff slowly broke until the corner of Turnagain Parkway and McCollie had slumped northward.

The two general types of vibrations produced by earthquakes are surface waves, which travel along the Earth's surface, and body waves, which travel through the Earth. Surface waves usually have the strongest vibrations and probably cause most of the damage done by earthquakes.

Body waves are of two types, compressional and shear. Both types pass through the Earth's interior from the focus of an earthquake to distant points on the surface, but only compressional waves travel through the Earth's molten core. Because compressional waves travel at great speeds and ordinarily reach the surface first, they are often called "primary waves" or simply "P" waves. P waves push tiny particles of Earth material directly ahead of them or displace the particles directly behind their line of travel.

Shear waves do not travel as rapidly through the Earth's crust and mantle as do compressional waves, and because they ordinarily reach the surface later they are called "secondary" or "S" waves. Instead of affecting material directly behind or ahead of their line of travel, shear waves displace material at right angles to their path and are therefore sometimes called "transverse" waves.

The first indication of an earthquake is often a sharp thud, signaling the arrival of compressional waves. This is followed by the shear waves and then the "ground roll" caused by the surface waves. A geologist who was at Valdez, Alaska, during the 1964 earthquake described this sequence: The first tremors were hard enough to stop a moving person, and shock waves were immediately noticeable on the surface of the ground. These shock waves continued with a rather long frequency, which gave the observer an impression of a rolling feeling rather than abrupt hard jolts. After about 1 minute the amplitude or strength of the shock waves increased in intensity and failures in buildings as well as the frozen ground surface began to occur.... After about 3½ minutes the severe shock waves ended and people began to react as could be expected.

Large earthquakes cause more damage east of the Rocky Mountains; this map shows areas that suffered major architectural damage (striped areas) and minor

The vibrations produced by earthquakes are detected, recorded, and measured by instruments called seismographs. The zig-zag line made by a seismograph, called a "seismogram," reflects the changing intensity of the vibrations by responding to the motion of the ground surface beneath the instrument. From the data expressed in seismograms, scientists can determine the time, the epicenter, the focal depth, and the type of faulting of an earthquake and can estimate how much energy was released. damage (dotted areas) during the magnitude-8 earthquakes in New Madrid and San Francisco and the smaller but still damaging quakes in Charleston and San Fernando.

The severity of an earthquake can be expressed in several ways. The magnitude of an earthquake, usually expressed by the Richter Scale, is a measure of the amplitude of the seismic waves. The moment magnitude of an earthquake is a measure of the amount of energy released—an amount that can be estimated from seismograph recordings. The intensity, as expressed by the Modified Mercalli Scale, is a subjective measure that describes how strong a shock was felt at a particular location.

The Richter Scale, named after Dr. Charles F. Richter of the California Institute of Technology, is the best known scale for measuring the magnitude of earthquakes. The scale is logarithmic so that a recording of 7, for example, indicates a disturbance with ground motion 10 times as large as a recording of 6. A quake of magnitude 2 is the smallest quake normally felt by people. Earthquakes with a Richter value of 6 or more are commonly considered major; great earthquakes have magnitudes of 8 or more on the Richter scale.

The Modified Mercalli Scale expresses the intensity of an earthquake's effects in a given locality in values ranging from I to XII. The most commonly used adaptation covers the range of intensity from the condition of "I—Not felt except by a very few under especially favorable conditions," to "XII—Damage total. Lines of sight and level are distorted. Objects thrown upward into the air." Evaluation of earthquake intensity can be made only after eyewitness reports and results of field investigations are studied and interpreted. The maximum intensity experienced in the Alaska earthquake of 1964 was X; damage from the San Francisco and New Madrid earthquakes reached a maximum intensity of XI.

Earthquakes of large magnitude do not necessarily cause the most intense surface effects. The effect in a given region depends to a large degree on local surface and subsurface geologic conditions. An area underlain by unstable ground (sand, clay, or other unconsolidated materials), for example, is likely to experience much more noticeable effects than an area equally distant from an earthquake's epicenter but underlain by firm ground such as granite. In general, earthquakes east of the Rocky Mountains affect a much larger area than earthquakes west of the Rockies.

An earthquake's destructiveness depends on many factors. In addition to magnitude and the local geologic conditions, these factors include the focal depth, the distance from the epicenter, and the design of buildings and other structures. The extent of damage also depends on the density of population and construction in the area shaken by the quake.

The Loma Prieta earthquake of 1989 demonstrated a wide range of effects. The Santa Cruz mountains suffered little damage from the seismic waves, even though they were close to the epicenter. The central core of the city of Santa Cruz, about 24 kilometers (15 miles) away from the epicenter, was almost completely destroyed. More than 80 kilometers (50 miles) away, the cities of San Francisco and Oakland suffered selective but severe damage, including the loss of more than 40 lives. The greatest destruction occurred in areas where roads and elevated structures were built on unstable ground underlain by loose, unconsolidated soils.

The Northridge, California, earthquake of 1994 also produced a wide variety of effects, even over distances of just a few hundred meters. Some buildings collapsed, while adjacent buildings of similar age and construction remained standing. Similarly, some highway spans collapsed, while others nearby did not.

Earthquakes are associated with volcanic eruptions. Abrupt increases in earthquake activity heralded eruptions at Mount St. Helens, Washington; Mount Spurr and Redoubt Volcano, Alaska; and Kilauea and Mauna Loa, Hawaii. The location and movement of swarms of tremors indicate the movement of magma through the volcano. Continuous records of seismic and tiltmeter (a device that measures ground tilting) data are maintained at U.S. Geological Survey volcano observatories in Hawaii, Alaska, California, and the Cascades, where study of these records enables specialists to make short-range predictions of volcanic eruptions. These warnings have been especially effective in Alaska, where the imminent eruption of a volcano requires the rerouting of international air traffic to enable airplanes to avoid volcanic clouds. Since 1982, at least seven jumbo jets, carrying more than 1,500 passengers, have lost power in the air after flying into clouds of volcanic ash. Though all flights were able to restart their engines eventually and no lives were lost, the aircraft suffered damages of tens of millions of dollars. As a result of these close calls, an international team of volcanologists, meteorologists,

dispatchers, pilots, and controllers have begun to work together to alert each other to imminent volcanic eruptions and to detect and track volcanic ash clouds.

The goal of earthquake prediction is to give warning of potentially damaging earthquakes early enough to allow appropriate response to the disaster, enabling people to minimize loss of life and property. The U.S. Geological Survey conducts and supports research on the likelihood of future earthquakes. This research includes field, laboratory, and theoretical investigations of earthquake mechanisms and fault zones. A primary goal of earthquake research is to increase the reliability of earthquake probability estimates. Ultimately, scientists would like to be able to specify a high probability for a specific earthquake on a particular fault within a particular year. Scientists estimate earthquake probabilities in two ways: by studying the history of large earthquakes in a specific area and the rate at which strain accumulates in the rock.

Scientists study the past frequency of large earthquakes in order to determine the future likelihood of similar large shocks. For example, if a region has experienced four magnitude 7 or larger earthquakes during 200 years of recorded history, and if these shocks occurred randomly in time, then scientists would assign a 50 percent probability (that is, just as likely to happen as not to happen) to the occurrence of another magnitude 7 or larger quake in the region during the next 50 years.

But in many places, the assumption of random occurrence with time may not be true, because when the strain is released along one part of the fault system, it may actually increase on another part. Four magnitude 6.8 or larger earthquakes and many magnitude 6-6.5 shocks occurred in the San Francisco Bay region during the 75 years between 1836 and 1911. For the next 68 years (until 1979), no earthquakes of magnitude 6 or larger occurred in the region. Beginning with a magnitude 6.0 shock in 1979, the earthquake activity in the region increased dramatically; between 1979 and 1989, there were four magnitude 6 or greater earthquakes, including the magnitude 7.1 Loma Prieta earthquake. This clustering of earthquakes leads scientists to estimate that the probability of a magnitude 6.8 or larger earthquake occurring during the next 30 years in the San Francisco Bay region is about 67 percent (twice as likely as not).

Another way to estimate the likelihood of future earthquakes is to study how fast strain accumulates. When plate movements build the strain in rocks to a critical level, like pulling a rubber band too tight, the rocks will suddenly break and slip to a new position. Scientists measure how much strain accumulates along a fault segment each year, how much time has passed since the last earthquake along the segment, and how much strain was released in the last earthquake. This information is then used to calculate the time required for the accumulating strain to build to the level that results in an earthquake. This simple model is complicated by the fact that such detailed information about faults is rare. In the United States, only the San Andreas fault system has adequate records for using this prediction method.

Both of these methods, and a wide array of monitoring techniques, are being tested along part of the San Andreas fault. For the past 150 years, earthquakes of about magnitude 6 have occurred an average of every 22 years on the San Andreas fault near Parkfield, California. The last shock was in 1966. Because of the consistency and similarity of these earthquakes, scientists have started an experiment to "capture" the next Parkfield earthquake. A dense web of monitoring instruments was deployed in the region during the late 1980s. The main goals of the ongoing Parkfield Earthquake Prediction Experiment are to record the geophysical signals before and after the expected earthquake; to issue a short-term prediction; and to develop effective methods of communication between earthquake scientists and community officials responsible for disaster response and mitigation. This project has already made important contributions to both earth science and public policy.

Scientific understanding of earthquakes is of vital importance to the Nation. As the population increases, expanding urban development and construction works encroach upon areas susceptible to earthquakes. With a greater understanding of the causes and effects of earthquakes, we may be able to reduce damage and loss of life from this destructive phenomenon.

1

What is the main purpose of this passage?

_____

2

What is the passage's tone?

_____

3

How would you summarize the passage?

_____

4

What is the authors' central thesis?

_____

5

How do the authors describe earthquakes?

_____

Jane Austen's *Emma* (1815) is a "comedy of manners," following the foibles of the titular Emma Woodhouse, "handsome, clever, and rich." *Emma* has been adapted repeatedly, perhaps best in the 1995 movie *Clueless*. This abridgement of *Emma* by Arthur Mee and J. A. Hammerton was published as part of the *The World's Greatest Books* collection in 1910.

Emma Woodhouse, handsome, clever, and rich, with a comfortable home and happy disposition, was the younger of the two daughters of a most affectionate and indulgent father, and had, in consequence of her sister's marriage, been mistress of his house from a very early period. Her mother had died too long ago for her to have more than an indistinct remembrance of her caresses, and her place had been supplied by Miss Taylor, who for sixteen years had been in Mr. Woodhouse's family, less as governess than friend, very fond of both daughters, but particularly of Emma. For years the two ladies had been living together, mutely attached, Emma doing just what she liked, highly esteeming Miss Taylor's judgment, but chiefly directed by her own.

The real evils, indeed, of Emma's situation were the power of having rather too much her own way, and a disposition to think a little too well of herself. The danger, however, was at present unperceived, and did not by any means rank as a misfortune with her.

Sorrow came--a gentle sorrow. Miss Taylor married. It was Miss Taylor's loss which first brought grief. It was on the wedding-day of this beloved friend, with the wedding over and the bride-people gone, that Emma first sat in mournful thought of any continuance. The event had every promise of happiness for her friend. Mr. Weston was a man of unexceptionable character, easy fortune, suitable age, and pleasant manners; and there was some satisfaction in considering with what self-denying, generous friendship she had always wished and promoted the match. But it was a black morning's work for her. The want of Miss Taylor would be felt every hour of every day. She had been a friend and companion such as few possessed: intelligent, well-informed, useful, gentle; knowing all the ways of the family, interested in all its concerns, and peculiarly interested in herself, in every pleasure, every scheme of hers--one to whom she could speak every thought, and who had such an affection for her as could never find fault.

How was Emma to bear the change? She was now in great danger of suffering from intellectual solitude. She dearly loved her father, but he was no companion for her. He could not meet her in conversation, rational or playful. The evil of the actual disparity in their ages (as Mr. Woodhouse had not married early) was much increased by his constitution and habits; for, having been a valetudinarian all his life, without activity of mind or body, he was a much older man in ways than in years; and though everywhere beloved for the friendliness of his heart and his amiable temper, his talents could not have recommended him at any time.

Emma's sister, though comparatively but little removed by matrimony, being settled in London, only sixteen miles off, was much beyond her daily reach; and it was quite three months before Christmas, that would bring the next visit from Isabella, her husband, and children.

Highbury, the large and populous village to which her house, Hartfield, really belonged, afforded her no equals. The Woodhouses were first in consequence there. All looked up to them; but there was not one of her acquaintances among them who could be accepted in lieu of Miss Taylor for even half a day. It was a melancholy change; and Emma could not but sigh over it, and wish for impossible things, till her father awoke from his usual after-dinner sleep, and made it necessary to be cheerful. His spirits required support. He was a nervous man, easily depressed; fond of everybody he was used to, and hating to part with them; hating change of every kind. Matrimony, as the origin of change, was always disagreeable to him; and he was not yet reconciled to his own daughter marrying, nor could ever speak of her but with compassion, though it had been entirely a match of affection, when he was now obliged to part with Miss Taylor, too.

He was pitying "poor Miss Taylor," and magnifying the half-mile's distance that separated Hartfield from Mr. Weston's place, Randalls, when a visitor walked in. This was Mr. George Knightley, the elder brother of Isabella's husband, and the owner of Donwell Abbey, the large estate of the district. He was a sensible man, about seven or eight and thirty, a very old and intimate friend of the family, and a frequent and always welcome visitor. He had returned to a late dinner after some days' absence in London, and had walked up to Hartfield to say that all was well with their relatives in Brunswick Square. They talked of the wedding. Emma congratulated herself on having made the match. Mr. Knightley demurred to this, remarking: "A straightforward, open-hearted man, like Weston, and a rational, unaffected woman, like Miss Taylor, may be safely left to manage their own concerns." And when Emma, in reply to entreaties from her father to make no more matches, answered, "Only one more, papa; only for Mr. Elton--you like Mr. Elton, papa; I must look about for a wife for him"--her old friend gave her the salutary advice: "Invite him to dinner, Emma, and help him to the best of the fish and the chicken; but leave him to choose his own wife. Depend upon it, a man of six or seven and twenty can take care of himself."

Emma lost no time in developing her schemes for the happiness of Mr. Elton. Through Mrs. Goddard, the mistress of the local boarding-school for girls, she struck up an acquaintance, which she contrived rapidly to develop into intimacy, with a Miss Harriet Smith--a plump, fair-haired, blue-eyed little beauty of seventeen, whose prettiness, docility, good-temper and simplicity might be allowed to balance her lack of intelligence and information.

Harriet was the natural daughter of somebody. Somebody had placed her several years back at Mrs. Goddard's school, and somebody had lately raised her from the condition of scholar to that of parlour-boarder. This was all that was generally known of her history. She had no visible friends but what had been acquired at Highbury, and was now just returned from a long visit in the country to some young ladies--the Misses Martin--who had been at school there with her.

The first step which Emma took in the education of Harriet was to cool her interest in the Martins. She pointed out that Mr. Robert Martin, who held a large farm from Mr. Knightley in Donwell parish, was too young to marry at twenty-four, that he had, besides, an awkward look, an abrupt manner, and an uncouth voice; and that, moreover, he was quite plain-looking and wholly ungenteel; whereas Mr. Elton, who was good-humoured, cheerful, obliging and gentle, was a pattern of good manners and good looks, and seemed to be taking quite an interest in Harriet. So indeed it appeared. Mr. Elton seemed delighted with being in the society of Emma and Harriet. He praised Harriet as a beautiful girl, congratulated Emma on the improvement she had wrought in her, contributed a charade to Harriet's riddle-book, and took a most animated interest in a portrait which Emma began to paint of her.

But Mr. Knightley was not so complacent. "I think Harriet," he said to Mrs. Weston, "the very worst sort of a companion that Emma could possibly have. She knows nothing herself, and looks upon Emma as knowing everything. Her ignorance is hourly flattery. How can Emma imagine she has anything to learn herself while Harriet is presenting such a delightful inferiority? And as for Harriet, Hartfield will only put her out of conceit with all the other places she belongs to. She will grow just refined enough to be uncomfortable with those among whom birth and circumstances have placed her."

This was in the early stages of the intimacy. Later in the day, when he learned that Emma had taken so decided a hand in the affairs of Harriet as to persuade her to decline a formal offer of marriage from Mr. Martin, he told her plainly:

"I have always thought it a very foolish intimacy, though I have kept my thoughts to myself; but now I perceive that it will be a very unfortunate one for Harriet. You will puff her up with such ideas of her own beauty, and what she has claim to, that, in a little while, nobody within her reach will be good enough for her. Robert Martin has no great loss if he can but think so; and I hope it will not be long before he does. Your views for Harriet are best known to yourself; but, as you make no secret of your love of match-making, I shall just hint to you as a friend that, if Elton is the man, I think it will be all labour in vain."

Emma laughed and disclaimed. "Depend upon it," he continued, "Elton will not do. Elton is a very good sort of a man, and a very respectable vicar of Highbury, but not at all likely to make an imprudent match. He is as well acquainted with his own claims as you can be with Harriet's; and I am convinced that he does not mean to throw himself away."

But despite this warning from Mr. George Knightley, despite a hint dropped by Mr. John Knightley, when he and his wife and children came to stop with the Woodhouses for Christmas--a hint to the effect that his sister-in-law would do well to consider whether Mr. Elton was not in love with her--Emma continued quite as ardent in her new friendship and in her hopes.

As to herself, she told Harriet that she was not going to be married at present, and had very little intention of ever marrying at all; though when Harriet reminded her of Miss Bates, who was the daughter of a former vicar of Highbury and lived in a very small way with her mother, a very old lady almost past everything but tea and quadrille, she confessed that if she thought she would ever be like Miss Bates, "so silly, so satisfied, so smiling, so prosing, so undistinguishing, so unfastidious, and so garrulous," she would marry to-morrow.

But Mr. Elton was unaware of Emma having thought of making such a self-denying ordinance; and so one night when the Woodhouses and the Knightleys were returning home from a party at Randalls he took advantage of his being alone in a carriage with her to propose to her, seeming never to doubt his being accepted. When he learned, however, for whom his hand had been destined, he became very indignant and contemptuous.

"Never, madam!" cried he. "Never, I assure you! I think seriously of Miss Smith! Miss Smith is a very good sort of girl; and I should be happy to see her respectably settled. I wish her extremely well; and, no doubt, there are men who might not object to-- Everybody has their level; but as for myself, I am not, I think, quite so much at a loss. I need not so totally despair of an equal alliance as to be addressing myself to Miss Smith! No, madam; my visits to Hatfield have been for yourself only."

Needless to say, Emma refused him, and they parted on terms of mutually deep mortification. Fortunately, the task of enlightening Harriet as to the state of Mr. Elton's feelings proved less troublesome than Emma had expected it to be. Harriet's tears fell abundantly, but otherwise she bore the intelligence very meekly and well.

As if to make up for the absence of Mr. Elton, who went to spend a few weeks in Bath, in an endeavour to cure his wounded affections. Highbury society was shortly enlarged by the arrival of two such welcome additions as Miss Jane Fairfax and Mr. Frank Churchill.

Miss Fairfax, who was the orphan daughter of Lieutenant Fairfax, and Miss Janes Bates had for many years been living with her father's brother-officer, Colonel Campbell, and his wife and daughter. A beautiful girl of nineteen, with only a few hundred pounds of her own, and no monetary expectations from her adoptive father, she had received such an education as qualified her to become a governess; and though as long as Colonel and Mrs. Campbell lived their home might always be hers, she had all along resolved to start earning her own living at one-and-twenty. Her friend, Miss Campbell, had recently married a rich and agreeable young man called Dixon; and though the Dixons had urgently invited her to join Colonel and Mrs. Campbell in a visit to them in Ireland, Jane preferred to spend three months' holiday with her aunt and grandmother at Highbury, with some vague intention of starting her scholastic career at the end of this period. Emma did not like Jane Fairfax, partly because Jane's aunt was always boring people by talking of her; partly, perhaps, because--as Mr. Knightley once told her--she saw in her the really accomplished young woman which she wanted to be thought herself. At any rate, she still found her as reserved as ever. Jane had been a little acquainted with Mr. Frank Churchill at Weymouth, but she either could not, or would not, tell Emma anything about him.

That gentleman, however, soon presented himself in person. He was the son of Mr. Weston by his first wife. At the age of three he had been adopted by his maternal uncle, Mr. Churchill; and so avowedly had he been brought up as their heir by Mr. and Mrs. Churchill--who had no children of their own--that on his coming of age he had assumed the name of Churchill. For some months he had been promising to pay a visit to his father and stepmother to compliment them on their marriage; but on the pretext of his not being able to leave Enscombe, his uncle's place, it had been repeatedly postponed.

Emma was inclined to make allowances for him as a young man dependent on the caprices of relations. But Mr. Knightley condemned his conduct roundly. "He cannot want money, he cannot want leisure," he said. "We know, on the contrary, that he has so much of both that he is glad to get rid of them at the idlest haunts in the kingdom." Notwithstanding, when he did arrive, Frank Churchill carried all before him by reason of his good looks, sprightliness, and amiability. Emma and he soon became great friends. He favoured an idea of hers, that Jane's refusal to go to the Dixons' in Ireland was due either to Mr. Dixon's attachment to her, or to her attachment to Mr. Dixon. When a Broadwood pianoforte arrived for Jane--which was generally taken to be a gift from Colonel Campbell--he agreed with her in thinking that this was another occurrence for which Mr. Dixon's love was responsible; and he was busily engaged in planning out the details of a projected ball at the Crown Inn when a letter from Mr. Churchill urging his instant departure compelled him to make a hurried return to Enscombe.

Meanwhile, while Emma was entertaining no doubt of her being in love with Frank, and only wondering how deep her feeling was, while she was content to think that Frank was very much in love with her, and was concluding every imaginary declaration on his side with a refusal of his proposals, Mr. Elton returned to Highbury with his bride. Miss Augusta Hawkins--to give Mrs. Elton her maiden name--was the younger of the two daughters of a Bristol tradesman, and was credited with having ten thousand pounds of her own. A self-important, presuming, familiar, ignorant, and ill-bred woman, with a little beauty and a little accomplishment, who was always expatiating on the charms of Mr. Suckling's--her brother-in-law's--place, Maple Grove, she soon excited disgust in Emma, who offended her by the scanty encouragement with which she received her proposals of intimacy, and was herself offended by the great fancy which Mrs. Elton took to Jane Fairfax. Long before Emma had forfeited her confidence, she was not satisfied with expressing a natural and reasonable admiration of Jane, but, without solicitation, or plea, or privilege, she must be wanting to assist and befriend her. The ill-feeling thus aroused found significant expression on the occasion of the long-talked-of ball at the Crown, which Mr. Weston was able to give one evening in May, thanks to the settlement of the Churchills at Richmond, and the consequent reappearance of Frank Churchill at Highbury. Indeed, Emma met with two annoyances on that famous evening. Mr. Weston had entreated her to come early, before any other person came, for the purpose of taking her opinion as to the propriety and comfort of the rooms; and when she got there, she found that quite half the company had come, by particular desire, to help Mr. Weston's judgment. She felt that to be the favourite and intimate of a man who had so many intimates was not the first distinction in the scale of vanity.

The other vexing circumstance was due to the conduct of Mr. Elton, who, asked by Mrs. Weston to dance with Harriet Smith, declined on the ground that he was an old married man, and that his dancing days were over. Fortunately, Mr. Knightley, who has recently disappointed Mrs. Weston, and pleased Emma by disclaiming any idea of being attached to Jane Fairfax, was able in some measure to redeem the situation by leading Harriet to the set himself. Emma had no opportunity of speaking to him till after supper; and then he said to her: "They aimed at wounding more than Harriet. Emma, why is it that they are your enemies?" He looked with smiling penetration, and, on receiving no answer, added: "She ought not to be angry with you, I suspect, whatever he may be. To that surmise you say nothing, of course; but confess, Emma, that you did want him to marry Harriet." "I did," replied Emma, "and they cannot forgive me."

A day or two afterwards, Harriet figured as the heroine of another little scene. She was rescued by Frank Churchill from an encounter with some gipsies; and after telling Emma, in a very serious tone, a few days later, that she should never marry, confessed that she had come to this resolution because the person she might prefer to marry was one so greatly her superior in situation.

His own attentions, his father's hints, his stepmother's guarded silence, all seemed to declare that Emma was Frank Churchill's object. But while so many were devoting him to Emma, and Emma herself was making him over to Harriet, Mr. Knightley began to suspect him of some inclination to trifle with Jane Fairfax. When Mr. Knightley mentioned these suspicions to Emma, she declared them sheer imagination, and said that she could answer for there being no attachment on the side of the gentleman; while he himself, as if to ridicule the whole idea, flirted outrageously with Emma on an excursion to Box Hill at which Jane was present, and even asked the former lady to choose a wife for him. The next day Emma, calling on Miss Bates, learned that Jane, who, was at present too unwell to see her, had just accepted a post as governess, obtained for her by Mrs. Elton, and that

Frank Churchill had been summoned to return immediately to Richmond in consequence of Mrs. Churchill's state of health. On the following day an express arrived at Randalls to announce the death of Mrs. Churchill.

Emma, seeing in this latter event a circumstance favourable to the union of Frank and Harriet (for Mr. Churchill, independent of his wife, was feared by nobody), now only wished for some proof of the former's attachment to her friend. She could, however, for the moment do nothing for Harriet, whereas she could show some attention to Jane, whose prospects were closing, while Harriet's were opening. But here she proved to be mistaken; all her endeavours were to no purpose. The invalid refused everything that was offered, no matter what its character; and Emma had to console herself with the thought that her intentions were good, and would have satisfied even so strict an investigator of motives as Mr. Knightley.

One morning, about ten days after Mrs. Churchill's death, Emma was called downstairs to Mr. Weston, who asked her to come to Randalls as Mrs. Weston wanted to see her alone. Relieved to find that the matter was not one of illness, either there or at Brunswick Square, Emma resolved to wait patiently till she could see her old friend. But what was her surprise, on Mr. Weston leaving them together, when his wife revealed the fact that Frank and Jane had been secretly engaged since October of the previous year! It was almost greater than Mrs. Weston's relief when she learned, to her joy, that Emma now cared nothing at all for Frank, and so had been in no wise injured by this clandestine understanding, the divulgence of which was due, it seemed, to the fact that, immediately on hearing of Jane's agreement to take up the post of governess, Frank had gone to his uncle, told him of the engagement, and with little difficulty obtained his consent to it.

It was with a heavy heart that Emma went home to give Harriet the news that must blast her hopes of happiness once more. But, again, a surprise was in store for her. Harriet had already been told by Mr. Weston, and seemed to bear her misfortune quite stoically, the reason being that the person of "superior situation" whom she despaired of securing was not Mr. Frank Churchill, but Mr. George Knightley.

Emma was not prepared for this development. It darted through her, with the speed of an arrow, that Mr. Knightley must marry no one but herself! Which desirable consummation was brought about at their next interview; for, after trying to console her for the abominable conduct of Frank Churchill, under the mistaken impression that that young gentleman had succeeded in engaging her affections, Mr. Knightley proposed marriage to her, and was accepted. As for Harriet, she was invited, at Emma's suggestion, to spend a fortnight with Mr. and Mrs. John Knightley in Brunswick Square, and there, meeting Mr. Robert Martin, through Mr. George Knightley's contrivance, was easily persuaded to become his wife.

About this same time, too, Mrs. Weston's husband and friends were all made happy by knowing her to be the mother of a little girl; while Emma and Mrs. Weston were enabled to take a more lenient view of Frank Churchill's conduct, thanks to a long letter which he wrote to the latter lady in which he apologised for his equivocal conduct to Emma, and expressed his regret that those attentions should have caused such poignant distress to the lady whom he was shortly to make his wife. The much discussed pianoforte had been his gift.

1

What is the main purpose of this passage?

_____

2

What is the passage's tone?

_____

3

How would you summarize the passage?

_____

4

How would you describe Emma?

_____

Thomas Malthus's *An Essay on the Principle of Population*, first published in 1798. His "Iron Law of Population Growth" and the "Malthusian Trap" reflect the theory that population, unchecked, must lead to starvation and war.

It has been said that the great question is now at issue, whether man shall henceforth start forwards with accelerated velocity towards illimitable, and hitherto unconceived improvement, or be condemned to a perpetual oscillation between happiness and misery, and after every effort remain still at an immeasurable distance from the wished-for goal.

Yet, anxiously as every friend of mankind must look forwards to the termination of this painful suspense, and eagerly as the inquiring mind would hail every ray of light that might assist its view into futurity, it is much to be lamented that the writers on each side of this momentous question still keep far aloof from each other. Their mutual arguments do not meet with a candid examination. The question is not brought to rest on fewer points, and even in theory scarcely seems to be approaching to a decision.

The advocate for the present order of things is apt to treat the sect of speculative philosophers either as a set of artful and designing knaves who preach up ardent benevolence and draw captivating pictures of a happier state of society only the better to enable them to destroy the present establishments and to forward their own deep-laid schemes of ambition, or as wild and mad-headed enthusiasts whose silly speculations and absurd paradoxes are not worthy the attention of any reasonable man.

The advocate for the perfectibility of man, and of society, retorts on the defender of establishments a more than equal contempt. He brands him as the slave of the most miserable and narrow prejudices; or as the defender of the abuses. of civil society only because he profits by them. He paints him either as a character who prostitutes his understanding to his interest, or as one whose powers of mind are not of a size to grasp any thing great and noble, who cannot see above five yards before him, and who must therefore be utterly unable to take in the views of the enlightened benefactor of mankind.

In this unamicable contest the cause of truth cannot but suffer. The really good arguments on each side of the question are not allowed to have their proper weight. Each pursues his own theory, little solicitous to correct or improve it by an attention to what is advanced by his opponents.

The friend of the present order of things condemns all political speculations in the gross. He will not even condescend to examine the grounds from which the perfectibility of society is inferred. Much less will he give himself the trouble in a fair and candid manner to attempt an exposition of their fallacy.

The speculative philosopher equally offends against the cause of truth. With eyes fixed on a happier state of society, the blessings of which he paints in the most captivating colours, he allows himself to indulge in the most bitter invectives against every present establishment, without applying his talents to consider the best and safest means of removing abuses and without seeming to be aware of the tremendous obstacles that threaten, even in theory, to oppose the progress of man towards perfection.

It is an acknowledged truth in philosophy that a just theory will always be confirmed by experiment. Yet so much friction, and so many minute circumstances occur in practice, which it is next to impossible for the most enlarged and penetrating mind to foresee, that on few subjects can any theory be pronounced just, till all the arguments against it have been maturely weighed and clearly and consistently refuted.

I have read some of the speculations on the perfectibility of man and of society with great pleasure. I have been warmed and delighted with the enchanting picture which they hold forth. I ardently wish for such happy improvements. But I see great, and, to my understanding, unconquerable difficulties in the way to them. These difficulties it is my present purpose to state, declaring, at the same time, that so far from exulting in them, as a cause of triumph over the friends of innovation, nothing would give me greater pleasure than to see them completely removed.

The most important argument that I shall adduce is certainly not new. The principles on which it depends have been explained in part by Hume, and more at large by Dr. Adam Smith. It has been advanced and applied to the present subject, though not with its proper weight, or in the most forcible point of view, by Mr. Wallace, and it may probably have been stated by many writers that I have never met with. I should certainly therefore not think of advancing it again, though I mean to place it in a point of view in some degree different from any that I have hitherto seen, if it had ever been fairly and satisfactorily answered.

The cause of this neglect on the part of the advocates for the perfectibility of mankind is not easily accounted for. I cannot doubt the talents of such men as Godwin and Condorcet. I am unwilling to doubt their candour. To my understanding, and probably to that of most others, the difficulty appears insurmountable. Yet these men of acknowledged ability and penetration scarcely deign to notice it, and hold on their course in such speculations with unabated ardour and undiminished confidence. I have certainly no right to say that they purposely shut their eyes to such arguments. I ought rather to doubt the validity of them, when neglected by such men, however forcibly their truth may strike my own mind. Yet in this respect it must be acknowledged that we are all of us too prone to err. If I saw a glass of wine repeatedly presented to a man, and he took no notice of it, I should be apt to think that he was blind or uncivil. A juster philosophy might teach me rather to think that my eyes deceived me and that the offer was not really what I conceived it to be.

In entering upon the argument I must premise that I put out of the question, at present, all mere conjectures, that is, all suppositions, the probable realization of which cannot be inferred upon any just philosophical grounds. A writer may tell me that he thinks man will ultimately become an ostrich. I cannot properly contradict him. But before he can expect to bring any reasonable person over to his opinion, he ought to shew that the necks of mankind have been gradually elongating, that the lips have grown harder and more prominent, that the legs and feet are daily altering their shape, and that the hair is beginning to change into stubs of feathers. And till the probability of so wonderful a conversion can be shewn, it is surely lost time and lost eloquence to expatiate on the happiness of man in such a state; to describe his powers, both of running and flying, to paint him in a condition where all narrow luxuries would be contemned, where he would be employed only in collecting the necessaries of life, and where, consequently, each man's share of labour would be light, and his portion of leisure ample.

I think I may fairly make two postulata.

First, That food is necessary to the existence of man.

Secondly, That the passion between the sexes is necessary and will remain nearly in its present state.

These two laws, ever since we have had any knowledge of mankind, appear to have been fixed laws of our nature, and, as we have not hitherto seen any alteration in them, we have no right to conclude that they will ever cease to be what they now are, without an immediate act of power in that Being who first arranged the system of the universe, and for the advantage of his creatures, still executes, according to fixed laws, all its various operations.

I do not know that any writer has supposed that on this earth man will ultimately be able to live without food. But Mr. Godwin has conjectured that the passion between the sexes may in time be extinguished. As,

however, he calls this part of his work a deviation into the land of conjecture, I will not dwell longer upon it at present than to say that the best arguments for the perfectibility of man are drawn from a contemplation of the great progress that he has already made from the savage state and the difficulty of saying where he is to stop. But towards the extinction of the passion between the sexes, no progress whatever has hitherto been made. It appears to exist in as much force at present as it did two thousand or four thousand years ago. There are individual exceptions now as there always have been. But, as these exceptions do not appear to increase in number, it would surely be a very unphilosophical mode of arguing to infer, merely from the existence of an exception, that the exception would, in time, become the rule, and the rule the exception.

Assuming then my postulata as granted, I say, that the power of population is indefinitely greater than the power in the earth to produce subsistence for man.

Population, when unchecked, increases in a geometrical ratio. Subsistence increases only in an arithmetical ratio. A slight acquaintance with numbers will shew the immensity of the first power in comparison of the second.

By that law of our nature which makes food necessary to the life of man, the effects of these two unequal powers must be kept equal.

This implies a strong and constantly operating check on population from the difficulty of subsistence. This difficulty must fall somewhere and must necessarily be severely felt by a large portion of mankind.

Through the animal and vegetable kingdoms, nature has scattered the seeds of life abroad with the most profuse and liberal hand. She has been comparatively sparing in the room and the nourishment necessary to rear them. The germs of existence contained in this spot of earth, with ample food, and ample room to expand in, would fill millions of worlds in the course of a few thousand years. Necessity, that imperious all pervading law of nature, restrains them within the prescribed bounds. The race of plants and the race of animals shrink under this great restrictive law. And the race of man cannot, by any efforts of reason, escape from it. Among plants and animals its effects are waste of seed, sickness, and premature death. Among mankind, misery and vice. The former, misery, is an absolutely necessary consequence of it. Vice is a highly probable consequence, and we therefore see it abundantly prevail, but it ought not, perhaps, to be called an absolutely necessary consequence. The ordeal of virtue is to resist all temptation to evil.

This natural inequality of the two powers of population and of production in the earth, and that great law of our nature which must constantly keep their effects equal, form the great difficulty that to me appears insurmountable in the way to the perfectibility of society. All other arguments are of slight and subordinate consideration in comparison of this. I see no way by which man can escape from the weight of this law which pervades all animated nature. No fancied equality, no agrarian regulations in their utmost extent, could remove the pressure of it even for a single century. And it appears, therefore, to be decisive against the possible existence of a society, all the members of which should live in ease, happiness, and comparative leisure; and feel no anxiety about providing the means of subsistence for themselves and families.

Consequently, if the premises are just, the argument is conclusive against the perfectibility of the mass of mankind.

I have thus sketched the general outline of the argument, but I will examine it more particularly, and I think it will be found that experience, the true source and foundation of all knowledge, invariably confirms its truth.

The different ratio in which population and food increase—The necessary effects of these different ratios of increase—Oscillation produced by them in the condition of the lower classes of society - Reasons why this oscillation has not been so much observed as might be expected—Three propositions on which the general argument of the Essay depends—The different states in which mankind have been known to exist proposed to be examined with reference to these three propositions.

I said that population, when unchecked, increased in a geometrical ratio, and subsistence for man in an arithmetical ratio.

Let us examine whether this position be just. I think it will be allowed, that no state has hitherto existed (at least that we have any account of) where the manners were so pure and simple, and the means of subsistence so abundant, that no check whatever has existed to early marriages, among the lower classes, from a fear of not providing well for their families, or among the higher classes, from a fear of lowering their condition in life. Consequently in no state that we have yet known has the power of population been left to exert itself with perfect freedom.

Whether the law of marriage be instituted or not, the dictate of nature and virtue seems to be an early attachment to one woman. Supposing a liberty of changing in the case of an unfortunate choice, this liberty would not affect population till it arose to a height greatly vicious; and we are now supposing the existence of a society where vice is scarcely known.

In a state therefore of great equality and virtue, where pure and simple manners prevailed, and where the means of subsistence were so abundant that no part of the society could have any fears about providing amply for a family, the power of population being left to exert itself unchecked, the increase of the human species would evidently be much greater than any increase that has been hitherto known.

In the United States of America, where the means of subsistence have been more ample, the manners of the people more pure, and consequently the checks to early marriages fewer, than in any of the modern states of Europe, the population has been found to double itself in twenty-five years.

This ratio of increase, though short of the utmost power of population, yet as the result of actual experience, we will take as our rule, and say, that population, when unchecked, goes on doubling itself every twenty-five years or increases in a geometrical ratio.

Let us now take any spot of earth, this Island for instance, and see in what ratio the subsistence it affords can be supposed to increase. We will begin with it under its present state of cultivation.

If I allow that by the best possible policy, by breaking up more land and by great encouragements to agriculture, the produce of this Island may be doubled in the first twenty-five years, I think it will be allowing as much as any person can well demand.

In the next twenty-five years, it is impossible to suppose that the produce could be quadrupled. It would be contrary to all our knowledge of the qualities of land. The very utmost that we can conceive, is, that the increase in the second twenty-five years might equal the present produce. Let us then take this for our rule, though certainly far beyond the truth, and allow that, by great exertion, the whole produce of the Island might be increased every twenty-five years, by a quantity of subsistence equal to what it at present produces. The most enthusiastic speculator cannot suppose a greater increase than this. In a few centuries it would make every acre of land in the Island like a garden.

Yet this ratio of increase is evidently arithmetical.

It may be fairly said, therefore, that the means of subsistence increase in an arithmetical ratio. Let us now bring the effects of these two ratios together.

The population of the Island is computed to be about seven millions, and we will suppose the present produce equal to the support of such a number. In the first twenty-five years the population would be fourteen millions, and the food being also doubled, the means of subsistence would be equal to this increase. In the next twenty-five years the population would be twenty-eight millions, and the means of subsistence only equal to the support of twenty-one millions. In the next period, the population would be fifty-six millions, and the means of subsistence just sufficient for half that number. And at the conclusion of the first century the population would be one hundred and twelve millions and the means of subsistence only equal to the support of thirty-five millions, which would leave a population of seventy-seven millions totally unprovided for.

A great emigration necessarily implies unhappiness of some kind or other in the country that is deserted. For few persons will leave their families, connections, friends, and native land, to seek a settlement in untried foreign climes, without some strong subsisting causes of uneasiness where they are, or the hope of some great advantages in the place to which they are going.

But to make the argument more general and less interrupted by the partial views of emigration, let us take the whole earth, instead of one spot, and suppose that the restraints to population were universally removed. If the subsistence for man that the earth affords was to be increased every twenty-five years by a quantity equal to what the whole world at present produces, this would allow the power of production in the earth to be absolutely unlimited, and its ratio of increase much greater than we can conceive that any possible exertions of mankind could make it.

Taking the population of the world at any number, a thousand millions, for instance, the human species would increase in the ratio of -- 1, 2, 4, 8, 16, 32, 64, 128, 256, 512, etc. and subsistence as -- 1, 2, 3, 4, 5, 6, 7, 8, 9, 10, etc. In two centuries and a quarter, the population would be to the means of subsistence as 512 to 10: in three centuries as 4096 to 13, and in two thousand years the difference would be almost incalculable, though the produce in that time would have increased to an immense extent.

No limits whatever are placed to the productions of the earth; they may increase for ever and be greater than any assignable quantity. yet still the power of population being a power of a superior order, the increase of the human species can only be kept commensurate to the increase of the means of subsistence by the constant operation of the strong law of necessity acting as a check upon the greater power.

The effects of this check remain now to be considered.

Among plants and animals the view of the subject is simple. They are all impelled by a powerful instinct to the increase of their species, and this instinct is interrupted by no reasoning or doubts about providing for their offspring. Wherever therefore there is liberty, the power of increase is exerted, and the superabundant effects are repressed afterwards by want of room and nourishment, which is common to animals and plants, and among animals by becoming the prey of others.

The effects of this check on man are more complicated. Impelled to the increase of his species by an equally powerful instinct, reason interrupts his career and asks him whether he may not bring beings into the world for whom he cannot provide the means of subsistence. In a state of equality, this would be the simple question. In the present state of society, other considerations occur. Will he not lower his rank in life? Will he not subject himself to greater difficulties than he at present feels? Will he not be obliged to labour harder? and if he has a large family, will his utmost exertions enable him to support them? May he not see his offspring in rags and misery, and clamouring for bread that he cannot give them? And may he not be reduced to the grating necessity of forfeiting his independence, and of being obliged to the sparing hand of charity for support?

These considerations are calculated to prevent, and certainly do prevent, a very great number in all civilized nations from pursuing the dictate of nature in an early attachment to one woman. And this restraint almost necessarily, though not absolutely so, produces vice. Yet in all societies, even those that are most vicious, the tendency to a virtuous attachment is so strong that there is a constant effort towards an increase of population. This constant effort as constantly tends to subject the lower classes of the society to distress and to prevent any great permanent amelioration of their condition.

The way in which, these effects are produced seems to be this. We will suppose the means of subsistence in any country just equal to the easy support of its inhabitants. The constant effort towards population, which is found to act even in the most vicious societies, increases the number of people before the means of subsistence are increased. The food therefore which before supported seven millions must now be divided among seven millions and a half or eight millions. The poor consequently must live much worse, and many of them be reduced to severe distress. The number of labourers also being above the proportion of the work in the market, the price of labour must tend toward a decrease, while the price of provisions would at the same time tend to rise. The labourer therefore must work harder to earn the same as he did before. During this season of distress, the discouragements to marriage, and the difficulty of rearing a family are so great that population is at a stand. In the mean time the cheapness of labour, the plenty of labourers, and the necessity of an increased industry amongst them, encourage cultivators to employ more labour upon their land, to turn up fresh soil, and to manure and improve more completely what is already in tillage, till ultimately the means of subsistence become in the same proportion to the population as at the period from which we set out. The situation of the labourer being then again tolerably comfortable, the restraints to population are in some degree loosened, and the same retrograde and progressive movements with respect to happiness are repeated.

This sort of oscillation will not be remarked by superficial observers, and it may be difficult even for the most penetrating mind to calculate its periods. Yet that in all old states some such vibration does exist, though from various transverse causes, in a much less marked, and in a much more irregular manner than I have described it, no reflecting man who considers the subject deeply can well doubt.

Many reasons occur why this oscillation has been less obvious, and less decidedly confirmed by experience, than might naturally be expected.

One principal reason is that the histories of mankind that we possess are histories only of the higher classes. We have but few accounts that can be depended upon of the manners and customs of that part of mankind where these retrograde and progressive movements chiefly take place. A satisfactory history of this kind, on one people, and of one period, would require the constant and minute attention of an observing mind during a long life. Some of the objects of inquiry would be, in what proportion to the number of adults was the number of marriages, to what extent vicious customs prevailed in consequence of the restraints upon matrimony, what was the comparative mortality among the children of the most distressed part of the community and those who lived rather more at their ease, what were the variations in the real price of labour, and what were the observable differences in the state of the lower classes of society with respect to ease and happiness, at different times during a certain period.

Such a history would tend greatly to elucidate the manner in which the constant check upon population acts and would probably prove the existence of the retrograde and progressive movements that have been mentioned, though the times of their vibrations must necessarily be rendered irregular from the operation of many interrupting causes, such as the introduction or failure of certain manufactures, a greater or less prevalent spirit of agricultural enterprise, years of plenty, or years of scarcity, wars and pestilence, poor laws, the invention of processes for shortening labour without the proportional extension of the market for the commodity, and, particularly, the difference between the nominal and real price of labour, a circumstance which has perhaps more than any other

contributed to conceal this oscillation from common view.

It very rarely happens that the nominal price of labour universally falls, but we well know that it frequently remains the same, while the nominal price of provisions has been gradually increasing. This is, in effect, a real fall in the price of labour, and during this period the condition of the lower orders of the community must gradually grow worse and worse. But the farmers and capitalists are growing rich from the real cheapness of labour. Their increased capitals enable them to employ a greater number of men. Work therefore may be plentiful, and the price of labour would consequently rise. But the want of freedom in the market of labour, which occurs more or less in all communities, either from parish laws, or the more general cause of the facility of combination among the rich, and its difficulty among the poor, operates to prevent the price of labour from rising at the natural period, and keeps it down some time longer; perhaps till a year of scarcity, when the clamour is too loud and the necessity too apparent to be resisted.

The true cause of the advance in the price of labour is thus concealed, and the rich affect to grant it as an act of compassion and favour to the poor, in consideration of a year of scarcity, and, when plenty returns, indulge themselves in the most unreasonable of all complaints, that the price does not again fall, when a little rejection would shew them that it must have risen long before but from an unjust conspiracy of their own.

But though the rich by unfair combinations contribute frequently to prolong a season of distress among the poor, yet no possible form of society could prevent the almost constant action of misery upon a great part of mankind, if in a state of inequality, and upon all, if all were equal.

The theory on which the truth of this position depends appears to me so extremely clear that I feel at a loss to conjecture what part of it can be denied.

That population cannot increase without the means of subsistence is a proposition so evident that it needs no illustration.

That population does invariably increase where there are the means of subsistence, the history of every people that have ever existed will abundantly prove.

And that the superior power of population cannot be checked without producing misery or vice, the ample portion of these too bitter ingredients in the cup of human life and the continuance of the. physical causes that seem to have produced them bear too convincing a testimony.

But, in order more fully to ascertain the validity of these three propositions, let us examine the different states in which mankind have been known to exist. Even a cursory review will, I think, be sufficient to convince us that these propositions are incontrovertible truths.

1

What is the main purpose of this passage?

_____

2

What is the passage's tone?

_____

3

How would you summarize the passage?

_____

4

What is the author's central thesis?

_____

"THE FAD OF THE FISHERMAN" – G. K. CHESTERTON

The following passage is adapted from G. K. Chesterton's *The Man Who Knew Too Much*. Chesterton (1874–1936) was an English author and philosopher. *The Man Who Knew Too Much* centers on Horne Fisher, a man all too connected with the British aristocracy and its seedy backroom politics.

A thing can sometimes be too extraordinary to be remembered. If it is clean out of the course of things, and has apparently no causes and no consequences, subsequent events do not recall it, and it remains only a subconscious thing, to be stirred by some accident long after. It drifts apart like a forgotten dream; and it was in the hour of many dreams, at daybreak and very soon after the end of dark, that such a strange sight was given to a man sculling a boat down a river in the West country. The man was awake; indeed, he considered himself rather wide awake, being the political journalist, Harold March, on his way to interview various political celebrities in their country seats. But the thing he saw was so inconsequent that it might have been imaginary. It simply slipped past his mind and was lost in later and utterly different events; nor did he even recover the memory till he had long afterward discovered the meaning.

Pale mists of morning lay on the fields and the rushes along one margin of the river; along the other side ran a wall of tawny brick almost overhanging the water. He had shipped his oars and was drifting for a moment with the stream, when he turned his head and saw that the monotony of the long brick wall was broken by a bridge; rather an elegant eighteenth-century sort of bridge with little columns of white stone turning gray. There had been floods and the river still stood very high, with dwarfish trees waist deep in it, and rather a narrow arc of white dawn gleamed under the curve of the bridge.

As his own boat went under the dark archway he saw another boat coming toward him, rowed by a man as solitary as himself. His posture prevented much being seen of him, but as he neared the bridge he stood up in the boat and turned round. He was already so close to the dark entry, however, that his whole figure was black against the morning light, and March could see nothing of his face except the end of two long whiskers or mustaches that gave something sinister to the silhouette, like horns in the wrong place. Even these details March would never have noticed but for what happened in the same instant. As the man came under the low bridge he made a leap at it and hung, with his legs dangling, letting the boat float away from under him. March had a momentary vision of two black kicking legs; then of one black kicking leg; and then of nothing except the eddying stream and the long perspective of the wall. But whenever he thought of it again, long afterward, when he understood the story in which it figured, it was always fixed in that one fantastic shape—as if those wild legs were a grotesque graven ornament of the bridge itself, in the manner of a gargoyle. At the moment he merely passed, staring, down the stream. He could see no flying figure on the bridge, so it must have already fled; but he was half conscious of some faint significance in the fact that among the trees round the bridgehead opposite the wall he saw a lamp-post; and, beside the lamp-post, the broad blue back of an unconscious policeman.

Even before reaching the shrine of his political pilgrimage he had many other things to think of besides the odd incident of the bridge; for the management of a boat by a solitary man was not always easy even on such a solitary stream. And indeed it was only by an unforeseen accident that he was solitary. The boat had been purchased and the whole expedition planned in conjunction with a friend, who had at the last moment been forced to alter all his arrangements. Harold March was to have traveled with his friend Horne Fisher on that inland voyage to Willowood Place, where the Prime Minister was a guest at the moment. More and more people were hearing of Harold March, for his striking political articles were opening to him the doors of larger and larger salons; but he had never met the Prime Minister yet. Scarcely anybody among the general public had ever heard of Horne Fisher; but he had known the Prime Minister all his life. For these reasons, had the two taken the projected journey together, March might have been slightly disposed to hasten it and Fisher vaguely content to lengthen it out. For Fisher was one of those people who are born knowing the Prime Minister. The knowledge seemed to have no very exhilarant effect, and in his case bore some resemblance to being born tired. But he was distinctly annoyed to receive, just as he was doing a little light packing of fishing tackle and cigars for the journey, a telegram from Willowood asking him to come down at once by train, as the Prime Minister had to leave that night. Fisher knew that his friend the journalist could not possibly start till the next day, and he liked his friend the journalist, and had looked forward to a few days on the river. He did not particularly like or dislike the Prime Minister, but he intensely disliked the alternative of a few hours in the train. Nevertheless, he accepted Prime Ministers as he accepted railway trains—as part of a system which he, at least, was not the revolutionist sent on earth to destroy. So he telephoned to March, asking him, with many apologetic curses and faint damns, to take the boat down the river as arranged, that they might meet at Willowood by the time settled; then he went outside and hailed a taxicab to take him to the railway station. There he paused at the bookstall to add to his light luggage a number of cheap murder stories, which he read with great pleasure, and without any premonition that he was about to walk into as strange a story in real life.

A little before sunset he arrived, with his light suitcase in hand, before the gate of the long riverside gardens of Willowood Place, one of the smaller seats of Sir Isaac Hook, the master of much shipping and many newspapers. He entered by the gate giving on the road, at the opposite side to the river, but there was a mixed quality in all that watery landscape which perpetually reminded a traveler that the river was near. White gleams of water would shine suddenly like swords or spears in the green thickets. And even in the garden itself, divided into courts and curtained with hedges and high garden trees, there hung everywhere in the air the music of water. The first of the green courts which he entered appeared to be a somewhat neglected croquet lawn, in which was a solitary young man playing croquet against himself. Yet he was not an enthusiast for the game, or even for the garden; and his sallow but well-featured face looked rather sullen than otherwise. He was only one of those young men who cannot support the burden of consciousness unless they are doing something, and whose conceptions of doing something are limited to a game of some kind. He was dark and well dressed in a light holiday fashion, and Fisher recognized him at once as a young man named James Bullen, called, for some unknown reason, Bunker. He was the nephew of Sir Isaac; but, what was much more important at the moment, he was also the private secretary of the Prime Minister.

"Hullo, Bunker!" observed Horne Fisher. "You're the sort of man I wanted to see. Has your chief come down yet?"

"He's only staying for dinner," replied Bullen, with his eye on the yellow ball. "He's got a great speech to-morrow at Birmingham and he's going straight through to-night. He's motoring himself there; driving the car, I mean. It's the one thing he's really proud of."

"You mean you're staying here with your uncle, like a good boy?" replied Fisher. "But what will the Chief do at Birmingham without the epigrams whispered to him by his brilliant secretary?"

"Don't you start ragging me," said the young man called Bunker. "I'm only too glad not to go trailing after him. He doesn't know a thing about maps or money or hotels or anything, and I have to dance

about like a courier. As for my uncle, as I'm supposed to come into the estate, it's only decent to be here sometimes."

"Very proper," replied the other. "Well, I shall see you later on," and, crossing the lawn, he passed out through a gap in the hedge.

He was walking across the lawn toward the landing stage on the river, and still felt all around him, under the dome of golden evening, an Old World savor and reverberation in that riverhaunted garden. The next square of turf which he crossed seemed at first sight quite deserted, till he saw in the twilight of trees in one corner of it a hammock and in the hammock a man, reading a newspaper and swinging one leg over the edge of the net.

Him also he hailed by name, and the man slipped to the ground and strolled forward. It seemed fated that he should feel something of the past in the accidents of that place, for the figure might well have been an early-Victorian ghost revisiting the ghosts of the croquet hoops and mallets. It was the figure of an elderly man with long whiskers that looked almost fantastic, and a quaint and careful cut of collar and cravat. Having been a fashionable dandy forty years ago, he had managed to preserve the dandyism while ignoring the fashions. A white top-hat lay beside the Morning Post in the hammock behind him. This was the Duke of Westmoreland, the relic of a family really some centuries old; and the antiquity was not heraldry but history. Nobody knew better than Fisher how rare such noblemen are in fact, and how numerous in fiction. But whether the duke owed the general respect he enjoyed to the genuineness of his pedigree or to the fact that he owned a vast amount of very valuable property was a point about which Mr. Fisher's opinion might have been more interesting to discover.

"You were looking so comfortable," said Fisher, "that I thought you must be one of the servants. I'm looking for somebody to take this bag of mine; I haven't brought a man down, as I came away in a hurry."

"Nor have I, for that matter," replied the duke, with some pride. "I never do. If there's one animal alive I loathe it's a valet. I learned to dress myself at an early age and was supposed to do it decently. I may be in my second childhood, but I've not go so far as being dressed like a child."

"The Prime Minister hasn't brought a valet; he's brought a secretary instead," observed Fisher. "Devilish inferior job. Didn't I hear that Harker was down here?"

"He's over there on the landing stage," replied the duke, indifferently, and resumed the study of the Morning Post.

Fisher made his way beyond the last green wall of the garden on to a sort of towing path looking on the river and a wooden island opposite. There, indeed, he saw a lean, dark figure with a stoop almost like that of a vulture, a posture well known in the law courts as that of Sir John Harker, the Attorney-General. His face was lined with headwork, for alone among the three idlers in the garden he was a man who had made his own way; and round his bald brow and hollow temples clung dull red hair, quite flat, like plates of copper.

"I haven't seen my host yet," said Horne Fisher, in a slightly more serious tone than he had used to the others, "but I suppose I shall meet him at dinner."

"You can see him now; but you can't meet him," answered Harker.

He nodded his head toward one end of the island opposite, and, looking steadily in the same direction, the other guest could see the dome of a bald head and the top of a fishing rod, both equally motionless, rising out of the tall undergrowth against the background of the stream beyond. The fisherman seemed to be seated against the stump of a tree and facing toward the other bank, so that his face could not be seen, but the shape of his head was unmistakable.

"He doesn't like to be disturbed when he's fishing," continued Harker. "It's a sort of fad of his to eat nothing but fish, and he's very proud of catching his own. Of course he's all for simplicity, like so many of these millionaires. He likes to come in saying he's worked for his daily bread like a laborer."

"Does he explain how he blows all the glass and stuffs all the upholstery," asked Fisher, "and makes all the silver forks, and grows all the grapes and peaches, and designs all the patterns on the carpets? I've always heard he was a busy man."

"I don't think he mentioned it," answered the lawyer. "What is the meaning of this social satire?"

"Well, I am a trifle tired," said Fisher, "of the Simple Life and the Strenuous Life as lived by our little set. We're all really dependent in nearly everything, and we all make a fuss about being independent in something. The Prime Minister prides himself on doing without a chauffeur, but he can't do without a factotum and Jack-of-all-trades; and poor old Bunker has to play the part of a universal genius, which God knows he was never meant for. The duke prides himself on doing without a valet, but, for all that, he must give a lot of people an infernal lot of trouble to collect such extraordinary old clothes as he wears. He must have them looked up in the British Museum or excavated out of the tombs. That white hat alone must require a sort of expedition fitted out to find it, like the North Pole. And here we have old Hook pretending to produce his own fish when he couldn't produce his

own fish knives or fish forks to eat it with. He may be simple about simple things like food, but you bet he's luxurious about luxurious things, especially little things. I don't include you; you've worked too hard to enjoy playing at work."

"I sometimes think," said Harker, "that you conceal a horrid secret of being useful sometimes. Haven't you come down here to see Number One before he goes on to Birmingham?"

Horne Fisher answered, in a lower voice: "Yes; and I hope to be lucky enough to catch him before dinner. He's got to see Sir Isaac about something just afterward."

"Hullo!" exclaimed Harker. "Sir Isaac's finished his fishing. I know he prides himself on getting up at sunrise and going in at sunset."

The old man on the island had indeed risen to his feet, facing round and showing a bush of gray beard with rather small, sunken features, but fierce eyebrows and keen, choleric eyes. Carefully carrying his fishing tackle, he was already making his way back to the mainland across a bridge of flat stepping-stones a little way down the shallow stream; then he veered round, coming toward his guests and civilly saluting them. There were several fish in his basket and he was in a good temper.

"Yes," he said, acknowledging Fisher's polite expression of surprise, "I get up before anybody else in the house, I think. The early bird catches the worm."

"Unfortunately," said Harker, "it is the early fish that catches the worm."

"But the early man catches the fish," replied the old man, gruffly.

"But from what I hear, Sir Isaac, you are the late man, too," interposed Fisher. "You must do with very little sleep."

"I never had much time for sleeping," answered Hook, "and I shall have to be the late man to-night, anyhow. The Prime Minister wants to have a talk, he tells me, and, all things considered, I think we'd better be dressing for dinner."

Dinner passed off that evening without a word of politics and little enough but ceremonial trifles. The Prime Minister, Lord Merivale, who was a long, slim man with curly gray hair, was gravely complimentary to his host about his success as a fisherman and the skill and patience he displayed; the conversation flowed like the shallow stream through the stepping-stones.

"It wants patience to wait for them, no doubt," said Sir Isaac, "and skill to play them, but I'm generally pretty lucky at it."

"Does a big fish ever break the line and get away?" inquired the politician, with respectful interest.

"Not the sort of line I use," answered Hook, with satisfaction. "I rather specialize in tackle, as a matter of fact. If he were strong enough to do that, he'd be strong enough to pull me into the river."

"A great loss to the community," said the Prime Minister, bowing.

Fisher had listened to all these futilities with inward impatience, waiting for his own opportunity, and when the host rose he sprang to his feet with an alertness he rarely showed. He managed to catch Lord Merivale before Sir Isaac bore him off for the final interview. He had only a few words to say, but he wanted to get them said.

He said, in a low voice as he opened the door for the Premier, "I have seen Montmirail; he says that unless we protest immediately on behalf of Denmark, Sweden will certainly seize the ports."

Lord Merivale nodded. "I'm just going to hear what Hook has to say about it," he said.

"I imagine," said Fisher, with a faint smile, "that there is very little doubt what he will say about it."

Merivale did not answer, but lounged gracefully toward the library, whither his host had already preceded him. The rest drifted toward the billiard room, Fisher merely remarking to the lawyer: "They won't be long. We know they're practically in agreement."

"Hook entirely supports the Prime Minister," assented Harker.

"Or the Prime Minister entirely supports Hook," said Horne Fisher, and began idly to knock the balls about on the billiard table.

Horne Fisher came down next morning in a late and leisurely fashion, as was his reprehensible habit; he had evidently no appetite for catching worms. But the other guests seemed to have felt a similar indifference, and they helped themselves to breakfast from the sideboard at intervals during the hours verging upon lunch. So that it was not many hours later when the first sensation of that strange day came upon them. It came in the form of a young man with light hair and a candid expression, who came sculling down the river and disembarked at the landing stage. It was, in fact, no other than Mr. Harold March, whose journey had begun far away up the river in the earliest hours of that day. He arrived late in the afternoon, having stopped for tea in a large riverside town, and he had a pink evening paper sticking out of his pocket. He fell on the riverside garden like a quiet and well-behaved thunderbolt, but he was a thunderbolt without knowing it.

The first exchange of salutations and introductions was commonplace enough, and consisted, indeed, of the inevitable repetition of excuses for the eccentric seclusion of the host. He had gone fishing again, of course, and must not be disturbed till the appointed hour, though he sat within a stone's throw of where they stood.

"You see it's his only hobby," observed Harker, apologetically, "and, after all, it's his own house; and he's very hospitable in other ways."

"I'm rather afraid," said Fisher, in a lower voice, "that it's becoming more of a mania than a hobby. I know how it is when a man of that age begins to collect things, if it's only collecting those rotten little river fish. You remember Talbot's uncle with his toothpicks, and poor old Buzzy and the waste of cigar ashes. Hook has done a lot of big things in his time—the great deal in the Swedish timber trade and the Peace Conference at Chicago—but I doubt whether he cares now for any of those big things as he cares for those little fish."

"Oh, come, come," protested the Attorney-General. "You'll make Mr. March think he has come to call on a lunatic. Believe me, Hook only does it for fun, like any other sport, only he's of the kind that takes his fun sadly. But I bet if there were big news about timber or shipping, he would drop his fun and his fish all right."

"Well, I wonder," said Horne Fisher, looking sleepily at the island in the river.

"By the way, is there any news of anything?" asked Harker of Harold March. "I see you've got an evening paper; one of those enterprising evening papers that come out in the morning."

"The beginning of Lord Merivale's Birmingham speech," replied March, handing him the paper. "It's only a paragraph, but it seems to me rather good."

Harker took the paper, flapped and refolded it, and looked at the "Stop Press" news. It was, as March had said, only a paragraph. But it was a paragraph that had a peculiar effect on Sir John Harker. His lowering brows lifted with a flicker and his eyes blinked, and for a moment his leathery jaw was loosened. He looked in some odd fashion like a very old man. Then, hardening his voice and handing the paper to Fisher without a tremor, he simply said:

"Well, here's a chance for the bet. You've got your big news to disturb the old man's fishing."

Horne Fisher was looking at the paper, and over his more languid and less expressive features a change also seemed to pass. Even that little paragraph had two or three large headlines, and his eye encountered, "Sensational Warning to Sweden," and, "We Shall Protest."

"What the devil—" he said, and his words softened first to a whisper and then a whistle.

"We must tell old Hook at once, or he'll never forgive us," said Harker. "He'll probably want to see Number One instantly, though it may be too late now. I'm going across to him at once. I bet I'll make him forget his fish, anyhow." And, turning his back, he made his way hurriedly along the riverside to the causeway of flat stones.

March was staring at Fisher, in amazement at the effect his pink paper had produced.

"What does it all mean?" he cried. "I always supposed we should protest in defense of the Danish ports, for their sakes and our own. What is all this botheration about Sir Isaac and the rest of you? Do you think it bad news?"

"Bad news!" repeated Fisher, with a sort of soft emphasis beyond expression.

"Is it as bad as all that?" asked his friend, at last.

"As bad as all that?" repeated Fisher. "Why of course it's as good as it can be. It's great news. It's glorious news! That's where the devil of it comes in, to knock us all silly. It's admirable. It's inestimable. It is also quite incredible."

He gazed again at the gray and green colors of the island and the river, and his rather dreary eye traveled slowly round to the hedges and the lawns.

"I felt this garden was a sort of dream," he said, "and I suppose I must be dreaming. But there is grass growing and water moving; and something impossible has happened."

Even as he spoke the dark figure with a stoop like a vulture appeared in the gap of the hedge just above him.

"You have won your bet," said Harker, in a harsh and almost croaking voice. "The old fool cares for nothing but fishing. He cursed me and told me he would talk no politics."

"I thought it might be so," said Fisher, modestly. "What are you going to do next?"

"I shall use the old idiot's telephone, anyhow," replied the lawyer. "I must find out exactly what has happened. I've got to speak for the Government myself to-morrow." And he hurried away toward the house.

In the silence that followed, a very bewildering silence so far as March was concerned, they saw the quaint figure of the Duke of Westmoreland, with his white hat and whiskers, approaching them across the garden. Fisher instantly stepped toward him with the pink paper in his hand, and, with a few words, pointed out the apocalyptic paragraph. The duke, who had been walking slowly, stood quite still, and for some seconds he looked like a tailor's dummy standing and staring outside some antiquated shop. Then March heard his voice, and it was high and almost hysterical:

"But he must see it; he must be made to understand. It cannot have been put to him properly." Then, with a certain recovery of fullness and even pomposity in the voice, "I shall go and tell him myself."

Among the queer incidents of that afternoon, March always remembered something almost comical about the clear picture of the old gentleman in his wonderful white hat carefully stepping from stone to stone across the river, like a figure crossing the traffic in Piccadilly. Then he disappeared behind the trees of the island, and March and Fisher turned to meet the Attorney-General, who was coming out of the house with a visage of grim assurance.

"Everybody is saying," he said, "that the Prime Minister has made the greatest speech of his life. Peroration and loud and prolonged cheers. Corrupt financiers and heroic peasants. We will not desert Denmark again."

Fisher nodded and turned away toward the towing path, where he saw the duke returning with a rather dazed expression. In answer to questions he said, in a husky and confidential voice:

"I really think our poor friend cannot be himself. He refused to listen; he—ah—suggested that I might frighten the fish."

A keen ear might have detected a murmur from Mr. Fisher on the subject of a white hat, but Sir John Harker struck it more decisively:

"Fisher was quite right. I didn't believe it myself, but it's quite clear that the old fellow is fixed on this fishing notion by now. If the house caught fire behind him he would hardly move till sunset."

Fisher had continued his stroll toward the higher embanked ground of the towing path, and he now swept a long and searching gaze, not toward the island, but toward the distant wooded heights that were the walls of the valley. An evening sky as clear as that of the previous day was settling down all over the dim landscape, but toward the west it was now red rather than gold; there was scarcely any sound but the monotonous music of the river. Then came the sound of a half-stifled exclamation from Horne Fisher, and Harold March looked up at him in wonder.

"You spoke of bad news," said Fisher. "Well, there is really bad news now. I am afraid this is a bad business."

"What bad news do you mean?" asked his friend, conscious of something strange and sinister in his voice.

"The sun has set," answered Fisher.

He went on with the air of one conscious of having said something fatal. "We must get somebody to go across whom he will really listen to. He may be mad, but there's method in his madness. There nearly always is method in madness. It's what drives men mad, being methodical. And he never goes on sitting there after sunset, with the whole place getting dark. Where's his nephew? I believe he's really fond of his nephew."

"Look!" cried March, abruptly. "Why, he's been across already.
There he is coming back."

And, looking up the river once more, they saw, dark against the sunset reflections, the figure of James Bullen stepping hastily and rather clumsily from stone to stone. Once he slipped on a stone with a slight splash. When he rejoined the group on the bank his olive face was unnaturally pale.

The other four men had already gathered on the same spot and almost simultaneously were calling out to him, "What does he say now?"

"Nothing. He says—nothing."

Fisher looked at the young man steadily for a moment; then he started from his immobility and, making a motion to March to follow him, himself strode down to the river crossing. In a few moments they were on the little beaten track that ran round the wooded island, to the other side of it where the fisherman sat. Then they stood and looked at him, without a word.

Sir Isaac Hook was still sitting propped up against the stump of the tree, and that for the best of reasons. A length of his own infallible fishing line was twisted and tightened twice round his throat and then twice round the wooden prop behind him. The leading investigator ran forward and touched the fisherman's hand, and it was as cold as a fish.

"The sun has set," said Horne Fisher, in the same terrible tones, "and he will never see it rise again."

Ten minutes afterward the five men, shaken by such a shock, were again together in the garden, looking at one another with white but watchful faces. The lawyer seemed the most alert of the group; he was articulate if somewhat abrupt.

"We must leave the body as it is and telephone for the police," he said. "I think my own authority will stretch to examining the servants and the poor fellow's papers, to see if there is anything that concerns them. Of course, none of you gentlemen must leave this place."

Perhaps there was something in his rapid and rigorous legality that suggested the closing of a net or trap. Anyhow, young Bullen suddenly broke down, or perhaps blew up, for his voice was like an explosion in the silent garden.

"I never touched him," he cried. "I swear I had nothing to do with it!"

"Who said you had?" demanded Harker, with a hard eye. "Why do you cry out before you're hurt?"

"Because you all look at me like that," cried the young man, angrily. "Do you think I don't know you're always talking about my damned debts and expectations?"

Rather to March's surprise, Fisher had drawn away from this first collision, leading the duke with him to another part of the garden. When he was out of earshot of the others he said, with a curious simplicity of manner:

"Westmoreland, I am going straight to the point."

"Well?" said the other, staring at him stolidly.

"You have a motive for killing him," said Fisher.

The duke continued to stare, but he seemed unable to speak.

"I hope you had a motive for killing him," continued Fisher, mildly. "You see, it's rather a curious situation. If you have a motive for murdering, you probably didn't murder. But if you hadn't any motive, why, then perhaps, you did."

"What on earth are you talking about?" demanded the duke, violently.

"It's quite simple," said Fisher. "When you went across he was either alive or dead. If he was alive, it might be you who killed him, or why should you have held your tongue about his death? But if he was dead, and you had a reason for killing him, you might have held your tongue for fear of being accused." Then after a silence he added, abstractedly: "Cyprus is a beautiful place, I believe. Romantic scenery and romantic people. Very intoxicating for a young man."

The duke suddenly clenched his hands and said, thickly, "Well, I had a motive."

"Then you're all right," said Fisher, holding out his hand with an air of huge relief. "I was pretty sure you wouldn't really do it; you had a fright when you saw it done, as was only natural. Like a bad dream come true, wasn't it?"

While this curious conversation was passing, Harker had gone into the house, disregarding the demonstrations of the sulky nephew, and came back presently with a new air of animation and a sheaf of papers in his hand.

"I've telephoned for the police," he said, stopping to speak to Fisher, "but I think I've done most of their work for them. I believe I've found out the truth. There's a paper here—" He stopped, for Fisher was looking at him with a singular expression; and it was Fisher who spoke next:

"Are there any papers that are not there, I wonder? I mean that are not there now?" After a pause he added: "Let us have the cards on the table. When you went through his papers in such a hurry, Harker, weren't you looking for something to—to make sure it shouldn't be found?"

Harker did not turn a red hair on his hard head, but he looked at the other out of the corners of his eyes.

"And I suppose," went on Fisher, smoothly, "that is why you, too, told us lies about having found Hook alive. You knew there was something to show that you might have killed him, and you didn't dare tell us he was killed. But, believe me, it's much better to be honest now."

Harker's haggard face suddenly lit up as if with infernal flames.

"Honest," he cried, "it's not so damned fine of you fellows to be honest. You're all born with silver spoons in your mouths, and then you swagger about with everlasting virtue because you haven't got other people's spoons in your pockets. But I was born in a Pimlico lodging house and I had to make my spoon, and there'd be plenty to say I only spoiled a horn or an honest man. And if a struggling man staggers a bit over the line in his youth, in the lower parts of the law which are pretty dingy, anyhow, there's always some old vampire to hang on to him all his life for it."

"Guatemalan Golcondas, wasn't it?" said Fisher, sympathetically.

Harker suddenly shuddered. Then he said, "I believe you must know everything, like God Almighty."

"I know too much," said Horne Fisher, "and all the wrong things."

The other three men were drawing nearer to them, but before they came too near, Harker said, in a voice that had recovered all its firmness:

"Yes, I did destroy a paper, but I really did find a paper, too; and
I believe that it clears us all."

"Very well," said Fisher, in a louder and more cheerful tone; "let us all have the benefit of it."

"On the very top of Sir Isaac's papers," explained Harker, "there was a threatening letter from a man named Hugo. It threatens to kill our unfortunate friend very much in the way that he was actually killed. It is a wild letter, full of taunts; you can see it for yourselves; but it makes a particular point of poor Hook's habit of fishing from the island. Above all, the man professes to be writing from a boat. And, since we alone went across to him," and he smiled in a rather ugly fashion, "the crime must have been committed by a man passing in a boat."

"Why, dear me!" cried the duke, with something almost amounting to animation. "Why, I remember the man called Hugo quite well! He was a sort of body servant and bodyguard of Sir Isaac. You see, Sir Isaac was in some fear of assault. He was—he was not very popular with several people. Hugo was discharged after some row or other; but I remember him well. He was a great big Hungarian fellow with great mustaches that stood out on each side of his face."

A door opened in the darkness of Harold March's memory, or, rather, oblivion, and showed a shining

landscape, like that of a lost dream. It was rather a waterscape than a landscape, a thing of flooded meadows and low trees and the dark archway of a bridge. And for one instant he saw again the man with mustaches like dark horns leap up on to the bridge and disappear.

"Good heavens!" he cried. "Why, I met the murderer this morning!"

* * *

Horne Fisher and Harold March had their day on the river, after all, for the little group broke up when the police arrived. They declared that the coincidence of March's evidence had cleared the whole company, and clinched the case against the flying Hugo. Whether that Hungarian fugitive would ever be caught appeared to Horne Fisher to be highly doubtful; nor can it be pretended that he displayed any very demoniac detective energy in the matter as he leaned back in the boat cushions, smoking, and watching the swaying reeds slide past.

"It was a very good notion to hop up on to the bridge," he said. "An empty boat means very little; he hasn't been seen to land on either bank, and he's walked off the bridge without walking on to it, so to speak. He's got twenty-four hours' start; his mustaches will disappear, and then he will disappear. I think there is every hope of his escape."

"Hope?" repeated March, and stopped sculling for an instant.

"Yes, hope," repeated the other. "To begin with, I'm not going to be exactly consumed with Corsican revenge because somebody has killed Hook. Perhaps you may guess by this time what Hook was. A damned blood-sucking blackmailer was that simple, strenuous, self-made captain of industry. He had secrets against nearly everybody; one against poor old Westmoreland about an early marriage in Cyprus that might have put the duchess in a queer position; and one against Harker about some flutter with his client's money when he was a young solicitor. That's why they went to pieces when they found him murdered, of course. They felt as if they'd done it in a dream. But I admit I have another reason for not wanting our Hungarian friend actually hanged for the murder."

"And what is that?" asked his friend.

"Only that he didn't commit the murder," answered Fisher.

Harold March laid down the oars and let the boat drift for a moment.

"Do you know, I was half expecting something like that," he said. "It was quite irrational, but it was hanging about in the atmosphere, like thunder in the air."

"On the contrary, it's finding Hugo guilty that's irrational," replied Fisher. "Don't you see that they're condemning him for the very reason for which they acquit everybody else? Harker and Westmoreland were silent because they found him murdered, and knew there were papers that made them look like the murderers. Well, so did Hugo find him murdered, and so did Hugo know there was a paper that would make him look like the murderer. He had written it himself the day before."

"But in that case," said March, frowning, "at what sort of unearthly hour in the morning was the murder really committed? It was barely daylight when I met him at the bridge, and that's some way above the island."

"The answer is very simple," replied Fisher. "The crime was not committed in the morning. The crime was not committed on the island."

March stared at the shining water without replying, but Fisher resumed like one who had been asked a question:

"Every intelligent murder involves taking advantage of some one uncommon feature in a common situation. The feature here was the fancy of old Hook for being the first man up every morning, his fixed routine as an angler, and his annoyance at being disturbed. The murderer strangled him in his own house after dinner on the night before, carried his corpse, with all his fishing tackle, across the stream in the dead of night, tied him to the tree, and left him there under the stars. It was a dead man who sat fishing there all day. Then the murderer went back to the house, or, rather, to the garage, and went off in his motor car. The murderer drove his own motor car."

Fisher glanced at his friend's face and went on. "You look horrified, and the thing is horrible. But other things are horrible, too. If some obscure man had been hag-ridden by a blackmailer and had his family life ruined, you wouldn't think the murder of his persecutor the most inexcusable of murders. Is it any worse when a whole great nation is set free as well as a family? By this warning to Sweden we shall probably prevent war and not precipitate it, and save many thousand lives rather more valuable than the life of that viper. Oh, I'm not talking sophistry or seriously justifying the thing, but the slavery that held him and his country was a thousand times less justifiable. If I'd really been sharp I should have guessed it from his smooth, deadly smiling at dinner that night. Do you remember that silly talk about how old Isaac could always play his fish? In a pretty hellish sense he was a fisher of men."

Harold March took the oars and began to row again.

"I remember," he said, "and about how a big fish might break the line and get away."

1 What is the main purpose of this passage?

_____

2 What is the passage's tone?

_____

3 How would you summarize the passage?

_____

4 How would you describe Horne Fisher?

_____

THE FARMER AND THE FARMER REFUTED – SAMUEL SEABURY AND ALEXANDER HAMILTON

Passage 1 is from Samuel Seabury, *Letters of a Westchester Farmer*, published in January 1775. Passage 2 is from Alexander Hamilton, *A Farmer Refuted*, published in February 1775.

Letters of a Westchester Farmer

Honourable Gentlemen,

WHEN you reflect upon the present confused and distressed state of this, and the other colonies, I am persuaded, that you will think no apology necessary for the liberty I have taken, of addressing you on that subject. The unhappy contention we have entered into with our parent state, would inevitably be attended with many disagreeable circumstances, with many and great inconveniences to us, even were it conducted on our part, with propriety and moderation. What then must be the case, when all proper and moderate measures are rejected? When not even the appearance of decency is regarded? When nothing seems to be consulted, but how to perplex, irritate, and affront, the British Ministry, Parliament, Nation and King? When every scheme that tends to peace, is branded with ignominy; as being the machination of slavery! When nothing is called FREEDOM but SEDITION! Nothing LIBERTY but REBELLION!

I will not presume to encroach so far upon your time, as to attempt to point out the causes of our unnatural contention with Great Britain. You are well acquainted with them—Nor will I attempt to trace out the progress of that infatuation, which hath so deeply, so miserably, infected the Colonies. You must have observed its rise, and noted its rapid growth. But I intreat your patience and candour, while I make some observations on the conduct of the Colonies in general, and of this Colony in particular, in the present dispute with our mother country: By which it will appear, that most, if not all the measures that have been adopted, have been illegal in their beginning, tyrannical in their operation—and that they must be ineffectual in the event.

It is the happiness of the British Government, and of all the British Colonies, that the people have a right to share in the legislature. This right they exercise by choosing representatives; and thereby constituting one branch of the legislative authority. But when they have chosen their representatives, that right, which was before diffused through the whole people, centers in their Representatives alone; and can legally be exercised by none but them. They become the guardians of the lives, the liberties, the rights and properties, of the people: And as they are under the most sacred obligations to discharge their trust with prudence and fidelity, so the people are under the strongest obligations to treat them with honour and respect; and to look to them for redress of all those grievances that they can justly complain of.

But in the present dispute with Great Britain, the representatives of the people have not only been utterly disregarded, but their dignity has been trampled upon, and their authority contravened.

A committee, chosen in a tumultuous, illegal manner, usurped the most despotic authority over the province. They entered into contracts, compacts, combinations, treaties of alliance, with the other colonies, without any power from the legislature of the province. They agreed with the other Colonies to send Delegates to meet in convention at Philadelphia, to determine upon the rights and liberties of the good people of this province, unsupported by any Law. They issued notifications to the several supervisors through the colony, desiring them to assemble the people, in order to choose committees, to choose Delegates to represent them in the Congress. They directed, or encouraged, or abetted a mob, in perpetrating a crime, which the laws of the province forbid, under the severest penalty, viz: the robbing Captain Etherington, an Officer in his Majesty's service, of a number of sheep, which he had purchased, to carry with him to St. Vincent's. They had the insolence to direct the manner in which the Delegates should be chosen in the counties: And the greater insolence, to count all the friends to order and good government—those namely, who did not choose to obey their seditious mandate,-- as being of their party, and as acquiescing in the New-York choice.

When the Delegates had met at Philadelphia, instead of settling a reasonable plan of accommodation with the parent country, they employed themselves in censuring acts of the British parliament, which were principally intended to prevent smuggling, and all illicit trade;--in writing addresses to the people of Great-Britain, to the inhabitants of the colonies in general, and to those of the province of Quebec, in particular; with the evident design of making them dissatisfied with their present government; and of exciting clamours, and raising seditions and rebellions against the state;--and in exercising a legislative authority over all the colonies. They had the insolence to proclaim themselves "A FULL AND FREE REPRESENTATION OF"--"HIS MAJESTY'S

FAITHFUL SUBJECTS IN ALL THE COLONIES "FROM NOVA-SCOTIA TO GEORGIA;" and, as such, have laid a tax on all those colonies, viz. the profits arising from the sales of all goods imported from Great-Britain, Ireland, &c. during the months of December and January: Which tax is to be employed for the relief of the Boston poor. They adopted a mad set of resolves, framed by an arch rebel, who hath since fled his country, for fear of being apprehended, and imposed afterwards upon the deluded people of the county of Suffolk in the province of Massachusetts-Bay; approving their wisdom and fortitude, and recommending "a perseverance in the same "firm and temperate conduct, as expressed in the" said resolves,— notwithstanding those resolves entirely unhinged the civil government of that province, fomented a spirit of dissatisfaction to Great-Britain, and of rebellion against the state; and declared that the people of that county would not act always on the defensive, against the King's troops.

I must beg leave to enumerate a few of the effects of the measures of the Congress—The government of Rhode-Island have dismantled the fort in their harbour, and carried off the cannon, in order to employ them against his Majesty's forces. The inhabitants of New-Hampshire have, under the command of Major SULLIVAN, one of the Delegates, attacked, and by force of arms taken a FORT at Portsmouth, belonging to his Majesty, and carried off all the powder and small arms found in it. The people of Maryland have had a provincial Congress who have assessed that colony in the sum of £. 10,000, to be expended in arming and disciplining the inhabitants, to fight against the King. The people in New-England are raising, arming and disciplining men, for the same loyal and Christian purpose. The people of New-York have, in obedience to the Congress, chosen a new Committee, consisting of no less than SIXTY persons; to act, first, in the capacity of tax-gatherers, to collect the duties imposed by the Congress for the benefit of the Boston poor, by distress and sale of the goods imported during the last and the present month: and secondly, as spies and informers; to see that the non-importation, non-consumption, and non-exportation schemes, decreed by the Congress, be carried into due execution.

By the first of these schemes, we are in danger of being deprived of many of the comforts, and of some of the necessaries of life. We lie at the mercy of the merchants, who may strip US of every farthing, by demanding what they shall think only a reasonable profit on their goods. By the second, our very mode of living is made subject to their inspection; and we shall probably soon see these lordly Committee-men condescend to go pimping, and peeping, and peering,

into tea-canisters and molasses jugs. By the third scheme, an embargo is to take place, after the tenth of September next, on all the farmers produce of EVERY KIND. So that should their whole plan be carried fully into execution, the laborious, necessary and numerous body of FARMERS would soon be reduced to distress and beggary.

The state to which the GRAND CONGRESS, and the subordinate Committees, have reduced the colonies, is really deplorable. They have introduced a system of the most oppressive tyranny that can possibly be imagined;—a tyranny, not only over the actions, but over the words, thoughts, and mils, of the good people of this province. People have been threatened with the vengeance of a mob, for speaking in support of order and good government. Every method has been used to intimidate the printers from publishing any thing, which tended to peace, or seem'd in favour of government; while the most detestable libels against the King, the British parliament, and Ministry, have been eagerly read, and extravagantly commended, as the matchless productions of some heaven-born genius, glowing with the pure flame of civil liberty. They not only oblige people to pay the tax assessed on their goods for the benefit of the Boston poor, but they also oblige them to say, that they are willing to do it; when it is notorious that many, if not most of them, would refuse if they dared.

Behold, Gentlemen, behold the wretched state to which we are reduced! A foreign power is brought in to govern this province. Laws made at Philadelphia, by factious men from New-England, New-Jersey, Pennsylvania, Maryland, Virginia, and the Carolinas, are imposed upon us by the most imperious menaces. Money is levied upon us without the consent of our representatives: which very money, under colour of relieving the poor people of Boston, it is too probable will be employed to raise an army against the King. Mobs and riots are encouraged, in order to force submission to the tyranny of the Congress. A very respectable gentleman, who serves his King in an honourable employment, has been threatened with ASSASSINATION, by the SONS OF LIBERTY, only for—doing his duty—for securing a number of muskets, illegally imported, and which were intended to arm the people of New England against their lawful Sovereign.

To YOU, Gentlemen, the good people of this province look for relief: on YOU they have fixed their hopes: from YOU they expect deliverance from this intolerable state of slavery. They have chosen YOU to be the guardians of their rights and liberties. You have hitherto executed the important trust committed to you, with such fidelity and prudence, as entitle you to their most grateful acknowledgments, and encourage them to depend upon you with the utmost confidence. They know well that all the insidous arts that evil-minded and designing men can possibly make use of, will be employed, to lead you away from that rectitude of conduct, which hath hitherto marked all your actions; and they anxiously wait the issue of your deliberations. If you assert your own dignity--If you maintain your own rights and privileges, we shall again be a free and happy, and, I trust, not an ungrateful people: but if you prostitute the dignity of your House;--if you betray the rights of your constituents, by confirming the decrees of the Congress;--you will thereby introduce a foreign power to govern and tax this province, and we shall be, of all men, the most wretched.--If laws made, and decrees passed, at Philadelphia, by the enthusiastic republicans of New-England and Virginia, are to bind the people of this province, and extort money from them, why, Gentlemen, do you meet? Is it barely to register their edicts, and to rivet the fetters of their tyranny on your constituents? Your constituents, in that case, would be better without you. You would be an useless burthen upon them: worse than useless; a snare and a trap to them. Your duty requires you to interpose your authority, and to break up this horrid combination of seditious men, which has already enslaved this province; and which was intended to draw the faithful subjects of our most gracious Sovereign into REBELLION and a CIVIL WAR. The CONGRESS address themselves to the people of this province, among others, in the following words: "We think ourselves "bound in duty to observe to you, that the schemes agitated 'against the colonies have been so conducted, as to render it "prudent, that you should extend your views to mournful "events, and be in all respects prepared for every contingency." They had war in their hearts when this sentiment was conceived, and rebellion dictated the expression.

What, I beseech you, will be the consequence of pursuing the mode of conduct, which they have delineated? It will procure the redress of no one grievance we complain of. It will not intimidate the people of Great-Britain. We see no appearance of fear on their part; but every circumstance shews a settled design to assert the supremacy and vindicate the authority of the empire. The measures of the Congress will irritate them, but never can conciliate their affections. Should they in some degree distress their trade and manufactures, they will distress us much more severely. The schemes of the Congress will, from their very nature, operate but slowly against the government and people of Great-Britain; and before they can produce their full effect, the present contention will probably be settled. The very next

summer will finish the dispute, either peaceably, or by force of arms. Should we oblige them to recur to this latter mode of acting, the Parliament will probably make a constitution for us, without consulting our inclinations; and force us to accept it, at the mouths of their cannon. Is it not better to make some reasonable proposals, to take some prudent step towards an accommodation, before matters come to this dreadful extremity? Suppose you do not; but adopt the mad measures of the Congress; or suffer them to proceed, and bring their delirious machinations to effect: The consequence will be, that you will establish the most ignominious, and abominable tyranny over your constituents, and over yourselves, that ever was invented. They have already made, and are now, by means of the New-York Committee of sixty, executing laws which contravene your authority. They are levying money on your constituents, without your consent. They have impudently encroached on the PRIVILEGES OF YOUR HOUSE, by dictating to your Agent, EDMUND BURKE, Esq; how he shall act in this dispute, without ever asking your advice, or waiting for your opinion^. Their abettors and supporters are frequently insinuating the incapacity and inability of the Honourable House of Assembly, to do anything of real consequence towards settling this unnatural contention.

Now, if they treat the Representatives of the province in this disrespectful manner, what are the people to expect? We shall not dare to eat, or drink, or sleep, or act, or speak, or think, but in the precise mode which they shall direct. They have already regulated our trade and commerce, our manner of living, and our diversions; and, if their VINDICATOR is to be credited, the next Congress is to regulate our courts of justice.— Then will their tyranny be established; a tyranny of the most dreadful kind;--which makes laws and executes them without check or controul. Then will our happy constitution be destroyed, and a REPUBLIC be raised on its ruins. Then will You, Gentlemen, become an useless body; and it will be a matter of no consequence whether you ever meet again, or not.

There is one consideration which, in particular, I must mention; and which, I think, ought to have great weight with you, and with every person. The people in New-England have wrested the command of the MILITIA from their Governors, which they are diligently training, and forming for action. Whatever may be their ostensible reason, the real one undoubtedly is, to oppose the King's troops, and to support a rebellion against their Sovereign. The people of Maryland, and of the Lower Counties on Delaware, are following their example. The Pennsylvanians are calling together a Provincial Congress, to meet the 23d instant. They have taken this step even while their Assembly is sitting. But I wonder not at this: That Assembly, by approving, and, as far as their power extends, confirming the measures of the GRAND CONGRESS, have prostituted their own dignity, and betrayed the rights of their constituents;

and unless some superior power interposes, they will shortly find themselves absolutely controlled by these grand Continental, and petty Provincial CONGRESSES.

The design of the projectors of this provincial congress in Pennsylvania, is undoubtedly to concert a plan for embodying a militia, to act in concert with the New-Englanders, Marylanders, &c. Take care, Gentlemen, that this procedure does not spread, and infect this province by the contagion of its example! I cannot conceive a worse state of thraldom, than a military power in any government, unchecked, and uncontrollable by the civil power. And this must be the case, with respect to a militia upon such an establishment as that of Maryland and New England. The laws of the congress, not the laws of the province, will be the rule of its conduct. Enthusiastic delegates, and brain-sick committee-men, will be its commanders; and the friends of order and good government, the devoted victims of its power.

We have been taught to consider the colonies, as being of the utmost consequence to Great-Britain. We have been told that her very existence, as a sovereign state, depends upon them. Let us suppose this to be true. Let us also suppose that Great-Britain views the colonies in the same light that we do; the consequence will be, that she will exert her utmost ability to retain them under her dominion. She will send every man, and every ship that she can spare, rather than suffer them to be torn from her. A considerable army of British troops is already in America. All accounts from England agree in affirming that a larger body will be sent hither early in the spring.

Suppose our opposition to the British government should bring on a war, and that the power of Great Britain, as is most probable, should prevail; will she immediately recall her troops? Will she subject herself to the expence of transporting another army to America, a few years hence? Will she not think it more prudent to keep a considerable military force in this country, to support the civil power, and to prevent the American republicans from throwing all into confusion again, that they may accomplish their rebellious purposes?

Suppose 20,000 men should be fixed upon an American establishment; who is to cloathe, feed and pay them? Great-Britain or the Colonies? By driving matters to extremity, we shall oblige Great-Britain to do the very thing that we are endeavouring, at least are pretending to endeavour, by our mad schemes, to prevent. We shall oblige her to raise a revenue upon us to support an army, to retain us in our dependance on her imperial authority.

If the other colonies run madly into such measures as must bring ruin upon them, are we obliged to imitate and follow them? If the people of New England will kindle a fire, and then rush into it, have we no way to shew our regard and affection for them, but to jump in after them? Let us rather keep out, that we may have it in our power to pull them out, before they are burnt to death. A little scorching I believe will not hurt them. It may do them good: it may make them dread the fire hereafter; for, like children, they seem incapable of learning from any experience but their own.

We, Gentlemen, have no alternative left, but either to join the other colonies in a war against Great-Britain, or to make the best terms that we can, for ourselves. The former may have the most old Oliverian glory in it, but the latter is certainly the most prudent course. It will save this province, and probably the whole continent, from desolation and destruction.

On you, Gentlemen, it depends, under the good providence of Almighty God, whether this war meditated by the Congress, shall blaze out in America, or not. All the Colonies in New-England, and some to the southward, have run head-long, under the influence of the Congress, into such measures, as evidently tend to a war against our mother-country, and our gracious Sovereign. This province, as yet, hath taken no decisive step. You have it in your power to establish it in peace and felicity; to secure it by a firm constitution; to make it the mediatrix with Great-Britain, for all the other Colonies, and to prevent the rage of slaughter, and the effusion of human blood.

Act now, I beseech you, as you ever have done, as the faithful representatives of the people; as the real guardians of their Rights and Liberties. Give them deliverance from the tyranny of the Congress and Committees: Secure them against the horrid carnage of a civil war: And endeavour to obtain for them You know whether, and how far, the people of this province are aggrieved by any acts of the British Parliament; and we look to you to procure us such relief as you shall think effectual. We know of no representatives but you, whom we have legally chosen. On your wisdom and integrity we can rely. We have long known, and often tried you. From you alone we expect the means of redressing our grievances, and of guarding our happy form of government, against all oppression from without, and all violence and insidious innovations from within. From you, we expect some plan of accommodating our unhappy disputes with our mother country, and of preventing a renewal of them, by obtaining such a line of government as shall establish the sovereign authority of Great-Britain over all the British dominions, and at the same time secure the rights and liberties of the Colonists: And your prudence and abilities we know are equal to the task.

Be assured, Gentlemen, that a very great majority of your constituents disapprove of the late violent proceedings, and will support you in the pursuit of more moderate measures, as soon as You have delivered Them from the tyranny of Committees, from the fear of violence, and the dread of mobs. Recur boldly to your good, old, legal and successful way of proceeding, by petition and remonstrance.

Address yourselves to the King and the two Houses of Parliament. Let your representations be decent and firm, and principally directed to obtain a solid American Constitution; such as we can accept with safety, and Great-Britain can grant with dignity. Try the experiment, and you will assuredly find that our most gracious Sovereign and both Houses of Parliament will readily meet you in the paths of peace. Only shew your willingness towards an accommodation, by acknowledging the supreme legislative authority of Great-Britain, and I dare confidently pronounce the attainment of whatever YOU with propriety, can ask, and the LEGISLATURE OF GREAT-BRITAIN with honour concede.

A Farmer Refuted

…I have not only disproved the existence of that parliamentary authority, of which you are so zealous an abettor, I have also shewn, that the mode you have proposed, for the accomodation of our disputes, would be destructive to American freedom. My next business is to vindicate the Congress, by a few natural inferences; and such reflections, on the state of our commercial conexion, with the mother country, as are necessary to shew the insignificancy of your objections to my former arguments, on this head.

Since it has been proved, that the British parliament has no right, either to the legislation, or taxation of America; and since neither could be ceded, without betraying our liberties, the Congress would have acted inconsistent with their duty to their country, had they done it. Their conduct, therefore, so far from being reprehensible, was perfectly justifiable and laudable.

The regulation of our trade, in the sense it is now admitted, is the only power we can, with justice to ourselves, permit the British parliament to exercise; and it is a privilege of so important a nature, so beneficial and lucrative to Great-Britain, that she ought, in equity, to be contented with it, and not attempt to grasp at any thing more. The Congress,

therefore, have made the only concession which the welfare and prosperity of America would warrant, or which Great Britain, in reason could expect.

All your clamours, therefore, against them, for not having drawn some proper line, are groundless and ridiculous. They have drawn the only line which American freedom will authorize, or which the relation between the parent state and the colonies requires.

It is a necessary consequence, and not an assumed point, that the claim of parliament to *bind us by statutes in all cases whatsoever*, is unconstitutional, unjust and tyrannical; and the repeated attempts to carry it into execution, evince a fixed inveterate design to exterminate the liberties of America.

Mr. Grenville, during his administration, was the projector of this scheme. His conduct as a minister has been severely arraigned, by his successors in office, and by the nation in general; but, notwithstanding this, a measure, which disgraces his character more, than any thing else, has been steadily pursued, ever since.

The Stamp Act was the commencement of our misfortunes; which, in consequence of the *spirited* opposition made by us, was repealed. The revenue act, imposing duties on Paper, Glass, &c. came next; and was also partly repealed on the same account: A part, however, was left to be the instrument of some future attack. The present minister, in conjunction with a mercenary tribe of merchants attempted to effect, by stratagem, which could not be done by an open undisguised manner of proceeding: His emissaries, every where, were set to work. They endeavored, by every possible device, to allure us into the snare. The act, passed for the purpose, was misrepresented; and we were assured with all the parade of pretended patriotism, that our liberties were in no danger. The advantage, we should receive, from the probable cheapness of English tea, was played off, with every exaggeration of falshood; and specious declamations, on the criminality of illicit trade, served as a gilding for the whole. Thus truth and its opposite were blended. The men, who could make just reflections, on the sanctity of an oath, were yet base enough to strike at the vitals of those rights, which ought to be held sacred by every rational being.

It so happened, that the first tea ship arrived at Boston. The Assembly of that province, justly alarmed at the consequences, made repeated applications to the consignees, for the East-India company, requesting them to send back the tea. They, as often refused to comply. The ship was detained, 'till the time was elapsed, after which the tea must have been landed, and the duties paid, or it would have been seized, by the Custom-house. To prevent this, a part of the citizens of Boston assembled, proceeded to the ship, and threw the tea into the river.

The scheme of the ministry was disappointed, on all hands. The tea was returned from all the colonies, except South-Carolina. It was landed there; but such precautions were taken, as equally served to baffle their attempt.

This abortion of their favourite plan inflamed the ministerial ire. They breathed nothing, but vengeance against America: Menaces of punishment resounded, through both houses of parliament. The commons of Great-Britain spoke more in the supercilious tone of masters, than in the becoming language of fellow subjects. To all the judicious reasonings of a Burke, or Barry, no other answer was returned, than an idle tale of *lenity* and *severity*. Much was said of their past forbearance and of their future resentment: This was the burthen of the song. The Quixot minister too, promised to bring America to his feet. Humiliating idea! and such as ought to be spurned by every free-born American!

Boston was the first victim to the meditated vengeance: An act was passed to block up her ports, and destroy her commerce, with every aggravating circumstance that can be imagined. It was not left at her option to elude the stroke, by paying for the tea; but she was also to make such satisfaction to the officers of his Majesty's revenue and others, who might have suffered as should be judged *reasonable by the governor*. Nor is this all, before her commerce could be restored, she must have submitted to the authority claimed and exercised by the parliament.

Had the rest of America passively looked on, while a sister colony was subjugated, the same fate would gradually have overtaken all. The safety of the whole depends upon the mutual protection of every part. If the sword of oppression be permitted to lop off one limb without opposition, reiterated strokes will soon dismember the whole body. Hence it was the duty and interest of all the colonies to succour and support the one which was suffering. It is sometimes sagaciously urged, that we ought to commisserate the distresses of the people of Massachusetts; but not intermeddle in their affairs, so far, as perhaps to bring ourselves into like circumstances with them. This might be good reasoning, if our neutrality would not be more dangerous, than our participation: But I am unable to conceive how the colonies in general would have any security against oppression, if they were once to content themselves, with barely *pitying* each other, while parliament was prosecuting and enforcing its demands. Unless they continually protect and assist each other, they must all inevitably fall a prey to their enemies.

Extraordinary emergencies, require extraordinary expedients. The best mode of opposition was that in which there might be an union of councils. This was necessary to ascertain the boundaries of our rights; and to give weight and dignity to our measures, both in Britain and America. A Congress was accordingly proposed, and universally agreed to.

You, Sir, triumph in the supposed *illegality* of this body; but, granting your supposition were true, it would be a matter of no real importance. When the first principles of civil society are violated, and the rights of a whole people are invaded, the common forms of municipal law are not to be regarded. Men may then betake themselves to the law of nature; and, if they but conform their actions, to that standard, all cavils against them, betray either ignorance or dishonesty. There are some events in society, to which human laws cannot extend; but when applied to them lose all their force and efficacy. In short, when human laws contradict or discountenance the means, which are necessary to preserve the essential rights of any society, they defeat the proper end of all laws, and so become null and void.

But you have barely asserted, not proved this *illegality*. If, by the term, you mean a contrariety to law, I desire you to produce the law against it, and maintain, there is none in being. If you mean, that there is no law, the intention of which may authorise such a convention, I deny this also. It has been always a principle of the law that subjects have a right to state their grievances, and petition the King for redress. This is explicitly acknowledged by an act of the first of William and Mary; and "all prosecutions and commitments for such petitioning," are declared to be illegal. So far then the Congress was a body founded in law; for if subjects have such a right they may undoubtedly elect and depute persons from among themselves to act for them.

As to the particular agreements entered into, with respect to our commerce, the law makes no provision for, or against them: They are perfectly indifferent, in a *legal* sense. We may, or may not trade, as is most suitable to our own circumstances.

The deputies, chosen in the several provinces met at Philadelphia, according to appointment; and framed a set of resolves declarative of the rights of America, all which, I have by general arguments proved, are consonant to reason and nature; to the spirit of the British constitution and to the intention of our charters. They made the only concession (as I have also shewn) that their duty to themselves and their country would justify, or that the connection, between Britain and the colonies, demanded.

They solicited the King, for a redress of grievances; but justly concluding, from past experience, from the behaviour and declarations of the majority, in both Houses of Parliament, and from the known character and avowed designs of the Minister, that little or no dependence was to be placed upon bare entreaties, they thought it necessary to second them by restrictions on trade.

In my former defence of the measures of the Congress, I proved in a manner you never will be able to invalidate, that petitions and remonstrances, would certainly be unavailing. I will now examine your frivolous and prevaricating reply.

You answer thus: "In the commotions, occasioned by the stamp act, we recurred to petitions and remonstrances, our grievances were pointed out, and redress solicited with temper and decency. They were heard, they were attended to, and the disagreeable act repealed. The same mode of application succeeded, with regard to the duties laid upon glass, painters colours, &c: You say indeed, that our addresses on this occasion were treated with contempt and neglect. But I beseech you, were not our addresses received, read and debated upon? And was not the repeal of those acts the consequence? *The fact you know is as I state it.* If these acts were not only disagreeable to the Americans; but were also found to militate against the commercial interests of Great-Britain, it proves what I asserted above, that duties, which injure our trade, will soon be felt in England; and then there will be no difficulty in getting them repealed."

I entirely deny the fact to be, as you state it; and you are conscious it is not. Our addresses were not heard, attended to, and the disagreeable act repealed in consequence of them: If this had been the case, why was no notice taken of them in the repealing act? Why were not our complaints assigned as the inducement to it? On the contrary, these are the express words of the first repeal, to which the second is also similar. "Whereas the continuance of the said act would be attended *with many inconveniencies,* and *may be productive of consequences greatly detrimental to the commercial interests of Great-Britain,* may it, therefore, please your most excellent Majesty, by and with the advice and consent, &c. that from and after the first day of May, 1766, the above mentioned act, and the several matters and things, therein contained, shall be, and is, and are, hereby, repealed, and made void, to all intents and purposes, whatsoever."

The inconveniences, and the ill-consequences to Great-Britain, are the only reasons, given for the revocation of the act. How then can you pretend to say it was in compliance with our petitions? You must think the complaisance of your readers very great, to imagine they will credit your assertions, at the expence of their own understandings.

Neither is the use you make of the assigned reason, at all just. The consequences, so detrimental to the commercial interests of Great-Britain, are not such as would have resulted from the natural operation of the act, had it been submitted to; but from the opposition made by us, and the cessation of imports, which had taken place.

A non-importation, (to which you have so violent an aversion) was the only thing, that procured us redress, on preceding occasions. We did not formerly, any more, than now, confine ourselves to petitions only; but took care to adopt a more prevailing method, to wit, a suspension of trade.

But what proves, to a demonstration, that our former petitions were unsuccessful is, that the grand object, they aimed at, was never obtained. This was an exemption from parliamentary taxation. Our addresses turned entirely upon this point. And so far were they from succeeding, that immediately upon the repeal of the stamp-act, a subsequent act was passed, declaring the right of Parliament to bind us, by statutes, in all cases whatsoever. This declaration of the unlimited universal authority of Parliament was a direct denial of the leading claim held up in our petition; and of course a rejection of the petition itself.

1

What is the main purpose of *Letters of a Westchester Farmer*?

_____

2

What is the tone of *Letters of a Westchester Farmer*?

_____

3

What is the central claim of *Letters of a Westchester Farmer*?

_____

4

What is the main purpose of *A Farmer Refuted*?

_____

5

What is the tone of *A Farmer Refuted*?

_____

6

What is the central claim of *A Farmer Refuted*?

_____

7

What is the relationship between the passages?

_____

The first passage is adapted from Abraham Lincoln's first inaugural address, at the advent of the US civil war. The second passage is adapted from Abraham Lincoln's second inaugural address in the final days of the US civil war.

First Inaugural Address

Fellow citizens of the United States:

In compliance with a custom as old as the government itself, I appear before you to address you briefly, and to take, in your presence, the oath prescribed by the Constitution of the United States, to be taken by the President "before he enters on the execution of his office."

I do not consider it necessary, at present, for me to dis`cuss those matters of administration about which there is no special anxiety, or excitement.

Apprehension seems to exist among the people of the Southern States, that by the accession of a Republican Administration, their property, and their peace, and personal security, are to be endangered. There has never been any reasonable cause for such apprehension. Indeed. the most ample evidence to the contrary has all the while existed. And been open to their inspection. It is found in nearly all the published speeches of him who now addresses —you. I do but quote from one of those speeches when I declare that "I have no purpose, directly or indirectly, to interfere with the institution of slavery in the States where it exists. I believe I have no lawful right to do so, and I have no inclination to do so." Those who nominated and elected me did so with full knowledge that I had made this, and many similar declarations, and had never recanted them. And more than this, they placed in the platform, for my acceptance, and as a law to themselves, and to me, the clear and emphatic resolution which I now read:

"Resolved, That the maintenance inviolate of the rights of the States, and especially the right of each State to order and control its own domestic institutions according to its own judgment exclusively, is essential to that balance of power on which the perfection and endurance of our political fabric depend; and we denounce the lawless invasion by armed force of the soil of any State or Territory, no matter under what pretext, as among the gravest of crimes."

I now reiterate these sentiments: and in doing so, I only press upon the public attention the most conclusive evidence of which the case is susceptible, that the property, peace and security of no section are to be in anywise endangered by the now incoming Administration. I add too, that all the protection which, consistently with the Constitution and the laws, can be given, will be cheerfully given to all the States when lawfully demanded, for whatever cause—as cheerfully to one section, as to another.

There is much controversy about the delivering up of fugitives from service or labor. The clause I now read is as plainly written in the Constitution as any other of its provisions:

"No person held to service or labor in one State, under the laws thereof, escaping into another, shall, in consequence of any law or regulation therein, be discharged from such service or labor, but shall be delivered up on claim of the party to whom such service or labor may be due."

It is scarcely questioned that this provision was intended by those who made it, for the reclaiming of what we call fugitive slaves; and the intention of the law—giver is the law. All members of Congress swear their support to the whole Constitution—to this provision as much as to any other. To the proposition, then, that slaves whose cases come within the terms of this clause, "shall be delivered up," their oaths are unanimous. Now, if they would make the effort in good temper, could they not, with nearly equal unanimity, frame and pass a law, by means of which to keep good that unanimous oath?

There is some difference of opinion whether this clause should be enforced by national or by state authority; but surely that difference is not a very material one. If the slave is to be surrendered, it can be of but little consequence to him, or to others, by which authority it is done. And should any one, in any case, be content that his oath shall go unkept, on a merely unsubstantial controversy as to how it shall be kept?

Again, in any law upon this subject, ought not all the safeguards of liberty known in civilized and humane jurisprudence to be introduced. so that a free man be not, in any case. surrendered as a slave? And might it not be well, at the same time. to provide by law for the enforcement of that clause in the Constitution which guaranties that "The citizens of each State shall be entitled to all privileges and immunities of citizens in the several States?" I take the official oath today, with no mental reservations, and with no purpose to construe the Constitution or laws, by any hypercritical rules. And while I do not choose now to specify particular acts of Congress as proper to be enforced, I do suggest, that it will be much safer for all, both in official and private stations, to conform to and abide by, all those acts which stand unrepealed, than to violate any of them, trusting to find impunity in having them held to be unconstitutional.

It is seventy—two years since the first inauguration of a President under our national Constitution. During that period fifteen different and greatly distinguished citizens, have, in succession, administered the executive branch of the government. They have conducted it through many perils; and, generally, with great success. Yet, with all this scope for precedent, I now enter upon the same task for the brief constitutional term of four years, under great and peculiar difficulty. A disruption of the Federal Union heretofore only menaced, is now formidably attempted.

I hold, that in contemplation of universal law, and of the Constitution, the Union of these States is perpetual. Perpetuity is implied, if not expressed, in the fundamental law of all national governments. It is safe to assert that no government proper, ever had a Provision in its organic law for its own termination. Continue to execute all the express provisions of our national Constitution, and the Union will endure forever—it being impossible to destroy it, except by some action not provided for in the instrument itself.

Again, if the United States be not a government proper, but an association of States in the nature of contract merely, can it, as a contract, be peaceably unmade, by less than all the parties who made it? One party to a contract may violate it—break it, so to speak; but does it not require all to lawfully rescind it?

Descending from these general principles, we find the proposition that, in legal contemplation, the Union is perpetual, confirmed by the history of the Union itself. The Union is much older than the Constitution. It was formed in fact, by the Articles of Association in 1774. It was matured and continued by the Declaration of Independence in 1776. It was further matured and the faith of all the then thirteen States expressly plighted and engaged that it should be perpetual, by the Articles of Confederation in 1778. And finally, in 1787, one of the declared objects for ordaining and establishing the Constitution, was "to form a more perfect union."

But if destruction of the Union, by one, or by a part only, of the States, be lawfully possible, the Union is less perfect than before the Constitution, having lost the vital element of perpetuity.

It follows from these views that no State, upon its own mere motion, can lawfully get out of the Union,—that resolves and ordinances to that effect are legally void; and that acts of violence, within any State or States, against the authority of the United States, are insurrectionary or revolutionary, according to circumstances.

I therefore consider that, in view of the Constitution and the laws, the Union is unbroken; and, to the extent of my ability, I shall take care, as the Constitution itself expressly enjoins upon me, that the laws of the Union be faithfully executed in all the States. Doing this I deem to be only a simple duty on my part; and I shall perform it, so far as practicable, unless my rightful masters, the American people, shall withhold the requisite means, or, in some authoritative manner, direct the contrary. I trust this will not be regarded as a menace, but only as the declared purpose of the Union that it will constitutionally defend, and maintain itself.

In doing this there needs to be no bloodshed or violence; and there shall be none, unless it be forced upon the national authority. The power confided to me, will be used to hold, occupy, and possess the property, and places belonging to the government, and to collect the duties and imposts; but beyond what may be necessary for these objects, there will be no invasion—no using of force against, or among the people anywhere. Where hostility to the United States, in any interior locality, shall be so great and so universal, as to prevent competent resident citizens from holding the Federal offices, there will be no attempt to force obnoxious strangers among the people for that object. While the strict legal might may exist in the government to enforce the exercise of these offices, the attempt to do so would be so irritating, and so nearly impracticable with all, that I deem it better to forego, for the time, the uses of such offices.

The mails, unless repelled, will continue to be furnished in all parts of the Union. So far as possible, the people everywhere shall have that sense of perfect security which is most favorable to calm thought and reflection. The course here indicated will be followed, unless current events, and experience, shall show a modification, or change, to be proper; and in every case and exigency, my best discretion will be exercised, according to circumstances actually existing, and with a view and a hope of a peaceful solution of the national troubles, and the restoration of fraternal sympathies and affections.

That there are persons in one section, or another who seek to destroy the Union at all events, and are glad of any pretext to do it, I will neither affirm or deny; but if there be such, I need address no word to them. To those, however, who really love the Union, may I not speak?

Before entering upon so grave a matter as the destruction of our national fabric, with all its benefits, its memories, and its hopes, would it not be wise to ascertain precisely why we do it? Will you hazard so desperate a step, while there is any possibility that any portion of the ills you fly from, have no real existence? Will you, while the certain ills you fly to, are greater than all the real ones you fly from? Will you risk the commission of so fearful a mistake?

All profess to be content in the Union, if all constitutional rights can be maintained. Is it true, then, that any right, plainly written in the Constitution, has been denied? I think not. Happily the human mind is so constituted, that no party can reach to the audacity of doing this. Think, if you can, of a single instance in which a plainly written provision of the Constitution has ever been denied. If, by the mere force of numbers, a majority should deprive a minority of any clearly written constitutional right, it might, in a moral point of view, justify revolution—certainly would, if such right were a vital one. But such is not our case. All the vital rights of minorities, and of individuals, are so plainly assured to them, by affirmations and negations, Warranties and prohibitions, in the Constitution, that controversies never arise concerning them. But no organic law can ever be framed with a provision specifically applicable to every question which may occur in practical administration. No foresight can anticipate, nor any document of reasonable length contain express provisions for all possible questions. Shall fugitives from labor be surrendered by national or by State authority? The Constitution does not expressly say. May Congress prohibit slavery in the territories? The Constitution does not expressly say. Must Congress protect slavery in the territories? The Constitution does not expressly say.

From questions of this class spring all our constitutional controversies, and we divide upon them into majorities and minorities. If the minority will not acquiesce, the majority must, or the government must cease. There is no other alternative; for continuing the government, is acquiescence on one side or the other. If a minority, in such case, will secede rather than acquiesce, they make a precedent which, in turn, will divide and ruin them; for a minority of their own will secede from them, whenever a majority refuses to be controlled by such minority. For instance, why may not any portion of a new confederacy, a year or two hence, arbitrarily secede again, precisely as portions of the present Union now claim to secede from it. All who cherish disunion sentiments, are now being educated to the exact temper of doing this. Is there such perfect identity of interests among the States to compose a new Union, as to produce harmony only, and prevent renewed secession?

Plainly, the central idea of secession, is the essence of anarchy. A majority, held in restraint by constitutional checks, and limitations, and always changing easily, with deliberate changes of popular opinions and sentiments, is the only true sovereign of a free people, Whoever rejects it, does, of necessity, fly to anarchy or to despotism. Unanimity is impossible; the rule of a minority, as a permanent arrangement, is wholly inadmissible; so that, rejecting the majority principle, anarchy, or despotism in some form, is all that is left.

I do not forget the position assumed by some, that constitutional questions are to be decided by the Supreme Court; nor do I deny that such decisions must be binding in any case, upon the parties to a suit, as to the object of that suit, while they are also entitled to very high respect and consideration, in all parallel cases, by all other departments of the government. And while it is obviously possible that such decision may be erroneous in any given case, still the evil effect following it, being limited to that particular case, with the chance that it may be over-ruled, and never become a precedent for other cases, can better be borne than could the evils of a different practice. At the same time the candid citizen must confess that if the policy of the government, upon vital questions, affecting the whole people, is to be irrevocably fixed by decisions of the Supreme Court, the instant they are made, in ordinary litigation between parties, in personal actions, the people will have ceased, to be their own rulers, having, to that extent, practically resigned their government, into the hands of that eminent tribunal. Nor is there, in this view, any assault upon the court, or the judges. It is a duty, from which they may not shrink, to decide cases properly brought before them; and it is no fault of theirs, if others seek to turn their decisions to political purposes.

One section of our country believes slavery is right, and ought to be extended, while the other believes it is wrong, and ought not to be extended. This is the only substantial dispute. The fugitive slave clause of the Constitution, and the law for the suppression of the foreign slave trade, are each as well enforced, perhaps, as any law can ever be in a community where the moral sense of the people imperfectly supports the law itself. The great body of the people abide by the dry legal obligation in both cases, and a few break over in each. This, I think, cannot be perfectly cured; and it would be worse in both cases after the separation of the sections, than before. The foreign slave trade, now imperfectly suppressed, would be ultimately revived without restriction, in one section; while fugitive slaves, now only partially surrendered, would not be surrendered at all, by the other.

Physically speaking, we cannot separate. We cannot remove our respective sections from each other, nor build an impassable wall between them. A husband and wife may be divorced, and go out of the presence, and beyond the reach of each other; but the different parts of our country cannot do this. They cannot but remain face to face; and intercourse, either amicable or hostile, must continue between them. Is it possible then to make that intercourse more advantageous, or more satisfactory, after separation than before? Can aliens make treaties easier than friends can make laws? Can treaties be more faithfully enforced between aliens, than laws can among friends? Suppose you go to war, you cannot fight always; and when, after much loss on both sides, and no gain on either, you cease fighting, the identical old questions, as to terms of intercourse, are again upon you.

This country, with its institutions, belongs to the people who inhabit it. Whenever they shall grow weary of the existing government, they can exercise their constitutional right of amending it, or their revolutionary right to dismember, or overthrow it. I cannot be ignorant of the fact that many woryour, and patriotic citizens are desirous of having the national constitution amended. While I make no recommendation of amendments, I fully recognize the rightful authority of the people over the whole subject, to be exercised in either of the modes prescribed in the instrument itself; and I should, under existing circumstances, favor, rather than oppose, a fair opportunity being afforded the people to act upon it.

I will venture to add that, to me, the convention mode seems preferable, in that it allows amendments to originate with the people themselves, instead of only permitting them to take, or reject, propositions, originated by others, not especially chosen for the purpose, and which might not be precisely such, as they would wish to either accept or refuse. I understand a proposed amendment to the Constitution—which amendment, however, I have not seen, has passed Congress, to the effect that the federal government, shall never interfere with the domestic institutions of the States, including that of persons held to service. To avoid misconstruction of what I have said, I depart from my purpose not to speak of particular amendments, so far as to say that, holding such a provision to now be implied constitutional law, I have no objection to its being made express, and irrevocable.

The Chief Magistrate derives all his authority from the people, and they have conferred none upon him to fix terms for the separation of the States. The people themselves can do this also if they choose; but the executive, as such, has nothing to do with it. His duty is to administer the present government, as it came to his hands, and to transmit it, unimpaired by him, to his successor.

Why should there not be a patient confidence in the ultimate justice of the people? Is there any better, or equal hope, in the world? In our present differences, is either party without faith of being in the right? If the Almighty Ruler of nations, with his eternal truth and justice, be on your side of the North, or on yours of the South, that truth, and that justice, will surely prevail, by the judgment of this great tribunal, the American people.

By the frame of the government under which we live, this same people have wisely given their public servants but little power for mischief; and have, with equal wisdom, provided for the return of that little to their own hands at very short intervals.

While the people retain their virtue, and vigilance, no administration, by any extreme of wickedness or folly, can very seriously injure the government, in the short space of four years.

My countrymen, one and all, think calmly and well, upon this whole subject. Nothing valuable can be lost by taking time. If there be an object to hurry any of you, in hot haste, to a step which you would never take deliberately, that object will be frustrated by taking time; but no good object can be frustrated by it. Such of you as are now dissatisfied, still have the old Constitution unimpaired, and, on the sensitive point, the laws of your own framing under it; while the new administration will have no immediate power, if it would, to change either. If it were admitted that You who are dissatisfied, hold the right side in the dispute, there still is no single good reason for precipitate action. Intelligence, patriotism, Christianity, and a firm reliance on Him, who has never yet forsaken this favored land, are still competent to adjust, in the best way, all our present difficulty.

In your hands, my dissatisfied fellow countrymen, and not in mine, is the momentous issue of civil war. The government will not assail you, You can have no conflict, without being yourselves the aggressors. You have no oath registered in Heaven to destroy the government, while I shall have the most solemn one to preserve, protect and defend" it.

I am loth to close. We are not enemies, but friends. We must not be enemies. Though passion may have strained, it must not break our bonds of affection. The mystic chords of memory, stretching from every battle—field, and patriot grave, to every living" heart and hearthstone, all over this broad land, will yet swell the chorus of the Union, when again touched, as surely they will be, by the better angels of our nature.

Second Inaugural Address

Fellow-countrymen: At this second appearing to take the oath of the presidential office, there is less occasion for an extended address than there was at the first. Then a statement, somewhat in detail, of a course to be pursued, seemed fitting and proper. Now, at the expiration of four years, during which public declarations have been constantly called forth on every point and phase of the great contest which still absorbs the attention and engrosses the energies of the nation, little that is new could be presented. The progress of our arms, upon which all else chiefly depends, is as well known to the public as to myself; and it is, I trust, reasonably satisfactory and encouraging to all. With high hope for the future, no prediction in regard to it is ventured.

On the occasion corresponding to this four years ago, all thoughts were anxiously directed to an impending civil war. All dreaded it—all sought to avert it. While the inaugural address was being delivered from this place, devoted altogether to saving the Union without war, insurgent agents were in the city seeking to destroy it without war—seeking to dissolve the Union, and divide effects, by negotiation. Both parties deprecated war; but one of them would make war rather than let the nation survive; and the other would accept war rather than let it perish. And the war came.

One-eighth of the whole population were colored slaves, not distributed generally over the Union, but localized in the Southern part of it. These slaves constituted a peculiar and powerful interest. All knew that this interest was, somehow, the cause of the war. To strengthen, perpetuate, and extend this interest was the object for which the insurgents would rend the Union, even by war; while the government claimed no right to do more than to restrict the territorial enlargement of it.

Neither party expected for the war the magnitude or the duration which it has already attained. Neither anticipated that the cause of the conflict might cease with, or even before, the conflict itself should cease. Each looked for an easier triumph, and a result less fundamental and astounding. Both read the same Bible, and pray to the same God; and each invokes his aid against the other. It may seem strange that any men should dare to ask a just God's assistance in wringing their bread from the sweat of other men's faces; but let us judge not, that we be not judged. The prayers of both could not be answered—that of neither has been answered fully.

The Almighty has his own purposes. "Woe unto the world because of offenses! for it must needs be that offenses come; but woe to that man by whom the offense cometh." If we shall suppose that American slavery is one of those offenses which, in the providence of God, must needs come, but which, having continued through his appointed time, he now wills to remove, and that he gives to both North and South this terrible war, as the woe due to those by whom the offense came, shall we discern therein any departure from those divine attributes which the believers in a living God always ascribe to him? Fondly do we hope—fervently do we pray—that this mighty scourge of war may speedily pass away. Yet, if God wills that it continue until all the wealth piled by the bondman's two hundred and fifty years of unrequited toil shall be sunk, and until every drop of blood drawn with the lash shall be paid by another drawn with the sword, as was said three thousand years ago, so still it must be said, "The judgments of the Lord are true and righteous altogether."

With malice toward none; with charity for all; with firmness in the right, as God gives us to see the right, let us strive on to finish the work we are in; to bind up the nation's wounds; to care for him who shall have borne the battle, and for his widow, and his orphan—to do all which may achieve and cherish a just and lasting peace among ourselves, and with all nations.

1

What is the main purpose of the first inaugural address?

_____

2

What is the first address's tone?

_____

3

What is the central claim of the first address?

_____

4

What is the main purpose of the second inaugural address?

_____

5

What is the second address's tone?

_____

6

What is the central claim of the second address?

_____

7

What is the relationship between the addresses?

_____

www.professorscompanion.com

THE HANGING STRANGER – PHILIP K. DICK

Philip K. Dick (1928-1982) was a pioneer of Science Fiction writing. His works have been adapted into some of the most popular televisions shows and movies, including *Blade Runner* (1982 and 2017), *Total Recall* (1990, 2012), *The Minority Report* (2002), and *The Man in the High Castle* (Amazon).

At five o'clock Ed Loyce washed up, tossed on his hat and coat, got his car out and headed across town toward his TV sales store. He was tired. His back and shoulders ached from digging dirt out of the basement and wheeling it into the back yard. But for a forty-year-old man he had done okay. Janet could get a new vase with the money he had saved; and he liked the idea of repairing the foundations himself.

It was getting dark. The setting sun cast long rays over the scurrying commuters, tired and grim-faced, women loaded down with bundles and packages, students, swarming home from the university, mixing with clerks and businessmen and drab secretaries. He stopped his Packard for a red light and then started it up again. The store had been open without him; he'd arrive just in time to spell the help for dinner, go over the records of the day, maybe even close a couple of sales himself. He drove slowly past the small square of green in the center of the street, the town park. There were no parking places in front of LOYCE TV SALES AND SERVICE. He cursed under his breath and swung the car in a U-turn. Again he passed the little square of green with its lonely drinking fountain and bench and single lamppost.

From the lamppost something was hanging. A shapeless dark bundle, swinging a little with the wind. Like a dummy of some sort. Loyce rolled down his window and peered out. What the hell was it? A display of some kind? Sometimes the Chamber of Commerce put up displays in the square.

Again he made a U-turn and brought his car around. He passed the park and concentrated on the dark bundle. It wasn't a dummy. And if it was a display it was a strange kind. The hackles on his neck rose and he swallowed uneasily. Sweat slid out on his face and hands.

It was a body. A human body.

"Look at it!" Loyce snapped. "Come on out here!"

Don Fergusson came slowly out of the store, buttoning his pin-stripe coat with dignity. "This is a big deal, Ed. I can't just leave the guy standing there."

"See it?" Ed pointed into the gathering gloom. The lamppost jutted up against the sky—the post and the bundle swinging from it. "There it is. How the hell long has it been there?" His voice rose excitedly.

"What's wrong with everybody? They just walk on past!"

Don Fergusson lit a cigarette slowly. "Take it easy, old man. There must be a good reason, or it wouldn't be there."

"A reason! What kind of a reason?"

Fergusson shrugged. "Like the time the Traffic Safety Council put that wrecked Buick there. Some sort of civic thing. How would I know?"

Jack Potter from the shoe shop joined them. "What's up, boys?"

"There's a body hanging from the lamppost," Loyce said. "I'm going to call the cops."

"They must know about it," Potter said. "Or otherwise it wouldn't be there."

"I got to get back in." Fergusson headed back into the store. "Business before pleasure."

Loyce began to get hysterical. "You see it? You see it hanging there? A man's body! A dead man!" "Sure, Ed. I saw it this afternoon when I went out for coffee."

"You mean it's been there all afternoon?"

"Sure. What's the matter?" Potter glanced at his watch. "Have to run. See you later, Ed."

Potter hurried off, joining the flow of people moving along the sidewalk. Men and women, passing by the park. A few glanced up curiously at the dark bundle—and then went on. Nobody stopped. Nobody paid any attention.

"I'm going nuts," Loyce whispered. He made his way to the curb and crossed out into traffic, among the cars. Horns honked angrily at him. He gained the curb and stepped up onto the little square of green.

The man had been middle-aged. His clothing was ripped and torn, a gray suit, splashed and caked with dried mud. A stranger. Loyce had never seen him before. Not a local man. His face was partly turned away, and in the evening wind he spun a little, turning gently, silently. His skin was gouged and cut. Red gashes, deep scratches of congealed blood. A pair of steel-rimmed glasses hung from one ear, dangling foolishly. His eyes bulged. His mouth was open, tongue thick and ugly blue.

"For Heaven's sake," Loyce muttered, sickened. He pushed down his nausea and made his way back to the sidewalk. He was shaking all over, with revulsion—and fear.

Why? Who was the man? Why was he hanging there? What did it mean?

And—why didn't anybody notice?

He bumped into a small man hurrying along the sidewalk. "Watch it!" the man grated. "Oh, it's you, Ed."

Ed nodded dazedly. "Hello, Jenkins."

"What's the matter?" The stationery clerk caught Ed's aim "You look sick."

"The body. There in the park."

"Sure, Ed." Jenkins led him into the alcove of LOYCE TV SALES AND SERVICE. "Take it easy."

Margaret Henderson from the jewelry store joined them. "Something wrong?"

"Ed's not feeling well."

Loyce yanked himself free. "How can you stand here? Don't you see it? For God's sake—" "What's he talking about?" Margaret asked nervously.

"The body!" Ed shouted. "The body hanging there!"

More people collected. "Is he sick? It's Ed Loyce. You okay, Ed?"

"The body!" Loyce screamed, struggling to get past them. Hands caught at him. He tore loose. "Let me go! The police! Get the police!"

"Ed—"

"Better get a doctor!"

"He must be sick."

"Or drunk."

Loyce fought his way through the people. He stumbled and half fell. Through a blur he saw rows of faces, curious, concerned, anxious. Men and women halting to see what the disturbance was. He fought past them toward his store. He could see Fergusson inside talking to a man, showing him an Emerson TV set. Pete Foley in the back at the service counter, setting up a new Philco. Loyce shouted at them frantically. His voice was lost in the roar of traffic and the murmuring around him.

"Do something!" he screamed. "Don't stand there! Do something! Something's wrong! Something's happened! Things are going on!" The crowd melted respectfully for the two heavy-set cops moving efficiently toward Loyce.

"Name?" the cop with the notebook murmured.

"Loyce." He mopped his forehead wearily. "Edward C. Loyce. Listen to me. Back there—"

"Address?" the cop demanded. The police car moved swiftly through traffic, shooting among the cars and buses. Loyce sagged against the seat, exhausted and confused. He took a deep shuddering breath.

"1368 Hurst Road."

"That's here in Pikeville?"

"That's right." Loyce pulled himself up with a violent effort. "Listen to me. Back there. In the square. Hanging from the lamppost—"

"Where were you today?" the cop behind the wheel demanded.

"Where?" Loyce echoed.

"You weren't in your shop, were you?"

"No." He shook his head. "No, I was home. Down in the basement."

"In the basement?"

"Digging. A new foundation. Getting out the dirt to pour a cement frame. Why? What has that to do with—"

"Was anybody else down there with you?"

"No. My wife was downtown. My kids were at school." Loyce looked from one heavy-set cop to the other. Hope flickered across his face, wild hope. "You mean because I was down there I missed—the explanation? I didn't get in on it? Like everybody else?" After a pause the cop with the notebook said: "That's right. You missed the explanation."

"Then it's official? The body—it's supposed to be hanging there?"

"It's supposed to be hanging there. For everybody to see."

Ed Loyce grinned weakly. "Good Lord. I guess I sort of went off the deep end. I thought maybe something had happened. You know, something like the Ku Klux Klan. Some kind of violence. Communists or Fascists taking over." He wiped his face with his breast-pocket handkerchief, his hands shaking. "I'm glad to know it's on the level."

"It's on the level." The police car was getting near the Hall of Justice. The sun had set. The streets were gloomy and dark. The lights had not yet come on.

"I feel better," Loyce said. "I was pretty excited there, for a minute. I guess I got all stirred up. Now that I understand, there's no need to take me in, is there?"

The two cops said nothing.

"I should be back at my store. The boys haven't had dinner. I'm all right, now. No more trouble. Is there any need of—" "This won't take long," the cop behind the wheel interrupted. "A short process. Only a few minutes."

"I hope it's short," Loyce muttered. The car slowed down for a stoplight. "I guess I sort of disturbed the peace. Funny, getting excited like that and—"

Loyce yanked the door open. He sprawled out into the street and rolled to his feet. Cars were moving all around him, gaining speed as the light changed. Loyce leaped onto the curb and raced among the people, burrowing into the swarming crowds. Behind him he heard sounds, snouts, people running.

They weren't cops. He had realized that right away. He knew every cop in Pikeville. A man couldn't own a store, operate a business in a small town for twenty-five years without getting to know all the cops.

They weren't cops—and there hadn't been any explanation. Potter, Fergusson, Jenkins, none of them knew why it was there. They didn't know—and they didn't care. That was the strange part.

Loyce ducked into a hardware store. He raced toward the back, past the startled clerks and customers, into the shipping room and through the back door. He tripped over a garbage can and ran up a flight of concrete steps. He climbed over a fence and jumped down on the other side, gasping and panting.

There was no sound behind him. He had got away.

He was at the entrance of an alley, dark and strewn with boards and ruined boxes and tires. He could see the street at the far end. A street light wavered and came on. Men and women. Stores. Neon signs. Cars.

And to his right—the police station.

He was close, terribly close. Past the loading platform of a grocery store rose the white concrete side of the Hall of Justice. Barred windows. The police antenna. A great concrete wall rising up in the darkness. A bad place for him to be near. He was too close. He had to keep moving, get farther away from them.

Them?

Loyce moved cautiously down the alley. Beyond the police station was the City Hall, the old-fashioned yellow structure of wood and gilded brass and broad cement steps. He could see the endless rows of offices, dark windows, the cedars and beds of flowers on each side of the entrance.

And—something else.

Above the City Hall was a patch of darkness, a cone of gloom denser than the surrounding night. A prism of black that spread out and was lost into the sky.

He listened. Good God, he could hear something. Something that made him struggle frantically to close his ears, his mind, to shut out the sound. A buzzing. A distant, muted hum like a great swarm of bees.

Loyce gazed up, rigid with horror. The splotch of darkness, hanging over the City Hall. Darkness so thick it seemed almost solid. In the vortex something moved. Flickering shapes. Things, descending from the sky, pausing momentarily above the City Hall, fluttering over it in a dense swarm and then dropping silently onto the roof.

Shapes. Fluttering shapes from the sky. From the crack of darkness that hung above him. He was seeing—them.

For a long time Loyce watched, crouched behind a sagging fence in a pool of scummy water.

They were landing. Coming down in groups, landing on the roof of the City Hall and disappearing inside. They had wings. Like giant insects of some kind. They flew and fluttered and came to rest—and then crawled crab-fashion, sideways, across the roof and into the building.

He was sickened. And fascinated. Cold night wind blew around him and he shuddered. He was tired,

dazed with shock. On the front steps of the City Hall were men, standing here and there. Groups of men coming out of the building and halting for a moment before going on.

Were there more of them?

It didn't seem possible. What he saw descending from the black chasm weren't men. They were alien—from some other world, some other dimension. Sliding through this slit, this break in the shell of the universe. Entering through this gap, winged insects from another realm of being.

On the steps of the City Hall a group of men broke up. A few moved toward a waiting car. One of the remaining shapes started to re-enter the City Hall. It changed its mind and turned to follow the others.

Loyce closed his eyes in horror. His senses reeled. He hung on tight, clutching at the sagging fence. The shape, the man-shape, had abruptly fluttered up and flapped after the others. It flew to the sidewalk and came to rest among them.

Pseudo-men. Imitation men. Insects with ability to disguise themselves as men. Like other insects familiar to Earth. Protective coloration. Mimicry.

Loyce pulled himself away. He got slowly to his feet. It was night. The alley was totally dark. But maybe they could see in the dark. Maybe darkness made no difference to them.

He left the alley cautiously and moved out onto the street. Men and women flowed past, but not so many, now. At the bus stops stood waiting groups. A huge bus lumbered along the street, its lights flashing in the evening gloom.

Loyce moved forward. He pushed his way among those waiting and when the bus halted he boarded it and took a seat in the rear, by the door. A moment later the bus moved into life and rumbled down the street.

Loyce relaxed a little. He studied the people around him. Dulled, tired faces. People going home from work. Quite ordinary faces. None of them paid any attention to him. All sat quietly, sunk down in their seats, jiggling with the motion of the bus. The man sitting next to him unfolded a newspaper. He began to read the sports section, his lips moving. An ordinary man. Blue suit. Tie. A businessman, or a salesman. On his way home to his wife and family.

Across the aisle a young woman, perhaps twenty. Dark eyes and hair, a package on her lap. Nylons and heels. Red coat and white Angora sweater. Gazing absently ahead of her.

A high school boy in jeans and black jacket.

A great triple-chinned woman with an immense shopping bag loaded with packages and parcels. Her thick face dim with weariness. Ordinary people. The kind that rode the bus every evening. Going home to their families. To dinner.

Going home—with their minds dead. Controlled, filmed over with the mask of an alien being that had appeared and taken possession of them, their town, their lives. Himself, too. Except that he happened to be deep in his cellar instead of in the store. Somehow, he had been overlooked. They had missed him. Their control wasn't perfect, foolproof.

Maybe there were others.

Hope flickered in Loyce. They weren't omnipotent. They had made a mistake, not got control of him. Their net, their field of control, had passed over him. He had emerged from his cellar as he had gone down. Apparently their power-zone was limited. A few seats down the aisle a man was watching him. Loyce broke off his chain of thought. A slender man, with dark hair and a small mustache. Well-dressed, brown suit and shiny shoes. A book between his small hands. He was watching Loyce, studying him intently. He turned quickly away.

Loyce tensed. One of them? Or—another they had missed?

The man was watching him again. Small dark eyes, alive and clever. Shrewd. A man too shrewd for them—or one of the things itself, an alien insect from beyond.

The bus halted. An elderly man got on slowly and dropped his token into the box. He moved down the aisle and took a seat opposite Loyce.

The elderly man caught the sharp-eyed man's gaze. For a split second something passed between them. A look rich with meaning.

Loyce got to his feet. The bus was moving. He ran to the door. One step down into the well. He yanked the emergency door release. The rubber door swung open.

"Hey!" the driver shouted, jamming on the brakes. "What the hell—?"

Loyce squirmed through. The bus was slowing down. Houses on all sides. A residential district, lawns and tall apartment buildings. Behind him, the bright-eyed man had leaped up. The elderly man was also on his feet. They were coming after him. Loyce leaped. He hit the pavement with terrific force and rolled against the curb. Pain lapped over him. Pain and a vast tide of blackness. Desperately, he fought it off. He struggled to his knees and then slid down again. The bus had stopped. People were getting off.

Loyce groped around. His fingers closed over something. A rock, lying in the gutter. He crawled to his feet, grunting with pain. A shape loomed before him. A man, the bright-eyed man with the book.

Loyce kicked. The man gasped and fell. Loyce brought the rock down. The man screamed and tried to roll away. "Stop! For God's sake listen—"

He struck again. A hideous crunching sound. The man's voice cut off and dissolved in a bubbling wail. Loyce scrambled up and back. The others were there, now. All around him. He ran, awkwardly, down the sidewalk, up a driveway. None of them followed him. They had stopped and were bending over the inert body of the man with the book, the bright-eyed man who had come after him.

Had he made a mistake?

But it was too late to worry about that. He had to get out—away from them. Out of Pikeville, beyond the crack of darkness, the rent between their world and his.

"Ed!" Janet Loyce backed away nervously. "What is it? What—"

Ed Loyce slammed the door behind him and came into the living room. "Pull down the shades. Quick." Janet moved toward the window. "But—"

"Do as I say. Who else is here besides you?"

"Nobody. Just the twins. They're upstairs in their room. What's happened? You look so strange. Why are you home?"

Ed locked the front door. He prowled around the house, into the kitchen. From the drawer under the sink he slid out the big butcher knife and ran his finger along it. Sharp. Plenty sharp. He returned to the living room.

"Listen to me," he said. "I don't have much time. They know I escaped and they'll be looking for me."

"Escaped?" Janet's face twisted with bewilderment and fear. "Who?"

"The town has been taken over. They're in control. I've got it pretty well figured out. They started at the top, at the City Hall and police department. What they did with the real humans they—"

"What are you talking about?"

"We've been invaded. From some other universe, some other dimension. They're insects. Mimicry. And more. Power to control minds. Your mind."

"My mind?"

"Their entrance is here, in Pikeville. They've taken over all of you. The whole town—except me. We're up against an incredibly powerful enemy, but they have their limitations. That's our hope. They're limited! They can make mistakes!" Janet shook her head. "I don't understand, Ed. You must be insane."

"Insane? No. Just lucky. If I hadn't been down in the basement I'd be like all the rest of you." Loyce peered out the window. "But I can't stand here talking. Get your coat."

"My coat?"

"We're getting out of here. Out of Pikeville. We've got to get help. Fight this thing. They can be beaten. They're not infallible. It's going to be close—but we may make it if we hurry. Come on!" He grabbed her arm roughly. "Get your coat and call the twins. We're all leaving. Don't stop to pack. There's no time for that."

White-faced, his wife moved toward the closet and got down her coat. "Where are we going?"

Ed pulled open the desk drawer and spilled the contents out onto the floor. He grabbed up a road map and spread it open. "They'll have the highway covered, of course. But there's a back road. To Oak Grove. I got onto it once. It's practically abandoned. Maybe they'll forget about it."

"The old Ranch Road? Good Lord—it's completely closed. Nobody's supposed to drive over it."

"I know." Ed thrust the map grimly into his coat. "That's our best chance. Now call down the twins and let's get going. Your car is full of gas, isn't it?"

Janet was dazed.

"The Chevy? I had it filled up yesterday afternoon." Janet moved toward the stairs. "Ed, I—"

"Call the twins!" Ed unlocked the front door and peered out. Nothing stirred. No sign of life. All right so far.

"Come on downstairs," Janet called in a wavering voice. "We're—going out for a while."

"Now?" Tommy's voice came.

"Hurry up," Ed barked. "Get down here, both of you."

Tommy appeared at the top of the stairs. "I was doing my homework. We're starting fractions. Miss Parker says if we don't get this done—"

"You can forget about fractions." Ed grabbed his son as he came down the stairs and propelled him toward the door. "Where's Jim?"

"He's coming."

Jim started slowly down the stairs. "What's up, Dad?"

"We're going for a ride."

"A ride? Where?"

Ed turned to Janet. "We'll leave the lights on. And the TV set. Go turn it on." He pushed her toward the set. "So they'll think we're still—"

He heard the buzz. And dropped instantly, the long butcher knife out. Sickened, he saw it coming down the stairs at him, wings a blur of motion as it aimed itself. It still bore a vague resemblance to Jimmy. It was small, a baby one. A brief glimpse—the thing hurtling at him, cold, multi-lensed inhuman eyes. Wings, body still clothed in yellow T-shirt and jeans, the mimic outline still stamped on it. A strange half-turn of its body as it reached him. What was it doing?

A stinger.

Loyce stabbed wildly at it. It retreated, buzzing frantically. Loyce rolled and crawled toward the door. Tommy and Janet stood still as statues, faces blank. Watching without expression. Loyce stabbed again. This time the knife connected. The thing shrieked and faltered. It bounced against the wall and fluttered down.

Something lapped through his mind. A wall of force, energy, an alien mind probing into him. He was suddenly paralyzed. The mind entered his own, touched against him briefly, shockingly. An utter alien presence, settling over him—and then it flickered out as the thing collapsed in a broken heap on the rug.

It was dead. He turned it over with his foot. It was an insect, a fly of some kind. Yellow T-shirt, jeans. His son Jimmy... He closed his mind tight. It was too late to think about that. Savagely he scooped up his knife and headed toward the door. Janet and Tommy stood stone-still, neither of them moving.

The car was out. He'd never get through. They'd be waiting for him. It was ten miles on foot. Ten long miles over rough ground, gulleys and open fields and hills of uncut forest. He'd have to go alone.

Loyce opened the door. For a brief second he looked back at his wife and son. Then he slammed the door behind him and raced down the porch steps.

A moment later he was on his way, hurrying swiftly through the darkness toward the edge of town.

The early morning sunlight was blinding. Loyce halted, gasping for breath, swaying back and forth. Sweat ran down in his eyes. His clothing was torn, shredded by the brush and thorns through which he had crawled. Ten miles—on his hands and knees. Crawling, creeping through the night. His shoes were mud-caked. He was scratched and limping, utterly exhausted. But ahead of him lay Oak Grove.

He took a deep breath and started down the hill. Twice he stumbled and fell, picking himself up and trudging on. His ears rang. Everything receded and wavered. But he was there. He had got out, away from Pikeville.

A farmer in a field gaped at him. From a house a young woman watched in wonder. Loyce reached the road and turned onto it. Ahead of him was a gasoline station and a drive-in. A couple of trucks, some chickens pecking in the dirt, a dog tied with a string.

The white-clad attendant watched suspiciously as he dragged himself up to the station. "Thank God." He caught hold of the wall. "I didn't think I was going to make it. They followed me most of the way. I could hear them buzzing. Buzzing and flitting around behind me."

"What happened?" the attendant demanded. "You in a wreck? A holdup?"

Loyce shook his head wearily. "They have the whole town. The City Hall and the police station. They hung a man from the lamppost. That was the first thing I saw. They've got all the roads blocked. I saw them hovering over the cars coming in. About four this morning I got beyond them. I knew it right away. I could feel them leave. And then the sun came up."

The attendant licked his lip nervously. "You're out of your head. I better get a doctor."

"Get me into Oak Grove," Loyce gasped. He sank down on the gravel. "We've got to get started—cleaning them out. Got to get started right away."

They kept a tape recorder going all the time he talked. When he had finished the Commissioner snapped off the recorder and got to his feet. He stood for a moment, deep in thought. Finally he got out his cigarettes and lit up slowly, a frown on his beefy face.

"You don't believe me," Loyce said.

The Commissioner offered him a cigarette. Loyce pushed it impatiently away. "Suit yourself." The Commissioner moved over to the window and stood for a time looking out at the town of Oak Grove. "I believe you," he said abruptly.

Loyce sagged. "Thank God."

"So you got away." The Commissioner shook his head. "You were down in your cellar instead of at work. A freak chance. One in a million."

Loyce sipped some of the black coffee they had brought him. "I have a theory," he murmured.

"What is it?"

"About them. Who they are. They take over one area at a time. Starting at the top—the highest level of authority. Working down from there in a widening circle. When they're firmly in control they go on to the next town. They spread, slowly, very gradually. I think it's been going on for a long time."

"A long time?"

"Thousands of years. I don't think it's new."

"Why do you say that?"

"When I was a kid... A picture they showed us in Bible League. A religious picture—an old print. The enemy gods, defeated by Jehovah. Moloch, Beelzebub, Moab, Baalin, Ashtaroth—"

"So?"

"They were all represented by figures." Loyce looked up at the Commissioner. "Beelzebub was represented as—a giant fly."

The Commissioner grunted. "An old struggle."

"They've been defeated. The Bible is an account of their defeats. They make gains—but finally they're defeated."

"Why defeated?"

"They can't get everyone. They didn't get me. And they never got the Hebrews. The Hebrews carried the message to the whole world. The realization of the danger. The two men on the bus. I think they understood. Had escaped, like I did." He clenched his fists. "I killed one of them. I made a mistake. I was afraid to take a chance."

The Commissioner nodded. "Yes, they undoubtedly had escaped, as you did. Freak accidents. But the rest of the town was firmly in control." He turned from the window, "Well, Mr. Loyce. You seem to have figured everything out."

"Not everything. The hanging man. The dead man hanging from the lamppost. I don't understand that. Why? Why did they deliberately hang him there?"

"That would seem simple." The Commissioner smiled faintly. "Bait."

Loyce stiffened. His heart stopped beating. "Bait? What do you mean?"

"To draw you out. Make you declare yourself. So they'd know who was under control—and who had escaped."

Loyce recoiled with horror. "Then they expected failures! They anticipated—" He broke off. "They were ready with a trap." "And you showed yourself. You reacted. You made yourself known." The Commissioner abruptly moved toward the door. "Come along, Loyce. There's a lot to do. We must get moving. There's no time to waste."

Loyce started slowly to his feet, numbed. "And the man. Who was the man? I never saw him before. He wasn't a local man. He was a stranger. All muddy and dirty, his face cut, slashed—"

There was a strange look on the Commissioner's face as he answered, "Maybe," he said softly, "you'll understand that, too. Come along with me, Mr. Loyce." He held the door open, his eyes gleaming. Loyce caught a glimpse of the street in front of the police station. Policemen, a platform of some sort. A telephone pole—and a rope! "Right this way," the Commissioner said, smiling coldly.

*****

As the sun set, the vice-president of the Oak Grove Merchants' Bank came up out of the vault, threw the heavy time locks, put on his hat and coat, and hurried outside onto the sidewalk. Only a few people were there, hurrying home to dinner.

"Good night," the guard said, locking the door after him.

"Good night," Clarence Mason murmured. He started along the street toward his car. He was tired. He had been working all day down in the vault, examining the lay-out of the safety deposit boxes to see if there was room for another tier. He was glad to be finished.

At the corner he halted. The street lights had not yet come on. The street was dim. Everything was vague. He looked around—and froze.

From the telephone pole in front of the police station, something large and shapeless hung. It moved a little with the wind. What the hell was it?

Mason approached it warily. He wanted to get home. He was tired and hungry. He thought of his wife, his kids, a hot meal on the dinner table. But there was something about the dark bundle, something ominous and ugly.

The light was bad; he couldn't tell what it was. Yet it drew him on, made him move closer for a better look. The shapeless thing made him uneasy. He was frightened by it. Frightened—and fascinated.

And the strange part was that nobody else seemed to notice it.

1

What is the main purpose of this passage?

_____

2

What is the passage's tone?

_____

3

How would you summarize the passage?

_____

4

How would you describe Mr. Loyce?

_____

Narratives about King Arthur, a legendary 5th century ruler of Britain, began emerging in the 12th century. These passages are adapted from Thomas Malory's *Le Morte d'Arthur*, first published in 1485. This version from 1892 has been updated with 19th century spelling.

The Marriage of Arthur and Guinevere and the Founding of the Round Table

It befell upon a certain day, that King Arthur said to Merlin, "My lords and knights do daily pray me now to take a wife; but I will have none without your counsel, for you hast ever helped me since I came first to this crown."

"It is well," said Merlin, "that you should take a wife, for no man of bounteous and noble nature should live without one; but is there any lady whom you lovest better than another?"

"Yea," said King Arthur, "I love Guinevere, the daughter of King Leodegrance, of Camelgard, who also holds in his house the Round Table that he had from my father Uther; and as I think, that damsel is the gentlest and the fairest lady living."

"Sir," answered Merlin, "as for her beauty, she is one of the fairest that do live; but if you had not loved her as you do, I would gladly have had you choose some other who was both fair and good. But where a man's heart is set, he will be loth to leave." This Merlin said, knowing the misery that should hereafter happen from this marriage.

Then King Arthur sent word to King Leodegrance that he mightily desired to wed his daughter, and how that he had loved her since he saw her first, when with Kings Ban and Bors he rescued Leodegrance from King Ryence of North Wales.

When King Leodegrance heard the message, he cried out, "These be the best tidings I have heard in all my life—so great and worshipful a prince to seek my daughter for his wife! I would gladly give him half my lands with her straightway, but that he needs none—and better will it please him that I send him the Round Table of King Uther, his father, with a hundred good knights towards the furnishing of it with guests, for he will soon find means to gather more, and make the table full."

Then King Leodegrance delivered his daughter Guinevere to the messengers of King Arthur, and also the Round Table with the hundred knights.

So they rode royally and freshly, sometimes by water and sometimes by land, towards Camelot. And as they rode along in the spring weather, they made full many sports and pastimes. And, in all those sports and games, a young knight lately come to Arthur's court, Sir Lancelot by name, was passing strong, and won praise from all, being full of grace and hardihood; and Guinevere also ever looked on him with joy. And always in the eventide, when the tents were set beside some stream or forest, many minstrels came and sang before the knights and ladies as they sat in the tent-doors, and many knights would tell adventures; and still Sir Lancelot was foremost, and told the knightliest tales, and sang the goodliest songs, of all the company.

And when they came to Camelot, King Arthur made great joy, and all the city with him; and riding forth with a great retinue he met Guinevere and her company, and led her through the streets all filled with people, and in the midst of all their shoutings and the ringing of church bells, to a palace hard by his own.

Then, in all haste, the king commanded to prepare the marriage and the coronation with the stateliest and most honorable pomp that could be made. And when the day was come, the archbishops led the king to the cathedral, whereto he walked, clad in his royal robes, and having four kings, bearing four golden swords, before him; a choir of passing sweet music going also with him.

In another part, was the queen dressed in her richest ornaments, and led by archbishops and bishops to the Chapel of the Virgins, the four queens also of the four kings last mentioned walked before her, bearing four white doves, according to ancient custom; and after her there followed many damsels, singing and making every sign of joy.

And when the two processions were come to the churches, so wondrous was the music and the singing, that all the knights and barons who were there pressed on each other, as in the crowd of battle, to hear and see the most they might.

When the king was crowned, he called together all the knights that came with the Round Table from Camelgard, and twenty-eight others, great and valiant men, chosen by Merlin out of all the realm, towards making up the full number of the table. Then the Archbishop of Canterbury blessed the seats of all the knights, and when they rose again therefrom to pay their homage to King Arthur, there was found upon the back of each knight's seat his name, written in letters of gold. But upon one seat was found written, "This is the Siege Perilous, wherein if any man shall sit save him whom Heaven hath chosen, he shall be devoured by fire."

Anon came young Gawain, the king's nephew, praying to be made a knight, whom the king knighted then and there. Soon after came a poor man, leading with him a tall fair lad of eighteen years of age, riding on a lean mare. And falling at the king's feet, the poor man said, "Lord, it was told me, that at this time of your marriage you would give to any man the gift he asked for, so it were not unreasonable."

"That is the truth," replied King Arthur, "and I will make it good."

"You speak graciously and nobly," said the poor man. "Lord, I ask nothing else but that you wilt make my son here a knight."

"It is a great thing that you ask," said the king. "What is your name?"

"Aries, the cowherd," answered he.

"Does this prayer come from you or from your son?" inquired King Arthur.

"Nay, lord, not from myself," said he, "but from him only, for I have thirteen other sons, and all of them will fall to any labor that I put them to. But this one will do no such work for anything that I or my wife may do, but is for ever shooting or fighting, and running to see knights and joustings, and torments me both night and day that he be made a knight."

"What is your name?" said the king to the young man.

"My name is Tor," said he.

Then the king, looking at him steadfastly, was well pleased with his face and figure, and with his look of nobleness and strength.

"Fetch all your other sons before me," said the king to Aries. But when he brought them, none of them resembled Tor in size or shape or feature.

Then the king knighted Tor, saying, "Be you to your life's end a good knight and a true, as I pray God you maybe; and if you prove woryour, and of prowess, one day you shalt be counted in the Round Table." Then turning to Merlin, Arthur said, "Prophesy now, O Merlin, shall Sir Tor become a woryour knight, or not?"

"Yea, lord," said Merlin, "so he ought to be, for he is the son of that King Pellinore whom you hast met, and proved to be one of the best knights living. He is no cowherd's son."

Presently after came in King Pellinore, and when he saw Sir Tor he knew him for his son, and was more pleased than words can tell to find him knighted by the king. And Pellinore did homage to King Arthur, and was gladly and graciously accepted of the king; and then was led by Merlin to a high seat at the Table Round, near to the Perilous Seat.

But Sir Gawain was full of anger at the honor done King Pellinore, and said to his brother Gaheris, "He slew our father, King Lot, therefore will I slay him."

"Do it not yet," said he; "wait till I also be a knight, then will I help you in it: it is best you suffer him to go

at this time, and not trouble this high feast with bloodshed."

"As you will, be it," said Sir Gawain.

Then rose the king and spake to all the Table Round, and charged them to be ever true and noble knights, to do neither outrage nor murder, nor any unjust violence, and always to flee treason; also by no means ever to be cruel, but give mercy unto him that asked for mercy, upon pain of forfeiting the liberty of his court forevermore. Moreover, at all times, on pain of death, to give all succor unto ladies and young damsels; and lastly, never to take part in any wrongful quarrel, for reward or payment. And to all this he swore them knight by knight.

Then he ordained that, every year at Pentecost, they should all come before him, wheresoever he might appoint a place, and give account of all their doings and adventures of the past twelve-month. And so, with prayer and blessing, and high words of cheer, he instituted the most noble order of the Round Table, whereto the best and bravest knights in all the world sought afterwards to find admission.

Then was the high feast made ready, and the king and queen sat side by side, before the whole assembly; and great and royal was the banquet and the pomp.

And as they sat, each man in his place, Merlin went round and said, "Sit still awhile, for you shall see a strange and marvelous adventure."

So as they sat, there suddenly came running through the hall, a white hart, with a white hound next after him, and thirty couple of black running hounds, making full cry; and the hart made circuit of the Table Round, and past the other tables; and suddenly the white hound flew upon him and bit him fiercely, and tore out a piece from his haunch. Whereat the hart sprang suddenly with a great leap, and overthrew a knight sitting at the table, who rose forthwith, and, taking up the hound, mounted, and rode fast away.

But no sooner had he left, than there came in a lady, mounted on a white palfrey, who cried out to the king, "Lord, suffer me not to have this injury!—the hound is mine which that knight taketh." And as she spake, a knight rode in all armed, on a great horse, and suddenly took up the lady and rode away with her by force, although she greatly cried and moaned.

Then the king desired Sir Gawain, Sir Tor, and King Pellinore to mount and follow this adventure to the uttermost; and told Sir Gawain to bring back the hart, Sir Tor the hound and knight, and King Pellinore the knight and the lady.

So Sir Gawain rode forth at a swift pace, and with him Gaheris, his brother, for a squire. And as they went, they saw two knights fighting on horseback, and when they reached them they divided them and asked the reason of their quarrel. "We fight for a foolish matter," one replied, "for we be brethren; but there came by a white hart this way, chased by many hounds, and thinking it was an adventure for the high feast of King Arthur, I would have followed it to have gained worship; whereat my younger brother here declared he was the better knight and would go after it instead, and so we fight to prove which of us be the better knight."

"This is a foolish thing," said Sir Gawain. "Fight with all strangers, if you will, but not brother with brother. Take my advice, set on against me, and if you yield to me, as I shall do my best to make you, you shall go to King Arthur and yield you to his grace."

"Sir knight," replied the brothers, "we are weary, and will do your wish without encountering you; but by whom shall we tell the king that we were sent?"

"By the knight that follows the quest of the white hart," said Sir Gawain. "And now tell me your names, and let us part."

"Sorlous and Brian of the Forest," they replied; and so they went their way to the king's court.

Then Sir Gawain, still following his quest by the distant baying of the hounds, came to a great river, and saw the hart swimming over and near to the further bank. And as he was about to plunge in and swim after, he saw a knight upon the other side, who cried, "Come not over here, Sir knight, after that hart, save you wilt joust with me."

"I will not fail for that," said Sir Gawain; and swam his horse across the stream.

Anon they got their spears, and ran against each other fiercely; and Sir Gawain smote the stranger off his horse, and turning, bade him yield.

"Nay," replied he, "not so; for though you have the better of me on horseback, I pray you, valiant knight, alight, and let us match together with our swords on foot."

"What is your name?" quoth Gawain.

"Allardin of the Isles," replied the stranger.

Then they fell on each other; but soon Sir Gawain struck him through the helm, so deeply and so hard, that all his brains were scattered, and Sir Allardin fell dead. "Ah," said Gaheris, "that was a mighty stroke for a young knight!"

Then did they turn again to follow the white hart, and let slip three couple of greyhounds after him; and at the last they chased him to a castle, and there they overtook and slew him, in the chief courtyard.

At that there rushed a knight forth from a chamber, with a drawn sword in his hand, and slew two of the hounds before their eyes, and chased the others from the castle, crying, "Oh, my white hart! alas, that you art dead! for you my sovereign lady gave to me, and evil have I kept you; but if I live, your death shall be dear

bought." Anon he went within and armed, and came out fiercely, and met Sir Gawain face to face.

"Why have you slain my hounds?" said Sir Gawain; "they did but after their nature: and you had better have taken vengeance on me than on the poor dumb beasts."

"I will avenge me on you, also," said the other, "ere you depart this place."

Then did they fight with each other savagely and madly, till the blood ran down to their feet. But at last Sir Gawain had the better, and felled the knight of the castle to the ground. Then he cried out for mercy, and yielded to Sir Gawain, and besought him as he was a knight and gentleman to save his life. "You shalt die," said Sir Gawain, "for slaying my hounds."

"I will make you all amends within my power," replied the knight.

But Sir Gawain would have no mercy, and unlaced his helm to strike his head off; and so blind was he with rage, that he saw not where a lady ran out from her chamber and fell down upon his enemy. And making a fierce blow at him, he smote off by mischance the lady's head.

"Alas!" cried Gaheris, "foully and shamefully have you done—the shame shall never leave you! Why give you not your mercy unto them that ask it? a knight without mercy is without worship also."

Then Sir Gawain was sore amazed at that fair lady's death, and knew not what to do, and said to the fallen knight, "Arise, for I will give you mercy."

"Nay, nay," said he, "I care not for your mercy now, for you hast slain my lady and my love—that of all earthly things I loved the best."

"I repent me sorely of it," said Sir Gawain, "for I meant to have struck you: but now shalt you go to King Arthur and tell him this adventure, and how you hast been overcome by the knight that follows the quest of the white hart."

"I care not whether I live or die, or where I go," replied the knight.

So Sir Gawain sent him to the court to Camelot, making him bear one dead greyhound before and one behind him on his horse. "Tell me your name before we part," said he.

"My name is Athmore of the Marsh," he answered.

Then went Sir Gawain into the castle, and prepared to sleep there and began to unarm; but Gaheris upbraided him, saying, "Will you disarm in this strange country? bethink you, you must needs have many enemies about."

No sooner had he spoken than there came out suddenly four knights, well armed, and assailed them hard, saying to Sir Gawain, "You new-made knight, how hast you shamed your knighthood! a knight without mercy is dishonored! Slayer of fair ladies, shame to you evermore! Doubt not you shalt yourself have need of mercy ere we leave you."

Then were the brothers in great jeopardy, and feared for their lives, for they were but two to four, and weary with traveling; and one of the four knights shot Sir Gawain with a bolt, and hit him through the arm, so that he could fight no more. But when there was nothing left for them but death, there came four ladies forth and prayed the four knights' mercy for the strangers. So they gave Sir Gawain and Gaheris their lives, and made them yield themselves prisoners.

On the morrow, came one of the ladies to Sir Gawain, and talked with him, saying, "Sir knight, what cheer?"

"Not good," said he.

"It is your own default, sir," said the lady, "for you have done a passing foul deed in slaying that fair damsel yesterday—and ever shall it be great shame to you. But you be not of King Arthur's kin."

"Yea, truly am I," said he; "my name is Gawain, son of King Lot of Orkney, whom King Pellinore slew—and my mother, Belisent, is half-sister to the king."

When the lady heard that, she went and presently got leave for him to quit the castle; and they gave him the head of the white hart to take with him, because it was in his quest; but made him also carry the dead lady with him—her head hung round his neck and her body lay before him on his horse's neck.

So in that fashion he rode back to Camelot; and when the king and queen saw him, and heard tell of his adventures, they were heavily displeased, and, by order of the queen, he was put upon his trial before a court of ladies—who judged him to be evermore, for all his life, the knight of ladies' quarrels, and to fight always on their side, and never against any, except he fought for one lady and his adversary for another; also they charged him never to refuse mercy to him that asked it, and swore him to it on the Holy Gospels. Thus ended the adventure of the white hart.

***

Meanwhile, Sir Tor had made him ready, and followed the knight who rode away with the hound. And as he went, there suddenly met him in the road a dwarf, who struck his horse so viciously upon the head with a great staff, that he leaped backwards a spear's length.

"Wherefore so smite you my horse, foul dwarf?" shouted Sir Tor.

"Because you shalt not pass this way," replied the dwarf, "unless you fight for it with yonder knights in those pavilions," pointing to two tents, where two great spears stood out, and two shields hung upon two trees hard by.

"I may not tarry, for I am on a quest I needs must follow," said Sir Tor.

"You shalt not pass," replied the dwarf, and therewith blew his horn. Then rode out quickly at Sir Tor one armed on horseback, but Sir Tor was quick as he, and riding at him bore him from his horse, and made him yield. Directly after came another still more fiercely, but with a few great strokes and buffets Sir Tor unhorsed him also, and sent them both to Camelot to King Arthur. Then came the dwarf and begged Sir Tor to take him in his service, "for," said he, "I will serve no more recreant knights."

"Take then a horse, and come with me," said Tor.

"Ride you after the knight with the white hound?" said the dwarf; "I can soon bring you where he is."

So they rode through the forest till they came to two more tents. And Sir Tor alighting, went into the first, and saw three damsels lie there, sleeping. Then went he to the other, and found another lady also sleeping, and at her feet the white hound he sought for, which instantly began to bay and bark so loudly, that the lady woke. But Sir Tor had seized the hound and given it to the dwarf's charge.

"What will you do, Sir knight?" cried out the lady; "will you take away my hound from me by force?"

"Yea, lady," said Sir Tor; "for so I must, having the king's command; and I have followed it from King Arthur's court, at Camelot, to this place."

"Well," said the lady, "you will not go far before you be ill handled, and will repent you of the quest."

"I shall cheerfully abide whatsoever adventure cometh, by the grace of God," said Sir Tor; and so mounted his horse and began to ride back on his way. But night coming on, he turned aside to a hermitage that was in the forest, and there abode till the next day, making but sorrowful cheer of such poor food as the hermit had to give him, and hearing a Mass devoutly before he left on the morrow.

And in the early morning, as he rode forth with the dwarf towards Camelot, he heard a knight call loudly after him, "Turn, turn! Abide, Sir knight, and yield me up the hound you took from my lady." At which he turned, and saw a great and strong knight, armed full splendidly, riding down upon him fiercely through a glade of the forest.

Now Sir Tor was very ill provided, for he had but an old courser, which was as weak as himself, because of the hermit's scanty fare. He waited, nevertheless, for the strange knight to come, and at the first onset with their spears, each unhorsed the other, and then fell to with their swords like two mad lions. Then did they smite through one another's shields and helmets till the fragments flew on all sides, and their blood ran out in streams; but yet they carved and rove through the thick armor of the hauberks, and gave each other great and ghastly wounds. But in the end, Sir Tor, finding the strange knight faint, doubled his strokes until he beat him to the earth. Then did he bid him yield to his mercy.

"That will I not," replied Abellius, "while my life lasts and my soul is in my body, unless you give me first the hound."

"I cannot," said Sir Tor, "and will not, for it was my quest to bring again that hound and you unto King Arthur, or otherwise to slay you."

With that there came a damsel riding on a palfrey, as fast as she could drive, and cried out to Sir Tor with a loud voice, "I pray you, for King Arthur's love, give me a gift."

"Ask," said Sir Tor, "and I will give you."

"Gramercy," said the lady, "I ask the head of this false knight Abellius, the most outrageous murderer that lives."

"I repent me of the gift I promised," said Sir Tor. "Let him make you amends for all his trespasses against you."

"He cannot make amends," replied the damsel, "for he hath slain my brother, a far better knight than he, and scorned to give him mercy, though I kneeled for half an hour before him in the mire, to beg it, and though it was but by a chance they fought, and for no former injury or quarrel. I require my gift of you as a true knight, or else will I shame you in King Arthur's court; for this Abellius is the falsest knight alive, and a murderer of many."

When Abellius heard this, he trembled greatly, and was sore afraid, and yielded to Sir Tor, and prayed his mercy.

"I cannot now, Sir knight," said he, "lest I be false to my promise. You would not take my mercy when I offered it; and now it is too late."

Therewith he unlaced his helmet, and took it off; but Abellius, in dismal fear, struggled to his feet, and fled, until Sir Tor overtook him, and smote off his head entirely with one blow.

"Now, sir," said the damsel, "it is near night, I pray you come and lodge at my castle hard by."

"I will, with a good will," said he, for both his horse and he had fared but poorly since they left Camelot.

So he went to the lady's castle and fared sumptuously, and saw her husband, an old knight, who greatly thanked him for his service, and urged him oftentimes to come again.

On the morrow he departed, and reached Camelot by noon, where the king and queen rejoiced to see him, and the king made him Earl; and Merlin prophesied that these adventures were but little to the things he should achieve hereafter.

***

Now while Sir Gawain and Sir Tor had fulfilled their quests, King Pellinore pursued the lady whom the knight had seized away from the wedding-feast. And as he rode through the woods, he saw in a valley a fair young damsel sitting by a well-side, and a wounded knight lying in her arms, and King Pellinore saluted her as he passed by.

As soon as she perceived him she cried out, "Help, help me, knight, for our Lord's sake!" But Pellinore was far too eager in his quest to stay or turn, although she cried a hundred times to him for help; at which she prayed to heaven he might have such sore need before he died as she had now. And presently thereafter her knight died in her arms; and she, for grief and love, slew herself with his sword.

But King Pellinore rode on till he met a poor man, and asked him had he seen a knight pass by that way, leading by force a lady with him.

"Yea, surely," said the man, "and greatly did she moan and cry; but even now another knight is fighting with him to deliver the lady; ride on and you shalt find them fighting still."

At that King Pellinore rode swiftly on, and came to where he saw the two knights fighting, hard by where two pavilions stood. And when he looked in one of them, he saw the lady that was his quest, and with her the two squires of the two knights who fought.

"Fair lady," said he, "you must come with me unto King Arthur's court."

"Sir knight," said the two squires, "yonder be two knights fighting for this lady; go part them, and get their consent to take her, ere you touch her."

"You say well," said King Pellinore, and rode between the combatants, and asked them why they fought.

"Sir knight," said the one, "yon lady is my cousin, mine aunt's daughter, whom I met borne away against her will, by this knight here, with whom I therefore fight to free her."

"Sir knight," replied the other, whose name was Hantzlake of Wentland, "this lady got I, by my arms and prowess, at King Arthur's court to-day."

"That is false," said King Pellinore; "you stole the lady suddenly, and fled away with her, before any knight could arm to stay you. But it is my service to take her back again. Neither of you shall therefore have her; but if you will fight for her, fight with me now and here."

"Well," said the knights, "make ready, and we will assail you with all our might."

Then Sir Hantzlake ran King Pellinore's horse through with his sword, so that they might be all alike on foot. But King Pellinore at that was passing wroth, and ran upon Sir Hantzlake, with a cry, "Keep well your head!" and gave him such a stroke upon the helm

www.professorscompanion.com

as clove him to the chin, so that he fell dead to the ground. When he saw that, the other knight refused to fight, and kneeling down said, "Take my cousin the lady with you, as your quest is; but as you art a true knight, suffer her to come to neither shame nor harm."

So the next day King Pellinore departed for Camelot, and took the lady with him; and as they rode in a valley full of rough stones, the damsel's horse stumbled and threw her, so that her arms were sorely bruised and hurt. And as they rested in the forest for the pain to lessen, night came on, and there they were compelled to make their lodging. A little before midnight they heard the trotting of a horse. "Be you still," said King Pellinore, "for now we may hear of some adventure," and therewith he armed her. Then he heard two knights meet and salute each other, in the dark; one riding from Camelot, the other from the north.

"What tidings at Camelot?" said one.

"By my head," said the other, "I have but just left there, and have espied King Arthur's court, and such a fellowship is there as never may be broke or overcome; for wellnigh all the chivalry of the world is there, and all full loyal to the king, and now I ride back homewards to the north to tell our chiefs, that they waste not their strength in wars against him."

"As for all that," replied the other knight, "I am but now from the north, and bear with me a remedy, the deadliest poison that ever was heard tell of, and to Camelot will I with it; for there we have a friend close to the king, and greatly cherished of him, who hath received gifts from us to poison him, as he hath promised soon to do."

"Beware," said the first knight, "of Merlin, for he knows all things, by the devil's craft."

"I will not fear for that," replied the other, and so rode on his way.

Anon King Pellinore and the lady passed on again; and when they came to the well at which the lady with the wounded knight had sat, they found both knight and damsel utterly devoured by lions and wild beasts, all save the lady's head.

When King Pellinore saw that, he wept bitterly, saying, "Alas! I might have saved her life had I but tarried a few moments in my quest."

"Wherefore make so much sorrow now?" said the lady.

"I know not," answered he, "but my heart grieves greatly for this poor lady's death, so fair she was and young."

Then he required a hermit to bury the remains of the bodies, and bare the lady's head with him to Camelot, to the court.

When he was arrived, he was sworn to tell the truth of his quest before the King and Queen, and when he had entered the Queen somewhat upbraided him, saying, "You were much to blame that you saved not that lady's life."

"Madam," said he, "I shall repent it all my life."

"Ay, king," quoth Merlin, who suddenly came in, "and so you ought to do, for that lady was your daughter, not seen since infancy by you. And she was on her way to court, with a right good young knight, who would have been her husband, but was slain by treachery of a felon knight, Lorraine le Savage, as they came; and because you wouldst not abide and help her, your best friend shall fail you in thine hour of greatest need, for such is the penance ordained you for that deed."

Then did King Pellinore tell Merlin secretly of the treason he had heard in the forest, and Merlin by his craft so ordered that the knight who bare the poison was himself soon after slain by it, and so King Arthur's life was saved.

1

What is the main purpose of this passage?

_____

2

What is the passage's tone?

_____

3

How would you summarize the passage?

_____

4

How would you describe Sir Gawain?

_____

5

How would you describe Sir Tor?

_____

6

How would you describe King Pellinore?

_____

Now after the quest of the Sangreal was fulfilled and all the knights who were left alive were come again to the Round Table, there was great joy in the court. And passing glad were King Arthur and Queen Guinevere to see Sir Lancelot and Sir Bors, for they had been long absent in that quest.

And so greatly was Sir Lancelot's fame now spread abroad that many ladies and damsels daily resorted to him and besought him for their champion; and all right quarrels did he gladly undertake for the pleasure of our Lord Christ. And always as much as he might he withdrew him from the queen.

Wherefore Queen Guinevere, who counted him for her own knight, grew wroth with him, and on a certain day she called him to her chamber, and said thus: "Sir Lancelot, I daily see your loyalty to me doth slack, for ever you art absent from this court, and take other ladies' quarrels on you more than ever you wert wont. Now do I understand you, false knight, and therefore shall I never trust you more. Depart now from my sight, and come no more within this court upon pain of your head." With that she turned from him and would hear no excuses.

So Sir Lancelot departed in heaviness of heart, and calling Sir Bors, Sir Ector, and Sir Lionel, he told them how the queen had dealt with him.

"Fair sir," replied Sir Bors, "remember what honor you have in this country, and how you are called the noblest knight in the world; wherefore go not, for women are hasty, and do often what they sore repent of afterwards. Be ruled by my advice. Take horse and ride to the hermitage beside Windsor, and there abide till I send you better tidings."

To that Sir Lancelot consented, and departed with a sorrowful countenance.

Now when the queen heard of his leaving she was inwardly sorry, but made no show of grief, bearing a proud visage outwardly. And on a certain day she made a costly banquet to all the knights of the Round Table, to show she had as great joy in all others as in Sir Lancelot. And at the banquet were Sir Gawain, and his brothers Sir Agravaine, Sir Gaheris, and Sir Gareth; also Sir Modred, Sir Bors, Sir Blamor, Sir Bleoberis, Sir Ector, Sir Lionel, Sir Palomedes, Sir Mador de la Port, and his cousin Sir Patrice—a knight of Ireland, Sir Pinell le Savage, and many more.

Now Sir Pinell hated Sir Gawain because he had slain one of his kinsmen by treason; and Sir Gawain had a great love for all kinds of fruit, which, when Sir Pinell knew, he poisoned certain apples that were set upon the table, with intent to slay him. And so it chanced as they ate and made merry, Sir Patrice, who sat next to Sir Gawain, took one of the poisoned apples and eat it, and when he had eaten he suddenly swelled up and fell down dead.

At that every knight leapt from the board ashamed and enraged nigh out of their wits, for they knew not what to say, yet seeing that the queen had made the banquet they all had suspicion of her.

"My lady the queen," said Sir Gawain, "I wit well this fruit was meant for me, for all men know my love for it, and now had I been nearly slain; wherefore, I fear me, you will be ashamed."

"This shall not end so," cried Sir Mador de la Port; "now have I lost a noble knight of my own blood, and for this despite and shame I will be revenged to the uttermost."

Then he challenged Queen Guinevere concerning the death of his cousin, but she stood still, sore abashed, and anon with her sorrow and dread, she swooned.

At the noise and sudden cry came in King Arthur, and to him appealed Sir Mador, and impeached the queen.

"Fair lords," said he, "full sorely am I troubled at this matter, for I must be rightful judge, and therein it repents me I may not do battle for my wife, for, as I deem, this deed was none of hers. But I suppose she will not lack a champion, and some good knight surely will put his body in jeopardy to save her."

But all who had been bidden to the banquet said they could not hold the queen excused, or be her champions, for she had made the feast, and either by herself or servants must it have come.

"Alas!" said the queen, "I made this dinner for a good intent, and no evil, so God help me in my need."

"My lord the king," said Sir Mador, "I require you heartily as you be a righteous king give me a day when I may have justice."

"Well," said the king, "I give you this day fifteen days, when you shall be ready and armed in the meadow beside Westminster, and if there be a knight to fight with you, God speed the right, and if not, then must my queen be burnt."

When the king and queen were alone together he asked her how this case befell.

"I wot not how or in what manner," answered she.

"Where is Sir Lancelot?" said King Arthur, "for he would not grudge to do battle for you."

"Sir," said she, "I cannot tell you, but all his kinsmen deem he is not in this realm."

"These be sad tidings," said the king; "I counsel you to find Sir Bors, and pray him for Sir Lancelot's sake to do this battle for you."

So the queen departed and sent for Sir Bors to her chamber, and besought his succor.

"Madam," said he, "what would you have me do? for I may not with my honor take this matter on me, for I was at that same dinner, and all the other knights would have me ever in suspicion. Now do you miss Sir Lancelot, for he would not have failed you in right nor yet in wrong, as you have often proved, but now you have driven him from the country."

"Alas! fair knight," said the queen, "I put me wholly at your mercy, and all that is done amiss I will amend as you will counsel me."

And therewith she kneeled down upon both her knees before Sir Bors, and besought him to have mercy on her.

Anon came in King Arthur also, and prayed him of his courtesy to help her, saying, "I require you for the love of Lancelot."

"My lord," said he, "you require the greatest thing of me that any man can ask, for if I do this battle for the queen I shall anger all my fellows of the Table Round; nevertheless, for my lord Sir Lancelot's sake, and for yours, I will that day be the queen's champion, unless there chance to come a better knight than I am to do battle for her." And this he promised on his faith.

Then were the king and queen passing glad, and thanked him heartily, and so departed.

But Sir Bors rode in secret to the hermitage where Sir Lancelot was, and told him all these tidings.

"It has chanced as I would have it," said Sir Lancelot; "yet make you ready for the battle, but tarry till you see me come."

"Sir," said Sir Bors, "doubt not but you shall have your will."

But many of the knights were greatly wroth with him when they heard he was to be the queen's champion, for there were few in the court but deemed her guilty.

Then said Sir Bors, "Wit you will, fair lords, it were a shame to us all to suffer so fair and noble a lady to be burnt for lack of a champion, for ever hath she proved herself a lover of good knights; wherefore I doubt not she is guiltless of this treason."

At that were some well pleased, but others rested passing wroth.

And when the day was come, the king and queen and all the knights went to the meadow beside Westminster, where the battle should be fought. Then the queen was put in ward, and a great fire was made round the iron stake, where she must be burnt if Sir Mador won the day.

So when the heralds blew, Sir Mador rode forth, and took oath that Queen Guinevere was guilty of Sir Patrice's death, and his oath he would prove with his body against any who would say the contrary. Then came forth Sir Bors, and said, "Queen Guinevere is in the right, and that will I prove with my hands."

With that they both departed to their tents to make ready for the battle. But Sir Bors tarried long, hoping Sir Lancelot would come, till Sir Mador cried out to King Arthur, "Bid your champion come forth, unless he dare not." Then was Sir Bors ashamed, and took his horse and rode to the end of the lists.

But ere he could meet Sir Mador he was aware of a knight upon a white horse, armed at all points, and with a strange shield, who rode to him and said, "I pray you withdraw from this quarrel, for it is mine, and I have ridden far to fight in it."

Thereat Sir Bors rode to King Arthur, and told him that another knight was come who would do battle for the queen.

"Who is he?" said King Arthur.

"I may not tell you," said Sir Bors; "but he made a covenant with me to be here to-day, wherefore I am discharged."

Then the king called that knight, and asked him if he would fight for the queen.

"Therefore came I hither, Sir king," answered he; "but let us tarry no longer, for anon I have other matters to do. But wit you well," said he to the Knights of the Round Table, "it is shame to you for such a courteous queen to suffer this dishonor."

And all men marveled who this knight might be, for none knew him save Sir Bors.

Then Sir Mador and the knight rode to either end of the lists, and couching their spears, ran one against the other with all their might; and Sir Mador's spear broke short, but the strange knight bore both him and his horse down to the ground. Then lightly they leaped from their saddles and drew their swords, and so came eagerly to the battle, and either gave the other many sad strokes and sore and deep wounds.

Thus they fought nigh an hour, for Sir Mador was a full strong and valiant knight. But at last the strange knight smote him to the earth, and gave him such a buffet on the helm as wellnigh killed him. Then did Sir Mador yield, and prayed his life.

"I will but grant it you," said the strange knight, "if you wilt release the queen from this quarrel forever, and promise that no mention shall be made upon Sir Patrice's tomb that ever she consented to that treason."

"All this shall be done," said Sir Mador.

Then the knights parters took up Sir Mador and led him to his tent, and the other knight went straight to the stair foot of King Arthur's throne; and by that time was the queen come to the king again, and kissed him lovingly.

Then both the king and she stooped down, and thanked the knight, and prayed him to put off his helm and rest him, and to take a cup of wine. And when he put his helmet off to drink, all people saw it was Sir Lancelot. But when the queen beheld him she sank almost to the ground weeping for sorrow and for joy, that he had done her such great goodness when she had showed him such unkindness.

Then the knights of his blood gathered round him, and there was great joy and mirth in the court. And Sir Mador and Sir Lancelot were soon healed of their wounds; and not long after came the Lady of the Lake to the court, and told all there by her enchantments how Sir Pinell, and not the queen, was guilty of Sir Patrice's death. Whereat the queen was held excused of all men, and Sir Pinell fled the country.

So Sir Patrice was buried in the church of Winchester, and it was written on his tomb that Sir Pinell slew him with a poisoned apple, in error for Sir Gawain. Then, through Sir Lancelot's favor, the queen was reconciled to Sir Mador, and all was forgiven.

Now fifteen days before the Feast of the Assumption of our Lady, the king proclaimed a tourney to be held that feast-day at Camelot, whereat himself and the King of Scotland would joust with all who should come against them. So thither went the King of North Wales, and King Anguish of Ireland, and Sir Galahaut the noble prince, and many other nobles of divers countries.

And King Arthur made ready to go, and would have had the queen go with him, but she said that she was sick. Sir Lancelot, also, made excuses, saying he was not yet whole of his wounds.

At that the king was passing heavy and grieved, and so departed alone towards Camelot. And by the way he lodged in a town called Astolat, and lay that night in the castle.

As soon as he had gone, Sir Lancelot said to the queen, "This night I will rest, and to-morrow betimes will I take my way to Camelot; for at these jousts I will be against the king and his fellowship."

"You may do as you list," said Queen Guinevere; "but by my counsel you will not be against the king, for in his company are many hardy knights, as you well know."

"Madam," said Sir Lancelot, "I pray you be not displeased with me, for I will take the adventure that God may send me."

And on the morrow he went to the church and heard mass, and took his leave of the queen, and so departed.

Then he rode long till he came to Astolat, and there lodged at the castle of an old baron called Sir Bernard of Astolat, which was near the castle where King Arthur lodged. And as Sir Lancelot entered the king espied him, and knew him. Then said he to the knights, "I have just seen a knight who will fight full well at the joust toward which we go."

"Who is it?" asked they.

"As yet you shall not know," he answered smiling.

When Sir Lancelot was in his chamber unarming the old baron came to him, saluting him, though as yet he knew not who he was.

Now Sir Bernard had a daughter passing beautiful, called the Fair Maid of Astolat, and when she saw Sir Lancelot she loved him from that instant with her whole heart, and could not stay from gazing on him.

On the morrow, Sir Lancelot asked the old baron to lend him a strange shield. "For," said he, "I would be unknown."

"Sir," said his host, "you shall have your desire, for here is the shield of my eldest son, Sir Torre, who was hurt the day he was made knight, so that he cannot ride; and his shield, therefore, is not known. And, if it please you, my youngest son, Sir Lavaine, shall ride with you to the jousts, for he is of his age full strong and mighty; and I deem you be a noble knight, wherefore I pray you tell me your name."

"As to that," said Sir Lancelot, "you must hold me excused at this time, but if I speed well at the jousts, I will come again and tell you; but in anywise let me have your son, Sir Lavaine, with me, and lend me his brother's shield."

Then, ere they departed, came Elaine, the baron's daughter, and said to Sir Lancelot, "I pray you, gentle knight, to wear my token at to-morrow's tourney."

"If I should grant you that, fair damsel," said he, "you might say that I did more for you than ever I have done for lady or damsel."

Then he bethought him that if he granted her request he would be the more disguised, for never before had he worn any lady's token. So anon he said, "Fair damsel, I will wear your token on my helmet if you wilt show it me."

Thereat was she passing glad, and brought him a scarlet sleeve broidered with pearls, which Sir Lancelot took, and put upon his helm. Then he prayed her to keep his shield for him until he came again, and taking Sir Torre's shield instead, rode forth with Sir Lavaine towards Camelot.

On the morrow the trumpets blew for the tourney, and there was a great press of dukes and earls and barons and many noble knights; and King Arthur sat in a gallery to behold who did the best. So the King of Scotland and his knights, and King Anguish of Ireland rode forth on King Arthur's side; and against them came the King of North Wales, the King of a Hundred Knights, the King of Northumberland, and the noble prince Sir Galahaut.

But Sir Lancelot and Sir Lavaine rode into a little wood behind the party which was against King Arthur, to watch which side should prove the weakest.

Then was there a strong fight between the two parties, for the King of a Hundred Knights smote down the King of Scotland; and Sir Palomedes, who was on King Arthur's side, overthrew Sir Galahaut. Then came fifteen Knights of the Round Table and beat back the Kings of Northumberland and North Wales with their knights.

"Now," said Sir Lancelot to Sir Lavaine, "if you will help me, you shall see yonder fellowship go back as fast as they came."

"Sir," said Sir Lavaine, "I will do what I can."

Then they rode together into the thickest of the press, and there, with one spear, Sir Lancelot smote down five Knights of the Round Table, one after other, and Sir Lavaine overthrew two. And taking another spear, for his own was broken, Sir Lancelot smote down four more knights, and Sir Lavaine a fifth. Then, drawing his sword, Sir Lancelot fought fiercely on the right hand and the left, and unhorsed Sir Safire, Sir Epinogris, and Sir Galleron. At that the Knights of the Round Table withdrew themselves as well as they were able.

"Now, mercy," said Sir Gawain, who sat by King Arthur; "what knight is that who doth such marvelous deeds of arms? I should deem him by his force to be Sir Lancelot, but that he wears a lady's token on his helm as never Lancelot doth."

"Let him be," said King Arthur; "he will be better known, and do more ere he depart."

Thus the party against King Arthur prospered at this time, and his knights were sore ashamed. Then Sir Bors, Sir Ector, and Sir Lionel called together the knights of their blood, nine in number, and agreed to join together in one band against the two strange knights. So they encountered Sir Lancelot all at once, and by main force smote his horse to the ground; and by misfortune Sir Bors struck Sir Lancelot through the shield into the side, and the spear broke off and left the head in the wound.

When Sir Lavaine saw that, he ran to the King of Scotland and struck him off his horse, and brought it to Sir Lancelot, and helped him to mount. Then Sir Lancelot bore Sir Bors and his horse to the ground, and in like manner served Sir Ector and Sir Lionel; and turning upon three other knights he smote them down also; while Sir Lavaine did many gallant deeds.

But feeling himself now sorely wounded Sir Lancelot drew his sword, and proffered to fight with Sir Bors, who, by this time, was mounted anew. And as they met, Sir Ector and Sir Lionel came also, and the swords of all three drave fiercely against him. When he felt their buffets, and his wound that was so grievous, he determined to do all his best while he could yet endure, and smote Sir Bors a blow that bent his head down nearly to the ground and razed his helmet off and pulled him from his horse.

Then rushing at Sir Ector and Sir Lionel, he smote them down, and might have slain all three, but when he saw their faces his heart forbade him. Leaving them, therefore, on the field, he hurled into the thickest of the press, and did such feats of arms as never were beheld before.

And Sir Lavaine was with him through it all, and overthrew ten knights; but Sir Lancelot smote down more than thirty, and most of them Knights of the Round Table.

Then the king ordered the trumpets to blow for the end of the tourney, and the prize to be given by the heralds to the knight with the white shield who bore the red sleeve.

But ere Sir Lancelot was found by the heralds, came the King of the Hundred Knights, the King of North Wales, the King of Northumberland, and Sir Galahaut, and said to him, "Fair knight, God bless you, for much have you done this day for us; wherefore we pray you come with us and receive the honor and the prize as you have worshipfully deserved it."

"My fair lords," said Sir Lancelot, "wit you well if I have deserved thanks, I have sore bought them, for I am like never to escape with my life; therefore pray you let me depart, for I am sore hurt. I take no thought of honor, for I had rather rest me than be lord of all the world." And therewith he groaned piteously, and rode a great gallop away from them.

And Sir Lavaine rode after him, sad at heart, for the broken spear still stuck fast in Sir Lancelot's side, and the blood streamed sorely from the wound. Anon they came near a wood more than a mile from the lists, where he knew he could be hidden.

Then said he to Sir Lavaine, "O gentle knight, help me to pull out this spear-head from my side, for the pain thereof nigh kills me."

"Dear lord," said he, "I gladly would help you; but I dread to draw it forth, lest you should die for loss of blood."

"I charge you as you love me," said Sir Lancelot, "draw it out."

So they dismounted, and with a mighty wrench Sir Lavaine drew the spear forth from Sir Lancelot's side; whereat he gave a marvelous great shriek and ghastly groan, and all his blood leaped forth in a full stream. Then he sank swooning to the earth, with a visage pale as death.

"Alas!" cried Sir Lavaine, "what shall I do now?"

And then he turned his master's face towards the wind, and sat by him nigh half an hour while he lay quiet as one dead. But at the last he lifted up his eyes, and said, "I pray you bear me on my horse again, and lead me to a hermit who dwells within two miles hence, for he was formerly a knight of Arthur's court, and now hath mighty skill in medicine and herbs."

So with great pain Sir Lavaine got him to his horse, and led him to the hermitage within the wood, beside a stream. Then knocked he with his spear upon the door, and prayed to enter. At that a child came out, to whom he said, "Fair child, pray the good man your master to come hither and let in a knight who is sore wounded."

Anon came out the knight-hermit, whose name was Sir Baldwin, and asked, "Who is this wounded knight?"

"I know not," said Sir Lavaine, "save that he is the noblest knight I ever met with, and hath done this day such marvelous deeds of arms against King Arthur that he hath won the prize of the tourney."

Then the hermit gazed long on Sir Lancelot, and hardly knew him, so pale he was with bleeding, yet said he at the last, "Who art you, lord?"

Sir Lancelot answered feebly, "I am a stranger knight adventurous, who labors through many realms to win worship."

"Why hide you your name, dear lord, from me?" cried Sir Baldwin; "for in sooth I know you now to be the noblest knight in all the world—my lord Sir Lancelot du Lake, with whom I long had fellowship at the Round Table."

"Since you know me, fair sir," said he, "I pray you, for Christ's sake, to help me if you may."

"Doubt not," replied he, "that you shall live and fare right well."

Then he staunched his wound, and gave him strong medicines and cordials till he was refreshed from his faintness and came to himself again.

Now after the jousting was done King Arthur held a feast, and asked to see the knight with the red sleeve that he might take the prize. So they told him how that knight had ridden from the field wounded nigh to death. "These be the worst tidings I have heard for many years," cried out the king; "I would not for my kingdom he were slain."

Then all men asked, "Know you him, lord?"

"I may not tell you at this time," said he; "but would to God we had good tidings of him."

Then Sir Gawain prayed leave to go and seek that knight, which the king gladly gave him. So forthwith he mounted and rode many leagues round Camelot, but could hear no tidings.

Within two days thereafter King Arthur and his knights returned from Camelot, and Sir Gawain chanced to lodge at Astolat, in the house of Sir Bernard. And there came in the fair Elaine to him, and prayed him news of the tournament, and who won the prize. "A knight with a white shield," said he, "who bare a red sleeve in his helm, smote down all comers and won the day."

At that the visage of Elaine changed suddenly from white to red, and heartily she thanked our Lady.

Then said Sir Gawain, "Know you that knight?" and urged her till she told him that it was her sleeve he wore. So Sir Gawain knew it was for love that she had given it; and when he heard she kept his proper shield he prayed to see it.

As soon as it was brought he saw Sir Lancelot's arms thereon, and cried, "Alas! now am I heavier of heart than ever yet."

"Wherefore?" said fair Elaine.

"Fair damsel," answered he, "know you not that the knight you love is of all knights the noblest in the world, Sir Lancelot du Lake? With all my heart I pray you may have joy of each other, but hardly dare I think that you shall see him in this world again, for he is so sore wounded he may scarcely live, and is gone out of sight where none can find him."

Then was Elaine nigh mad with grief and sorrow, and with piteous words she prayed her father that she might go seek Sir Lancelot and her brother. So in the end her father gave her leave, and she departed.

And on the morrow came Sir Gawain to the court, and told how he had found Sir Lancelot's shield in Elaine's keeping, and how it was her sleeve which he had worn; whereat all marveled, for Sir Lancelot had done for her more than he had ever done for any woman.

But when Queen Guinevere heard it she was beside herself with wrath, and sending privily for Sir Bors, who sorrowed sorely that through him Sir Lancelot had been hurt—"Have you now heard," said she, "how falsely Sir Lancelot hath betrayed me?"

"I beseech you, madam," said he, "speak not so, for else I may not hear you."

"Shall I not call him traitor," cried she, "who hath worn another lady's token at the jousting?"

"Be sure he did it, madam, for no ill intent," replied Sir Bors, "but that he might be better hidden, for never did he in that wise before."

"Now shame on him, and you who would help him," cried the queen.

"Madam, say what you will," said he; "but I must haste to seek him, and God send me soon good tidings of him."

So with that he departed to find Sir Lancelot.

Now Elaine had ridden with full haste from Astolat, and come to Camelot, and there she sought throughout the country for any news of Lancelot. And so it chanced that Sir Lavaine was riding near the hermitage to exercise his horse, and when she saw him she ran up and cried aloud, "How doth my lord Sir Lancelot fare?"

Then said Sir Lavaine, marveling greatly, "How know you my lord's name, fair sister?"

So she told him how Sir Gawain had lodged with Sir Bernard, and knew Sir Lancelot's shield.

Then prayed she to see his lord forthwith, and when she came to the hermitage and found him lying there sore sick and bleeding, she swooned for sorrow. Anon, as she revived, Sir Lancelot kissed her, and said, "Fair maid, I pray you take comfort, for, by God's grace, I shall be shortly whole of this wound, and if you be come to tend me, I am heartily bounden to your great kindness." Yet was he sore vexed to hear Sir Gawain had discovered him, for he knew Queen Guinevere would be full wroth because of the red sleeve.

So Elaine rested in the hermitage, and ever night and day she watched and waited on Sir Lancelot, and would let none other tend him. And as she saw him more, the more she set her love upon him, and could by no means withdraw it. Then said Sir Lancelot to Sir Lavaine, "I pray you set some to watch for the good knight Sir Bors, for as he hurt me, so will he surely seek for me."

Now Sir Bors by this time had come to Camelot, and was seeking for Sir Lancelot everywhere, so Sir Lavaine soon found him, and brought him to the hermitage.

And when he saw Sir Lancelot pale and feeble, he wept for pity and sorrow that he had given him that grievous wound. "God send you a right speedy cure, dear lord," said he; "for I am of all men most unhappy to have wounded you, who art our leader, and the noblest knight in all the world."

"Fair cousin," said Sir Lancelot, "be comforted, for I have but gained what I sought, and it was through pride that I was hurt, for had I warned you of my coming it had not been; wherefore let us speak of other things."

So they talked long together, and Sir Bors told him of the queen's anger. Then he asked Sir Lancelot, "Was it from this maid who tends you so lovingly you had the token?"

"Yea," said Sir Lancelot; "and would I could persuade her to withdraw her love from me."

"Why should you do so?" said Sir Bors; "for she is passing fair and loving. I would to heaven you could love her."

"That may not be," replied he; "but it repents me in sooth to grieve her."

Then they talked of other matters, and of the great jousting at Allhallowtide next coming, between King Arthur and the King of North Wales.

"Abide with me till then," said Sir Lancelot, "for by that time I trust to be all whole again, and we will go together."

So Elaine daily and nightly tending him, within a month he felt so strong he deemed himself full cured. Then on a day, when Sir Bors and Sir Lavaine were from the hermitage, and the knight-hermit also was gone forth, Sir Lancelot prayed Elaine to bring him some herbs from the forest.

When she was gone he rose and made haste to arm himself, and try if he were whole enough to joust, and mounted on his horse, which was fresh with lack of labor for so long a time. But when he set his spear in the rest and tried his armor, the horse bounded and leapt beneath him, so that Sir Lancelot strained to keep him back. And therewith his wound, which was not wholly healed, burst forth again, and with a mighty groan he sank down swooning on the ground.

At that came fair Elaine and wept and piteously moaned to see him lying so. And when Sir Bors and Sir Lavaine came back, she called them traitors to let him rise, or to know any rumor of the tournament. Anon the hermit returned and was wroth to see Sir Lancelot risen, but within a while he recovered him from his swoon and staunched the wound. Then Sir Lancelot told him how he had risen of his own will to assay his strength for the tournament. But the hermit bade him rest and let Sir Bors go alone, for else would he sorely peril his life. And Elaine, with tears, prayed him in the same wise, so that Sir Lancelot in the end consented.

So Sir Bors departed to the tournament, and there he did such feats of arms that the prize was given between him and Sir Gawain, who did like valiantly.

And when all was over he came back and told Sir Lancelot, and found him so nigh well that he could rise and walk. And within a while thereafter he departed from the hermitage and went with Sir Bors, Sir Lavaine, and fair Elaine to Astolat, where Sir Bernard joyfully received them.

But after they had lodged there a few days Sir Lancelot and Sir Bors must needs depart and return to King Arthur's court.

So when Elaine knew Sir Lancelot must go, she came to him and said, "Have mercy on me, fair knight, and let me not die for your love."

Then said Sir Lancelot, very sad at heart, "Fair maid, what would you that I should do for you?"

"If I may not be your wife, dear lord," she answered, "I must die."

"Alas!" said he, "I pray heaven that may not be; for in sooth I may not be your husband. But gladly would I show you what thankfulness I can for all your love and kindness to me. And ever will I be your knight, fair maiden; and if it chance that you shall ever wed some noble knight, right heartily will I give you such a dower as half my lands will bring."

"Alas! what shall that aid me?" answered she; "for I must die," and therewith she fell to the earth in a deep swoon.

Then was Sir Lancelot passing heavy of heart, and said to Sir Bernard and Sir Lavaine, "What shall I do for her?"

"Alas!" said Sir Bernard, "I know well that she will die for your sake."

And Sir Lavaine said, "I marvel not that she so sorely mourns your departure, for truly I do as she doth, and since I once have seen you, lord, I cannot leave you."

So anon, with a full sorrowful heart, Sir Lancelot took his leave, and Sir Lavaine rode with him to the court. And King Arthur and the Knights of the Round Table joyed greatly to see him whole of his wound, but Queen Guinevere was sorely wroth, and neither spake with him nor greeted him.

Now when Sir Lancelot had departed, the Maid of Astolat could neither eat, nor drink, nor sleep for sorrow; and having thus endured ten days, she felt within herself that she must die.

Then sent she for a holy man, and was shriven and received the sacrament. But when he told her she must leave her earthly thoughts, she answered, "Am I not an earthly woman? What sin is it to love the noblest knight of all the world? And, by my truth, I am not able to withstand the love whereof I die; wherefore, I pray the High Father of Heaven to have mercy on my soul."

Then she besought Sir Bernard to indict a letter as she should devise, and said, "When I am dead put this within my hand, and dress me in my fairest clothes, and lay me in a barge all covered with black samite, and steer it down the river till it reach the court. Thus, father, I beseech you let it be."

Then, full of grief, he promised her it should be so. And anon she died, and all the household made a bitter lamentation over her.

Then did they as she had desired, and laid her body, richly dressed, upon a bed within the barge, and a trusty servant steered it down the river towards the court.

Now King Arthur and Queen Guinevere sat at a window of the palace, and saw the barge come floating with the tide, and marveled what was laid therein, and sent a messenger to see, who, soon returning, prayed them to come forth.

When they came to the shore they marveled greatly, and the king asked of the serving-man who steered the barge what this might mean. But he made signs that he was dumb, and pointed to the letter in the damsel's hands. So King Arthur took the letter from the hand of the corpse, and found thereon written, "To the noble knight, Sir Lancelot du Lake."

Then was Sir Lancelot sent for, and the letter read aloud by a clerk, and thus it was written:—

"Most noble knight, my lord Sir Lancelot, now hath death forever parted us. I, whom men call the Maid of Astolat, set my love upon you, and have died for your sake. This is my last request, that you pray for my soul and give me burial. Grant me this, Sir Lancelot, as you art a peerless knight."

At these words the queen and all the knights wept sore for pity.

Then said Sir Lancelot, "My lord, I am right heavy for the death of this fair damsel; and God knows that right unwillingly I caused it, for she was good as she was fair, and much was I beholden to her; but she loved me beyond measure, and asked me that I could not give her."

"You might have shown her gentleness enough to save her life," answered the queen.

"Madam," said he, "she would but be repaid by my taking her to wife, and that I could not grant her, for love coms of the heart and not by constraint."

"That is true," said the king; "for love is free."

"I pray you," said Sir Lancelot, "let me now grant her last asking, to be buried by me."

So on the morrow, he caused her body to be buried richly and solemnly, and ordained masses for her soul, and made great sorrow over her.

Then the queen sent for Sir Lancelot, and prayed his pardon for her wrath against him without cause. "This is not the first time it hath been so," answered he; "yet must I ever bear with you, and so do I now forgive you."

So Queen Guinevere and Sir Lancelot were made friends again; but anon such favor did she show him, as in the end brought many evils on them both and all the realm.

1

What is the main purpose of this passage?

_____

2

What is the passage's tone?

_____

3

How would you summarize the passage?

_____

4

How would you describe Sir Lancelot?

_____

5

How would you describe Elaine?

_____

Within a while thereafter was a jousting at the court, wherein Sir Lancelot won the prize. And two of those he smote down were Sir Agravaine, the brother of Sir Gawain, and Sir Modred, his false brother—King Arthur's son by Belisent. And because of his victory they hated Sir Lancelot, and sought how they might injure him.

So on a night, when King Arthur was hunting in the forest, and the queen sent for Sir Lancelot to her chamber, they two espied him; and thinking now to make a scandal and a quarrel between Lancelot and the king, they found twelve others, and said Sir Lancelot was ever now in the queen's chamber, and King Arthur was dishonored.

Then, all armed, they came suddenly round the queen's door, and cried, "Traitor! now art you taken."

"Madam, we be betrayed," said Sir Lancelot; "yet shall my life cost these men dear."

Then did the queen weep sore, and dismally she cried, "Alas! there is no armor here whereby you might withstand so many; wherefore you will be slain, and I be burnt for the dread crime they will charge on me."

But while she spake the shouting of the knights was heard without, "Traitor, come forth, for now you art snared!"

"Better were twenty deaths at once than this vile outcry," said Sir Lancelot.

Then he kissed her and said, "Most noble lady, I beseech you, as I have ever been your own true knight, take courage; pray for my soul if I be now slain, and trust my faithful friends, Sir Bors and Sir Lavaine, to save you from the fire."

But ever bitterly she wept and moaned, and cried, "Would God that they would take and slay me, and that you could escape."

"That shall never be," said he. And wrapping his mantle round his arm he unbarred the door a little space, so that but one could enter.

Then first rushed in Sir Chalaunce, a full strong knight, and lifted up his sword to smite Sir Lancelot; but lightly he avoided him, and struck Sir Chalaunce, with his hand, such a sore buffet on the head as felled him dead upon the floor.

Then Sir Lancelot pulled in his body and barred the door again, and dressed himself in his armor, and took his drawn sword in his hand.

But still the knights cried mightily without the door, "Traitor, come forth!"

"Be silent and depart," replied Sir Lancelot; "for be you sure you will not take me, and to-morrow will I meet you face to face before the king."

"You shall have no such grace," they cried; "but we will slay you, or take you as we list."

"Then save yourselves who may," he thundered, and therewith suddenly unbarred the door and rushed forth at them. And at the first blow he slew Sir Agravaine, and after him twelve other knights, with twelve more mighty buffets. And none of all escaped him save Sir Modred, who, sorely wounded, flew away for life.

Then returned he to the queen, and said, "Now, madam, will I depart, and if you be in any danger I pray you come to me."

"Surely will I stay here, for I am queen," she answered; "yet if to-morrow any harm come to me I trust to you for rescue."

"Have you no doubt of me," said he, "for ever while I live am I your own true knight."

Therewith he took his leave, and went and told Sir Bors and all his kindred of this adventure. "We will be with you in this quarrel," said they all; "and if the queen be sentenced to the fire, we certainly will save her."

Meanwhile Sir Modred, in great fear and pain, fled from the court, and rode until he found King Arthur, and told him all that had befallen. But the king would scarce believe him till he came and saw the bodies of Sir Agravaine and all the other knights.

Then felt he in himself that all was true, and with his passing grief his heart nigh broke. "Alas!" cried he, "now is the fellowship of the Round Table forever broken: yea, woe is me! I may not with my honor spare my queen."

Anon it was ordained that Queen Guinevere should be burned to death, because she had dishonored King Arthur.

But when Sir Gawain heard thereof, he came before the king, and said, "My lord, I counsel you be not too hasty in this matter, but stay the judgment of the queen a season, for it may well be that Sir Lancelot was in her chamber for no evil, seeing she is greatly beholden to him for so many deeds done for her sake, and peradventure she had sent to him to thank him, and did it secretly that she might avoid slander."

But King Arthur answered, full of grief, "Alas! I may not help her; she is judged as any other woman."

Then he required Sir Gawain and his brethren, Sir Gaheris and Sir Gareth, to be ready to bear the queen to-morrow to the place of execution.

"Nay, noble lord," replied Sir Gawain, "that can I never do; for neither will my heart suffer me to see the queen die, nor shall men ever say I was of your counsel in this matter."

Then said his brother, "You may command us to be there, but since it is against our will, we will be without arms, that we may do no battle against her."

So on the morrow was Queen Guinevere led forth to die by fire, and a mighty crowd was there, of knights and nobles, armed and unarmed. And all the lords and ladies wept sore at that piteous sight. Then was she shriven by a priest, and the men came nigh to bind her to the stake and light the fire.

At that Sir Lancelot's spies rode hastily and told him and his kindred, who lay hidden in a wood hard by; and suddenly, with twenty knights, he rushed into the midst of all the throng to rescue her.

But certain of King Arthur's knights rose up and fought with them, and there was a full great battle and confusion. And Sir Lancelot drave fiercely here and there among the press, and smote on every side, and at every blow struck down a knight, so that many were slain by him and his fellows.

Then was the queen set free, and caught up on Sir Lancelot's saddle and fled away with him and all his company to the Castle of La Joyous Garde.

Now so it chanced that, in the turmoil of the fighting, Sir Lancelot had unawares struck down and slain the two good knights Sir Gareth and Sir Gaheris, knowing it not, for he fought wildly, and saw not that they were unarmed.

When King Arthur heard thereof, and of all that battle, and the rescue of the queen, he sorrowed heavily for those good knights, and was passing wroth with Lancelot and the queen.

But when Sir Gawain heard of his brethren's death he swooned for sorrow and wrath, for he wist that Sir Lancelot had killed them in malice. And as soon as he recovered he ran in to the king, and said, "Lord king and uncle, hear this oath which now I swear, that from this day I will not fail Sir Lancelot till one of us hath slain the other. And now, unless you haste to war with him, that we may be avenged, will I myself alone go after him."

Then the king, full of wrath and grief, agreed thereto, and sent letters throughout the realm to summon all his knights, and went with a vast army to besiege the Castle of La Joyous Garde. And Sir Lancelot, with his knights, mightily defended it; but never would he suffer any to go forth and attack one of the king's army, for he was right loth to fight against him.

So when fifteen weeks were passed, and King Arthur's army wasted itself in vain against the castle, for it was passing strong, it chanced upon a day Sir Lancelot was looking from the walls and espied King Arthur and Sir Gawain close beside.

"Come forth, Sir Lancelot," said King Arthur right fiercely, "and let us two meet in the midst of the field."

"God forbid that I should encounter with you, lord, for you didst make me a knight," replied Sir Lancelot.

Then cried Sir Gawain, "Shame on you, traitor and false knight, yet be you well assured we will regain the queen and slay you and your company; yea, double shame on you to slay my brother Gaheris unarmed, Sir Gareth also, who loved you so well. For that treachery, be sure I am thine enemy till death."

"Alas!" cried Sir Lancelot, "that I hear such tidings, for I knew not I had slain those noble knights, and right sorely now do I repent it with a heavy heart. Yet abate your wrath, Sir Gawain, for you know full well I did it by mischance, for I loved them ever as my own brothers."

"You liest, false recreant," cried Sir Gawain, fiercely.

At that Sir Lancelot was wroth, and said, "I well see you art now mine enemy, and that there can be no more peace with you, or with my lord the king, else would I gladly give back the queen."

Then the king would gladly have listened to Sir Lancelot, for more than all his own wrong did he grieve at the sore waste and damage of the realm, but Sir Gawain persuaded him against it, and ever cried out foully on Sir Lancelot.

When Sir Bors and the other knights of Lancelot's party heard the fierce words of Sir Gawain, they were passing wroth, and prayed to ride forth and be avenged on him, for they were weary of so long waiting to no good. And in the end Sir Lancelot, with a heavy heart, consented.

So on the morrow the hosts on either side met in the field, and there was a great battle. And Sir Gawain prayed his knights chiefly to set upon Sir Lancelot; but Sir Lancelot commanded his company to forbear King Arthur and Sir Gawain.

So the two armies jousted together right fiercely, and Sir Gawain proffered to encounter with Sir Lionel, and overthrew him. But Sir Bors and Sir Blamor, and Sir Palomedes, who were on Sir Lancelot's side, did great feats of arms, and overthrew many of King Arthur's knights.

Then the king came forth against Sir Lancelot, but Sir Lancelot forbore him and would not strike again.

At that Sir Bors rode up against the king and smote him down. But Sir Lancelot cried, "Touch him not on pain of your head," and going to King Arthur he alighted and gave him his own horse, saying, "My lord, I pray you forbear this strife, for it can bring to neither of us any honor."

And when King Arthur looked on him the tears came to his eyes as he thought of his noble courtesy, and he said within himself, "Alas! that ever this war began."

But on the morrow Sir Gawain led forth the army again, and Sir Bors commanded on Sir Lancelot's side. And they two struck together so fiercely that both fell to the ground sorely wounded; and all the day they fought till night fell, and many were slain on both sides, yet in the end neither gained the victory.

But by now the fame of this fierce war spread through all Christendom, and when the Pope heard thereof he sent a Bull, and charged King Arthur to make peace with Lancelot, and receive back Queen Guinevere; and for the offense imputed to her absolution should be given by the Pope.

Thereto would King Arthur straightway have obeyed, but Sir Gawain ever urged him to refuse.

When Sir Lancelot heard thereof, he wrote thus to the king: "It was never in my thought, lord, to withhold your queen from you; but since she was condemned for my sake to death, I deemed it but a just and knightly part to rescue her therefrom; wherefore I recommend me to your grace, and within eight days will I come to you and bring the queen in safety."

Then, within eight days, as he had said, Sir Lancelot rode from out the castle with Queen Guinevere, and a hundred knights for company, each carrying an olive branch, in sign of peace. And so they came to the court, and found King Arthur sitting on his throne, with Sir Gawain and many other knights around him. And when Sir Lancelot entered with the queen, they both kneeled down before the king.

Anon Sir Lancelot rose and said, "My lord, I have brought hither my lady the queen again, as right requires, and by commandment of the Pope and you. I pray you take her to your heart again and forget the past. For myself I may ask nothing, and for my sin I shall have sorrow and sore punishment; yet I would to heaven I might have your grace."

But ere the king could answer, for he was moved with pity at his words, Sir Gawain cried aloud, "Let the king do as he will, but be sure, Sir Lancelot, you and I shall never be accorded while we live, for you has slain my brethren traitorously and unarmed."

"As heaven is my help," replied Sir Lancelot, "I did it ignorantly, for I loved them well, and while I live I shall bewail their death; but to make war with me were no avail, for I must needs fight with you if you assailest, and peradventure I might kill you also, which I were right loth to do."

"I will forgive you never," cried Sir Gawain, "and if the king accords with you he shall lose my service."

Then the knights who stood near tried to reconcile Sir Gawain to Sir Lancelot, but he would not hear them. So, at the last, Sir Lancelot said, "Since peace is vain, I will depart, lest I bring more evil on my fellowship."

And as he turned to go, the tears fell from him, and he said, "Alas, most noble Christian realm, which I have loved above all others, now shall I see you never more!" Then said he to the queen, "Madam, now must I leave you and this noble fellowship forever. And, I beseech you, pray for me, and if you ever be defamed of any, let me hear thereof, and as I have been ever your true knight in right and wrong, so will I be again."

With that he kneeled and kissed King Arthur's hands, and departed on his way. And there was none in all that court, save Sir Gawain alone, but wept to see him go.

So he returned with all his knights to the Castle of La Joyous Garde, and, for his sorrow's sake, he named it Dolorous Garde thenceforth.

Anon he left the realm, and went with many of his fellowship beyond the sea to France, and there divided all his lands among them equally, he sharing but as the rest.

And from that time forward peace had been between him and King Arthur, but for Sir Gawain, who left the king no rest, but constantly persuaded him that Lancelot was raising mighty hosts against him.

So in the end his malice overcame the king, who left the government in charge of Modred, and made him guardian of the queen, and went with a great army to invade Sir Lancelot's lands.

Yet Sir Lancelot would make no war upon the king, and sent a message to gain peace on any terms King Arthur chose. But Sir Gawain met the herald ere he reached the king, and sent him back with taunting and bitter words. Whereat Sir Lancelot sorrowfully called his knights together and fortified the Castle of Benwicke, and there was shortly besieged by the army of King Arthur.

And every day Sir Gawain rode up to the walls, and cried out foully on Sir Lancelot, till, upon a time, Sir Lancelot answered him that he would meet him in the field and put his boasting to the proof. So it was agreed on both sides that there should none come nigh them or separate them till one had fallen or yielded; and they two rode forth.

Then did they wheel their horses apart, and turning, came together as it had been thunder, so that both horses fell, and both their lances broke. At that they drew their swords and set upon each other fiercely, with passing grievous strokes.

Now Sir Gawain had through magic a marvelous great gift. For every day, from morning till noon, his strength waxed to the might of seven men, but after that waned to his natural force. Therefore till noon he gave Sir Lancelot many mighty buffets, which scarcely he endured. Yet greatly he forbore Sir Gawain, for he was aware of his enchantment, and smote him slightly till his own knights marveled. But after noon Sir Gawain's strength sank fast, and then, with one full blow, Sir Lancelot laid him on the earth. Then Sir Gawain cried out, "Turn not away, you traitor knight, but slay me if you wilt, or else I will arise and fight with you again some other time."

"Sir knight," replied Sir Lancelot, "I never yet smote a fallen man."

At that they bore Sir Gawain sorely wounded to his tent, and King Arthur withdrew his men, for he was loth to shed the blood of so many knights of his own fellowship.

But now came tidings to King Arthur from across the sea, which caused him to return in haste. For thus the news ran, that no sooner was Sir Modred set up in his regency, than he had forged false tidings from abroad that the king had fallen in a battle with Sir Lancelot. Whereat he had proclaimed himself the king, and had been crowned at Canterbury, where he had held a coronation feast for fifteen days. Then he had gone to Winchester, where Queen Guinevere abode, and had commanded her to be his wife; whereto, for fear and sore perplexity, she had feigned consent, but, under pretext of preparing for the marriage, had fled in haste to London and taken shelter in the Tower, fortifying it and providing it with all manner of victuals, and defending it against Sir Modred, and answering to all his threats that she would rather slay herself than be his queen.

Thus was it written to King Arthur. Then, in passing great wrath and haste, he came with all his army swiftly back from France and sailed to England. But when Sir Modred heard thereof, he left the Tower and marched with all his host to meet the king at Dover.

Then fled Queen Guinevere to Amesbury to a nunnery, and there she clothed herself in sackcloth, and spent her time in praying for the king and in good deeds and fasting. And in that nunnery evermore she lived, sorely repenting and mourning for her sin, and for the ruin she had brought on all the realm. And there anon she died.

And when Sir Lancelot heard thereof, he put his knightly armor off, and bade farewell to all his kin, and went a mighty pilgrimage for many years, and after lived a hermit till his death.

When Sir Modred came to Dover, he found King Arthur and his army but just landed; and there they fought a fierce and bloody battle, and many great and noble knights fell on both sides.

But the king's side had the victory, for he was beyond himself with might and passion, and all his knights so fiercely followed him, that, in spite of all

their multitude, they drove Sir Modred's army back with fearful wounds and slaughter, and slept that night upon the battle-field.

But Sir Gawain was smitten by an arrow in the wound Sir Lancelot gave him, and wounded to the death. Then was he borne to the king's tent, and King Arthur sorrowed over him as it had been his own son. "Alas!" said he; "in Sir Lancelot and in you I had my greatest earthly joy, and now is all gone from me."

And Sir Gawain answered, with a feeble voice, "My lord and king, I know well my death is come, and through my own wilfulness, for I am smitten in the wound Sir Lancelot gave me. Alas! that I have been the cause of all this war, for but for me you hadst been now at peace with Lancelot, and then had Modred never done this treason. I pray you, therefore, my dear lord, be now agreed with Lancelot, and tell him, that although he gave me my death-wound, it was through my own seeking; wherefore I beseech him to come back to England, and here to visit my tomb, and pray for my soul."

When he had thus spoken, Sir Gawain gave up his ghost, and the king grievously mourned for him.

Then they told him that the enemy had camped on Barham Downs, whereat, with all his hosts, he straightway marched there, and fought again a bloody battle, and overthrew Sir Modred utterly. Howbeit, he raised yet another army, and retreating ever from before the king, increased his numbers as he went, till at the farthest west in Lyonesse, he once more made a stand.

Now, on the night of Trinity Sunday, being the eve of the battle, King Arthur had a vision, and saw Sir Gawain in a dream, who warned him not to fight with Modred on the morrow, else he would be surely slain; and prayed him to delay till Lancelot and his knights should come to aid him.

So when King Arthur woke he told his lords and knights that vision, and all agreed to wait the coming of Sir Lancelot. Then a herald was sent with a message of truce to Sir Modred, and a treaty was made that neither army should assail the other.

But when the treaty was agreed upon, and the heralds returned, King Arthur said to his knights, "Beware, lest Sir Modred deceive us, for I in no wise trust him, and if swords be drawn be ready to encounter!" And Sir Modred likewise gave an order, that if any man of the king's army drew his sword, they should begin to fight.

And as it chanced, a knight of the king's side was bitten by an adder in the foot, and hastily drew forth his sword to slay it. That saw Sir Modred, and forthwith commanded all his army to assail the king's.

So both sides rushed to battle, and fought passing fiercely. And when the king saw there was no hope to stay them, he did right mightily and nobly as a king should do, and ever, like a lion, raged in the thickest of the press, and slew on the right hand and on the left, till his horse went fetlock deep in blood. So all day long they fought, and stinted not till many a noble knight was slain.

But the king was passing sorrowful to see his trusty knights lie dead on every side. And at the last but two remained beside him, Sir Lucan, and his brother, Sir Bedivere, and both were sorely wounded.

"Now am I come to mine end," said King Arthur; "but, lo! that traitor Modred lives yet, and I may not die till I have slain him. Now, give me my spear, Sir Lucan."

"Lord, let him be," replied Sir Lucan; "for if you pass through this unhappy day, you shall be right well revenged upon him. My good lord, remember well your dream, and what the spirit of Sir Gawain did forewarn you."

"Betide me life, betide me death," said the king; "now I see him yonder alone, he shall never escape my hands, for at a better vantage shall I never have him."

"God speed you well," said Sir Bedivere.

Then King Arthur got his spear in both his hands, and ran towards Sir Modred, crying, "Traitor, now is your death-day come!" And when Sir Modred heard his words, and saw him come, he drew his sword and stood to meet him. Then King Arthur smote Sir Modred through the body more than a fathom. And when Sir Modred felt he had his death wound, he thrust himself with all his might up to the end of King Arthur's spear, and smote his father, Arthur, with his sword upon the head, so that it pierced both helm and brain-pan.

And therewith Sir Modred fell down stark dead to the earth, and King Arthur fell down also in a swoon, and swooned many times.

Then Sir Lucan and Sir Bedivere came and bare him away to a little chapel by the sea-shore. And there Sir Lucan sank down with the bleeding of his own wounds, and fell dead.

And King Arthur lay long in a swoon, and when he came to himself, he found Sir Lucan lying dead beside him, and Sir Bedivere weeping over the body of his brother.

Then said the king to Sir Bedivere, "Weeping will avail no longer, else would I grieve forevermore. Alas! now is the fellowship of the Round Table dissolved forever, and all my realm I have so loved is wasted with war. But my time comes fast, wherefore take you Excalibur, my good sword, and go therewith to yonder water-side and throw it in, and bring me word what thing you seest."

So Sir Bedivere departed; but as he went he looked upon the sword, the hilt whereof was all inlaid with precious stones exceeding rich. And presently he said within himself, "If I now throw this sword into the water, what good should come of it?" So he hid the sword among the reeds, and came again to the king.

"What did you see?" said he to Sir Bedivere.

"Lord," said he, "I saw nothing else but wind and waves."

"You hast untruly spoken," said the king; "wherefore go lightly back and throw it in, and spare not."

Then Sir Bedivere returned again, and took the sword up in his hand; but when he looked on it, he thought it sin and shame to throw away a thing so noble. Wherefore he hid it yet again, and went back to the king.

"What saw you?" said King Arthur.

"Lord," answered he, "I saw nothing but the water ebbing and flowing."

"Oh, traitor and untrue!" cried out the king; "twice hast you now betrayed me. Art you called of men a noble knight, and would betray me for a jewelled sword? Now, therefore, go again for the last time, for your tarrying hath put me in sore peril of my life, and I fear my wound hath taken cold; and if you do it not this time, by my faith I will arise and slay you with my hands."

Then Sir Bedivere ran quickly and took up the sword, and went down to the water's edge, and bound the girdle round the hilt and threw it far into the water. And lo! an arm and hand came forth above the water, and caught the sword, and brandished it three times, and vanished.

So Sir Bedivere came again to the king and told him what he had seen.

"Help me from hence," said King Arthur; "for I dread me I have tarried over long."

Then Sir Bedivere took the king up in his arms, and bore him to the water's edge. And by the shore they saw a barge with three fair queens therein, all dressed in black, and when they saw King Arthur they wept and wailed.

"Now put me in the barge," said he to Sir Bedivere, and tenderly he did so.

Then the three queens received him, and he laid his head upon the lap of one of them, who cried, "Alas! dear brother, why have you tarried so long, for your wound hath taken cold?"

With that the barge put from the land, and when Sir Bedivere saw it departing, he cried with a bitter cry, "Alas! my lord King Arthur, what shall become of me now you have gone from me?"

"Comfort yourself," said King Arthur, "and be strong, for I may no more help you. I go to the Vale of

Avilion to heal me of my grievous wound, and if you see me no more, pray for my soul."

Then the three queens kneeled down around the king and sorely wept and wailed, and the barge went forth to sea, and departed slowly out of Sir Bedivere's sight.

1

What is the main purpose of these passages?

_____

2

What is the overall tone of the passages?

_____

3

How would you summarize the passages?

_____

4

How would you describe Arthur?

_____

5

How would you describe Guinevere?

_____

6

How would you describe Sir Lancelot?

_____

7

How would you describe Sir Gawain?

_____

8

How would you describe Sir Modrd?

_____

9

How would you describe Sir Bedivere?

_____

10

How would you describe chivalry?

_____

"LETTER FROM BIRMINGHAM JAIL" – REV. DR. MARTIN LUTHER KING, JR.

This passage is adapted from Martin Luther King, Jr.'s open letter to eight white clergymen in Birmingham, Alabama, who published "A Call for Unity." This letter is King's response, written while jailed for protesting.

My dear Fellow Clergymen,

While confined here in the Birmingham City Jail, I came across your recent statement calling our present activities "unwise and untimely." Seldom, if ever, do I pause to answer criticism of my work and ideas. If I sought to answer all the criticisms that cross my desk, my secretaries would be engaged in little else in the course of the day and I would have no time for constructive work. But since I feel that you are men of genuine goodwill and your criticisms are sincerely set forth, I would like to answer your statement in what I hope will be patient and reasonable terms.

I think I should give the reason for my being in Birmingham, since you have been influenced by the argument of "outsiders coming in." I have the honor of serving as president of the Southern Christian Leadership Conference, an organization operating in every Southern state with headquarters in Atlanta, Georgia. We have some eighty-five affiliate organizations all across the South—one being the Alabama Christian Movement for Human Rights. Whenever necessary and possible we share staff, educational, and financial resources with our affiliates. Several months ago our local affiliate here in Birmingham invited us to be on call to engage in a nonviolent direct action program if such were deemed necessary. We readily consented and when the hour came we lived up to our promises. So I am here, along with several members of my staff, because we were invited here. I am here because I have basic organizational ties here. Beyond this, I am in Birmingham because injustice is here. Just as the eighth century prophets left their little villages and carried their "thus saith the Lord" far beyond the boundaries of their home town, and just as the Apostle Paul left his little village of Tarsus and carried the gospel of Jesus Christ to practically every hamlet and city of the Graeco-Roman world, I too am compelled to carry the gospel of freedom beyond my particular home town. Like Paul, I must constantly respond to the Macedonian call for aid.

Moreover, I am cognizant of the interrelatedness of all communities and states. I cannot sit idly by in Atlanta and not be concerned about what happens in Birmingham. Injustice anywhere is a threat to justice everywhere. We are caught in an inescapable network of mutuality tied in a single garment of destiny. Whatever affects one directly affects all indirectly.

Never again can we afford to live with the narrow, provincial "outside agitator" idea. Anyone who lives inside the United States can never be considered an outsider anywhere in this country.

You deplore the demonstrations that are presently taking place in Birmingham. But I am sorry that your statement did not express a similar concern for the conditions that brought the demonstrations into being. I am sure that each of you would want to go beyond the superficial social analyst who looks merely at effects, and does not grapple with underlying causes. I would not hesitate to say that it is unfortunate that so-called demonstrations are taking place in Birmingham at this time, but I would say in more emphatic terms that it is even more unfortunate that the white power structure of this city left the Negro community with no other alternative.

In any nonviolent campaign there are four basic steps: (1) Collection of the facts to determine whether injustices are alive; (2) Negotiation; (3) Self-purification; and (4) Direct action. We have gone through all of these steps in Birmingham. There can be no gainsaying of the fact that racial injustice engulfs this community. Birmingham is probably the most thoroughly segregated city in the United States. Its ugly record of police brutality is known in every section of this country. Its unjust treatment of Negroes in the courts is a notorious reality. There have been more unsolved bombings of Negro homes and churches in Birmingham than any city in this nation. These are the hard, brutal, and unbelievable facts. On the basis of these conditions Negro leaders sought to negotiate with the city fathers. But the political leaders consistently refused to engage in good faith negotiation.

Then came the opportunity last September to talk with some of the leaders of the economic community. In these negotiating sessions certain promises were made by the merchants—such as the promise to remove the humiliating racial signs from the stores. On the basis of these promises Rev. Shuttlesworth and the leaders of the Alabama Christian Movement for Human Rights agreed to call a moratorium on any type of demonstrations. As the weeks and months unfolded we realized that we were the victims of a broken promise. The signs remained. As in so many experiences of the past we were confronted with blasted hopes, and the dark shadow of a deep disappointment settled upon us. So we had no alternative except that of preparing for direct action, whereby we would present our very bodies as a means of laying our case before the conscience of the local and national community. We were not unmindful of the difficulties involved. So we decided to go through a process of self-purification. We started having workshops on nonviolence and repeatedly asked ourselves the questions, "Are you able to accept blows without retaliating?" "Are you able to endure the ordeals of jail?"

We decided to set our direct-action program around the Easter season, realizing that with the exception of Christmas, this was the largest shopping period of the year. Knowing that a strong economic withdrawal program would be the by-product of direct action, we felt that this was the best time to bring pressure on the merchants for the needed changes. Then it occurred to us that the March election was ahead, and so we speedily decided to postpone action until after election day. When we discovered that Mr. Connor was in the run-off, we decided again to postpone action so that the demonstrations could not be used to cloud the issues. At this time we agreed to begin our nonviolent witness the day after the run-off.

This reveals that we did not move irresponsibly into direct action. We too wanted to see Mr. Connor defeated; so we went through postponement after postponement to aid in this community need. After this we felt that direct action could be delayed no longer.

You may well ask, Why direct action? Why sit-ins, marches, etc.? Isn't negotiation a better path?" You are exactly right in your call for negotiation. Indeed, this is the purpose of direct action. Nonviolent direct action seeks to create such a crisis and establish such creative tension that a community that has constantly refused to negotiate is forced to confront the issue. It seeks so to dramatize the issue that it can no longer be ignored. I just referred to the creation of tension as a part of the work of the nonviolent resister. This may sound rather shocking. But I must confess that I am not afraid of the word tension. I have earnestly worked and preached against violent tension, but there is a type of constructive nonviolent tension that is necessary for growth. Just as Socrates felt that it was necessary to create a tension in the mind so that individuals could rise from the bondage of myths and half-truths to the unfettered realm of creative analysis and objective appraisal, we must see the need of having nonviolent gadflies to create the kind of tension in society that will help men rise from the dark depths of prejudice and racism to the majestic heights of understanding and brotherhood. So the purpose of the direct action is to create a situation so crisis-packed that it will inevitably open the door to negotiation. We, therefore, concur with you in your call for negotiation. Too long has our beloved Southland been bogged down in the tragic attempt to live in monologue rather than dialogue.

One of the basic points in your statement is that our acts are untimely. Some have asked, "Why didn't you give the new administration time to act?" The only answer that I can give to this inquiry is that the new administration must be prodded about as much as the outgoing one before it acts. We will be sadly mistaken if we feel that the election of Mr. Boutwell will bring the millennium to Birmingham. While Mr. Boutwell is much more articulate and gentle than Mr. Connor, they are both segregationists dedicated to the task of maintaining the status quo. The hope I see in Mr. Boutwell is that he will be reasonable enough to see the futility of massive resistance to desegregation. But he will not see this without pressure from the devotees of civil rights. My friends, I must say to you that we have not made a single gain in civil rights without determined legal and nonviolent pressure. History is the long and tragic story of the fact that privileged groups seldom give up their privileges voluntarily. Individuals may see the moral light and voluntarily give up their unjust posture; but as Reinhold Niebuhr has reminded us, groups are more immoral than individuals.

We know through painful experience that freedom is never voluntarily given by the oppressor; it must be demanded by the oppressed. Frankly I have never yet engaged in a direct action movement that was "well timed," according to the timetable of those who have not suffered unduly from the disease of segregation. For years now I have heard the word "Wait!" It rings in the ear of every Negro with a piercing familiarity. This "wait" has almost always meant "never." It has been a tranquilizing thalidomide, relieving the emotional stress for a moment, only to give birth to an ill-formed infant of frustration. We must come to see with the distinguished jurist of yesterday that "justice too long delayed is justice denied." We have waited for more than three hundred and forty years for our constitutional and God-given rights. The nations of Asia and Africa are moving with jet-like speed toward the goal of political independence, and we still creep at horse and buggy pace toward the gaining of a cup of coffee at a lunch counter.

I guess it is easy for those who have never felt the stinging darts of segregation to say wait. But when you have seen vicious mobs lynch your mothers and fathers at will and drown your sisters and brothers at whim; when you have seen hate filled policemen curse, kick, brutalize, and even kill your black brothers and sisters with impunity; when you see the vast majority of your twenty million Negro brothers smothering in an air-tight cage of poverty in the midst of an affluent society; when you suddenly find your tongue twisted and your speech stammering as you seek to explain to your six-year-old daughter why she can't go to the public amusement park that has just been advertised on television, and see tears welling up in her little eyes when she is told that Funtown is closed to colored children, and see the depressing clouds of inferiority begin to form in her little mental sky, and see her begin to distort her little personality by unconsciously developing a bitterness toward white people; when you have to concoct an answer for a five-year-old son asking in agonizing pathos: "Daddy, why do white people treat colored people so mean?"; when you take a cross-country drive and find it necessary to sleep night after night in the uncomfortable corners of your automobile because no motel will accept you; when you are humiliated day in and day out by nagging signs reading "white" men and "colored"; when your first name becomes "nigger" and your middle name becomes "boy" (however old you are) and your last name becomes "John," and when your wife and mother are never given the respected title "Mrs."; when you are harried by day and haunted by night by the fact that you are a Negro, living constantly at tip-toe stance never quite knowing what to expect next, and plagued with inner fears and outer resentments; when you are forever fighting a degenerating sense of "nobodiness"—then you will understand why we find it difficult to wait. There comes a time when the cup of endurance runs over, and men are no longer willing to be plunged into an abyss of injustice where they experience the bleakness of corroding despair. I hope, sirs, you can understand our legitimate and unavoidable impatience.

You express a great deal of anxiety over our willingness to break laws. This is certainly a legitimate concern. Since we so diligently urge people to obey the Supreme Court's decision of 1954 outlawing segregation in the public schools, it is rather strange and paradoxical to find us consciously breaking laws. One may well ask: "How can you advocate breaking some laws and obeying others?" The answer is found in the fact that there are two types of laws: There are just laws and there are unjust laws. I would be the first to advocate obeying just laws. One has not only a legal but moral responsibility to obey just laws. Conversely, one has a moral responsibility to disobey unjust laws. I would agree with Saint Augustine that "An unjust law is no law at all."

Now what is the difference between the two? How does one determine when a law is just or unjust? A just law is a man-made code that squares with the moral law or the law of God. An unjust law is a code that is out of harmony with the moral law. To put it in the terms of Saint Thomas Aquinas, an unjust law is a human law that is not rooted in eternal and natural law. Any law that uplifts human personality is just.

Any law that degrades human personality is unjust. All segregation statutes are unjust because segregation distorts the soul and damages the personality. It gives the segregator a false sense of superiority and the segregated a false sense of inferiority. To use the words of Martin Buber, the great Jewish philosopher, segregation substitutes an "I-it" relationship for an "I-you" relationship, and ends up relegating persons to the status of things. So segregation is not only politically, economically, and sociologically unsound, but it is morally wrong and sinful. Paul Tillich has said that sin is separation. Isn't segregation an existential expression of man's tragic separation, an expression of his awful estrangement, his terrible sinfulness? So I can urge men to obey the 1954 decision of the Supreme Court because it is morally right, and I can urge them to disobey segregation ordinances because they are morally wrong.

Let us turn to a more concrete example of just and unjust laws. An unjust law is a code that a majority inflicts on a minority that is not binding on itself. This is difference made legal. On the other hand a just law is a code that a majority compels a minority to follow that it is willing to follow itself. This is sameness made legal.

Let me give another explanation. An unjust law is a code inflicted upon a minority which that minority had no part in enacting or creating because they did not have the unhampered right to vote. Who can say that the legislature of Alabama which set up the segregation laws was democratically elected? Throughout the state of Alabama all types of conniving methods are used to prevent Negroes from becoming registered voters and there are some counties without a single Negro registered to vote despite the fact that the Negro constitutes a majority of the population. Can any law set up in such a state be considered democratically structured?

These are just a few examples of unjust and just laws. There are some instances when a law is just on its face but unjust in its application. For instance, I was arrested Friday on a charge of parading without a permit. Now there is nothing wrong with an ordinance which requires a permit for a parade, but when the ordinance is used to preserve segregation and to deny citizens the First Amendment privilege of peaceful assembly and peaceful protest, then it becomes unjust.

I hope you can see the distinction I am trying to point out. In no sense do I advocate evading or defying the law as the rabid segregationist would do. This would lead to anarchy. One who breaks an unjust law must do it openly, lovingly (not hatefully as the white mothers did in New Orleans when they were seen on television screaming "nigger, nigger, nigger") and with a willingness to accept the penalty. I submit that an individual who breaks a law that conscience tells him is unjust, and willingly accepts the penalty by staying in jail to arouse the conscience of the community over its injustice, is in reality expressing the very highest respect for law.

Of course there is nothing new about this kind of civil disobedience. It was seen sublimely in the refusal of Shadrach, Meshach, and Abednego to obey the laws of Nebuchadnezzar because a higher moral law was involved. It was practiced superbly by the early Christians who were willing to face hungry lions and the excruciating pain of chopping blocks, before submitting to certain unjust laws of the Roman Empire. To a degree academic freedom is a reality today because Socrates practiced civil disobedience.

We can never forget that everything Hitler did in Germany was "legal" and everything the Hungarian freedom fighters did in Hungary was "illegal." It was "illegal" to aid and comfort a Jew in Hitler's Germany. But I am sure that, if I had lived in Germany during that time, I would have aided and comforted my Jewish brothers even though it was illegal. If I lived in a communist country today where certain principles dear to the Christian faith are suppressed, I believe I would openly advocate disobeying these anti-religious laws.

I must make two honest confessions to you, my Christian and Jewish brothers. First, I must confess that over the last few years I have been gravely disappointed with the white moderate. I have almost reached the regrettable conclusion that the Negroes' great stumbling block in the stride toward freedom is not the White Citizen's "Counciler" or the Ku Klux Klanner, but the white moderate who is more devoted to "order" than to justice; who prefers a negative peace which is the absence of tension to a positive peace which is the presence of justice; who constantly says "I agree with you in the goal you seek, but I can't agree with your methods of direct action"; who paternalistically feels that he can set the timetable for another man's freedom; who lives by the myth of time and who constantly advises the Negro to wait until a "more convenient season." Shallow understanding from people of good will is more frustrating than absolute misunderstanding from people of ill will. Lukewarm acceptance is much more bewildering than outright rejection.

I had hoped that the white moderate would understand that law and order exist for the purpose of establishing justice, and that when they fail to do this they become dangerously structured dams that block the flow of social progress. I had hoped that the white moderate would understand that the present tension in the South is merely a necessary phase of the transition from an obnoxious negative peace, where the Negro passively accepted his unjust plight, to a substance-filled positive peace, where all men will respect the dignity and worth of human personality. Actually, we who engage in nonviolent direct action are not the creators of tension. We merely bring to the surface the hidden tension that is already alive. We bring it out in the open where it can be seen and dealt with. Like a boil that can never be cured as long as it is covered up but must be opened with all its pus-flowing ugliness to the natural medicines of air and light, injustice must likewise be exposed, with all of the tension its exposing creates, to the light of human conscience and the air of national opinion before it can be cured.

In your statement you asserted that our actions, even though peaceful, must be condemned because they precipitate violence. But can this assertion be logically made? Isn't this like condemning the robbed man because his possession of money precipitated the evil act of robbery? Isn't this like condemning Socrates because his unswerving commitment to truth and his philosophical delvings precipitated the misguided popular mind to make him drink the hemlock? Isn't this like condemning Jesus because His unique God consciousness and never-ceasing devotion to His will precipitated the evil act of crucifixion? We must come to see, as federal courts have consistently affirmed, that it is immoral to urge an individual to withdraw his efforts to gain his basic constitutional rights because the quest precipitates violence. Society must protect the robbed and punish the robber.

I had also hoped that the white moderate would reject the myth of time. I received a letter this morning from a white brother in Texas which said: "All Christians know that the colored people will receive equal rights eventually, but is it possible that you are in too great of a religious hurry? It has taken Christianity almost 2,000 years to accomplish what it has. The teachings of Christ take time to come to earth." All that is said here grows out of a tragic misconception of time. It is the strangely irrational notion that there is something in the very flow of time that will inevitably cure all ills. Actually time is neutral. It can be used either destructively or constructively. I am coming to feel that the people of ill will have used time much more effectively than the people of good will. We will have to repent in this generation not merely for the vitriolic words and actions of the bad people, but for the appalling silence of the good people. We must come to see that human progress never rolls in on wheels of inevitability. It comes through the tireless efforts and persistent work of men willing to be co-workers with God, and without this hard work time itself becomes an ally of the forces of social stagnation.

We must use time creatively, and forever realize that the time is always ripe to do right. Now is the time to make real the promise of democracy, and transform our pending national elegy into a creative psalm of brotherhood. Now is the time to lift our national policy from the quicksand of racial injustice to the solid rock of human dignity.

You spoke of our activity in Birmingham as extreme. At first I was rather disappointed that fellow clergymen would see my nonviolent efforts as those of the extremist. I started thinking about the fact that I stand in the middle of two opposing forces in the Negro community. One is a force of complacency made up of Negroes who, as a result of long years of oppression, have been so completely drained of self-respect and a sense of "somebodiness" that they have adjusted to segregation, and of a few Negroes in the middle class who, because of a degree of academic and economic security, and because at points they profit by segregation, have unconsciously become insensitive to the problems of the masses. The other force is one of bitterness and hatred and comes perilously close to advocating violence. It is expressed in the various black nationalist groups that are springing up over the nation, the largest and best known being Elijah Muhammad's Muslim movement. This movement is nourished by the contemporary frustration over the continued existence of racial discrimination. It is made up of people who have lost faith in America, who have absolutely repudiated Christianity, and who have concluded that the white man is an incurable "devil." I have tried to stand between these two forces saying that we need not follow the "do-nothingism" of the complacent or the hatred and despair of the black nationalist. There is the more excellent way of love and nonviolent protest. I'm grateful to God that, through the Negro church, the dimension of nonviolence entered our struggle. If this philosophy had not emerged I am convinced that by now many streets of the South would be flowing with floods of blood. And I am further convinced that if our white brothers dismiss us as "rabble rousers" and "outside agitators"—those of us who are working through the channels of nonviolent direct action—and refuse to support our nonviolent efforts, millions of Negroes, out of frustration and despair, will seek solace and security in black-nationalist ideologies, a development that will lead inevitably to a frightening racial nightmare.

Oppressed people cannot remain oppressed forever. The urge for freedom will eventually come. This is what has happened to the American Negro. Something within has reminded him of his birthright of freedom; something without has reminded him that he can gain it. Consciously and unconsciously, he has been swept in by what the Germans call the Zeitgeist, and with his black brothers of Africa, and his brown and yellow brothers of Asia, South America, and the Caribbean, he is moving with a sense of cosmic urgency toward the promised land of racial justice. Recognizing this vital urge that has engulfed the Negro community, one should readily understand public demonstrations. The Negro has many pent-up resentments and latent frustrations. He has to get them out. So let him march sometime; let him have his prayer pilgrimages to the city hall; understand why he must have sit-ins and freedom rides. If his repressed emotions do not come out in these nonviolent ways, they will come out in ominous expressions of violence. This is not a threat; it is a fact of history. So I have not said to my people, "Get rid of your discontent." But I have tried to say that this normal and heal your discontent can be channeled through the creative outlet of nonviolent direct action. Now this approach is being dismissed as extremist. I must admit that I was initially disappointed in being so categorized.

But as I continued to think about the matter I gradually gained a bit of satisfaction from being considered an extremist. Was not Jesus an extremist in love? "Love your enemies, bless them that curse you, pray for them that despitefully use you." Was not Amos an extremist for justice—"Let justice roll down like waters and righteousness like a mighty stream." Was not Paul an extremist for the gospel of Jesus Christ—"I bear in my body the marks of the Lord Jesus." Was not Martin Luther an extremist—"Here I stand; I can do none other so help me God." Was not John Bunyan an extremist—"I will stay in jail to the end of my days before I make a butchery of my conscience." Was not Abraham Lincoln an extremist—"This nation cannot survive half slave and half free." Was not Thomas Jefferson an extremist—"We hold these truths to be self-evident, that all men are created equal." So the question is not whether we will be extremist but what kind of extremist will we be. Will we be extremists for hate or will we be extremists for love? Will we be extremists for the preservation of injustice—or will we be extremists for the cause of justice? In that dramatic scene on Calvary's hill three men were crucified. We must never forget that all three were crucified for the same crime—the crime of extremism. Two were extremists for immorality, and thus fell below their environment. The other, Jesus Christ, was an extremist for love, truth, and goodness, and thereby rose above His environment. So, after all, maybe the South, the nation, and the world are in dire need of creative extremists.

I had hoped that the white moderate would see this. Maybe I was too optimistic. Maybe I expected too much. I guess I should have realized that few members of a race that has oppressed another race can understand or appreciate the deep groans and passionate yearnings of those that have been oppressed, and still fewer have the vision to see that injustice must be rooted out by strong, persistent, and determined action. I am thankful, however, that some of our white brothers have grasped the meaning of this social revolution and committed themselves to it. They are still all too small in quantity, but they are big in quality. Some like Ralph McGill, Lillian Smith, Harry Golden, and James Dabbs have written about our struggle in eloquent, prophetic, and understanding terms. Others have marched with us down nameless streets of the South. They have languished in filthy, roach-infested jails, suffering the abuse and brutality of angry policemen who see them as "dirty nigger lovers." They, unlike so many of their moderate brothers and sisters, have recognized the urgency of the moment and sensed the need for powerful "action" antidotes to combat the disease of segregation.

Let me rush on to mention my other disappointment. I have been so greatly disappointed with the white Church and its leadership. Of course there are some notable exceptions. I am not unmindful of the fact that each of you has taken some significant stands on this issue. I commend you, Rev. Stallings, for your Christian stand on this past Sunday, in welcoming Negroes to your worship service on a non-segregated basis. I commend the Catholic leaders of this state for integrating Spring Hill College several years ago.

But despite these notable exceptions I must honestly reiterate that I have been disappointed with the Church. I do not say that as one of those negative critics who can always find something wrong with the Church. I say it as a minister of the gospel, who loves the Church; who was nurtured in its bosom; who has been sustained by its spiritual blessings and who will remain true to it as long as the cord of life shall lengthen.

I had the strange feeling when I was suddenly catapulted into the leadership of the bus protest in Montgomery several years ago that we would have the support of the white Church. I felt that the white ministers, priests, and rabbis of the South would be some of our strongest allies. Instead, some have been outright opponents, refusing to understand the freedom movement and misrepresenting its leaders; all too many others have been more cautious than courageous and have remained silent behind the anesthetizing security of the stained glass windows.

In spite of my shattered dreams of the past, I came to Birmingham with the hope that the white religious leadership of this community would see the justice of our cause and with deep moral concern, serve as the channel through which our just grievances could get to the power structure. I had hoped that each of you would understand. But again I have been disappointed.

I have heard numerous religious leaders of the South call upon their worshippers to comply with a desegregation decision because it is the law, but I have longed to hear white ministers say follow this decree because integration is morally right and the Negro is your brother. In the midst of blatant injustices inflicted upon the Negro, I have watched white churches stand on the sideline and merely mouth pious irrelevancies and sanctimonious trivialities. In the midst of a mighty struggle to rid our nation of racial and economic injustice, I have heard so many ministers say, "Those are social issues with which the gospel has no real concern," and I have watched so many churches commit themselves to a completely other-worldly religion which made a strange distinction between body and soul, the sacred and the secular.

So here we are moving toward the exit of the twentieth century with a religious community largely adjusted to the status quo, standing as a tail-light behind other community agencies rather than a headlight leading men to higher levels of justice.

I have travelled the length and breadth of Alabama, Mississippi and all the other southern states. On sweltering summer days and crisp autumn mornings I have looked at her beautiful churches with their spires pointing heavenward. I have beheld the impressive outlay of her massive religious education buildings. Over and over again I have found myself asking: "Who worships here? Who is their God? Where were their voices when the lips of Governor Barnett dripped with words of interposition and nullification? Where were they when Governor Wallace gave the clarion call for defiance and hatred? Where were their voices of support when tired, bruised, and weary Negro men and women decided to rise from the dark dungeons of complacency to the bright hills of creative protest?"

Yes, these questions are still in my mind. In deep disappointment, I have wept over the laxity of the church. But be assured that my tears have been tears of love. There can be no deep disappointment where there is not deep love. Yes, I love the Church; I love her sacred walls. How could I do otherwise? I am in the rather unique position of being the son, the grandson, and the great-grandson of preachers. Yes, I see the Church as the body of Christ. But, oh! How we have blemished and scarred that body through social neglect and fear of being nonconformist.

There was a time when the Church was very powerful. It was during that period when the early Christians rejoiced when they were deemed woryour to suffer for what they believed. In those days the Church was not merely a thermometer that recorded the ideas and principles of popular opinion; it was a thermostat that transformed the mores of society. Wherever the early Christians entered a town the power structure got disturbed and immediately sought to convict them for being "disturbers of the peace" and "outside agitators." But they went on with the conviction that they were "a colony of heaven" and had to obey God rather than man. They were small in number but big in commitment. They were too God-intoxicated to be "astronomically intimidated." They brought an end to such ancient evils as infanticide and gladiatorial contest.

Things are different now. The contemporary Church is so often a weak, ineffectual voice with an uncertain sound. It is so often the arch-supporter of the status quo. Far from being disturbed by the presence of the Church, the power structure of the average community is consoled by the Church's silent and often vocal sanction of things as they are.

But the judgment of God is upon the Church as never before. If the Church of today does not recapture the sacrificial spirit of the early Church, it will lose its authentic ring, forfeit the loyalty of millions, and be dismissed as an irrelevant social club with no meaning for the twentieth century. I am meeting young people every day whose disappointment with the Church has risen to outright disgust.

Maybe again I have been too optimistic. Is organized religion too inextricably bound to the status quo to save our nation and the world? Maybe I must turn my faith to the inner spiritual Church, the church within the Church, as the true ecclesia and the hope of the world. But again I am thankful to God that some noble souls from the ranks of organized religion have broken loose from the paralyzing chains of conformity and joined us as active partners in the struggle for freedom. They have left their secure congregations and walked the streets of Albany, Georgia, with us. They have gone through the highways of the South on torturous rides for freedom. Yes, they have gone to jail with us. Some have been kicked out of their churches and lost the support of their bishops and fellow ministers. But they have gone with the faith that right defeated is stronger than evil triumphant. These men have been the leaven in the lump of the race. Their witness has been the spiritual salt that has preserved the true meaning of the Gospel in these troubled times. They have carved a tunnel of hope through the dark mountain of disappointment.

I hope the Church as a whole will meet the challenge of this decisive hour. But even if the Church does not come to the aid of justice, I have no despair about the future. I have no fear about the outcome of our struggle in Birmingham, even if our motives are presently misunderstood. We will reach the goal of freedom in Birmingham and all over the nation, because the goal of America is freedom. Abused and scorned though we may be, our destiny is tied up with the destiny of America. Before the pilgrims landed at Plymouth, we were here. Before the pen of Jefferson etched across the pages of history the majestic words of the Declaration of Independence, we were here. For more than two centuries our foreparents labored in this country without wages; they made cotton "king"; and they built the homes of their masters in the midst of brutal injustice and shameful humiliation—and yet out of a bottomless vitality they continued to thrive and develop. If the inexpressible cruelties of slavery could not stop us, the opposition we now face will surely fail. We will win our freedom because the sacred heritage of our nation and the eternal will of God are embodied in our echoing demands.

I must close now. But before closing I am impelled to mention one other point in your statement that troubled me profoundly. You warmly commend the Birmingham police force for keeping "order" and "preventing violence." I don't believe you would have so warmly commended the police force if you had seen its angry violent dogs literally biting six unarmed, nonviolent Negroes. I don't believe you would so quickly commend the policemen if you would observe their ugly and inhuman treatment of Negroes here in the city jail; if you would watch them push and curse old Negro women and young Negro girls; if you would see them slap and kick old Negro men and young Negro boys; if you will observe them, as they did on two occasions, refuse to give us food because we wanted to sing our grace together. I'm sorry that I can't join you in your praise for the police department.

It is true that they have been rather disciplined in their public handling of the demonstrators. In this sense they have been rather publicly "nonviolent." But for what purpose? To preserve the evil system of segregation. Over the last few years I have consistently preached that nonviolence demands the means we use must be as pure as the ends we seek. So I have tried to make it clear that it is wrong to use immoral means to attain moral ends. But now I must affirm that it is just as wrong or even more so to use moral means to preserve immoral ends. Maybe Mr. Connor and his policemen have been rather publicly nonviolent, as Chief Pritchett was in Albany, Georgia, but they have used the moral means of nonviolence to maintain the immoral end of flagrant injustice. T. S. Eliot has said that there is no greater treason than to do the right deed for the wrong reason.

I wish you had commended the Negro sit-inners and demonstrators of Birmingham for their sublime courage, their willingness to suffer, and their amazing discipline in the midst of the most inhuman provocation. One day the South will recognize its real heroes. They will be the James Merediths, courageously and with a majestic sense of purpose, facing jeering and hostile mobs and the agonizing loneliness that characterizes the life of the pioneer. They will be old, oppressed, battered Negro women, symbolized in a seventy-two year old woman of Montgomery, Alabama, who rose up with a sense of dignity and with her people decided not to ride the segregated buses, and responded to one who inquired about her tiredness with ungrammatical profundity: "My feets is tired, but my soul is rested." They will be the young high school and college students, young ministers of the gospel and a host of their elders courageously and nonviolently sitting-in at lunch counters and willingly going to jail for conscience sake. One day the South will know that when these disinherited children of God sat down at lunch counters they were in reality standing up for the best in the American dream and the most sacred values in our Judaeo-Christian heritage, and thus carrying our whole nation back to great wells of democracy which were dug deep by the founding fathers in the formulation of the Constitution and the Declaration of Independence.

Never before have I written a letter this long (or should I say a book?). I'm afraid it is much too long to take your precious time. I can assure you that it would have been much shorter if I had been writing from a comfortable desk, but what else is there to do when you are alone for days in the dull monotony of a narrow jail cell other than write long letters, think strange thoughts, and pray long prayers?

If I have said anything in this letter that is an overstatement of the truth and is indicative of an unreasonable impatience, I beg you to forgive me. If I have said anything in this letter that is an understatement of the truth and is indicative of my having a patience that makes me patient with anything less than brotherhood, I beg God to forgive me.

I hope this letter finds you strong in the faith. I also hope that circumstances will soon make it possible for me to meet each of you, not as an integrationist or a civil rights leader, but as a fellow clergyman and a Christian brother. Let us all hope that the dark clouds of racial prejudice will soon pass away and the deep fog of misunderstanding will be lifted from our fear-drenched communities and in some not too distant tomorrow the radiant stars of love and brotherhood will shine over our great nation with all their scintillating beauty.

Yours for the cause of Peace and Brotherhood,
—Martin Luther King, Jr.

1

What is the main purpose of this passage?

_____

2

What is the passage's tone?

_____

3

How would you summarize the passage?

_____

4

What is Dr. King's central thesis?

_____

This passage is adapted from the National Security Council Paper NSC-68, a top secret report completed by the US Department of State's Policy Planning Staff on April 7, 1950. The 58-page memorandum is among the most influential documents composed by the US Government during the Cold War, and was not declassified until 1975.

Analysis

I. Background of the Present Crisis

Within the past thirty-five years the world has experienced two global wars of tremendous violence. It has witnessed two revolutions--the Russian and the Chinese--of extreme scope and intensity. It has also seen the collapse of five empires--the Ottoman, the Austro-Hungarian, German, Italian, and Japanese-- and the drastic decline of two major imperial systems, the British and the French. During the span of one generation, the international distribution of power has been fundamentally altered. For several centuries it had proved impossible for any one nation to gain such preponderant strength that a coalition of other nations could not in time face it with greater strength. The international scene was marked by recurring periods of violence and war, but a system of sovereign and independent states was maintained, over which no state was able to achieve hegemony.

Two complex sets of factors have now basically altered this historic distribution of power. First, the defeat of Germany and Japan and the decline of the British and French Empires have interacted with the development of the United States and the Soviet Union in such a way that power increasingly gravitated to these two centers. Second, the Soviet Union, unlike previous aspirants to hegemony, is animated by a new fanatic faith, anti-thetical to our own, and seeks to impose its absolute authority over the rest of the world. Conflict has, therefore, become endemic and is waged, on the part of the Soviet Union, by violent or non-violent methods in accordance with the dictates of expediency. With the development of increasingly terrifying weapons of mass destruction, every individual faces the ever-present possibility of annihilation should the conflict enter the phase of total war.

On the one hand, the people of the world yearn for relief from the anxiety arising from the risk of atomic war. On the other hand, any substantial further extension of the area under the domination of the Kremlin would raise the possibility that no coalition adequate to confront the Kremlin with greater strength could be assembled. It is in this context that this Republic and its citizens in the ascendancy of their strength stand in their deepest peril.

The issues that face us are momentous, involving the fulfillment or destruction not only of this Republic but of civilization itself. They are issues which will not await our deliberations. With conscience and resolution this Government and the people it represents must now take new and fateful decisions.

II. Fundamental Purpose of the United States

The fundamental purpose of the United States is laid down in the Preamble to the Constitution: "…to form a more perfect Union, establish justice, insure domestic Tranquility, provide for the common defence, promote the general Welfare, and secure the Blessings of Liberty to ourselves and our Posterity." In essence, the fundamental purpose is to assure the integrity and vitality of our free society, which is founded upon the dignity and worth of the individual.

Three realities emerge as a consequence of this purpose: Our determination to maintain the essential elements of individual freedom, as set forth in the Constitution and Bill of Rights; our determination to create conditions under which our free and democratic system can live and prosper; and our determination to fight if necessary to defend our way of life, for which as in the Declaration of Independence, "with a firm reliance on the protection of Divine Providence, we mutually pledge to each other our lives, our Fortunes, and our sacred Honor."

III. Fundamental Design of the Kremlin

The fundamental design of those who control the Soviet Union and the international communist movement is to retain and solidify their absolute power, first in the Soviet Union and second in the areas now under their control. In the minds of the Soviet leaders, however, achievement of this design requires the dynamic extension of their authority and the ultimate elimination of any effective opposition to their authority.

The design, therefore, calls for the complete subversion or forcible destruction of the machinery of government and structure of society in the countries of the non-Soviet world and their replacement by an apparatus and structure subservient to and controlled from the Kremlin. To that end Soviet efforts are now directed toward the domination of the Eurasian land mass. The United States, as the principal center of power in the non-Soviet world and the bulwark of opposition to Soviet expansion, is the principal enemy whose integrity and vitality must be subverted or destroyed by one means or another if the Kremlin is to achieve its fundamental design.

IV. The Underlying Conflict in the Realm of ideas and Values between the U.S. Purpose and the Kremlin Design

A. NATURE OF CONFLICT

The Kremlin regards the United States as the only major threat to the conflict between idea of slavery under the grim oligarchy of the Kremlin, which has come to a crisis with the polarization of power described in Section I, and the exclusive possession of atomic weapons by the two protagonists. The idea of freedom, moreover, is peculiarly and intolerably subversive of the idea of slavery. But the converse is not true. The implacable purpose of the slave state to eliminate the challenge of freedom has placed the two great powers at opposite poles. It is this fact which gives the present polarization of power the quality of crisis.

The free society values the individual as an end in himself, requiring of him only that measure of self-discipline and self-restraint which make the rights of each individual compatible with the rights of every other individual. The freedom of the individual has as its counterpart, therefore, the negative responsibility of the individual not to exercise his freedom in ways inconsistent with the freedom of other individuals and the positive responsibility to make constructive use of his freedom in the building of a just society.

From this idea of freedom with responsibility derives the marvelous diversity, the deep tolerance, the lawfulness of the free society. This is the explanation of the strength of free men. It constitutes the integrity and the vitality of a free and democratic system. The free society attempts to create and maintain an environment in which every individual has the opportunity to realize his creative powers. It also explains why the free society tolerates those within it who would use their freedom to destroy it. By the same token, in relations between nations, the prime reliance of the free society is on the strength and appeal of its idea, and it feels no compulsion sooner or later to bring all societies into conformity with it.

For the free society does not fear, it welcomes, diversity. It derives its strength from its hospitality even to antipathetic ideas. It is a market for free trade in ideas, secure in its faith that free men will take the best wares, and grow to a fuller and better realization of their powers in exercising their choice.

The idea of freedom is the most contagious idea in history, more contagious than the idea of submission to authority. For the breadth of freedom cannot be tolerated in a society which has come under the domination of an individual or group of individuals with a will to absolute power. Where the despot holds absolute power--the absolute power of the absolutely powerful will--all other wills must be subjugated in an act of willing submission, a degradation willed by the individual upon himself under the compulsion of a perverted faith. It is the first article of this faith that he finds and can only find the meaning of his existence in serving the ends of the system. The system becomes God, and submission to the will of God becomes submission to the will of the system. It is not enough to yield outwardly to the system--even Gandhian non-violence is not acceptable--for the spirit of resistance and the devotion to a higher authority might then remain, and the individual would not be wholly submissive.

The same compulsion which demands total power over all men within the Soviet state without a single exception, demands total power over all Communist Parties and all states under Soviet domination. Thus Stalin has said that the theory and tactics of Leninism as expounded by the Bolshevik party are mandatory for the proletarian parties of all countries. A true internationalist is defined as one who unhesitatingly upholds the position of the Soviet Union and in the satellite states true patriotism is love of the Soviet Union. By the same token the "peace policy" of the Soviet Union, described at a Party Congress as "a more advantageous form of fighting capitalism," is a device to divide and immobilize the non-Communist world, and the peace the Soviet Union seeks is the peace of total conformity to Soviet policy.

The antipathy of slavery to freedom explains the iron curtain, the isolation, the autarchy of the society whose end is absolute power. The existence and persistence of the idea of freedom is a permanent and continuous threat to the foundation of the slave society; and it therefore regards as intolerable the long continued existence of freedom in the world. What is new, what makes the continuing crisis, is the polarization of power which now inescapably confronts the slave society with the free.

The assault on free institutions is world-wide now, and in the context of the present polarization of power a defeat of free institutions anywhere is a defeat everywhere. The shock we sustained in the destruction of Czechoslovakia was not in the measure of Czechoslovakia's material importance to us. In a material sense, her capabilities were already at Soviet disposal. But when the integrity of Czechoslovak institutions was destroyed, it was in the intangible scale of values that we registered a loss more damaging than the material loss we had already suffered.

Thus unwillingly our free society finds itself mortally challenged by the Soviet system. No other value system is so wholly irreconcilable with ours, so implacable in its purpose to destroy ours, so capable of turning to its own uses the most dangerous and divisive trends in our own society, no other so skillfully and powerfully evokes the elements of irrationality in human nature everywhere, and no other has the support of a great and growing center of military power.

B. OBJECTIVES

The objectives of a free society are determined by its fundamental values and by the necessity for maintaining the material environment in which they flourish. Logically and in fact, therefore, the Kremlin's challenge to the United States is directed not only to our values but to our physical capacity to protect their environment. It is a challenge which encompasses both peace and war and our objectives in peace and war must take account of it.

Thus we must make ourselves strong, both in the way in which we affirm our values in the conduct of our national life, and in the development of our military and economic strength. We must lead in building a successfully functioning political and economic system in the free world. It is only by practical affirmation, abroad as well as at home, of our essential values, that we can preserve our own integrity, in which lies the real frustration of the Kremlin design. But beyond thus affirming our values our policy and actions must be such as to foster a fundamental change in the nature of the Soviet system, a change toward which the frustration of the design is the first and perhaps the most important step. Clearly it will not only be less costly but more effective if this change occurs to a maximum extent as a result of internal forces in Soviet society. In a shrinking world, which now faces the threat of atomic warfare, it is not an adequate objective merely to seek to check the Kremlin design, for the absence of order among nations is becoming less and less tolerable. This fact imposes on us, in our own interests, the responsibility of world leadership. It demands that we make the attempt, and accept the risks inherent in it, to bring about order and justice by means consistent with the principles of freedom and democracy. We should limit our requirement of the Soviet Union to its participation with other nations on the basis of equality and respect for the rights of others. Subject to this requirement, we must with our allies and the former subject peoples seek to create a world society based on the principle of consent. Its framework cannot be inflexible. It will consist of many national communities of great and varying abilities and resources, and hence of war potential. The seeds of conflicts will inevitably exist or will come into being. To acknowledge this is only to acknowledge the impossibility of a final solution. Not to acknowledge it

can be fatally dangerous in a world in which there are no final solutions.

All these objectives of a free society are equally valid and necessary in peace and war. But every consideration of devotion to our fundamental values and to our national security demands that we seek to achieve them by the strategy of the cold war. It is only by developing the moral and material strength of the free world that the Soviet regime will become convinced of the falsity of its assumptions and that the pre-conditions for workable agreements can be created. By practically demonstrating the integrity and vitality of our system the free world widens the area of possible agreement and thus can hope gradually to bring about a Soviet acknowledgement of realities which in sum will eventually constitute a frustration of the Soviet design. Short of this, however, it might be possible to create a situation which will induce the Soviet Union to accommodate itself, with or without the conscious abandonment of its design, to coexistence on tolerable terms with the non-Soviet world. Such a development would be a triumph for the idea of freedom and democracy. It must be an immediate objective of United States policy.

There is no reason, in the event of war, for us to alter our overall objectives. They do not include unconditional surrender, the subjugation of the Russian peoples or a Russia shorn of its economic potential. Such a course would irrevocably unite the Russian people behind the regime which enslaves them. Rather these objectives contemplate Soviet acceptance of the specific and limited conditions requisite to an international environment in which free institutions can flourish, and in which the Russian peoples will have a new chance to work out their own destiny. If we can make the Russian people our allies in the enterprise we will obviously have made our task easier and victory more certain.

The growing intensity of the conflict which has been imposed upon us, however, requires the changes of emphasis and the additions that are apparent. Coupled with the probable fission bomb capability and possible thermonuclear bomb capability of the Soviet Union, the intensifying struggle requires us to face the fact that we can expect no lasting abatement of the crisis unless and until a change occurs in the nature of the Soviet system.

C. MEANS

The free society is limited in its choice of means to achieve its ends.

Compulsion is the negation of freedom, except when it is used to enforce the rights common to all. The resort to force, internally or externally, is therefore a last resort for a free society. The act is permissible only when one individual or groups of individuals within it threaten the basic rights of other individuals or when another society seeks to impose its will upon it. The free society cherishes and protects as fundamental the rights of the minority against the will of a majority, because these rights are the inalienable rights of each and every individual.

The resort to force, to compulsion, to the imposition of its will is therefore a difficult and dangerous act for a free society, which is warranted only in the face of even greater dangers. The necessity of the act must be clear and compelling; the act must commend itself to the overwhelming majority as an inescapable exception to the basic idea of freedom; or the regenerative capacity of free men after the act has been performed will be endangered.

The Kremlin is able to select whatever means are expedient in seeking to carry out its fundamental design. Thus it can make the best of several possible worlds, conducting the struggle on those levels where it considers it profitable and enjoying the benefits of a pseudo-peace on those levels where it is not ready for a contest. At the ideological or psychological level, in the struggle for men's minds, the conflict is worldwide. At the political and economic level, within states and in the relations between states, the struggle for power is being intensified. And at the military level, the Kremlin has thus far been careful not to commit a technical breach of the peace, although using its vast forces to intimidate its neighbors, and to support an aggressive foreign policy, and not hesitating through its agents to resort to arms in favorable circumstances. The attempt to carry out its fundamental design is being pressed, therefore, with all means which are believed expedient in the present situation, and the Kremlin has inextricably engaged us in the conflict between its design and our purpose.

We have no such freedom of choice, and least of all in the use of force. Resort to war is not only a last resort for a free society, but it is also an act which cannot definitively end the fundamental conflict in the realm of ideas. The idea of slavery can only be overcome by the timely and persistent demonstration of the superiority of the idea of freedom. Military victory alone would only partially and perhaps only temporarily affect the fundamental conflict, for although the ability of the Kremlin to threaten our security might be for a time destroyed, the resurgence of totalitarian forces and the re-establishment of the Soviet system or its equivalent would not be long delayed unless great progress were made in the fundamental conflict.

Practical and ideological considerations therefore both impel us to the conclusion that we have no choice but to demonstrate the superiority of the idea of freedom by its constructive application, and to attempt to change the world situation by means short of war in such a way as to frustrate the Kremlin design and hasten the decay of the Soviet system.

For us the role of military power is to serve the national purpose by deterring an attack upon us while we seek by other means to create an environment in which our free society can flourish, and by fighting, if necessary, to defend the integrity and vitality of our free society and to defeat any aggressor. The Kremlin uses Soviet military power to back up and serve the Kremlin design. It does not hesitate to use military force aggressively if that course is expedient in the achievement of its design. The differences between our fundamental purpose and the Kremlin design, therefore, are reflected in our respective attitudes toward and use of military force.

Our free society, confronted by a threat to its basic values, naturally will take such action, including the use of military force, as may be required to protect those values. The integrity of our system will not be jeopardized by any measures, covert or overt, violent or non-violent, which serve the purposes of frustrating the Kremlin design, nor does the necessity for conducting ourselves so as to affirm our values in actions as well as words forbid such measures, provided only they are appropriately calculated to that end and are not so excessive or misdirected as to make us enemies of the people instead of the evil men who have enslaved them.

But if war comes, what is the role of force? Unless we so use it that the Russian people can perceive that our effort is directed against the regime and its power for aggression, and not against their own interests, we will unite the regime and the people in the kind of last ditch fight in which no underlying problems are solved, new ones are created, and where our basic principles are obscured and compromised. If we do not in the application of force demonstrate the nature of our objectives we will, in fact, have compromised from the outset our fundamental purpose. In the words of the Federalist (No. 28) "The means to be employed must be proportioned to the extent of the mischief." The mischief may be a global war or it may be a Soviet campaign for limited objectives. In either case we should take no avoidable initiative which would cause it to become a war of annihilation, and if we have the forces to defeat a Soviet drive for limited objectives it may well be to our interest not to let it become a global war. Our aim in applying force must be to compel the acceptance of terms consistent with our objectives, and our capabilities for the application of force should, therefore, within the limits of what we can sustain over the long pull, be congruent to the range of tasks which we may encounter.

[The following 27 pages indicate the current and potential armaments, including nuclear weaponry, for the United States and USSR.]

1

What is the main purpose of this passage?

_____

2

What is the passage's tone?

_____

3

How would you summarize the passage?

_____

4

What is the authors' central thesis?

_____

Possible Courses of Action

Introduction. Four possible courses of action by the United States in the present situation can be distinguished. They are:

a. Continuation of current policies, with current and currently projected programs for carrying out these policies; b. Isolation; c. War; and d. A more rapid building up of the political, economic, and military strength of the free world than provided under a, with the purpose of reaching, if possible, a tolerable state of order among nations without war and of preparing to defend ourselves in the event that the free world is attacked.

The role of negotiation. Negotiation must be considered in relation to these courses of action. A negotiator always attempts to achieve an agreement which is somewhat better than the realities of his fundamental position would justify and which is, in any case, not worse than his fundamental position requires. This is as true in relations among sovereign states as in relations between individuals. The Soviet Union possesses several advantages over the free world in negotiations on any issue:

a. It can and does enforce secrecy on all significant facts about conditions within the Soviet Union, so that it can be expected to know more about the realities of the free world's position than the free world knows about its position; b. It does not have to be responsive in any important sense to public opinion; c. It does not have to consult and agree with any other countries on the terms it will offer and accept; and d. It can influence public opinion in other countries while insulating the peoples under its control.

These are important advantages. Together with the unfavorable trend of our power position, they militate, as is shown in Section A below, against successful negotiation of a general settlement at this time. For although the United States probably now possesses, principally in atomic weapons, a force adequate to deliver a powerful blow upon the Soviet Union and to open the road to victory in a long war, it is not sufficient by itself to advance the position of the United States in the cold war.

The problem is to create such political and economic conditions in the free world, backed by force sufficient to inhibit Soviet attack, that the Kremlin will accommodate itself to these conditions, gradually withdraw, and eventually change its policies drastically. It has been shown [in the 27 page armament analysis] that truly effective control of atomic energy would require such an opening up of the Soviet Union and such evidence in other ways of its good faith and its intent to co-exist in peace as to reflect or at least initiate a change in the Soviet system.

Clearly under present circumstances we will not be able to negotiate a settlement which calls for a change in the Soviet system. What, then, is the role of negotiation?

In the first place, the public in the United States and in other free countries will require, as a condition to firm policies and adequate programs directed to the frustration of the Kremlin design, that the free world be continuously prepared to negotiate agreements with the Soviet Union on equitable terms. It is still argued by many people here and abroad that equitable agreements with the Soviet Union are possible, and this view will gain force if the Soviet Union begins to show signs of accommodation, even on unimportant issues.

The free countries must always, therefore, be prepared to negotiate and must be ready to take the initiative at times in seeking negotiation. They must develop a negotiating position which defines the issues and the terms on which they would be prepared--and at what stages--to accept agreements with the Soviet Union. The terms must be fair in the view of popular opinion in the free world. This means that they must be consistent with a positive program for peace--in harmony with the United Nations' Charter and providing, at a minimum, for the effective control of all armaments by the United Nations or a successor organization. The terms must not require more of the Soviet Union than such behavior and such participation in a world organization. The fact that such conduct by the Soviet Union is impossible without such a radical change in Soviet policies as to constitute a change in the Soviet system would then emerge as a result of the Kremlin's unwillingness to accept such terms or of its bad faith in observing them.

A sound negotiating position is, therefore, an essential element in the ideological conflict. For some time after a decision to build up strength, any offer of, or attempt at, negotiation of a general settlement along the lines of the Berkeley speech by the Secretary of State could be only a tactic. Nevertheless, concurrently with a decision and a start on building up the strength of the free world, it may be desirable to pursue this tactic both to gain public support for the program and to minimize the immediate risks of war. It is urgently necessary for the United States to determine its negotiating position and to obtain agreement with its major allies on the purposes and terms of negotiation.

In the second place, assuming that the United States in cooperation with other free countries decides and acts to increase the strength of the free world and assuming that the Kremlin chooses the path of accommodation, it will from time to time be necessary and desirable to negotiate on various specific issues with the Kremlin as the area of possible agreement widens.

The Kremlin will have three major objectives in negotiations with the United States. The first is to eliminate the atomic capabilities of the United States; the second is to prevent the effective mobilization of the superior potential of the free world in human and material resources; and the third is to secure a withdrawal of United States forces from, and commitments to, Europe and Japan. Depending on its evaluation of its own strengths and weaknesses as against the West's (particularly the ability and will of the West to sustain its efforts), it will or will not be prepared to make important concessions to achieve these major objectives. It is unlikely that the Kremlin's evaluation is such that it would now be prepared to make significant concessions.

The objectives of the United States and other free countries in negotiations with the Soviet Union (apart from the ideological objectives discussed above) are to record, in a formal fashion which will facilitate the consolidation and further advance of our position, the process of Soviet accommodation to the new political, psychological, and economic conditions in the world which will result from adoption of the fourth course of action and which will be supported by the increasing military strength developed as an integral part of that course of action. In short, our objectives are to record, where desirable, the gradual withdrawal of the Soviet Union and to facilitate that process by making negotiation, if possible, always more expedient than resort to force.

It must be presumed that for some time the Kremlin will accept agreements only if it is convinced that by acting in bad faith whenever and wherever there is an opportunity to do so with impunity, it can derive greater advantage from the agreements than the free world. For this reason, we must take care that any agreements are enforceable or that they are not susceptible of violation without detection and the possibility of effective countermeasures.

This further suggests that we will have to consider carefully the order in which agreements can be concluded. Agreement on the control of atomic energy would result in a relatively greater disarmament of the United States than of the Soviet Union, even assuming considerable progress in building up the strength of the free world in conventional forces and weapons. It might be accepted by the Soviet Union as part of a deliberate design to move against Western Europe and other areas of strategic importance with conventional forces and weapons. In this event, the United States would find itself at war, having previously disarmed itself in its most important weapon, and would be engaged in a race to redevelop atomic weapons.

This seems to indicate that for the time being the United States and other free countries would have to insist on concurrent agreement on the control of nonatomic forces and weapons and perhaps on the other elements of a general settlement, notably peace treaties with Germany, Austria, and Japan and the withdrawal of Soviet influence from the satellites. If, contrary to our expectations, the Soviet Union should accept agreements promising effective control of atomic energy and conventional armaments, without any other changes in Soviet policies, we would have to consider very carefully whether we could accept such agreements. It is unlikely that this problem will arise.

To the extent that the United States and the rest of the free world succeed in so building up their strength in conventional forces and weapons that a Soviet attack with similar forces could be thwarted or held, we will gain increased flexibility and can seek agreements on the various issues in any order, as they become negotiable.

In the third place, negotiation will play a part in the building up of the strength of the free world, apart from the ideological strength discussed above. This is most evident in the problems of Germany, Austria, and Japan. In the process of building up strength, it may be desirable for the free nations, without the Soviet Union, to conclude separate arrangements with Japan, Western Germany, and Austria which would enlist the energies and resources of these countries in support of the free world. This will be difficult unless it has been demonstrated by attempted negotiation with the Soviet Union that the Soviet Union is not prepared to accept treaties of peace which would leave these countries free, under adequate safeguards, to participate in the United Nations and in regional or broader associations of states consistent with the United Nations' Charter and providing security and adequate opportunities for the peaceful development of their political and economic life.

This demonstrates the importance, from the point of view of negotiation as well as for its relationship to the building up of the strength of the free world (see Section D below), of the problem of closer association--on a regional or a broader basis--among the free countries.

In conclusion, negotiation is not a possible separate course of action but rather a means of gaining support for a program of building strength, of recording, where necessary and desirable, progress in the cold war, and of facilitating further progress while helping to minimize the risks of war. Ultimately, it is our objective to negotiate a settlement with the Soviet Union (or a successor state or states) on which the world can place reliance as an enforceable instrument of peace. But it is important to emphasize that such a settlement can only record the progress which the free world will have made in creating a political and economic system in the world so successful that the frustration of the Kremlin's design for world domination will be complete. The analysis in the following sections indicates that the building of such a system requires expanded and accelerated programs for the carrying out of current policies.

A. THE FIRST COURSE--CONTINUATION OF CURRENT POLICIES, WITH CURRENT AND CURRENTLY PROJECTED PROGRAMS FOR CARRYING OUT THESE POLICIES

1. Military aspects. On the basis of current programs, the United States has a large potential military capability but an actual capability which, though improving, is declining relative to the USSR, particularly in light of its probable fission bomb capability and possible thermonuclear bomb capability. The same holds true for the free world as a whole relative to the Soviet world as a whole. If war breaks out in 1950 or in the next few years, the United States and its allies, apart from a powerful atomic blow, will be compelled to conduct delaying actions, while building up their strength for a general offensive. A frank evaluation of the requirements, to defend the United States and its vital interests and to support a vigorous initiative in the cold war, on the one hand, and of present capabilities, on the other, indicates that there is a sharp and growing disparity between them.

A review of Soviet policy shows that the military capabilities, actual and potential, of the United States and the rest of the free world, together with the apparent determination of the free world to resist further Soviet expansion, have not induced the Kremlin to relax its pressures generally or to give up the initiative in the cold war. On the contrary, the Soviet Union has consistently pursued a bold foreign policy, modified only when its probing revealed a determination and an ability of the free world to resist encroachment upon it. The relative military capabilities of the free world are declining, with the result that its determination to resist may also decline and that the security of the United States and the free world as a whole will be jeopardized.

From the military point of view, the actual and potential capabilities of the United States, given a continuation of current and projected programs, will become less and less effective as a war deterrent. Improvement of the state of readiness will become more and more important not only to inhibit the launching of war by the Soviet Union but also to support a national policy designed to reverse the present ominous trends in international relations. A building up of the military capabilities of the United States and the free world is a pre-condition to the achievement of the objectives outlined in this report and to the protection of the United States against disaster.

Fortunately, the United States military establishment has been developed into a unified and effective force as a result of the policies laid down by the Congress and the vigorous carrying out of these policies by the Administration in the fields of both organization and economy. It is, therefore, a base upon which increased strength can be rapidly built with maximum efficiency and economy.

2. Political aspects. The Soviet Union is pursuing the initiative in the conflict with the free world. Its atomic capabilities, together with its successes in the Far East, have led to an increasing confidence on its part and to an increasing nervousness in Western Europe and the rest of the free world. We cannot be sure, of course, how vigorously the Soviet Union will pursue its initiative, nor can we be sure of the strength or weakness of the other free countries in reacting to it. There are, however, ominous signs of further deterioration in the Far East. There are also some indications that a decline in morale and confidence in Western Europe may be expected. In particular, the situation in Germany is unsettled. Should the belief or suspicion spread that the free nations are not now able to prevent the Soviet Union from taking, if it chooses, the military actions outlined above, the determination of the free countries to resist probably would lessen and there would be an increasing temptation for them to seek a position of neutrality.

Politically, recognition of the military implications of a continuation of present trends will mean that the United States and especially other free countries will tend to shift to the defensive, or to follow a dangerous policy of bluff, because the maintenance of a firm initiative in the cold war is closely related to aggregate strength in being and readily available.

This is largely a problem of the incongruity of the current actual capabilities of the free world and the threat to it, for the free world has an economic and military potential far superior to the potential of the Soviet Union and its satellites. The shadow of Soviet force falls darkly on Western Europe and Asia and supports a policy of encroachment. The free world lacks adequate means--in the form of forces in being-- to thwart such expansion locally. The United States will therefore be confronted more frequently with the dilemma of reacting totally to a limited extension of Soviet control or of not reacting at all (except with ineffectual protests and half measures). Continuation of present trends is likely to lead, therefore, to a

gradual withdrawal under the direct or indirect pressure of the Soviet Union, until we discover one day that we have sacrificed positions of vital interest. In other words, the United States would have chosen, by lack of the necessary decisions and actions, to fall back to isolation in the Western Hemisphere. This course would at best result in only a relatively brief truce and would be ended either by our capitulation or by a defensive war--on unfavorable terms from unfavorable positions--against a Soviet Empire compromising all or most of Eurasia. (See Section B.)

3. Economic and social aspects. The present foreign economic policies and programs of the United States will not produce a solution to the problem of international economic equilibrium, notably the problem of the dollar gap, and will not create an economic base conducive to political stability in many important free countries.

The European Recovery Program has been successful in assisting the restoration and expansion of production in Western Europe and has been a major factor in checking the dry rot of Communism in Western Europe. However, little progress has been made toward the resumption by Western Europe of a position of influence in world affairs commensurate with its potential strength. Progress in this direction will require integrated political, economic, and military policies and programs, which are supported by the United States and the Western European countries and which will probably require a deeper participation by the United States than has been contemplated.

The Point IV Program and other assistance programs will not adequately supplement, as now projected, the efforts of other important countries to develop effective institutions, to improve the administration of their affairs, and to achieve a sufficient measure of economic development. The moderate regimes now in power in many countries, like India, Indonesia, Pakistan, and the Philippines, will probably be unable to restore or retain their popular support and authority unless they are assisted in bringing about a more rapid improvement of the economic and social structure than present programs will make possible.

The Executive Branch is now undertaking a study of the problem of the United States balance of payments and of the measures which might be taken by the United States to assist in establishing international economic equilibrium. This is a very important project and work on it should have a high priority. However, unless such an economic program is matched and supplemented by an equally far-sighted and vigorous political and military program, we will not be successful in checking and rolling back the Kremlin's drive.

4. Negotiation. In short, by continuing along its present course the free world will not succeed in making effective use of its vastly superior political, economic, and military potential to build a tolerable state of order among nations. On the contrary, the political, economic, and military situation of the free world is already unsatisfactory and will become less favorable unless we act to reverse present trends.

This situation is one which militates against successful negotiations with the Kremlin--for the terms of agreements on important pending issues would reflect present realities and would therefore be unacceptable, if not disastrous, to the United States and the rest of the free world. Unless a decision had been made and action undertaken to build up the strength, in the broadest sense, of the United States and the free world, an attempt to negotiate a general settlement on terms acceptable to us would be ineffective and probably long drawn out, and might thereby seriously delay the necessary measures to build up our strength.

This is true despite the fact that the United States now has the capability of delivering a powerful blow against the Soviet Union in the event of war, for one of the present realities is that the United States is not prepared to threaten the use of our present atomic superiority to coerce the Soviet Union into acceptable agreements. In light of present trends, the Soviet Union will not withdraw and the only conceivable basis for a general settlement would be spheres of influence and of no influenced "settlement" which the Kremlin could readily exploit to its great advantage. The idea that Germany or Japan or other important areas can exist as islands of neutrality in a divided world is unreal, given the Kremlin design for world domination.

B. THE SECOND COURSE--ISOLATION

Continuation of present trends, it has been shown above, will lead progressively to the withdrawal of the United States from most of its present commitments in Europe and Asia and to our isolation in the Western Hemisphere and its approaches. This would result not from a conscious decision but from a failure to take the actions necessary to bring our capabilities into line with our commitments and thus to a withdrawal under pressure. This pressure might come from our present Allies, who will tend to seek other "solutions" unless they have confidence in our determination to accelerate our efforts to build a successfully functioning political and economic system in the free world.

There are some who advocate a deliberate decision to isolate ourselves. Superficially, this has some

attractiveness as a course of action, for it appears to bring our commitments and capabilities into harmony by reducing the former and by concentrating our present, or perhaps even reduced, military expenditures on the defense of the United States.

This argument overlooks the relativity of capabilities. With the United States in an isolated position, we would have to face the probability that the Soviet Union would quickly dominate most of Eurasia, probably without meeting armed resistance. It would thus acquire a potential far superior to our own, and would promptly proceed to develop this potential with the purpose of eliminating our power, which would, even in isolation, remain as a challenge to it and as an obstacle to the imposition of its kind of order in the world. There is no way to make ourselves inoffensive to the Kremlin except by complete submission to its will. Therefore isolation would in the end condemn us to capitulate or to fight alone and on the defensive, with drastically limited offensive and retaliatory capabilities in comparison with the Soviet Union. (These are the only possibilities, unless we are prepared to risk the future on the hazard that the Soviet Empire, because of over-extension or other reasons, will spontaneously destroy itself from within.)

The argument also overlooks the imponderable, but nevertheless drastic, effects on our belief in ourselves and in our way of life of a deliberate decision to isolate ourselves. As the Soviet Union came to dominate free countries, it is clear that many Americans would feel a deep sense of responsibility and guilt for having abandoned their former friends and allies. As the Soviet Union mobilized the resources of Eurasia, increased its relative military capabilities, and heightened its threat to our security, some would be tempted to accept "peace" on its terms, while many would seek to defend the United States by creating a regimented system which would permit the assignment of a tremendous part of our resources to defense. Under such a state of affairs our national morale would be corrupted and the integrity and vitality of our system subverted.

Under this course of action, there would be no negotiation, unless on the Kremlin's terms, for we would have given up everything of importance.

It is possible that at some point in the course of isolation, many Americans would come to favor a surprise attack on the Soviet Union and the area under its control, in a desperate attempt to alter decisively the balance of power by an overwhelming blow with modern weapons of mass destruction. It appears unlikely that the Soviet Union would wait for such an attack before launching one of its own. But even if it did and even if our attack were successful, it is clear that the United States would face appalling tasks in establishing a tolerable state of order among nations after such a war and after Soviet occupation of all or most of Eurasia for some years. These tasks appear so enormous and success so unlikely that reason dictates an attempt to achieve our objectives by other means.

C. THE THIRD COURSE--WAR

Some Americans favor a deliberate decision to go to war against the Soviet Union in the near future. It goes without saying that the idea of "preventive" war-- in the sense of a military attack not provoked by a military attack upon us or our allies--is generally unacceptable to Americans. Its supporters argue that since the Soviet Union is in fact at war with the free world now and that since the failure of the Soviet Union to use all-out military force is explainable on grounds of expediency, we are at war and should conduct ourselves accordingly. Some further argue that the free world is probably unable, except under the crisis of war, to mobilize and direct its resources to the checking and rolling back of the Kremlin's drive for world dominion. This is a powerful argument in the light of history, but the considerations against war are so compelling that the free world must demonstrate that this argument is wrong. The case for war is premised on the assumption that the United States could launch and sustain an attack of sufficient impact to gain a decisive advantage for the free world in a long war and perhaps to win an early decision.

The ability of the United States to launch effective offensive operations is now limited to attack with atomic weapons. A powerful blow could be delivered upon the Soviet Union, but it is estimated that these operations alone would not force or induce the Kremlin to capitulate and that the Kremlin would still be able to use the forces under its control to dominate most or all of Eurasia. This would probably mean a long and difficult struggle during which the free institutions of Western Europe and many freedom-loving people would be destroyed and the regenerative capacity of Western Europe dealt a crippling blow.

Apart from this, however, a surprise attack upon the Soviet Union, despite the provocativeness of recent Soviet behavior, would be repugnant to many Americans. Although the American people would probably rally in support of the war effort, the shock of responsibility for a surprise attack would be morally corrosive. Many would doubt that it was a "just war" and that all reasonable possibilities for a peaceful settlement had been explored in good faith. Many more, proportionately, would hold such views in other countries, particularly in Western Europe and particularly after Soviet occupation, if only because the Soviet Union would liquidate articulate opponents. It would, therefore, be difficult after such a war to create

a satisfactory international order among nations. Victory in such a war would have brought us little if at all closer to victory in the fundamental ideological conflict.

These considerations are no less weighty because they are imponderable, and they rule out an attack unless it is demonstrably in the nature of a counter-attack to a blow which is on its way or about to be delivered. (The military advantages of landing the first blow become increasingly important with modern weapons, and this is a fact which requires us to be on the alert in order to strike with our full weight as soon as we are attacked, and, if possible, before the Soviet blow is actually delivered.) There is no "easy" solution and that the only sure victory lies in the frustration of the Kremlin design by the steady development of the moral and material strength of the free world and its projection into the Soviet world in such a way as to bring about an internal change in the Soviet system.

D. THE REMAINING COURSE OF ACTION--A RAPID BUILD-UP OF POLITICAL, ECONOMIC, AND MILITARY STRENGTH IN THE FREE WORLD

A more rapid build-up of political, economic, and military strength and thereby of confidence in the free world than is now contemplated is the only course which is consistent with progress toward achieving our fundamental purpose. The frustration of the Kremlin design requires the free world to develop a successfully functioning political and economic system and a vigorous political offensive against the Soviet Union. These, in turn, require an adequate military shield under which they can develop. It is necessary to have the military power to deter, if possible, Soviet expansion, and to defeat, if necessary, aggressive Soviet or Soviet-directed actions of a limited or total character. The potential strength of the free world is great; its ability to develop these military capabilities and its will to resist Soviet expansion will be determined by the wisdom and will with which it undertakes to meet its political and economic problems.

1. Military aspects. U.S. military capabilities are strategically more defensive in nature than offensive and are more potential than actual. It is evident, from an analysis of the past and of the trend of weapon development, that there is now and will be in the future no absolute defense. The history of war also indicates that a favorable decision can only be achieved through offensive action. Even a defensive strategy, if it is to be successful, calls not only for defensive forces to hold vital positions while mobilizing and preparing for the offensive, but also for offensive forces to attack the enemy and keep him off balance.

The two fundamental requirements which must be met by forces in being or readily available are support of foreign policy and protection against disaster. To meet the second requirement, the forces in being or readily available must be able, at a minimum, to perform certain basic tasks:

a. To defend the Western Hemisphere and essential allied areas in order that their war-making capabilities can be developed;

b. To provide and protect a mobilization base while the offensive forces required for victory are being built up;

c. To conduct offensive operations to destroy vital elements of the Soviet war-making capacity, and to keep the enemy off balance until the full offensive strength of the United States and its allies can be brought to bear;

d. To defend and maintain the lines of communication and base areas necessary to the execution of the above tasks; and

e. To provide such aid to allies as is essential to the execution of their role in the above tasks.

In the broadest terms, the ability to perform these tasks requires a build-up of military strength by the United States and its allies to a point at which the combined strength will be superior for at least these tasks, both initially and throughout a war, to the forces that can be brought to bear by the Soviet Union and its satellites. In specific terms, it is not essential to match item for item with the Soviet Union, but to provide an adequate defense against air attack on the United States and Canada and an adequate defense against air and surface attack on the United Kingdom and Western Europe, Alaska, the Western Pacific, Africa, and the Near and Middle East, and on the long lines of communication to these areas. Furthermore, it is mandatory that in building up our strength, we enlarge upon our technical superiority by an accelerated exploitation of the scientific potential of the United States and our allies.

Forces of this size and character are necessary not only for protection against disaster but also to support our foreign policy. In fact, it can be argued that larger forces in being and readily available are necessary to inhibit a would-be aggressor than to provide the nucleus of strength and the mobilization base on which the tremendous forces required for victory can be built. For example, in both World Wars I and 11 the ultimate victors had the strength, in the end, to win though they had not had the strength in being or readily available to prevent the outbreak of war. In part, at least, this was because they had not had the military strength on which to base a strong foreign policy. At any rate, it is clear that a substantial and rapid building up of strength in the free world is

necessary to support a firm policy intended to check and to roll back the Kremlin's drive for world domination.

Moreover, the United States and the other free countries do not now have the forces in being and readily available to defeat local Soviet moves with local action, but must accept reverses or make these local moves the occasion for war--for which we are not prepared. This situation makes for great uneasiness among our allies, particularly in Western Europe, for whom total war means, initially, Soviet occupation. Thus, unless our combined strength is rapidly increased, our allies will tend to become increasingly reluctant to support a firm foreign policy on our part and increasingly anxious to seek other solutions, even though they are aware that appeasement means defeat. An important advantage in adopting the fourth course of action lies in its psychological impact--the revival of confidence and hope in the future. It is recognized, of course, that any announcement of the recommended course of action could be exploited by the Soviet Union in its peace campaign and would have adverse psychological effects in certain parts of the free world until the necessary increase in strength has been achieved. Therefore, in any announcement of policy and in the character of the measures adopted, emphasis should be given to the essentially defensive character and care should be taken to minimize, so far as possible, unfavorable domestic and foreign reactions.

2. Political and economic aspects. The immediate objectives--to the achievement of which such a build-up of strength is a necessary though not a sufficient condition--are a renewed initiative in the cold war and a situation to which the Kremlin would find it expedient to accommodate itself, first by relaxing tensions and pressures and then by gradual withdrawal. The United States cannot alone provide the resources required for such a build-up of strength. The other free countries must carry their part of the burden, but their ability and determination to do it will depend on the action the United States takes to develop its own strength and on the adequacy of its foreign political and economic policies. Improvement in political and economic conditions in the free world, as has been emphasized above, is necessary as a basis for building up the will and the means to resist and for dynamically affirming the integrity and vitality of our free and democratic way of life on which our ultimate victory depends.

At the same time, we should take dynamic steps to reduce the power and influence of the Kremlin inside the Soviet Union and other areas under its control. The objective would be the establishment of friendly regimes not under Kremlin domination. Such action is essential to engage the Kremlin's attention, keep it off balance, and force an increased expenditure of Soviet resources in counteraction. In other words, it would be the current Soviet cold war technique used against the Soviet Union.

A program for rapidly building up strength and improving political and economic conditions will place heavy demands on our courage and intelligence; it will be costly; it will be dangerous. But half-measures will be more costly and more dangerous, for they will be inadequate to prevent and may actually invite war. Budgetary considerations will need to be subordinated to the stark fact that our very independence as a nation may be at stake.

A comprehensive and decisive program to win the peace and frustrate the Kremlin design should be so designed that it can be sustained for as long as necessary to achieve our national objectives. It would probably involve:

The development of an adequate political and economic framework for the achievement of our long-range objectives.

A substantial increase in expenditures for military purposes adequate to meet the requirements for the tasks listed in Section D-1.

A substantial increase in military assistance programs, designed to foster cooperative efforts, which will adequately and efficiently meet the requirements of our allies for the tasks referred to in Section D-l-e.

Some increase in economic assistance programs and recognition of the need to continue these programs until their purposes have been accomplished.

A concerted attack on the problem of the United States balance of payments, along the lines already approved by the President.

Development of programs designed to build and maintain confidence among other peoples in our strength and resolution, and to wage overt psychological warfare calculated to encourage mass defections from Soviet allegiance and to frustrate the Kremlin design in other ways.

Intensification of affirmative and timely measures and operations by covert means in the fields of economic warfare and political and psychological warfare with a view to fomenting and supporting unrest and revolt in selected strategic satellite countries.

Development of internal security and civilian defense programs.

Improvement and intensification of intelligence activities.

Reduction of Federal expenditures for purposes other than defense and foreign assistance, if necessary by the deferment of certain desirable programs.

Increased taxes.

Essential as prerequisites to the success of this program would be (a) consultations with Congressional leaders designed to make the program the object of non-partisan legislative support, and (b) a presentation to the public of a full explanation of the facts and implications of present international trends.

The program will be costly, but it is relevant to recall the disproportion between the potential capabilities of the Soviet and non-Soviet worlds. The Soviet Union is currently devoting about 40 percent of available resources (gross national product plus reparations, equal in 1949 to about $65 billion) to military expenditures (14 percent) and to investment (26 percent), much of which is in war-supporting industries. In an emergency the Soviet Union could increase the allocation of resources to these purposes to about 50 percent, or by one-fourth.

The United States is currently devoting about 22 percent of its gross national product ($255 billion in 1949) to military expenditures (6 percent), foreign assistance (2 percent), and investment (14 percent), little of which is in war-supporting industries. (The "fighting value" obtained per dollar of expenditure by the Soviet Union considerably exceeds that obtained by the United States, primarily because of the extremely low military and civilian living standards in the Soviet Union.) In an emergency the United States could devote upward of 50 percent of its gross national product to these purposes (as it did during the last war), an increase of several times present expenditures for direct and indirect military purposes and foreign assistance.

From the point of view of the economy as a whole, the program might not result in a real decrease in the standard of living, for the economic effects of the program might be to increase the gross national product by more than the amount being absorbed for additional military and foreign assistance purposes. One of the most significant lessons of our World War 11 experience was that the American economy, when it operates at a level approaching full efficiency, can provide enormous resources for purposes other than civilian consumption while simultaneously providing a high standard of living. After allowing for price changes, personal consumption expenditures rose by about one-fifth between 1939 and 1944, even though the economy had in the meantime increased the amount of resources going into Government use by $60 $65 billion (in 1939 prices).

This comparison between the potentials of the Soviet Union and the United States also holds true for the Soviet world and the free world and is of fundamental importance in considering the courses of action open to the United States.

The comparison gives renewed emphasis to the fact that the problems faced by the free countries in their efforts to build a successfully functioning system lie not so much in the field of economics as in the field of politics. The building of such a system may require more rapid progress toward the closer association of the free countries in harmony with the concept of the United Nations. It is clear that our long-range objectives require a strengthened United Nations, or a successor organization, to which the world can look for the maintenance of peace and order in a system based on freedom and justice. It also seems clear that a unifying ideal of this kind might awaken and arouse the latent spiritual energies of free men everywhere and obtain their enthusiastic support for a positive program for peace going far beyond the frustration of the Kremlin design and opening vistas to the future that would outweigh short-run sacrifices.

The threat to the free world involved in the development of the Soviet Union's atomic and other capabilities will rise steadily and rather rapidly. For the time being, the United States possesses a marked atomic superiority over the Soviet Union which, together with the potential capabilities of the United States and other free countries in other forces and weapons, inhibits aggressive Soviet action. This provides an opportunity for the United States, in cooperation with other free countries, to launch a build-up of strength which will support a firm policy directed to the frustration of the Kremlin design. The immediate goal of our efforts to build a successfully functioning political and economic system in the free world backed by adequate military strength is to postpone and avert the disastrous situation which, in light of the Soviet Union's probable fission bomb capability and possible thermonuclear bomb capability, might arise in 1954 on a continuation of our present programs. By acting promptly and vigorously in such a way that this date is, so to speak, pushed into the future, we would permit time for the process of accommodation, withdrawal and frustration to produce the necessary changes in the Soviet system. Time is short, however, and the risks of war attendant upon a decision to build up strength will steadily increase the longer we defer it.

1

What is the main purpose of this section of the passage?

2

What is this section's passage's tone?

3

How would you summarize this section?

4

What is the authors' central thesis?

Conclusions and Recommendations

The foregoing analysis indicates that the probable fission bomb capability and possible thermonuclear bomb capability of the Soviet Union have greatly intensified the Soviet threat to the security of the United States. This threat is of the same character as that described in NSC 20/4 (approved by the President on November 24, 1948) but is more immediate than had previously been estimated. In particular, the United States now faces the contingency that within the next four or five years the Soviet Union will possess the military capability of delivering a surprise atomic attack of such weight that the United States must have substantially increased general air, ground, and sea strength, atomic capabilities, and air and civilian defenses to deter war and to provide reasonable assurance, in the event of war, that it could survive the initial blow and go on to the eventual attainment of its objectives. In return, this contingency requires the intensification of our efforts in the fields of intelligence and research and development.

Allowing for the immediacy of the danger, the following statement of Soviet threats, contained in NSC 20/4, remains valid:

The gravest threat to the security of the United States within the foreseeable future stems from the hostile designs and formidable power of the USSR, and from the nature of the Soviet system.

The political, economic, and psychological warfare which the USSR is now waging has dangerous potentialities for weakening the relative world position of the United States and disrupting its traditional institutions by means short of war, unless sufficient resistance is encountered in the policies of this and other non-communist countries.

The risk of war with the USSR is sufficient to warrant, in common prudence, timely and adequate preparation by the United States. Even though present estimates indicate that the Soviet leaders probably do not intend deliberate armed action involving the United States at this time, the possibility of such deliberate resort to war cannot be ruled out. Now and for the foreseeable future there is a continuing danger that war will arise either through Soviet miscalculation of the determination of the United States to use all the means at its command to safeguard its security, through Soviet misinterpretation of our intentions, or through U.S. miscalculation of Soviet reactions to measures which we might take.

Soviet domination of the potential power of Eurasia, whether achieved by armed aggression or by political and subversive means, would be strategically and politically unacceptable to the United States.

The capability of the United States either in peace or in the event of war to cope with threats to its security or to gain its objectives would be severely weakened by internal development, important among which are: Serious espionage, subversion and sabotage, particularly by concerted and well-directed communist activity; Prolonged or exaggerated economic instability; Internal political and social disunity; Inadequate or excessive armament or foreign aid expenditure; An excessive or wasteful usage of our resources in time of peace; Lessening of U.S. prestige and influence through vacillation of appeasement or lack of skill and imagination in the conduct of its foreign policy or by shirking world responsibilities; Development of a false sense of security through a deceptive change in Soviet tactics.

Although such developments as those indicated above would severely weaken the capability of the United States and its allies to cope with the Soviet threat to their security, considerable progress has been made since 1948 in laying the foundation upon which adequate strength can now be rapidly built.

In the light of present and prospective Soviet atomic capabilities, the action which can be taken under present programs and plans, however, becomes dangerously inadequate, in both timing and scope, to accomplish the rapid progress toward the attainment of the United States political, economic, and military objectives which is now imperative.

A continuation of present trends would result in a serious decline in the strength of the free world relative to the Soviet Union and its satellites. This unfavorable trend arises from the inadequacy of current programs and plans rather than from any error in our objectives and aims. These trends lead in the direction of isolation, not by deliberate decision but by lack of the necessary basis for a vigorous initiative in the conflict with the Soviet Union.

Our position as the center of power in the free world places a heavy responsibility upon the United States for leadership. We must organize and enlist the energies and resources of the free world in a positive program for peace which will frustrate the Kremlin design for world domination by creating a situation in the free world to which the Kremlin will be compelled to adjust. Without such a cooperative effort, led by the United States, we will have to make gradual withdrawals under pressure until we discover one day that we have sacrificed positions of vital interest.

It is imperative that this trend be reversed by a much more rapid and concerted build-up of the actual strength of both the United States and the other nations of the free world. The analysis shows that this will be costly and will involve significant domestic financial and economic adjustments.

The execution of such a build-up, however, requires that the United States have an affirmative program beyond the solely defensive one of countering the threat posed by the Soviet Union. This program must light the path to peace and order among nations in a system based on freedom and justice, as contemplated in the Charter of the United Nations. Further, it must envisage the political and economic measures with which and the military shield behind which the free world can work to frustrate the Kremlin design by the strategy of the cold war; for every consideration of devotion to our fundamental values and to our national security demands that we achieve our objectives by the strategy of the cold war, building up our military strength in order that it may not have to be used. The only sure victory lies in the frustration of the Kremlin design by the steady development of the moral and material strength of the free world and its projection into the Soviet world in such a way as to bring about an internal change in the Soviet system. Such a positive program--harmonious with our fundamental national purpose and our objectives--is necessary if we are to regain and retain the initiative and to win and hold the necessary popular support and cooperation in the United States and the rest of the free world.

This program should include a plan for negotiation with the Soviet Union, developed and agreed with our allies and which is consonant with our objectives. The United States and its allies, particularly the United Kingdom and France, should always be ready to negotiate with the Soviet Union on terms consistent with our objectives. The present world situation, however, is one which militates against successful negotiations with the Kremlin--for the terms of agreements on important pending issues would reflect present realities and would therefore be unacceptable, if not disastrous, to the United States and the rest of the free world. After a decision and a start on building up the strength of the free world has been made, it might then be desirable for the United States to take an initiative in seeking negotiations in the hope that it might facilitate the process of accommodation by the Kremlin to the new situation. Failing that, the unwillingness of the Kremlin to accept equitable terms or its bad faith in observing them would assist in consolidating popular opinion in the free world in support of the measures necessary to sustain the build-up.

In summary, we must, by means of a rapid and sustained build-up of the political, economic, and military strength of the free world, and by means of an affirmative program intended to wrest the initiative from the Soviet Union, confront it with convincing evidence of the determination and ability of the free world to frustrate the Kremlin design of a world dominated by its will. Such evidence is the only means short of war which eventually may force the Kremlin to abandon its present course of action and to negotiate acceptable agreements on issues of major importance.

The whole success of the proposed program hangs ultimately on recognition by this Government, the American people, and all free peoples, that the cold war is in fact a real war in which the survival of the free world is at stake. Essential prerequisites to success are consultations with Congressional leaders designed to make the program the object of non-partisan legislative support, and a presentation to the public of a full explanation of the facts and implications of the present international situation. The prosecution of the program will require of us all the ingenuity, sacrifice, and unity demanded by the vital importance of the issue and the tenacity to persevere until our national objectives have been attained.

It is therefore recommended that the President:

a. Approve the foregoing Conclusions.

. Direct the National Security Council, under the continuing direction of the President, and with the participation of other Departments and Agencies as appropriate, to coordinate and insure the implementation of the Conclusions herein on an urgent and continuing basis for as long as necessary to achieve our objectives. For this purpose, representatives of the member Departments and Agencies, the Joint Chiefs of Staff or their deputies, and other Departments and Agencies as required should be constituted as a revised and strengthened staff organization under the National Security Council to develop coordinated programs for consideration by the National Security Council.

1

What is the main purpose of this passage?

_____

2

What is the passage's tone?

_____

3

How would you summarize the passage?

_____

4

What is the authors' central thesis?

_____

THE PIT AND THE PENDULUM – EDGAR ALLAN POE

Edgar Allan Poe (1809-1849) is best known for his tales of macabre and mysterious gothic literature. *The Pit and the Pendulum* was, remarkably, first published in *The Gift: A Christmas and New Year's Present* for 1843.

Impia tortorum longas hic turba furores
Sanguinis innocui non satiata, aluit.
Sospite nunc patria, fracto nunc funeris antro,
Mors ubi dira fuit vita salusque patent.[1]

- Quatrain composed for the gates of a market to be erected upon the site of the Jacobin Club House in Paris.

***

I was sick, sick unto death, with that long agony, and when they at length unbound me, and I was permitted to sit, I felt that my senses were leaving me. The sentence, the dread sentence of death, was the last of distinct accentuation which reached my ears. After that, the sound of the inquisitorial voices seemed merged in one dreamy indeterminate hum. It conveyed to my soul the idea of REVOLUTION, perhaps from its association in fancy with the burr of a mill-wheel. This only for a brief period, for presently I heard no more. Yet, for a while, I saw, but with how terrible an exaggeration! I saw the lips of the black-robed judges. They appeared to me white--whiter than the sheet upon which I trace these words--and thin even to grotesqueness; thin with the intensity of their expression of firmness, of immovable resolution, of stern contempt of human torture. I saw that the decrees of what to me was fate were still issuing from those lips. I saw them writhe with a deadly locution. I saw them fashion the syllables of my name, and I shuddered, because no sound succeeded. I saw, too, for a few moments of delirious horror, the soft and nearly imperceptible waving of the sable draperies which enwrapped the walls of the apartment; and then my vision fell upon the seven tall candles upon the table. At first they wore the aspect of charity, and seemed white slender angels who would save me: but then all at once there came a most deadly nausea over my spirit, and I felt every fibre in my frame thrill, as if I

had touched the wire of a galvanic battery, while the angel forms became meaningless spectres, with heads of flame, and I saw that from them there would be no help. And then there stole into my fancy, like a rich musical note, the thought of what sweet rest there must be in the grave. The thought came gently and stealthily, and it seemed long before it attained full appreciation; but just as my spirit came at length properly to feel and entertain it, the figures of the judges vanished, as if magically, from before me; the tall candles sank into nothingness; their flames went out utterly; the blackness of darkness superened; all sensations appeared swallowed up in a mad rushing descent as of the soul into Hades. Then silence, and stillness, and night were the universe.

I had swooned; but still will not say that all of consciousness was lost. What of it there remained I will not attempt to define, or even to describe; yet all was not lost. In the deepest slumber--no! In delirium--no! In a swoon--no! In death--no! Even in the grave all was not lost. Else there is no immortality for man. Arousing from the most profound of slumbers, we break the gossamer web of some dream. Yet in a second afterwards (so frail may that web have been) we remember not that we have dreamed. In the return to life from the swoon there are two stages; first, that of the sense of mental or spiritual; secondly, that of the sense of physical existence. It seems probable that if, upon reaching the second stage, we could recall the impressions of the first, we should find these impressions eloquent in memories of the gulf beyond. And that gulf is, what? How at least shall we distinguish its shadows from those of the tomb? But if the impressions of what I have termed the first stage are not at will recalled, yet, after long interval, do they not come unbidden, while we marvel whence they come? He who has never swooned is not he who finds strange palaces and wildly familiar faces in coals that glow; is not he who beholds floating in mid-air the sad visions that the many may not view; is not he who ponders over the perfume of some novel flower; is not he whose brain grows bewildered with the meaning of some musical cadence which has never before arrested his attention.

Amid frequent and thoughtful endeavours to remember, amid earnest struggles to regather some

---

[1] Here an unholy mob of torturers, with an unquenchable thirst
    for human blood, once fed their long frenzy.
Our homeland is safe now, the baneful pit destroyed,
    and what was once a place of savage death is now a scene of life and health.

token of the state of seeming nothingness into which my soul had lapsed, there have been moments when I have dreamed of success; there have been brief, very brief periods when I have conjured up remembrances which the lucid reason of a later epoch assures me could have had reference only to that condition of seeming unconsciousness. These shadows of memory tell indistinctly of tall figures that lifted and bore me in silence down--down--still down--till a hideous dizziness oppressed me at the mere idea of the interminableness of the descent. They tell also of a vague horror at my heart on account of that heart's unnatural stillness. Then comes a sense of sudden motionlessness throughout all things; as if those who bore me (a ghastly train!) had outrun, in their descent, the limits of the limitless, and paused from the wearisomeness of their toil. After this I call to mind flatness and dampness; and then all is MADNESS--the madness of a memory which busies itself among forbidden things.

Very suddenly there came back to my soul motion and sound--the tumultuous motion of the heart, and in my ears the sound of its beating. Then a pause in which all is blank. Then again sound, and motion, and touch, a tingling sensation pervading my frame. Then the mere consciousness of existence, without thought, a condition which lasted long. Then, very suddenly, THOUGHT, and shuddering terror, and earnest endeavour to comprehend my true state. Then a strong desire to lapse into insensibility. Then a rushing revival of soul and a successful effort to move. And now a full memory of the trial, of the judges, of the sable draperies, of the sentence, of the sickness, of the swoon. Then entire forgetfulness of all that followed; of all that a later day and much earnestness of endeavour have enabled me vaguely to recall.

So far I had not opened my eyes. I felt that I lay upon my back unbound. I reached out my hand, and it fell heavily upon something damp and hard. There I suffered it to remain for many minutes, while I strove to imagine where and what I could be. I longed, yet dared not, to employ my vision. I dreaded the first glance at objects around me. It was not that I feared to look upon things horrible, but that I grew aghast lest there should be NOTHING to see. At length, with a wild desperation at heart, I quickly unclosed my eyes. My worst thoughts, then, were confirmed. The blackness of eternal night encompassed me. I struggled for breath. The intensity of the darkness seemed to oppress and stifle me. The atmosphere was intolerably close. I still lay quietly, and made effort to exercise my reason. I brought to mind the inquisitorial proceedings, and attempted from that point to deduce my real condition. The sentence had passed, and it

appeared to me that a very long interval of time had since elapsed. Yet not for a moment did I suppose myself actually dead. Such a supposition, notwithstanding what we read in fiction, is altogether inconsistent with real existence;--but where and in what state was I? The condemned to death, I knew, perished usually at the auto-da-fes, and one of these had been held on the very night of the day of my trial. Had I been remanded to my dungeon, to await the next sacrifice, which would not take place for many months? This I at once saw could not be. Victims had been in immediate demand. Moreover my dungeon, as well as all the condemned cells at Toledo, had stone floors, and light was not altogether excluded.

A fearful idea now suddenly drove the blood in torrents upon my heart, and for a brief period I once more relapsed into insensibility. Upon recovering, I at once started to my feet, trembling convulsively in every fibre. I thrust my arms wildly above and around me in all directions. I felt nothing; yet dreaded to move a step, lest I should be impeded by the walls of a TOMB. Perspiration burst from every pore, and stood in cold big beads upon my forehead. The agony of suspense grew at length intolerable, and I cautiously moved forward, with my arms extended, and my eyes straining from their sockets, in the hope of catching some faint ray of light. I proceeded for many paces, but still all was blackness and vacancy. I breathed more freely. It seemed evident that mine was not, at least, the most hideous of fates.

And now, as I still continued to step cautiously onward, there came thronging upon my recollection a thousand vague rumours of the horrors of Toledo. Of the dungeons there had been strange things narrated-- fables I had always deemed them--but yet strange, and too ghastly to repeat, save in a whisper. Was I left to perish of starvation in this subterranean world of darkness; or what fate perhaps even more fearful awaited me? That the result would be death, and a death of more than customary bitterness, I knew too well the character of my judges to doubt. The mode and the hour were all that occupied or distracted me.

My outstretched hands at length encountered some solid obstruction. It was a wall, seemingly of stone masonry--very smooth, slimy, and cold. I followed it up; stepping with all the careful distrust with which certain antique narratives had inspired me. This process, however, afforded me no means of ascertaining the dimensions of my dungeon; as I might make its circuit, and return to the point whence I set out, without being aware of the fact, so perfectly uniform seemed the wall. I therefore sought the knife which had been in my pocket when led into the inquisitorial chamber, but it was gone; my clothes had been exchanged for a wrapper of coarse serge. I had thought of forcing the blade in some minute crevice of the masonry, so as to identify my point of departure. The difficulty, nevertheless, was but trivial, although, in the disorder of my fancy, it seemed at first insuperable. I tore a part of the hem from the robe, and placed the fragment at full length, and at right angles to the wall. In groping my way around the prison, I could not fail to encounter this rag upon completing the circuit. So, at least, I thought, but I had not counted upon the extent of the dungeon, or upon my own weakness. The ground was moist and slippery. I staggered onward for some time, when I stumbled and fell. My excessive fatigue induced me to remain prostrate, and sleep soon overtook me as I lay.

Upon awaking, and stretching forth an arm, I found beside me a loaf and a pitcher with water. I was too much exhausted to reflect upon this circumstance, but ate and drank with avidity. Shortly afterwards I resumed my tour around the prison, and with much toil came at last upon the fragment of the serge. Up to the period when I fell I had counted fifty-two paces, and upon resuming my walk I had counted forty-eight more, when I arrived at the rag. There were in all, then, a hundred paces; and, admitting two paces to the yard, I presumed the dungeon to be fifty yards in circuit. I had met, however, with many angles in the wall, and thus I could form no guess at the shape of the vault, for vault I could not help supposing it to be.

I had little object--certainly no hope--in these researches, but a vague curiosity prompted me to continue them. Quitting the wall, I resolved to cross the area of the enclosure. At first I proceeded with extreme caution, for the floor although seemingly of solid material was treacherous with slime. At length, however, I took courage and did not hesitate to step firmly--endeavouring to cross in as direct a line as possible. I had advanced some ten or twelve paces in this manner, when the remnant of the torn hem of my robe became entangled between my legs. I stepped on it, and fell violently on my face.

In the confusion attending my fall, I did not immediately apprehend a somewhat startling circumstance, which yet, in a few seconds afterward, and while I still lay prostrate, arrested my attention. It was this: my chin rested upon the floor of the prison, but my lips, and the upper portion of my head, although seemingly at a less elevation than the chin, touched nothing. At the same time, my forehead seemed bathed in a clammy vapour, and the peculiar smell of decayed fungus arose to my nostrils. I put forward my arm, and shuddered to find that I had fallen at the very brink of a circular pit, whose extent of course I had no means of ascertaining at the moment. Groping about the masonry just below the margin, I

succeeded in dislodging a small fragment, and let it fall into the abyss. For many seconds I hearkened to its reverberations as it dashed against the sides of the chasm in its descent; at length there was a sullen plunge into water, succeeded by loud echoes. At the same moment there came a sound resembling the quick opening, and as rapid closing of a door overhead, while a faint gleam of light flashed suddenly through the gloom, and as suddenly faded away.

I saw clearly the doom which had been prepared for me, and congratulated myself upon the timely accident by which I had escaped. Another step before my fall, and the world had seen me no more and the death just avoided was of that very character which I had regarded as fabulous and frivolous in the tales respecting the Inquisition. To the victims of its tyranny, there was the choice of death with its direst physical agonies, or death with its most hideous moral horrors. I had been reserved for the latter. By long suffering my nerves had been unstrung, until I trembled at the sound of my own voice, and had become in every respect a fitting subject for the species of torture which awaited me.

Shaking in every limb, I groped my way back to the wall--resolving there to perish rather than risk the terrors of the wells, of which my imagination now pictured many in various positions about the dungeon. In other conditions of mind I might have had courage to end my misery at once by a plunge into one of these abysses; but now I was the veriest of cowards. Neither could I forget what I had read of these pits--that the SUDDEN extinction of life formed no part of their most horrible plan.

Agitation of spirit kept me awake for many long hours; but at length I again slumbered. Upon arousing, I found by my side, as before, a loaf and a pitcher of water. A burning thirst consumed me, and I emptied the vessel at a draught. It must have been drugged, for scarcely had I drunk before I became irresistibly drowsy. A deep sleep fell upon me--a sleep like that of death. How long it lasted of course I know not; but when once again I unclosed my eyes the objects around me were visible. By a wild sulphurous lustre, the origin of which I could not at first determine, I was enabled to see the extent and aspect of the prison.

In its size I had been greatly mistaken. The whole circuit of its walls did not exceed twenty-five yards. For some minutes this fact occasioned me a world of vain trouble; vain indeed--for what could be of less importance, under the terrible circumstances which environed me than the mere dimensions of my dungeon? But my soul took a wild interest in trifles, and I busied myself in endeavours to account for the error I had committed in my measurement. The truth at length flashed upon me. In my first attempt at exploration I had counted fifty-two paces up to the period when I fell; I must then have been within a pace or two of the fragment of serge; in fact I had nearly performed the circuit of the vault. I then slept, and upon awaking, I must have returned upon my steps, thus supposing the circuit nearly double what it actually was. My confusion of mind prevented me from observing that I began my tour with the wall to the left, and ended it with the wall to the right.

I had been deceived too in respect to the shape of the enclosure. In feeling my way I had found many angles, and thus deduced an idea of great irregularity, so potent is the effect of total darkness upon one arousing from lethargy or sleep! The angles were simply those of a few slight depressions or niches at odd intervals. The general shape of the prison was square. What I had taken for masonry seemed now to be iron, or some other metal in huge plates, whose sutures or joints occasioned the depression. The entire surface of this metallic enclosure was rudely daubed in all the hideous and repulsive devices to which the charnel superstition of the monks has given rise. The figures of fiends in aspects of menace, with skeleton forms and other more really fearful images, overspread and disfigured the walls. I observed that the outlines of these monstrosities were sufficiently distinct, but that the colours seemed faded and blurred, as if from the effects of a damp atmosphere. I now noticed the floor, too, which was of stone. In the centre yawned the circular pit from whose jaws I had escaped; but it was the only one in the dungeon.

All this I saw indistinctly and by much effort, for my personal condition had been greatly changed during slumber. I now lay upon my back, and at full length, on a species of low framework of wood. To this I was securely bound by a long strap resembling a surcingle. It passed in many convolutions about my limbs and body, leaving at liberty only my head, and my left arm to such extent that I could by dint of much exertion supply myself with food from an earthen dish which lay by my side on the floor. I saw to my horror that the pitcher had been removed. I say to my horror, for I was consumed with intolerable thirst. This thirst it appeared to be the design of my persecutors to stimulate, for the food in the dish was meat pungently seasoned.

Looking upward, I surveyed the ceiling of my prison. It was some thirty or forty feet overhead, and constructed much as the side walls. In one of its panels a very singular figure riveted my whole attention. It was the painted figure of Time as he is commonly represented, save that in lieu of a scythe he held what at a casual glance I supposed to be the pictured image of a huge pendulum, such as we see on antique clocks.

There was something, however, in the appearance of this machine which caused me to regard it more attentively. While I gazed directly upward at it (for its position was immediately over my own), I fancied that I saw it in motion. In an instant afterward the fancy was confirmed. Its sweep was brief, and of course slow. I watched it for some minutes, somewhat in fear but more in wonder. Wearied at length with observing its dull movement, I turned my eyes upon the other objects in the cell.

A slight noise attracted my notice, and looking to the floor, I saw several enormous rats traversing it. They had issued from the well which lay just within view to my right. Even then while I gazed, they came up in troops hurriedly, with ravenous eyes, allured by the scent of the meat. From this it required much effort and attention to scare them away.

It might have been half-an-hour, perhaps even an hour (for I could take but imperfect note of time) before I again cast my eyes upward. What I then saw confounded and amazed me. The sweep of the pendulum had increased in extent by nearly a yard. As a natural consequence, its velocity was also much greater. But what mainly disturbed me was the idea that it had perceptibly DESCENDED. I now observed, with what horror it is needless to say, that its nether extremity was formed of a crescent of glittering steel, about a foot in length from horn to horn; the horns upward, and the under edge evidently as keen as that of a razor. Like a razor also it seemed massy and heavy, tapering from the edge into a solid and broad structure above. It was appended to a weighty rod of brass, and the whole HISSED as it swung through the air.

I could no longer doubt the doom prepared for me by monkish ingenuity in torture. My cognisance of the pit had become known to the inquisitorial agents-- THE PIT, whose horrors had been destined for so bold a recusant as myself, THE PIT, typical of hell, and regarded by rumour as the Ultima Thule of all their punishments. The plunge into this pit I had avoided by the merest of accidents, and I knew that surprise or entrapment into torment formed an important portion of all the grotesquerie of these dungeon deaths. Having failed to fall, it was no part of the demon plan to hurl me into the abyss, and thus (there being no alternative) a different and a milder destruction awaited me. Milder! I half smiled in my agony as I thought of such application of such a term.

What boots it to tell of the long, long hours of horror more than mortal, during which I counted the rushing oscillations of the steel! Inch by inch--line by line--with a descent only appreciable at intervals that seemed ages--down and still down it came! Days passed--it might have been that many days passed--ere it swept so closely over me as to fan me with its acrid breath. The odour of the sharp steel forced itself into my nostrils. I prayed--I wearied heaven with my prayer for its more speedy descent. I grew frantically mad, and struggled to force myself upward against the sweep of the fearful scimitar. And then I fell suddenly calm and lay smiling at the glittering death as a child at some rare bauble.

There was another interval of utter insensibility; it was brief, for upon again lapsing into life there had been no perceptible descent in the pendulum. But it might have been long--for I knew there were demons who took note of my swoon, and who could have arrested the vibration at pleasure. Upon my recovery, too, I felt very--oh! inexpressibly--sick and weak, as if through long inanition. Even amid the agonies of that period the human nature craved food. With painful effort I outstretched my left arm as far as my bonds permitted, and took possession of the small remnant which had been spared me by the rats. As I put a portion of it within my lips there rushed to my mind a half-formed thought of joy--of hope? Yet what business had I with hope? It was, as I say, a half-formed thought--man has many such, which are never completed. I felt that it was of joy--of hope; but I felt also that it had perished in its formation. In vain I struggled to perfect--to regain it. Long suffering had nearly annihilated all my ordinary powers of mind. I was an imbecile--an idiot.

The vibration of the pendulum was at right angles to my length. I saw that the crescent was designed to cross the region of the heart. It would fray the serge of my robe; it would return and repeat its operations-- again--and again. Notwithstanding its terrifically wide sweep (some thirty feet or more) and the hissing vigour of its descent, sufficient to sunder these very walls of iron, still the fraying of my robe would be all that, for several minutes, it would accomplish; and at this thought I paused. I dared not go farther than this reflection. I dwelt upon it with a pertinacity of attention--as if, in so dwelling, I could arrest HERE the descent of the steel. I forced myself to ponder upon the sound of the crescent as it should pass across the garment--upon the peculiar thrilling sensation which the friction of cloth produces on the nerves. I pondered upon all this frivolity until my teeth were on edge.

Down--steadily down it crept. I took a frenzied pleasure in contrasting its downward with its lateral velocity. To the right--to the left--far and wide--with the shriek of a damned spirit! to my heart with the stealthy pace of the tiger! I alternately laughed and howled, as the one or the other idea grew predominant.

Down--certainly, relentlessly down! It vibrated within three inches of my bosom! I struggled violently- -furiously--to free my left arm. This was free only from the elbow to the hand. I could reach the latter, from the platter beside me to my mouth with great effort, but no farther. Could I have broken the fastenings above the elbow, I would have seized and attempted to arrest the pendulum. I might as well have attempted to arrest an avalanche!

Down--still unceasingly--still inevitably down! I gasped and struggled at each vibration. I shrunk convulsively at its very sweep. My eyes followed its outward or upward whirls with the eagerness of the most unmeaning despair; they closed themselves spasmodically at the descent, although death would have been a relief, O, how unspeakable! Still I quivered in every nerve to think how slight a sinking of the machinery would precipitate that keen glistening axe upon my bosom. It was hope that prompted the nerve to quiver--the frame to shrink. It was HOPE--the hope that triumphs on the rack--that whispers to the death-condemned even in the dungeons of the Inquisition.

I saw that some ten or twelve vibrations would bring the steel in actual contact with my robe, and with this observation there suddenly came over my spirit all the keen, collected calmness of despair. For the first time during many hours, or perhaps days, I THOUGHT. It now occurred to me that the bandage or surcingle which enveloped me was UNIQUE. I was tied by no separate cord. The first stroke of the razor-like crescent athwart any portion of the band would so detach it that it might be unwound from my person by means of my left hand. But how fearful, in that case, the proximity of the steel! The result of the slightest struggle, how deadly! Was it likely, moreover, that the minions of the torturer had not foreseen and provided for this possibility! Was it probable that the bandage crossed my bosom in the track of the pendulum? Dreading to find my faint, and, as it seemed, my last hope frustrated, I so far elevated my head as to obtain a distinct view of my breast. The surcingle enveloped my limbs and body close in all directions save SAVE IN THE PATH OF THE DESTROYING CRESCENT.

Scarcely had I dropped my head back into its original position when there flashed upon my mind what I cannot better describe than as the unformed half of that idea of deliverance to which I have previously alluded, and of which a moiety only floated indeterminately through my brain when I raised food to my burning lips. The whole thought was now present--feeble, scarcely sane, scarcely definite, but still entire. I proceeded at once, with the nervous energy of despair, to attempt its execution.

For many hours the immediate vicinity of the low framework upon which I lay had been literally swarming with rats. They were wild, bold, ravenous, their red eyes glaring upon me as if they waited but for motionlessness on my part to make me their prey. "To what food," I thought, "have they been accustomed in the well?"

They had devoured, in spite of all my efforts to prevent them, all but a small remnant of the contents of the dish. I had fallen into an habitual see-saw or wave of the hand about the platter; and at length the unconscious uniformity of the movement deprived it of effect. In their voracity the vermin frequently fastened their sharp fangs in my fingers. With the particles of the oily and spicy viand which now remained, I thoroughly rubbed the bandage wherever I could reach it; then, raising my hand from the floor, I lay breathlessly still.

At first the ravenous animals were startled and terrified at the change--at the cessation of movement. They shrank alarmedly back; many sought the well. But this was only for a moment. I had not counted in vain upon their voracity. Observing that I remained without motion, one or two of the boldest leaped upon the frame-work and smelt at the surcingle. This seemed the signal for a general rush. Forth from the well they hurried in fresh troops. They clung to the wood, they overran it, and leaped in hundreds upon my person. The measured movement of the pendulum disturbed them not at all. Avoiding its strokes, they busied themselves with the annointed bandage. They pressed, they swarmed upon me in ever accumulating heaps. They writhed upon my throat; their cold lips sought my own; I was half stifled by their thronging pressure; disgust, for which the world has no name, swelled my bosom, and chilled with heavy clamminess my heart. Yet one minute and I felt that the struggle would be over. Plainly I perceived the loosening of the bandage. I knew that in more than one place it must be already severed. With a more than human resolution I lay STILL.

Nor had I erred in my calculations, nor had I endured in vain. I at length felt that I was FREE. The surcingle hung in ribands from my body. But the stroke of the pendulum already pressed upon my bosom. It had divided the serge of the robe. It had cut through the linen beneath. Twice again it swung, and a sharp sense of pain shot through every nerve. But the moment of escape had arrived. At a wave of my hand my deliverers hurried tumultously away. With a steady movement, cautious, sidelong, shrinking, and slow, I slid from the embrace of the bandage and beyond the reach of the scimitar. For the moment, at least I WAS FREE.

Free! and in the grasp of the Inquisition! I had scarcely stepped from my wooden bed of horror upon the stone floor of the prison, when the motion of the hellish machine ceased and I beheld it drawn up by some invisible force through the ceiling. This was a lesson which I took desperately to heart. My every motion was undoubtedly watched. Free! I had but escaped death in one form of agony to be delivered unto worse than death in some other. With that thought I rolled my eyes nervously around on the barriers of iron that hemmed me in. Something unusual--some change which at first I could not appreciate distinctly--it was obvious had taken place in the apartment. For many minutes of a dreamy and trembling abstraction I busied myself in vain, unconnected conjecture. During this period I became aware, for the first time, of the origin of the sulphurous light which illumined the cell. It proceeded from a fissure about half-an-inch in width extending entirely around the prison at the base of the walls which thus appeared, and were completely separated from the floor. I endeavoured, but of course in vain, to look through the aperture. As I arose from the attempt, the mystery of the alteration in the chamber broke at once upon my understanding. I have observed that although the outlines of the figures upon the walls were sufficiently distinct, yet the colours seemed blurred and indefinite. These colours had now assumed, and were momentarily assuming, a startling and most intense brilliancy, that give to the spectral and fiendish portraitures an aspect that might have thrilled even firmer nerves than my own. Demon eyes, of a wild and ghastly vivacity, glared upon me in a thousand directions where none had been visible before, and gleamed with the lurid lustre of a fire that I could not force my imagination to regard as unreal.

UNREAL! Even while I breathed there came to my nostrils the breath of the vapour of heated iron! A suffocating odour pervaded the prison! A deeper glow settled each moment in the eyes that glared at my agonies! A richer tint of crimson diffused itself over the pictured horrors of blood. I panted 'I gasped for breath! There could be no doubt of the design of my tormentors--oh most unrelenting! oh, most demoniac of men! I shrank from the glowing metal to the centre of the cell. Amid the thought of the fiery destruction that impended, the idea of the coolness of the well came over my soul like balm. I rushed to its deadly brink. I threw my straining vision below. The glare from the enkindled roof illumined its inmost recesses. Yet, for a wild moment, did my spirit refuse to comprehend the meaning of what I saw. At length it forced --it wrestled its way into my soul--it burned itself in upon my shuddering reason. O for a voice to speak!—oh, horror!—oh, any horror but this! With a shriek I rushed from the margin and buried my face in my hands--weeping bitterly.

The heat rapidly increased, and once again I looked up, shuddering as if with a fit of the ague. There had been a second change in the cell--and now the change was obviously in the FORM. As before, it was in vain that I at first endeavoured to appreciate or understand what was taking place. But not long was I left in doubt. The inquisitorial vengeance had been hurried by my two-fold escape, and there was to be no more dallying with the King of Terrors. The room had been square. I saw that two of its iron angles were now acute--two consequently, obtuse. The fearful difference quickly increased with a low rumbling or moaning sound. In an instant the apartment had shifted its form into that of a lozenge. But the alteration stopped not here--I neither hoped nor desired it to stop. I could have clasped the red walls to my bosom as a garment of eternal peace. "Death," I said "any death but that of the pit!" Fool! might I not have known that INTO THE PIT it was the object of the burning iron to urge me? Could I resist its glow? or if even that, could I withstand its pressure? And now, flatter and flatter grew the lozenge, with a rapidity that left me no time for contemplation. Its centre, and of course, its greatest width, came just over the yawning gulf. I shrank back-- but the closing walls pressed me resistlessly onward. At length for my seared and writhing body there was no longer an inch of foothold on the firm floor of the prison. I struggled no more, but the agony of my soul found vent in one loud, long, and final scream of despair. I felt that I tottered upon the brink--I averted my eyes--

There was a discordant hum of human voices! There was a loud blast as of many trumpets! There was a harsh grating as of a thousand thunders! The fiery walls rushed back! An outstretched arm caught my own as I fell fainting into the abyss. It was that of General Lasalle. The French army had entered Toledo. The Inquisition was in the hands of its enemies.

1

What is the main purpose of this passage?

_____

2

What is the passage's tone?

_____

3

How would you summarize the passage?

_____

4

How would you describe the narrator?

_____

The following three passages are short stories from Saki. "Saki" was the pen name of H. H. Munro (1870-1916), a British humorist. The literature passage on SAT practice test #3, is from his "Schartz-Metterklume Method." The following three short stories are among Saki's most popular.

"Toys of Peace"

"Harvey," said Eleanor Bope, handing her brother a cutting from a London morning paper of the 19th of March, "just read this about children's toys, please; it exactly carries out some of our ideas about influence and upbringing."

"In the view of the National Peace Council," ran the extract, "there are grave objections to presenting our boys with regiments of fighting men, batteries of guns, and squadrons of 'Dreadnoughts.' Boys, the Council admits, naturally love fighting and all the panoply of war . . . but that is no reason for encouraging, and perhaps giving permanent form to, their primitive instincts. At the Children's Welfare Exhibition, which opens at Olympia in three weeks' time, the Peace Council will make an alternative suggestion to parents in the shape of an exhibition of 'peace toys.' In front of a specially-painted representation of the Peace Palace at The Hague will be grouped, not miniature soldiers but miniature civilians, not guns but ploughs and the tools of industry . . . It is hoped that manufacturers may take a hint from the exhibit, which will bear fruit in the toy shops."

"The idea is certainly an interesting and very well-meaning one," said Harvey; "whether it would succeed well in practice—"

"We must try," interrupted his sister; "you are coming down to us at Easter, and you always bring the boys some toys, so that will be an excellent opportunity for you to inaugurate the new experiment. Go about in the shops and buy any little toys and models that have special bearing on civilian life in its more peaceful aspects. Of course you must explain the toys to the children and interest them in the new idea. I regret to say that the 'Siege of Adrianople' toy, that their Aunt Susan sent them, didn't need any explanation; they knew all the uniforms and flags, and even the names of the respective commanders, and when I heard them one day using what seemed to be the most objectionable language they said it was Bulgarian words of command; of course it may have been, but at any rate I took the toy away from them. Now I shall expect your Easter gifts to give quite a new impulse and direction to the children's minds; Eric is not

eleven yet, and Bertie is only nine-and-a-half, so they are really at a most impressionable age."

"There is primitive instinct to be taken into consideration, you know," said Harvey doubtfully, "and hereditary tendencies as well. One of their great-uncles fought in the most intolerant fashion at Inkerman—he was specially mentioned in dispatches, I believe—and their great-grandfather smashed all his Whig neighbours' hot houses when the great Reform Bill was passed. Still, as you say, they are at an impressionable age. I will do my best."

On Easter Saturday Harvey Bope unpacked a large, promising-looking red cardboard box under the expectant eyes of his nephews. "Your uncle has brought you the newest thing in toys," Eleanor had said impressively, and youthful anticipation had been anxiously divided between Albanian soldiery and a Somali camel-corps. Eric was hotly in favour of the latter contingency. "There would be Arabs on horseback," he whispered; "the Albanians have got jolly uniforms, and they fight all day long, and all night, too, when there's a moon, but the country's rocky, so they've got no cavalry."

A quantity of crinkly paper shavings was the first thing that met the view when the lid was removed; the most exiting toys always began like that. Harvey pushed back the top layer and drew forth a square, rather featureless building.

"It's a fort!" exclaimed Bertie.

"It isn't, it's the palace of the Mpret of Albania," said Eric, immensely proud of his knowledge of the exotic title; "it's got no windows, you see, so that passers-by can't fire in at the Royal Family."

"It's a municipal dust-bin," said Harvey hurriedly; "you see all the refuse and litter of a town is collected there, instead of lying about and injuring the health of the citizens."

In an awful silence he disinterred a little lead figure of a man in black clothes.

"That," he said, "is a distinguished civilian, John Stuart Mill. He was an authority on political economy."

"Why?" asked Bertie.

"Well, he wanted to be; he thought it was a useful thing to be."

Bertie gave an expressive grunt, which conveyed his opinion that there was no accounting for tastes.

Another square building came out, this time with windows and chimneys.

"A model of the Manchester branch of the Young Women's Christian Association," said Harvey.

"Are there any lions?" asked Eric hopefully. He had been reading Roman history and thought that where you found Christians you might reasonably expect to find a few lions.

"There are no lions," said Harvey. "Here is another civilian, Robert Raikes, the founder of Sunday schools, and here is a model of a municipal wash-house. These little round things are loaves baked in a sanitary bakehouse. That lead figure is a sanitary inspector, this one is a district councillor, and this one is an official of the Local Government Board."

"What does he do?" asked Eric wearily.

"He sees to things connected with his Department," said Harvey. "This box with a slit in it is a ballot-box. Votes are put into it at election times."

"What is put into it at other times?" asked Bertie.

"Nothing. And here are some tools of industry, a wheelbarrow and a hoe, and I think these are meant for hop-poles. This is a model beehive, and that is a ventilator, for ventilating sewers. This seems to be another municipal dust-bin—no, it is a model of a school of art and public library. This little lead figure is Mrs. Hemans, a poetess, and this is Rowland Hill, who introduced the system of penny postage. This is Sir John Herschel, the eminent astrologer."

"Are we to play with these civilian figures?" asked Eric.

"Of course," said Harvey, "these are toys; they are meant to be played with."

"But how?"

It was rather a poser. "You might make two of them contest a seat in Parliament," said Harvey, "an have an election—"

"With rotten eggs, and free fights, and ever so many broken heads!" exclaimed Eric.

"And noses all bleeding and everybody drunk as can be," echoed Bertie, who had carefully studied one of Hogarth's pictures.

"Nothing of the kind," said Harvey, "nothing in the least like that. Votes will be put in the ballot-box, and the Mayor will count them—and he will say which has received the most votes, and then the two candidates will thank him for presiding, and each will say that the contest has been conducted throughout in the pleasantest and most straightforward fashion, and they part with expressions of mutual esteem. There's a jolly game for you boys to play. I never had such toys when I was young."

"I don't think we'll play with them just now," said Eric, with an entire absence of the enthusiasm that his uncle had shown; "I think perhaps we ought to do a little of our holiday task. It's history this time; we've got to learn up something about the Bourbon period in France."

"The Bourbon period," said Harvey, with some disapproval in his voice.

"We've got to know something about Louis the Fourteenth," continued Eric; "I've learnt the names of all the principal battles already."

This would never do. "There were, of course, some battles fought during his reign," said Harvey, "but I fancy the accounts of them were much exaggerated; news was very unreliable in those days, and there were practically no war correspondents, so generals and commanders could magnify every little skirmish they engaged in till they reached the proportions of decisive battles. Louis was really famous, now, as a landscape gardener; the way he laid out Versailles was so much admired that it was copied all over Europe."

"Do you know anything about Madame Du Barry?" asked Eric; "didn't she have her head chopped off?"

"She was another great lover of gardening," said Harvey, evasively; "in fact, I believe the well known rose Du Barry was named after her, and now I think you had better play for a little and leave your lessons till later."

Harvey retreated to the library and spent some thirty or forty minutes in wondering whether it would be possible to compile a history, for use in elementary schools, in which there should be no prominent mention of battles, massacres, murderous intrigues, and violent deaths. The York and Lancaster period and the Napoleonic era would, he admitted to himself, present considerable difficulties, and the Thirty Years' War would entail something of a gap if you left it out altogether. Still, it would be something gained if, at a highly impressionable age, children could be got to fix their attention on the invention of calico printing instead of the Spanish Armada or the Battle of Waterloo.

It was time, he thought, to go back to the boys' room, and see how they were getting on with their peace toys. As he stood outside the door he could hear Eric's voice raised in command; Bertie chimed in now and again with a helpful suggestion.

"That is Louis the Fourteenth," Eric was saying, "that one in knee-breeches, that Uncle said invented Sunday schools. It isn't a bit like him, but it'll have to do."

"We'll give him a purple coat from my paintbox by and by," said Bertie.

"Yes, an' red heels. That is Madame de Maintenon, that one he called Mrs. Hemans. She begs Louis not to go on this expedition, but he turns a deaf ear. He takes Marshal Saxe with him, and we must pretend that they have thousands of men with them. The watchword is Qui vive? and the answer is L'état c'est moi—that was one of his favourite remarks, you know. They land at

Manchester in the dead of the night, and a Jacobite conspirator gives them the keys of the fortress."

Peeping in through the doorway Harvey observed that the municipal dust-bin had been pierced with holes to accommodate the muzzles of imaginary cannon, and now represented the principal fortified position in Manchester; John Stuart Mill had been dipped in red ink, and apparently stood for Marshal Saxe.

"Louis orders his troops to surround the Young Women's Christian Association and seize the lot of them. 'Once back at the Louvre and the girls are mine,' he exclaims. We must use Mrs. Hemans again for one of the girls; she says 'Never,' and stabs Marshal Saxe to the heart."

"He bleeds dreadfully," exclaimed Bertie, splashing red ink liberally over the façade of the Association building.

"The soldiers rush in and avenge his death with the utmost savagery. A hundred girls are killed"—here Bertie emptied the remainder of the red ink over the devoted building—"and the surviving five hundred are dragged off to the French ships. 'I have lost a Marshal,' says Louis, 'but I do not go back empty-handed.'"

Harvey stole away from the room, and sought out his sister.

"Eleanor," he said, "the experiment—"
"Yes?"
"Has failed. We have begun too late."

1

What is the main purpose of this passage?

2

What is the passage's tone?

3

How would you summarize the passage?

4

How would you describe Harvey and Eleanor?

5

How would you describe the children?

"The outlook is not encouraging for us smaller businesses," said Mr. Scarrick to the artist and his sister, who had taken rooms over his suburban grocery store. "These big concerns are offering all sorts of attractions to the shopping public which we couldn't afford to imitate, even on a small scale—reading-rooms and play-rooms and gramophones and Heaven knows what. People don't care to buy half a pound of sugar nowadays unless they can listen to Harry Lauder and have the latest Australian cricket scores ticked off before their eyes. With the big Christmas stock we've got in we ought to keep half a dozen assistants hard at work, but as it is my nephew Jimmy and myself can pretty well attend to it ourselves. It's a nice stock of goods, too, if I could only run it off in a few weeks time, but there's no chance of that—not unless the London line was to get snowed up for a fortnight before Christmas. I did have a sort of idea of engaging Miss Luffcombe to give recitations during afternoons; she made a great hit at the Post Office entertainment with her rendering of 'Little Beatrice's Resolve'."

"Anything less likely to make your shop a fashionable shopping centre I can't imagine," said the artist, with a very genuine shudder; "if I were trying to decide between the merits of Carlsbad plums and confected figs as a winter dessert it would infuriate me to have my train of thought entangled with little Beatrice's resolve to be an Angel of Light or a girl scout. No," he continued, "the desire to get something thrown in for nothing is a ruling passion with the feminine shopper, but you can't afford to pander effectively to it. Why not appeal to another instinct; which dominates not only the woman shopper but the male shopper—in fact, the entire human race?"

"What is that instinct, sir?" said the grocer.

* * * * *

Mrs. Greyes and Miss Fritten had missed the 2:18 to Town, and as there was not another train till 3:12 they thought that they might as well make their grocery purchases at Scarrick's. It would not be sensational, they agreed, but it would still be shopping.

For some minutes they had the shop almost to themselves, as far as customers were concerned, but while they were debating the respective virtues and blemishes of two competing brands of anchovy paste they were startled by an order, given across the counter, for six pomegranates and a packet of quail seed. Neither commodity was in general demand in that neighbourhood. Equally unusual was the style and appearance of the customer; about sixteen years old,

with dark olive skin, large dusky eyes, and thick, low-growing, blue-black hair, he might have made his living as an artist's model. As a matter of fact he did. The bowl of beaten brass that he produced for the reception of his purchases was distinctly the most astonishing variation on the string bag or marketing basket of suburban civilisation that his fellow-shoppers had ever seen. He threw a gold piece, apparently of some exotic currency, across the counter, and did not seem disposed to wait for any change that might be forthcoming.

"The wine and figs were not paid for yesterday," he said; "keep what is over of the money for our future purchases."

"A very strange-looking boy?" said Mrs. Greyes interrogatively to the grocer as soon as his customer had left.

"A foreigner, I believe," said Mr. Scarrick, with a shortness that was entirely out of keeping with his usually communicative manner.

"I wish for a pound and a half of the best coffee you have," said an authoritative voice a moment or two later. The speaker was a tall, authoritative-looking man of rather outlandish aspect, remarkable among other things for a full black beard, worn in a style more in vogue in early Assyria than in a London suburb of the present day.

"Has a dark-faced boy been here buying pomegranates?" he asked suddenly, as the coffee was being weighed out to him.

The two ladies almost jumped on hearing the grocer reply with an unblushing negative.

"We have a few pomegranates in stock," he continued, "but there has been no demand for them."

"My servant will fetch the coffee as usual," said the purchaser, producing a coin from a wonderful metal-work purse. As an apparent afterthought he fired out the question: "Have you, perhaps, any quail seed?"

"No," said the grocer, without hesitation, "we don't stock it."

"What will he deny next?" asked Mrs. Greyes under her breath. What made it seem so much worse was the fact that Mr. Scarrick had quite recently presided at a lecture on Savonarola.[1]

Turning up the deep astrachan[2] collar of his long coat, the stranger swept out of the shop, with the air, Miss Fritten afterwards described it, of a Satrap proroguing a Sanhedrim. Whether such a pleasant function ever fell to a Satrap's lot she was not quite certain, but the simile faithfully conveyed her meaning to a large circle of acquaintances.

---

[1] Savonarola (1452-1498) was an Italian friar who advocated for repentance and the rights of the poor.

[2] An exotic Russian fur

"Don't let's bother about the 3:12," said Mrs. Greyes; "let's go and talk this over at Laura Lipping's. It's her day."

When the dark-faced boy arrived at the shop next day with his brass marketing bowl there was quite a fair gathering of customers, most of whom seemed to be spinning out their purchasing operations with the air of people who had very little to do with their time. In a voice that was heard all over the shop, perhaps because everybody was intently listening, he asked for a pound of honey and a packet of quail seed.

"More quail seed!" said Miss Fritten. "Those quails must be voracious, or else it isn't quail seed at all."

"I believe it's opium, and the bearded man is a detective," said Mrs. Greyes brilliantly.

"I don't," said Laura Lipping; "I'm sure it's something to do with the Portuguese Throne."

"More likely to be a Persian intrigue on behalf of the ex-Shah," said Miss Fritten; "the bearded man belongs to the Government Party. The quail-seed is a countersign, of course; Persia is almost next door to Palestine, and quails come into the Old Testament, you know."

"Only as a miracle," said her well-informed younger sister; "I've thought all along it was part of a love intrigue."

The boy who had so much interest and speculation centred on him was on the point of departing with his purchases when he was waylaid by Jimmy, the nephew-apprentice, who, from his post at the cheese and bacon counter, commanded a good view of the street.

"We have some very fine Jaffa oranges," he said hurriedly, pointing to a corner where they were stored, behind a high rampart of biscuit tins. There was evidently more in the remark than met the ear. The boy flew at the oranges with the enthusiasm of a ferret finding a rabbit family at home after a long day of fruitless subterranean research. Almost at the same moment the bearded stranger stalked into the shop, and flung an order for a pound of dates and a tin of the best Smyrna halva across the counter. The most adventurous housewife in the locality had never heard of halva, but Mr. Scarrick was apparently able to produce the best Smyrna variety of it without a moment's hesitation.

"We might be living in the Arabian Nights," said Miss Fritten, excitedly.

"Hush! Listen," beseeched Mrs. Greyes.

"Has the dark-faced boy, of whom I spoke yesterday, been here to-day?" asked the stranger.

"We've had rather more people than usual in the shop to-day," said Mr. Scarrick, "but I can't recall a boy such as you describe."

Mrs. Greyes and Miss Fritten looked round triumphantly at their friends. It was, of course, deplorable that any one should treat the truth as an article temporarily and excusably out of stock, but they felt gratified that the vivid accounts they had given of Mr. Scarrick's traffic in falsehoods should receive confirmation at first hand.

"I shall never again be able to believe what he tells me about the absence of colouring matter in the jam," whispered an aunt of Mrs. Greyes tragically.

The mysterious stranger took his departure; Laura Lipping distinctly saw a snarl of baffled rage reveal itself behind his heavy moustache and upturned astrachan collar. After a cautious interval the seeker after oranges emerged from behind the biscuit tins, having apparently failed to find any individual orange that satisfied his requirements. He, too, took his departure, and the shop was slowly emptied of its parcel and gossip laden customers. It was Emily Yorling's "day", and most of the shoppers made their way to her drawing-room. To go direct from a shopping expedition to a tea party was what was known locally as "living in a whirl".

Two extra assistants had been engaged for the following afternoon, and their services were in brisk demand; the shop was crowded. People bought and bought, and never seemed to get to the end of their lists. Mr. Scarrick had never had so little difficulty in persuading customers to embark on new experiences in grocery wares. Even those women whose purchases were of modest proportions dawdled over them as though they had brutal, drunken husbands to go home to. The afternoon had dragged uneventfully on, and there was a distinct buzz of unpent excitement when a dark-eyed boy carrying a brass bowl entered the shop. The excitement seemed to have communicated itself to Mr. Scarrick; abruptly deserting a lady who was making insincere inquiries about the home life of the Bombay duck, he intercepted the newcomer on his way to the accustomed counter and informed him, amid a deathlike hush, that he had run out of quail seed.

The boy looked nervously round the shop, and turned hesitatingly to go. He was again intercepted, this time by the nephew, who darted out from behind his counter and said something about a better line of oranges. The boy's hesitation vanished; he almost scuttled into the obscurity of the orange corner. There was an expectant turn of public attention towards the door, and the tall, bearded stranger made a really effective entrance. The aunt of Mrs. Greyes declared afterwards that she found herself sub-consciously repeating "The Assyrian came down like a wolf on the fold" under her breath, and she was generally believed.

The newcomer, too, was stopped before he reached the counter, but not by Mr. Scarrick or his assistant. A heavily veiled lady, whom no one had hitherto noticed, rose languidly from a seat and greeted him in a clear, penetrating voice.

"Your Excellency does his shopping himself?" she said.

"I order the things myself," he explained; "I find it difficult to make my servants understand."

In a lower, but still perfectly audible, voice the veiled lady gave him a piece of casual information.

"They have some excellent Jaffa oranges here." Then with a tinkling laugh she passed out of the shop.

The man glared all round the shop, and then, fixing his eyes instinctively on the barrier of biscuit tins, demanded loudly of the grocer: "You have, perhaps, some good Jaffa oranges?"

Every one expected an instant denial on the part of Mr. Scarrick of any such possession. Before he could answer, however, the boy had broken forth from his sanctuary. Holding his empty brass bowl before him he passed out into the street. His face was variously described afterwards as masked with studied indifference, overspread with ghastly pallor, and blazing with defiance. Some said that his teeth chattered, others that he went out whistling the Persian National Hymn. There was no mistaking, however, the effect produced by the encounter on the man who had seemed to force it. If a rabid dog or a rattlesnake had suddenly thrust its companionship on him he could scarcely have displayed a greater access of terror. His air of authority and assertiveness had gone, his masterful stride had given way to a furtive pacing to and fro, as of an animal seeking an outlet for escape. In a dazed perfunctory manner, always with his eyes turning to watch the shop entrance, he gave a few random orders, which the grocer made a show of entering in his book. Now and then he walked out into the street, looked anxiously in all directions, and hurried back to keep up his pretence of shopping. From one of these sorties he did not return; he had dashed away into the dusk, and neither he nor the dark-faced boy nor the veiled lady were seen again by the expectant crowds that continued to throng the Scarrick establishment for days to come.

* * * * *

"I can never thank you and your sister sufficiently," said the grocer.

"We enjoyed the fun of it," said the artist modestly, "and as for the model, it was a welcome variation on posing for hours for 'The Lost Hylas'."

"At any rate," said the grocer, "I insist on paying for the hire of the black beard."

1

What is the main purpose of this passage?

_____

2

What is the passage's tone?

_____

3

How would you summarize the passage?

_____

4

How would you describe the grocer?

_____

5

How would you describe the crowds?

_____

"Tobermory"

It was a chill, rain-washed afternoon of a late August day, that indefinite season when partridges are still in security or cold storage, and there is nothing to hunt—unless one is bounded on the north by the Bristol Channel, in which case one may lawfully gallop after fat red stags. Lady Blemley's house-party was not bounded on the north by the Bristol Channel, hence there was a full gathering of her guests round the tea-table on this particular afternoon. And, in spite of the blankness of the season and the triteness of the occasion, there was no trace in the company of that fatigued restlessness which means a dread of the pianola and a subdued hankering for auction bridge. The undisguised open-mouthed attention of the entire party was fixed on the homely negative personality of Mr. Cornelius Appin. Of all her guests, he was the one who had come to Lady Blemley with the vaguest reputation. Some one had said he was "clever," and he had got his invitation in the moderate expectation, on the part of his hostess, that some portion at least of his cleverness would be contributed to the general entertainment. Until tea-time that day she had been unable to discover in what direction, if any, his cleverness lay. He was neither a wit nor a croquet champion, a hypnotic force nor a begetter of amateur theatricals. Neither did his exterior suggest the sort of man in whom women are willing to pardon a generous measure of mental deficiency. He had subsided into mere Mr. Appin, and the Cornelius seemed a piece of transparent baptismal bluff. And now he was claiming to have launched on the world a discovery beside which the invention of gunpowder, of the printing-press, and of steam locomotion were inconsiderable trifles. Science had made bewildering strides in many directions during recent decades, but this thing seemed to belong to the domain of miracle rather than to scientific achievement.

"And do you really ask us to believe," Sir Wilfrid was saying, "that you have discovered a means for instructing animals in the art of human speech, and that dear old Tobermory has proved your first successful pupil?"

"It is a problem at which I have worked for the last seventeen years," said Mr. Appin, "but only during the last eight or nine months have I been rewarded with glimmerings of success. Of course I have experimented with thousands of animals, but latterly only with cats, those wonderful creatures which have assimilated themselves so marvellously with our civilization while retaining all their highly developed feral instincts. Here and there among cats one comes across an outstanding superior intellect, just as one does among the ruck of human beings, and when I made the acquaintance of Tobermory a week ago I saw at once that I was in contact with a "Beyond-cat" of extraordinary intelligence. I had gone far along the road to success in recent experiments; with Tobermory, as you call him, I have reached the goal."

Mr. Appin concluded his remarkable statement in a voice which he strove to divest of a triumphant inflection. No one said "Rats," though Clovis's lips moved in a monosyllabic contortion, which probably invoked those rodents of disbelief.

"And do you mean to say," asked Miss Resker, after a slight pause, "that you have taught Tobermory to say and understand easy sentences of one syllable?"

"My dear Miss Resker," said the wonder-worker patiently, "one teaches little children and savages and backward adults in that piecemeal fashion; when one has once solved the problem of making a beginning with an animal of highly developed intelligence one has no need for those halting methods. Tobermory can speak our language with perfect correctness."

This time Clovis very distinctly said, "Beyond-rats!" Sir Wilfred was more polite but equally sceptical.

"Hadn't we better have the cat in and judge for ourselves?" suggested Lady Blemley.

Sir Wilfred went in search of the animal, and the company settled themselves down to the languid expectation of witnessing some more or less adroit drawing-room ventriloquism.

In a minute Sir Wilfred was back in the room, his face white beneath its tan and his eyes dilated with excitement.

"By Gad, it's true!"

His agitation was unmistakably genuine, and his hearers started forward in a thrill of wakened interest.

Collapsing into an armchair he continued breathlessly:

"I found him dozing in the smoking-room, and called out to him to come for his tea. He blinked at me in his usual way, and I said, 'Come on, Toby; don't keep us waiting' and, by Gad! he drawled out in a most horribly natural voice that he'd come when he dashed well pleased! I nearly jumped out of my skin!"

Appin had preached to absolutely incredulous hearers; Sir Wilfred's statement carried instant conviction. A Babel-like chorus of startled exclamation arose, amid which the scientist sat mutely enjoying the first fruit of his stupendous discovery.

In the midst of the clamour Tobermory entered the room and made his way with velvet tread and studied unconcern across the group seated round the tea-table.

A sudden hush of awkwardness and constraint fell on the company. Somehow there seemed an element of embarrassment in addressing on equal terms a domestic cat of acknowledged dental ability.

"Will you have some milk, Tobermory?" asked Lady Blemley in a rather strained voice.

"I don't mind if I do," was the response, couched in a tone of even indifference. A shiver of suppressed excitement went through the listeners, and Lady Blemley might be excused for pouring out the saucerful of milk rather unsteadily.

"I'm afraid I've spilt a good deal of it," she said apologetically.

"After all, it's not my Axminster," was Tobermory's rejoinder.

Another silence fell on the group, and then Miss Resker, in her best district-visitor manner, asked if the human language had been difficult to learn. Tobermory looked squarely at her for a moment and then fixed his gaze serenely on the middle distance. It was obvious that boring questions lay outside his scheme of life.

"What do you think of human intelligence?" asked Mavis Pellington lamely.

"Of whose intelligence in particular?" asked Tobermory coldly.

"Oh, well, mine for instance," said Mavis with a feeble laugh.

"You put me in an embarrassing position," said Tobermory, whose tone and attitude certainly did not suggest a shred of embarrassment. "When your inclusion in this house-party was suggested Sir Wilfrid protested that you were the most brainless woman of his acquaintance, and that there was a wide distinction between hospitality and the care of the feeble-minded. Lady Blemley replied that your lack of brain-power was the precise quality which had earned you your invitation, as you were the only person she could think of who might be idiotic enough to buy their old car. You know, the one they call 'The Envy of Sisyphus,' because it goes quite nicely up-hill if you push it."

Lady Blemley's protestations would have had greater effect if she had not casually suggested to Mavis only that morning that the car in question would be just the thing for her down at her Devonshire home.

Major Barfield plunged in heavily to effect a diversion.

"How about your carryings-on with the tortoise-shell puss up at the stables, eh?"

The moment he had said it every one realized the blunder.

"One does not usually discuss these matters in public," said Tobermory frigidly. "From a slight observation of your ways since you've been in this house I should imagine you'd find it inconvenient if I were to shift the conversation to your own little affairs."

The panic which ensued was not confined to the Major.

"Would you like to go and see if cook has got your dinner ready?" suggested Lady Blemley hurriedly, affecting to ignore the fact that it wanted at least two hours to Tobermory's dinner-time.

"Thanks," said Tobermory, "not quite so soon after my tea. I don't want to die of indigestion."

"Cats have nine lives, you know," said Sir Wilfred heartily.

"Possibly," answered Tobermory; "but only one liver."

"Adelaide!" said Mrs. Cornett, "do you mean to encourage that cat to go out and gossip about us in the servants' hall?"

The panic had indeed become general. A narrow ornamental balustrade ran in front of most of the bedroom windows at the Towers, and it was recalled with dismay that this had formed a favourite promenade for Tobermory at all hours, whence he could watch the pigeons—and heaven knew what else besides. If he intended to become reminiscent in his present outspoken strain the effect would be something more than disconcerting. Mrs. Cornett, who spent much time at her toilet table, and whose complexion was reputed to be of a nomadic though punctual disposition, looked as ill at ease as the Major. Miss Scrawen, who wrote fiercely sensuous poetry and led a blameless life, merely displayed irritation; if you are methodical and virtuous in private you don't necessarily want everyone to know it. Bertie van Tahn, who was so depraved at 17 that he had long ago given up trying to be any worse, turned a dull shade of gardenia white, but he did not commit the error of dashing out of the room like Odo Finsberry, a young gentleman who was understood to be reading for the Church and who was possibly disturbed at the thought of scandals he might hear concerning other people. Clovis had the presence of mind to maintain a composed exterior; privately he was calculating how long it would take to procure a box of fancy mice through the agency of the Exchange and Mart as a species of hush-money.

Even in a delicate situation like the present, Agnes Resker could not endure to remain long in the background.

"Why did I ever come down here?" she asked dramatically.

Tobermory immediately accepted the opening.

"Judging by what you said to Mrs. Cornett on the croquet-lawn yesterday, you were out of food. You described the Blemleys as the dullest people to stay with that you knew, but said they were clever enough to employ a first-rate cook; otherwise they'd find it difficult to get any one to come down a second time."

"There's not a word of truth in it! I appeal to Mrs. Cornett—" exclaimed the discomfited Agnes.

"Mrs. Cornett repeated your remark afterwards to Bertie van Tahn," continued Tobermory, "and said, 'That woman is a regular Hunger Marcher; she'd go anywhere for four square meals a day,' and Bertie van Tahn said—"

At this point the chronicle mercifully ceased. Tobermory had caught a glimpse of the big yellow tom from the Rectory working his way through the shrubbery towards the stable wing. In a flash he had vanished through the open French window.

With the disappearance of his too brilliant pupil Cornelius Appin found himself beset by a hurricane of bitter upbraiding, anxious inquiry, and frightened entreaty. The responsibility for the situation lay with him, and he must prevent matters from becoming worse. Could Tobermory impart his dangerous gift to other cats? was the first question he had to answer. It was possible, he replied, that he might have initiated his intimate friend the stable puss into his new accomplishment, but it was unlikely that his teaching could have taken a wider range as yet.

"Then," said Mrs. Cornett, "Tobermory may be a valuable cat and a great pet; but I'm sure you'll agree, Adelaide, that both he and the stable cat must be done away with without delay."

"You don't suppose I've enjoyed the last quarter of an hour, do you?" said Lady Blemley bitterly. "My husband and I are very fond of Tobermory—at least, we were before this horrible accomplishment was infused into him; but now, of course, the only thing is to have him destroyed as soon as possible."

"We can put some strychnine in the scraps he always gets at dinner-time," said Sir Wilfred, "and I will go and drown the stable cat myself. The coachman will be very sore at losing his pet, but I'll say a very catching form of mange has broken out in both cats and we're afraid of it spreading to the kennels."

"But my great discovery!" expostulated Mr. Appin; "after all my years of research and experiment—"

"You can go and experiment on the short-horns at the farm, who are under proper control," said Mrs. Cornett, "or the elephants at the Zoological Gardens. They're said to be highly intelligent, and they have this recommendation, that they don't come creeping about our bedrooms and under chairs, and so forth."

An archangel ecstatically proclaiming the Millennium, and then finding that it clashed unpardonably with Henley and would have to be indefinitely postponed, could hardly have felt more crestfallen than Cornelius Appin at the reception of his wonderful achievement. Public opinion, however, was against him—in fact, had the general voice been consulted on the subject it is probable that a strong minority vote would have been in favour of including him in the strychnine diet.

Defective train arrangements and a nervous desire to see matters brought to a finish prevented an immediate dispersal of the party, but dinner that evening was not a social success. Sir Wilfred had had rather a trying time with the stable cat and subsequently with the coachman. Agnes Resker ostentatiously limited her repast to a morsel of dry toast, which she bit as though it were a personal enemy; while Mavis Pellington maintained a vindictive silence throughout the meal. Lady Blemley kept up a flow of what she hoped was conversation, but her attention was fixed on the doorway. A plateful of carefully dosed fish scraps was in readiness on the sideboard, but the sweets and savoury and dessert went their way, and no Tobermory appeared in the dining-room or kitchen.

The sepulchral dinner was cheerful compared with the subsequent vigil in the smoking-room. Eating and drinking had at least supplied a distraction and cloak to the prevailing embarrassment. Bridge was out of the question in the general tension of nerves and tempers, and after Odo Finsberry had given a lugubrious rendering of 'Melisande in the Wood' to a frigid audience, music was tacitly avoided. At eleven the servants went to bed, announcing that the small window in the pantry had been left open as usual for Tobermory's private use. The guests read steadily through the current batch of magazines, and fell back gradually on the "Badminton Library" and bound volumes of Punch. Lady Blemley made periodic visits to the pantry, returning each time with an expression of listless depression which forestalled questioning.

At two o'clock Clovis broke the dominating silence.

"He won't turn up tonight. He's probably in the local newspaper office at the present moment, dictating the first installment of his reminiscences. Lady What's-her-name's book won't be in it. It will be the event of the day."

Having made this contribution to the general cheerfulness, Clovis went to bed. At long intervals the various members of the house-party followed his example.

The servants taking round the early tea made a uniform announcement in reply to a uniform question. Tobermory had not returned.

Breakfast was, if anything, a more unpleasant function than dinner had been, but before its conclusion the situation was relieved. Tobermory's corpse was brought in from the shrubbery, where a gardener had just discovered it. From the bites on his throat and the yellow fur which coated his claws it was evident that he had fallen in unequal combat with the big Tom from the Rectory.

By midday most of the guests had quitted the Towers, and after lunch Lady Blemley had sufficiently recovered her spirits to write an extremely nasty letter to the Rectory about the loss of her valuable pet.

Tobermory had been Appin's one successful pupil, and he was destined to have no successor. A few weeks later an elephant in the Dresden Zoological Garden, which had shown no previous signs of irritability, broke loose and killed an Englishman who had apparently been teasing it. The victim's name was variously reported in the papers as Oppin and Eppelin, but his front name was faithfully rendered Cornelius.

"If he was trying German irregular verbs on the poor beast," said Clovis, "he deserved all he got.

1

What is the main purpose of this passage?

2

What is the passage's tone?

3

How would you summarize the passage?

4

How would you describe Tobermory?

5

How would you describe Cornelius Appin?

THE YELLOW WALLPAPER – CHARLOTTE PERKINS GILMAN

This passage is adapted from Charlotte Perkins Gilman, *The Yellow Wallpaper*, 1892. Perkins had been prescribed "rest cure" and "to live as domestic a life as possible" as a treatment for hysteria.

It is very seldom that mere ordinary people like John and myself secure ancestral halls for the summer.

A colonial mansion, a hereditary estate, I would say a haunted house, and reach the height of romantic felicity,—but that would be asking too much of fate!

Still I will proudly declare that there is something queer about it.

Else, why should it be let so cheaply? And why have stood so long untenanted?

John laughs at me, of course, but one expects that in marriage.

John is practical in the extreme. He has no patience with faith, an intense horror of superstition, and he scoffs openly at any talk of things not to be felt and seen and put down in figures.

John is a physician, and perhaps—(I would not say it to a living soul, of course, but this is dead paper and a great relief to my mind)—perhaps that is one reason I do not get well faster.

You see, he does not believe I am sick!

And what can one do?

If a physician of high standing, and one's own husband, assures friends and relatives that there is really nothing the matter with one but temporary nervous depression,—a slight hysterical tendency,—what is one to do?

My brother is also a physician, and also of high standing, and he says the same thing.

So I take phosphates or phosphites,—whichever it is,—and tonics, and journeys, and air, and exercise, and am absolutely forbidden to "work" until I am well again.

Personally I disagree with their ideas.

Personally I believe that congenial work, with excitement and change, would do me good.

But what is one to do?

I did write for a while in spite of them; but it does exhaust me a good deal—having to be so sly about it, or else meet with heavy opposition.

I sometimes fancy that in my condition if I had less opposition and more society and stimulus—but John says the very worst thing I can do is to think about my condition, and I confess it always makes me feel bad.

So I will let it alone and talk about the house.

The most beautiful place! It is quite alone, standing well back from the road, quite three miles from the village. It makes me think of English places that you read about, for there are hedges and walls and gates that lock, and lots of separate little houses for the gardeners and people.

There is a delicious garden! I never saw such a garden—large and shady, full of box-bordered paths, and lined with long grape-covered arbors with seats under them.

There were greenhouses, too, but they are all broken now.

There was some legal trouble, I believe, something about the heirs and co-heirs; anyhow, the place has been empty for years.

That spoils my ghostliness, I am afraid; but I don't care—there is something strange about the house—I can feel it.

I even said so to John one moonlight evening, but he said what I felt was a draught, and shut the window.

I get unreasonably angry with John sometimes. I'm sure I never used to be so sensitive. I think it is due to this nervous condition.

But John says if I feel so I shall neglect proper self-control; so I take pains to control myself,—before him, at least—and that makes me very tired.

I don't like our room a bit. I wanted one downstairs that opened on the piazza and had roses all over the window, and such pretty, old-fashioned chintz hangings! but John would not hear of it.

He said there was only one window and not room for two beds, and no near room for him if he took another.

He is very careful and loving, and hardly lets me stir without special direction.

I have a schedule prescription for each hour in the day; he takes all care from me, and so I feel basely ungrateful not to value it more.

He said we came here solely on my account, that I was to have perfect rest and all the air I could get. "Your exercise depends on your strength, my dear," said he, "and your food somewhat on your appetite; but air you can absorb all the time." So we took the nursery, at the top of the house.

It is a big, airy room, the whole floor nearly, with windows that look all ways, and air and sunshine galore. It was nursery first and then playground and gymnasium, I should judge; for the windows are barred for little children, and there are rings and things in the walls.

The paint and paper look as if a boys' school had used it. It is stripped off—the paper—in great patches all around the head of my bed, about as far as I can reach, and in a great place on the other side of the room low down. I never saw a worse paper in my life.

One of those sprawling flamboyant patterns committing every artistic sin.

It is dull enough to confuse the eye in following, pronounced enough to constantly irritate, and provoke study, and when you follow the lame, uncertain curves for a little distance they suddenly commit suicide—plunge off at outrageous angles, destroy themselves in unheard-of contradictions.

The color is repellant, almost revolting; a smouldering, unclean yellow, strangely faded by the slow-turning sunlight.

It is a dull yet lurid orange in some places, a sickly sulphur tint in others.

No wonder the children hated it! I should hate it myself if I had to live in this room long.

There comes John, and I must put this away,—he hates to have me write a word.

We have been here two weeks, and I haven't felt like writing before, since that first day.

I am sitting by the window now, up in this atrocious nursery, and there is nothing to hinder my writing as much as I please, save lack of strength.

John is away all day, and even some nights when his cases are serious.

I am glad my case is not serious!

But these nervous troubles are dreadfully depressing.

John does not know how much I really suffer. He knows there is no reason to suffer, and that satisfies him.

Of course it is only nervousness. It does weigh on me so not to do my duty in any way!

I meant to be such a help to John, such a real rest and comfort, and here I am a comparative burden already!

Nobody would believe what an effort it is to do what little I am able—to dress and entertain, and order things.

It is fortunate Mary is so good with the baby. Such a dear baby!

And yet I cannot be with him, it makes me so nervous.

I suppose John never was nervous in his life. He laughs at me so about this wall paper!

At first he meant to repaper the room, but afterwards he said that I was letting it get the better of me, and that nothing was worse for a nervous patient than to give way to such fancies.

He said that after the wall paper was changed it would be the heavy bedstead, and then the barred windows, and then that gate at the head of the stairs, and so on.

"You know the place is doing you good," he said, "and really, dear, I don't care to renovate the house just for a three months' rental."

"Then do let us go downstairs," I said, "there are such pretty rooms there."

Then he took me in his arms and called me a blessed little goose, and said he would go down cellar if I wished, and have it whitewashed into the bargain.

But he is right enough about the beds and windows and things.

It is as airy and comfortable a room as any one need wish, and, of course, I would not be so silly as to make him uncomfortable just for a whim.

I'm really getting quite fond of the big room, all but that horrid paper.

Out of one window I can see the garden, those mysterious deep-shaded arbors, the riotous old-fashioned flowers, and bushes and gnarly trees.

Out of another I get a lovely view of the bay and a little private wharf belonging to the estate. There is a beautiful shaded lane that runs down there from the house. I always fancy I see people walking in these numerous paths and arbors, but John has cautioned me not to give way to fancy in the least. He says that with my imaginative power and habit of story-making a nervous weakness like mine is sure to lead to all manner of excited fancies, and that I ought to use my will and good sense to check the tendency. So I try.

I think sometimes that if I were only well enough to write a little it would relieve the press of ideas and rest me.

But I find I get pretty tired when I try.

It is so discouraging not to have any advice and companionship about my work. When I get really well John says we will ask Cousin Henry and Julia down for a long visit; but he says he would as soon put fire-works in my pillow-case as to let me have those stimulating people about now.

I wish I could get well faster.

But I must not think about that. This paper looks to me as if it knew what a vicious influence it had!

There is a recurrent spot where the pattern lolls like a broken neck and two bulbous eyes stare at you upside-down.

I got positively angry with the impertinence of it and the everlastingness. Up and down and sideways they crawl, and those absurd, unblinking eyes are everywhere. There is one place where two breadths didn't match, and the eyes go all up and down the line, one a little higher than the other.

I never saw so much expression in an inanimate thing before, and we all know how much expression they have! I used to lie awake as a child and get more entertainment and terror out of blank walls and plain furniture than most children could find in a toy-store.

I remember what a kindly wink the knobs of our big old bureau used to have, and there was one chair that always seemed like a strong friend.

I used to feel that if any of the other things looked too fierce I could always hop into that chair and be safe.

The furniture in this room is no worse than inharmonious, however, for we had to bring it all from downstairs. I suppose when this was used as a playroom they had to take the nursery things out, and no wonder! I never saw such ravages as the children have made here.

The wall paper, as I said before, is torn off in spots, and it sticketh closer than a brother—they must have had perseverance as well as hatred.

Then the floor is scratched and gouged and splintered, the plaster itself is dug out here and there, and this great heavy bed, which is all we found in the room, looks as if it had been through the wars.

But I don't mind it a bit—only the paper.

There comes John's sister. Such a dear girl as she is, and so careful of me! I must not let her find me writing.

She is a perfect, an enthusiastic housekeeper, and hopes for no better profession. I verily believe she thinks it is the writing which made me sick!

But I can write when she is out, and see her a long way off from these windows.

There is one that commands the road, a lovely, shaded, winding road, and one that just looks off over the country. A lovely country, too, full of great elms and velvet meadows.

This wall paper has a kind of sub-pattern in a different shade, a particularly irritating one, for you can only see it in certain lights, and not clearly then.

But in the places where it isn't faded, and where the sun is just so, I can see a strange, provoking, formless sort of figure, that seems to sulk about behind that silly and conspicuous front design.

There's sister on the stairs!

Well, the Fourth of July is over! The people are all gone and I am tired out. John thought it might do me good to see a little company, so we just had mother and Nellie and the children down for a week.

Of course I didn't do a thing. Jennie sees to everything now.

But it tired me all the same.

John says if I don't pick up faster he shall send me to Weir Mitchell in the fall.

But I don't want to go there at all. I had a friend who was in his hands once, and she says he is just like John and my brother, only more so!

Besides, it is such an undertaking to go so far.

I don't feel as if it was worth while to turn my hand over for anything, and I'm getting dreadfully fretful and querulous.

I cry at nothing, and cry most of the time.

Of course I don't when John is here, or anybody else, but when I am alone.

And I am alone a good deal just now. John is kept in town very often by serious cases, and Jennie is good and lets me alone when I want her to.

So I walk a little in the garden or down that lovely lane, sit on the porch under the roses, and lie down up here a good deal.

I'm getting really fond of the room in spite of the wall paper. Perhaps because of the wall paper.

It dwells in my mind so!

I lie here on this great immovable bed—it is nailed down, I believe—and follow that pattern about by the hour. It is as good as gymnastics, I assure you. I start, we'll say, at the bottom, down in the corner over there where it has not been touched, and I determine for the thousandth time that I will follow that pointless pattern to some sort of a conclusion.

I know a little of the principles of design, and I know this thing was not arranged on any laws of radiation, or alternation, or repetition, or symmetry, or anything else that I ever heard of.

It is repeated, of course, by the breadths, but not otherwise.

Looked at in one way, each breadth stands alone, the bloated curves and flourishes—a kind of "debased Romanesque" with delirium tremens—go waddling up and down in isolated columns of fatuity.

But, on the other hand, they connect diagonally, and the sprawling outlines run off in great slanting waves of optic horror, like a lot of wallowing seaweeds in full chase.

The whole thing goes horizontally, too, at least it seems so, and I exhaust myself in trying to distinguish the order of its going in that direction.

They have used a horizontal breadth for a frieze, and that adds wonderfully to the confusion.

There is one end of the room where it is almost intact, and there, when the cross-lights fade and the low sun shines directly upon it, I can almost fancy radiation, after all,—the interminable grotesques seem to form around a common centre and rush off in headlong plunges of equal distraction.

It makes me tired to follow it. I will take a nap, I guess.

I don't know why I should write this.

I don't want to.

I don't feel able.

And I know John would think it absurd. But I must say what I feel and think in some way—it is such a relief!

But the effort is getting to be greater than the relief.

Half the time now I am awfully lazy, and lie down ever so much.

John says I mustn't lose my strength, and has me take cod-liver oil and lots of tonics and things, to say nothing of ale and wine and rare meat.

Dear John! He loves me very dearly, and hates to have me sick. I tried to have a real earnest reasonable talk with him the other day, and tell him how I wished he would let me go and make a visit to Cousin Henry and Julia.

But he said I wasn't able to go, nor able to stand it after I got there; and I did not make out a very good case for myself, for I was crying before I had finished.

It is getting to be a great effort for me to think straight. Just this nervous weakness, I suppose.

And dear John gathered me up in his arms, and just carried me upstairs and laid me on the bed, and sat by me and read to me till he tired my head.

He said I was his darling and his comfort and all he had, and that I must take care of myself for his sake, and keep well.

He says no one but myself can help me out of it, that I must use my will and self-control and not let my silly fancies run away with me.

There's one comfort, the baby is well and happy, and does not have to occupy this nursery with the horrid wall paper.

If we had not used it that blessed child would have! What a fortunate escape! Why, I wouldn't have a child of mine, an impressionable little thing, live in such a room for worlds.

I never thought of it before, but it is lucky that John kept me here, after all. I can stand it so much easier than a baby, you see.

Of course I never mention it to them any more,— I am too wise,—but I keep watch of it all the same.

There are things in that paper that nobody knows but me, or ever will.

Behind that outside pattern the dim shapes get clearer every day.

It is always the same shape, only very numerous.

And it is like a woman stooping down and creeping about behind that pattern. I don't like it a bit. I wonder—I begin to think—I wish John would take me away from here!

It is so hard to talk with John about my case, because he is so wise, and because he loves me so.

But I tried it last night.

It was moonlight. The moon shines in all around, just as the sun does.

I hate to see it sometimes, it creeps so slowly, and always comes in by one window or another.

John was asleep and I hated to waken him, so I kept still and watched the moonlight on that undulating wall paper till I felt creepy.

The faint figure behind seemed to shake the pattern, just as if she wanted to get out.

I got up softly and went to feel and see if the paper did move, and when I came back John was awake.

"What is it, little girl?" he said. "Don't go walking about like that—you'll get cold."

I thought it was a good time to talk, so I told him that I really was not gaining here, and that I wished he would take me away.

"Why, darling!" said he, "our lease will be up in three weeks, and I can't see how to leave before.

"The repairs are not done at home, and I cannot possibly leave town just now. Of course if you were in any danger I could and would, but you really are better, dear, whether you can see it or not. I am a doctor, dear, and I know. You are gaining flesh and color, your appetite is better. I feel really much easier about you."

"I don't weigh a bit more," said I, "nor as much; and my appetite may be better in the evening, when you are here, but it is worse in the morning, when you are away."

"Bless her little heart!" said he with a big hug; "she shall be as sick as she pleases. But now let's improve the shining hours by going to sleep, and talk about it in the morning."

"And you won't go away?" I asked gloomily.

"Why, how can I, dear? It is only three weeks more and then we will take a nice little trip of a few days while Jennie is getting the house ready. Really, dear, you are better!"

"Better in body, perhaps"—I began, and stopped short, for he sat up straight and looked at me with such a stern, reproachful look that I could not say another word.

"My darling," said he, "I beg of you, for my sake and for our child's sake, as well as for your own, that you will never for one instant let that idea enter your mind! There is nothing so dangerous, so fascinating, to a temperament like yours. It is a false and foolish fancy. Can you not trust me as a physician when I tell you so?"

So of course I said no more on that score, and we went to sleep before long. He thought I was asleep first, but I wasn't,—I lay there for hours trying to decide whether that front pattern and the back pattern really did move together or separately.

On a pattern like this, by daylight, there is a lack of sequence, a defiance of law, that is a constant irritant to a normal mind.

The color is hideous enough, and unreliable enough, and infuriating enough, but the pattern is torturing.

You think you have mastered it, but just as you get well under way in following, it turns a back somersault, and there you are. It slaps you in the face, knocks you down, and tramples upon you. It is like a bad dream.

The outside pattern is a florid arabesque, reminding one of a fungus. If you can imagine a toadstool in joints, an interminable string of toadstools, budding and sprouting in endless convolutions,—why, that is something like it.

That is, sometimes!

There is one marked peculiarity about this paper, a thing nobody seems to notice but myself, and that is that it changes as the light changes.

When the sun shoots in through the east window— I always watch for that first long, straight ray—it changes so quickly that I never can quite believe it.

That is why I watch it always.

By moonlight—the moon shines in all night when there is a moon—I wouldn't know it was the same paper.

At night in any kind of light, in twilight, candlelight, lamplight, and worst of all by moonlight, it becomes bars! The outside pattern, I mean, and the woman behind it is as plain as can be.

I didn't realize for a long time what the thing was that showed behind,—that dim sub-pattern,—but now I am quite sure it is a woman.

By daylight she is subdued, quiet. I fancy it is the pattern that keeps her so still. It is so puzzling. It keeps me quiet by the hour.

I lie down ever so much now. John says it is good for me, and to sleep all I can.

Indeed, he started the habit by making me lie down for an hour after each meal.

It is a very bad habit, I am convinced, for, you see, I don't sleep.

And that cultivates deceit, for I don't tell them I'm awake,—oh, no!

The fact is, I am getting a little afraid of John.

He seems very queer sometimes, and even Jennie has an inexplicable look.

It strikes me occasionally, just as a scientific hypothesis, that perhaps it is the paper!

I have watched John when he did not know I was looking, and come into the room suddenly on the most innocent excuses, and I've caught him several times looking at the paper! And Jennie too. I caught Jennie with her hand on it once.

She didn't know I was in the room, and when I asked her in a quiet, a very quiet voice, with the most restrained manner possible, what she was doing with the paper she turned around as if she had been caught stealing, and looked quite angry—asked me why I should frighten her so!

Then she said that the paper stained everything it touched, that she had found yellow smooches on all my clothes and John's, and she wished we would be more careful!

Did not that sound innocent? But I know she was studying that pattern, and I am determined that nobody shall find it out but myself!

Life is very much more exciting now than it used to be. You see I have something more to expect, to look forward to, to watch. I really do eat better, and am more quiet than I was.

John is so pleased to see me improve! He laughed a little the other day, and said I seemed to be flourishing in spite of my wall paper.

I turned it off with a laugh. I had no intention of telling him it was because of the wall paper—he would make fun of me. He might even want to take me away.

I don't want to leave now until I have found it out. There is a week more, and I think that will be enough.

I'm feeling ever so much better! I don't sleep much at night, for it is so interesting to watch developments; but I sleep a good deal in the daytime.

In the daytime it is tiresome and perplexing.

There are always new shoots on the fungus, and new shades of yellow all over it. I cannot keep count of them, though I have tried conscientiously.

It is the strangest yellow, that wall paper! It makes me think of all the yellow things I ever saw—not beautiful ones like buttercups, but old foul, bad yellow things.

But there is something else about that paper—the smell! I noticed it the moment we came into the room, but with so much air and sun it was not bad. Now we have had a week of fog and rain, and whether the windows are open or not the smell is here.

It creeps all over the house.

I find it hovering in the dining-room, skulking in the parlor, hiding in the hall, lying in wait for me on the stairs.

It gets into my hair.

Even when I go to ride, if I turn my head suddenly and surprise it—there is that smell!

Such a peculiar odor, too! I have spent hours in trying to analyze it, to find what it smelled like.

It is not bad—at first, and very gentle, but quite the subtlest, most enduring odor I ever met.

In this damp weather it is awful. I wake up in the night and find it hanging over me.

It used to disturb me at first. I thought seriously of burning the house—to reach the smell.

But now I am used to it. The only thing I can think of that it is like is the color of the paper—a yellow smell!

There is a very funny mark on this wall, low down, near the mopboard. A streak that runs around the room. It goes behind every piece of furniture, except the bed, a long, straight, even smooch, as if it had been rubbed over and over.

I wonder how it was done and who did it, and what they did it for. Round and round and round—round and round and round—it makes me dizzy!

I really have discovered something at last.

Through watching so much at night, when it changes so, I have finally found out.

The front pattern does move—and no wonder! The woman behind shakes it!

Sometimes I think there are a great many women behind, and sometimes only one, and she crawls around fast, and her crawling shakes it all over.

Then in the very bright spots she keeps still, and in the very shady spots she just takes hold of the bars and shakes them hard.

And she is all the time trying to climb through. But nobody could climb through that pattern—it strangles so; I think that is why it has so many heads.

They get through, and then the pattern strangles them off and turns them upside-down, and makes their eyes white!

If those heads were covered or taken off it would not be half so bad.

I think that woman gets out in the daytime!

And I'll tell you why—privately—I've seen her!

I can see her out of every one of my windows!

It is the same woman, I know, for she is always creeping, and most women do not creep by daylight.

I see her in that long shaded lane, creeping up and down. I see her in those dark grape arbors, creeping all around the garden.

I see her on that long road under the trees, creeping along, and when a carriage comes she hides under the blackberry vines.

I don't blame her a bit. It must be very humiliating to be caught creeping by daylight!

I always lock the door when I creep by daylight. I can't do it at night, for I know John would suspect something at once.

And John is so queer, now, that I don't want to irritate him. I wish he would take another room! Besides, I don't want anybody to get that woman out at night but myself.

I often wonder if I could see her out of all the windows at once.

But, turn as fast as I can, I can only see out of one at one time.

And though I always see her she may be able to creep faster than I can turn!

I have watched her sometimes away off in the open country, creeping as fast as a cloud shadow in a high wind.

If only that top pattern could be gotten off from the under one! I mean to try it, little by little.

I have found out another funny thing, but I shan't tell it this time! It does not do to trust people too much.

There are only two more days to get this paper off, and I believe John is beginning to notice. I don't like the look in his eyes.

And I heard him ask Jennie a lot of professional questions about me. She had a very good report to give.

She said I slept a good deal in the daytime.

John knows I don't sleep very well at night, for all I'm so quiet!

He asked me all sorts of questions, too, and pretended to be very loving and kind.

As if I couldn't see through him!

Still, I don't wonder he acts so, sleeping under this paper for three months.

It only interests me, but I feel sure John and Jennie are secretly affected by it.

Hurrah! This is the last day, but it is enough. John is to stay in town over night, and won't be out until this evening.

Jennie wanted to sleep with me—the sly thing! but I told her I should undoubtedly rest better for a night all alone.

That was clever, for really I wasn't alone a bit! As soon as it was moonlight, and that poor thing began to crawl and shake the pattern, I got up and ran to help her.

I pulled and she shook, I shook and she pulled, and before morning we had peeled off yards of that paper.

A strip about as high as my head and half around the room.

And then when the sun came and that awful pattern began to laugh at me I declared I would finish it today!

We go away to-morrow, and they are moving all my furniture down again to leave things as they were before.

Jennie looked at the wall in amazement, but I told her merrily that I did it out of pure spite at the vicious thing.

She laughed and said she wouldn't mind doing it herself, but I must not get tired.

How she betrayed herself that time!

But I am here, and no person touches this paper but me—not alive!

She tried to get me out of the room—it was too patent! But I said it was so quiet and empty and clean now that I believed I would lie down again and sleep all I could; and not to wake me even for dinner—I would call when I woke.

So now she is gone, and the servants are gone, and the things are gone, and there is nothing left but that great bed-stead nailed down, with the canvas mattress we found on it.

We shall sleep downstairs to-night, and take the boat home to-morrow.

I quite enjoy the room, now it is bare again.

How those children did tear about here!

This bedstead is fairly gnawed!

But I must get to work.

I have locked the door and thrown the key down into the front path.

I don't want to go out, and I don't want to have anybody come in, till John comes.

I want to astonish him.

I've got a rope up here that even Jennie did not find. If that woman does get out, and tries to get away, I can tie her!

But I forgot I could not reach far without anything to stand on!

This bed will not move!

I tried to lift and push it until I was lame, and then I got so angry I bit off a little piece at one corner—but it hurt my teeth.

Then I peeled off all the paper I could reach standing on the floor. It sticks horribly and the pattern just enjoys it! All those strangled heads and bulbous eyes and waddling fungus growths just shriek with derision!

I am getting angry enough to do something desperate. To jump out of the window would be admirable exercise, but the bars are too strong even to try.

Besides, I wouldn't do it. Of course not. I know well enough that a step like that is improper and might be misconstrued.

I don't like to look out of the windows even—there are so many of those creeping women, and they creep so fast.

I wonder if they all come out of that wall paper, as I did?

But I am securely fastened now by my well-hidden rope—you don't get me out in the road there!

I suppose I shall have to get back behind the pattern when it comes night, and that is hard!

It is so pleasant to be out in this great room and creep around as I please!

I don't want to go outside. I won't, even if Jennie asks me to.

For outside you have to creep on the ground, and everything is green instead of yellow.

But here I can creep smoothly on the floor, and my shoulder just fits in that long smooch around the wall, so I cannot lose my way.

Why, there's John at the door!

It is no use, young man, you can't open it!

How he does call and pound!

Now he's crying for an axe.

It would be a shame to break down that beautiful door!

"John, dear!" said I in the gentlest voice, "the key is down by the front steps, under a plantain leaf!"

That silenced him for a few moments.

Then he said—very quietly indeed, "Open the door, my darling!"

"I can't," said I. "The key is down by the front door, under a plantain leaf!"

And then I said it again, several times, very gently and slowly, and said it so often that he had to go and see, and he got it, of course, and came in. He stopped short by the door.

"What is the matter?" he cried. "For God's sake, what are you doing?"

I kept on creeping just the same, but I looked at him over my shoulder.

"I've got out at last," said I, "in spite of you and Jane! And I've pulled off most of the paper, so you can't put me back!"

Now why should that man have fainted? But he did, and right across my path by the wall, so that I had to creep over him every time!

1

What is the main purpose of this passage?

2

What is the passage's tone?

3

How would you summarize the passage?

4

How would you describe John?

5

How would you describe the unnamed narrator?

WANT MORE? TEN BOOKS TO READ FOR FUN

The readings in this book are just the start. I hope this book has rekindled the fun of reading for you. To keep yourself going, here are ten of my favorite books for high school students to read. Not all of them are *literature* as such (though some are), but they are all *fun*. They are also all classics, readily available at your public or school library or available online or at your local bookstore. Feel free to visit www.professorscompanion.com/ for links and more suggestions.

Like this?	Try reading
The Handmaid's Tale	❑ *A Room of One's One*, by Virginia Woolf ❑ *Dragonflight & Dragonsong*, by Anne McCaffrey
Stranger Things	❑ *One Hundred Years of Solitude*, by Gabriel Garcia Marquez
The Outdoors	❑ *Silent Spring*, by Rachel Carson
Satire	❑ *The Princess Bride*, by William Goldman
Math and Science	❑ *Cosmos & Pale Blue Dot*, by Carl Sagan ❑ *Silent Spring*, by Rachel Carson
House of Cards	❑ *All the President's Men*, by Bob Woodward and Carl Bernstein
Comic Book Movies	❑ *Dragonflight & Dragonsong*, by Anne McCaffrey
Parks and Recreation	❑ *Silent Spring*, by Rachel Carson
Hamilton	❑ *Souls of Black Folk*, by W. E. B. Du Bois
Science Fiction	❑ *Dragonflight & Dragonsong*, by Anne McCaffrey
Game of Thrones	❑ *All the President's Men*, by Bob Woodward and Carl Bernstein ❑ *Dragonflight & Dragonsong*, by Anne McCaffrey
Literature	❑ *A Room of One's Own*, by Virginia Woolf
African American History	❑ *Souls of Black Folk*, by W. E. B. Du Bois
The Cold War	❑ *All the President's Men*, by Bob Woodward and Carl Bernstein
Philosophy	❑ *One Hundred Years of Solitude*, by Gabriel Garcia Marquez

Do you have suggestions for your peers? Send me an email at tom@theprofessorscompanion.com and you may find your suggestion featured on the website, in a newsletter, or in a future edition of this book!

Have fun reading!

– Tom

All the President's Men, by Carl Bernstein and Bob Woodward

In 1972, five operatives from CREEP, the Committee to Re-Elect the President (Richard Nixon), broke into the Democratic National Committee's headquarters at the Watergate office complex. A cover-up, orchestrated from the White House, brought down the president. *All the President's Men*, written by two of the *Washington Post* journalists who uncovered the conspiracy, chronicles the tumultuous Watergate years and the end of the Nixon presidency.

> *June 17, 1972. Nine o'clock Saturday morning. Early for the telephone. Woodward fumbled for the receiver and snapped awake. The city editor of the* Washington Post *was on the line. Five men had been arrested earlier that morning in a burglary at Democratic headquarters, carrying photographic equipment and electronic gear…*

Silent Spring, by Rachel Carson

Probably the most influential environmental science book, Rachel Carson's *Silent Spring* investigated the harmful effects of pesticides and is credited with bringing the environmentalist movement to popular consciousness.

> *As crude a weapon as the cave man's club, the chemical barrage has been hurled against the fabric of life—a fabric on the one hand delicate and destructible, on the other miraculously tough and resilient, and capable of striking back in unexpected ways. These extraordinary capacities of life have been ignored by the practitioners of chemical control who have brought to their task no 'high-minded orientation', no humility before the vast forces with which they tamper. The 'control of nature' is a phrase conceived in arrogance, born of the Neanderthal age of biology and philosophy, when it was supposed that nature exists for the convenience of man. The concepts and practices of applied entomology for the most part date from that Stone Age of science. It is our alarming misfortune that so primitive a science has armed itself with the most modern and terrible weapons, and that in turning them against the insects it has also turned them against the earth.*

The Souls of Black Folk, by W. E. B. Du Bois

W. E. B. Du Bois's 1903 anthology *The Souls of Black Folk* is a landmark of African American literature and the field of sociology. One of the Modern Library's 100 best works of non-fiction, *The Souls of Black Folk* describes the "double-consciousness" of African American identity, the idea that African Americans have a dual yet distinct identities (a concept that is related to today's concept of "intersectional" identities).

> *After the Egyptian and Indian, the Greek and Roman, the Teuton and Mongolian, the Negro is a sort of seventh son, born with a veil, and gifted with second-sight in this American world,—a world which yields him no true self-consciousness, but only lets him see himself through the revelation of the other world. It is a peculiar sensation, this double-consciousness, this sense of always looking at one's self through the eyes of others, of measuring one's soul by the tape of a world that looks on in*

amused contempt and pity. One ever feels his two-ness,—an American, a Negro; two souls, two thoughts, two unreconciled strivings; two warring ideals in one dark body, whose dogged strength alone keeps it from being torn asunder.

The Princess Bride: S. Morgenstern's Classic Tale of True Love and High Adventure, by William Goldman

Beloved as a movie, *The Princess Bride* is the "abridgment" of a fictitious Renaissance history of Guilder and Florin by S. Morgenstern. Its author, William Goldman, was also the Academy Award winning screenwriter of *Butch Cassidy and the Sundance Kid* and *All the President's Men*.

What happens when the most beautiful girl in the world marries the handsomest prince of all time and he turns out to be...well...a lot less than the man of her dreams? As a boy, William Goldman claims, he loved to hear his father read the "S. Morgenstern classic, The Princess Bride. *But as a grown-up he discovered that the boring parts were left out of good old Dad's recitation, and only the "good parts" reached his ears. Now Goldman does Dad one better. He's reconstructed the "Good Parts Version" to delight wise kids and wide-eyed grownups everywhere. What's it about? Fencing. Fighting. True Love. Strong Hate. Harsh Revenge. A Few Giants. Lots of Bad Men. Lots of Good Men. Five or Six Beautiful Women. Beasties Monstrous and Gentle. Some Swell Escapes and Captures. Death, Lies, Truth, Miracles, and a Little Sex. In short, it's about everything.*

Dragonflight and *Dragonsong*, by Anne McCaffrey

The Dragonriders of Pern is a long-running series of books and anthologies created by Anne McCaffrey, the first woman to win the Hugo and Nebula awards for science fiction and fantasy writing. The series chronicles the world of Pern, a planet settled by humans and plagued by deadly spores that fall from rogue planet every 200 years. *Dragoflight*, the first book of the series, tells of Lessa, a young girl who has sworn revenge against the man who murdered her father, an oath that Lessa must balance with her responsibilities to Pern. *Dragonsong* tells a different tale, the tale of a young fisherman's girl who longs to sing and write music, despite the fact that the profession of "harper" was closed to women.

When is a legend a legend? Why is a myth a myth? How old and disused must a fact be for it to be relegated to the category "Fairy-tale"? And why do certain facts remain incontrovertible while others lose their validity to assume a shabby, unsuitable character?

The winged, tailed, and fiery-breathed dragons (named for the Earth legend they resembled), their dragonmen, a breed apart, and the menace they battled, created a whole new group of legends and myths. Once relieved of imminent danger, Pern settled into a more comfortable way of life. The descendants of heroes fell into disfavor, as the legends fell into disrepute. This, then, is a tale of legends disbelieved and their restoration. Yet how goes a legend? Where is myth?

One Hundred Years of Solitude, by Gabriel Garcia Marquez

The *magnum opus* of Colombian author and Nobel Prize for Literature laureate Gabriel Garcia Marquez, *One Hundred Years of Solitude* is perhaps the best-known example of magical realism. Readers willing to press on through the quixotic tale of the town of Macondo and the Buendía family are rewarded with a complex tale of history and politics, economic and technological advancement, and mystery.

> *"Many years later, as he faced the firing squad, Colonel Aureliano Buendía was to remember that distant afternoon when his father took him to discover ice."*

Cosmos and *Pale Blue Dot: A Vision of the Human Future in Space*, by Carl Sagan

Carl Sagan, the public intellectual and astronomer, brought the sheer size of the universe to millions of bookshelves in America and around the world. *Cosmos* was an New York Times best seller in 1980, and in 1994, Sagan wrote *Pale Blue Dot* after reflecting on the Voyager One satellite's photograph of the planet Earth from 4 billion miles away.

> *Look again at that dot. That's here. That's home. That's us. On it everyone you love, everyone you know, everyone you ever heard of, every human being who ever was, lived out their lives. The aggregate of our joy and suffering, thousands of confident religions, ideologies, and economic doctrines, every hunter and forager, every hero and coward, every creator and destroyer of civilization, every king and peasant, every young couple in love, every mother and father, hopeful child, inventor and explorer, every teacher of morals, every corrupt politician, every "superstar," every "supreme leader," every saint and sinner in the history of our species lived there-on a mote of dust suspended in a sunbeam.*

A Room of One's Own, by Virginia Woolf

Virginia Woolf was a proto-feminist English author. Her *A Room of One's Own* advocates for women authors to have their own literal space and metaphorical freedom (through financial independence). In addition to her oft-quoted maxim, "One cannot think well, love well, sleep well, if one has not dined well," and the titular, "A woman must have money and a room of her own if she is to write fiction," *A Room of One's Own* concludes by encouraging women to write.

> *"Therefore I would ask you to write all kinds of books, hesitating at no subject however trivial or however vast. By hook or by crook, I hope that you will possess yourselves of money enough to travel and to idle, to contemplate the future or the past of the world, to dream over books and loiter at street corners and let the line of thought dip deep into the stream."*

WHAT DID I LIKE?

As you read, you should keep track of the passage you like and don't like. I typically start with a rating of my enjoyment on a scale of 1 to 5. You can then write a few comments about the passage. Don't go overboard with this, but it can be helpful to write down your thoughts. I can also help you find similar passages to try next (take a look at the table on page 6).

Short Reads	Comments	Rating
"Advice to Youth"		/5
The Dangers of Spaceflight		/5
The Division of Labor		/5
Don't Wait for the Translation		/5
Common Sense		/5
"Ex Oblivione"		/5
Flatland: A Romance of Many Dimensions		/5
"The King of Vultures"		/5
"On Nomination to the Supreme Court"		/5
"On My Impending Interview with Burr"		/5
The Prince		/5
The Story of an Hour		/5
"What to the Slave Is the Fourth of July?"		/5
War of the Worlds		/5
"Yosemite Fall"		/5
The Young Edda		/5

Medium Reads	Comments	Rating
"2-B-R-0-2-B"		/5
The Discovery of Radium		/5
Editorials from The Crisis		/5
A History of the Amazons		/5
Government Is the Problem		/5
"Ich bin ein Berliner" and "Tear Down this Wall"		/5
Macbeth: A Prose Adaptation		/5
"An Occurrence at Owl Creek Bridge"		/5
On the Separation of Powers		/5
"The Pendulum"		/5
Silly Novels by Lady Novelists		/5
"Where I Lived, and What I Lived For"		/5
"A Modest Proposal"		/5
"Women's Rights are Human Rights"		/5

Long Reads	Comments	Rating
To Build a Fire		/5
Earthquakes		/5
Emma (Abridged)		/5
An Essay on the Principle of Population		/5
"The Fad of the Fisherman"		/5
The Farmer and the Farmer Refuted		/5
Inaugural Addresses, Abraham Lincoln		/5
The Hanging Stranger		/5
Selections from The Death of King Arthur		/5
"Letter from Birmingham Jail"		/5
Report 68 – National Security Council		/5
The Pit and the Pendulum		/5
Three Satirical Stories by Saki		/5
The Yellow Wallpaper		/5